Political Ideologies

Neil McNaughton

Philip Allan Updates
Market Place
Deddington
Oxfordshire
OX15 0SE

Orders
Bookpoint Ltd, 130 Milton Park, Abingdon, Oxfordshire, OX14 4SB
tel: 01235 827720
fax: 01235 400454
e-mail: uk.orders@bookpoint.co.uk
Lines are open 9.00 a.m.–5.00 p.m., Monday to Saturday, with a 24-hour message
answering service. You can also order through the Philip Allan Updates website:
www.philipallan.co.uk

© Philip Allan Updates 2005

ISBN–13: 978-1-84489-215-0
ISBN–10: 1-84489-215-8

All photographs are reproduced by permission of Topfoto, except where otherwise
specified.

Design and illustrations by Neil Fozzard
Printed in Great Britain by CPI Bath

Philip Allan Updates' policy is to use papers that are natural, renewable and recyclable
products and made from wood grown in sustainable forests. The logging and manufac-
turing processes are expected to conform to the environmental regulations of the country
of origin.

P00919

Contents

Introduction

This A2 textbook reviews all the major ideologies covered in the exam board specifications. The first nine chapters each deal with an important ideology, describing both its development and its core values. This is designed to develop your understanding of the subject; it is important that you are aware of the historical context of each ideology, how it has changed over time and its enduring values and beliefs. Whenever new concepts and terms are introduced, concise explanations of these are given in the Key Term boxes highlighted within the text.

Brief biographies of important authorities on each ideology are included. These place topics in context and provide useful examples that can be deployed when answering examination questions. Quotations from leading figures add colour to your exam answers and give insights into how such people expressed themselves. However, the list of thinkers is not exhaustive and you should also undertake some additional, more specialised reading. To help you do this, a small number of recommended texts is included at the end of each chapter. These are core writings from which additional examples and knowledge can be gleaned.

Towards the end of each chapter there is a section on the key issues relating to the ideology concerned. This will assist you with answering commonly asked questions by identifying the most important controversies surrounding them. These sections include some comparative material, since an understanding of ideologies can always be improved by making comparisons and contrasts. For example, considering how different ideologies view the concept of equality can assist our comprehension of them.

These chapters finish by listing a number of typical examination questions. They are divided into short questions, which should be answered in 15 minutes, and long questions, which should take 45 minutes to answer. These questions can be answered by referring to the relevant chapter, and to the key issues section within that chapter in particular. The examples and quotations you should include can be found in the text too.

Chapter 10 summarises the current state of the concept of ideology. It describes various theories which suggest that ideology is now an outdated idea and that the progress of history has come to an end. The final chapter is a guide to answering typical examination questions on political ideologies. As well as offering general principles, it gives exemplars with detailed suggestions as to the content and structure of particular answers.

The bibliography that follows is divided into three parts. The first contains suggested extension reading to help you take your study of ideology further. The second gives useful websites. Finally, a list of classic works is included. It may interest you to go back to the primary texts, both to deepen your knowledge and to see how the great political thinkers throughout history have explained their theories. The comprehensive index that concludes this book is useful for quick references and highlights where the Key Terms feature in each chapter.

Tackling ideologies

The terms that make up most of the chapter headings in this textbook will be familiar to you. We all have ideas about what a liberal or a conservative is like. There are many images of anarchism or Marxism which we could conjure up — revolutionaries, sinister assassins or colourful demonstrators at international meetings. In the case of feminists and environmentalists, too, we may harbour stereotypes which can have little basis in fact.

Such images are often misleading. All ideologies have complex roots and include sophisticated ideas. In addition, they each have important variations and developments within them. It is therefore vital to guard against your own prejudices and keep an open mind. You may find some of the ideas in these ideologies objectionable; in some cases, they may even be repugnant. It is important, however, to try to get inside the minds of an ideology's adherents. Remember that all these ideas have, at some time or other, been extremely popular. You must therefore ask what was, or is, their appeal.

Fascism, for example, illustrates the need for objectivity. The evils of genocide, concentration camps, war and conquest, which were the manifestations of this philosophy in the twentieth century, can prevent an effective examination of the ideology. Millions of Germans and Italians supported fascism freely and enthusiastically. How did this come about? What was the appeal of fascism? It is important to understand that there were features of the fascist ideology which had nothing to do with the Final Solution or with Hitler's attempt to dominate Europe. For example, did the fascist critique of democracy have any validity? Is there a place in certain historical circumstances for the kind of dynamic leadership which fascism offers? Is there anything we can learn about how societies can be bound together in order to carry out some acceptable form of collective enterprise?

Anarchism, too, presents problems. To most observers, it is an impractical philosophy based on an overoptimistic view of humankind and an unworkable set of propositions.

However, anarchism provides a comprehensive critique of modern society. By examining the anarchist position, we can develop a deeper understanding of the workings of some societies. For example, what is the true nature and function of the state? How can private property be justified? What would humankind do if awarded complete, uninhibited freedom?

There are four questions that can be asked of each ideology:

1 What does it say about the fundamental nature of humankind?
2 How does it go about analysing society? For example, is its analysis based on social class, the nature of government, some view about a natural order or the historical development of the society in question?
3 Does it have any fundamental values which determine its thinking?
4 Does it base its ideas upon scientific analysis or simply upon basic principles?

You should also consider the main variations within each ideology. Some ideologies, such as liberalism, socialism and conservatism, have tended to change over time. Others have internal divisions that are based upon differences in underlying principles. For example, some anarchists have an individualistic view of human nature, while others believe that humankind is essentially social. This has led to two distinctive forms of the same ideology. Similarly, some feminists believe that the status of women will only be improved if there is a revolutionary change in the nature of male-dominated society. Others argue that the problem can be solved by reforming society in a more moderate fashion.

Note that these ideologies are not necessarily separate, discrete entities. There is a good deal of overlap and there are shared ideals between them. There are many examples of this, most strikingly that of neo-liberalism. This movement, which has dominated conservatism since the 1980s, is inspired by a brand of liberalism that was at its height in the mid-nineteenth century. Similarly, the ultimate goal of many anarchists is to create a communist form of society, which is reminiscent of the final stage of historical development foreseen by Marx.

This blurring of distinctions can be a source of confusion when considering political parties. Don't assume, for example, that the ideas of liberalism are only to be found in Liberal parties. The UK Conservative Party has from time to time been relatively progressive in its outlook, notably under Margaret Thatcher in the 1980s. Indeed, liberal philosophy has influenced all mainstream political parties in the developed world.

Finally, be cautious when using terms such as socialism and social democracy. These have been used by parties from time to time to describe themselves, but it is their own interpretation of the term that they are using. You need to take a more detached view.

The historical development of ideology

The term 'ideology' is believed to have been developed by the French philosopher Antoine de Tracy (1754–1836). He used it to mean the 'science of ideas'. This concept arose out of the Enlightenment period and the reconstruction of French society necessitated by the 1789 revolution.

The Enlightenment brought about new ways of understanding the world that were free from religious prejudices and the corruption of truth by absolute monarchies and aristocratic governments. For de Tracy, it was possible to study society, religion, politics and philosophy in an objective, scientific manner, and so comprehend society better. This was seen as a crucial development, since it was hoped that a rational form of society could result from a rational study of ideas. Thus, ideology did not begin life as a set of beliefs, but as a claim to understanding the world scientifically.

The new concept did not last long before it came under criticism. Far from being objective, it was argued, ideology was a utopian ideal — a vision of society not as it was, but as the advocates of ideological thinking wished it to be. A more vehement attack was provided by Karl Marx in the middle of the nineteenth century. He argued that ideology was merely a reflection of the ideas of the ruling class in any age, a corruption of truth designed to maintain the dominant position of that ruling class. For example, liberalism was the dominant ideology of capitalism. Its advocacy of individual liberty, free markets and the absence of government regulation all served the interests of the capitalist structure, its exploitative nature, and the bourgeois class which controlled it. Describing ideology as the ruling ideas of the age, Marx pointed out its links with the ruling class:

> The ideas of the ruling class are in every epoch the ruling ideas, i.e. the class which
> is the ruling material force of society, is at the same time its ruling intellectual force.
>
> From *The German Ideology*, 1846

However, Marx's critique of ideology was undermined by the success of his own philosophy. In a sense, the fact that Marxism itself became an ideology disproved his assertion that ideology must only be the possession of the ruling class.

Moreover, the dominant liberal ideology of capitalism came to be challenged by a range of ideologies, including socialism, anarchism and conservative forms of nationalism. This gave rise to a new perspective on the concept. The Marxists themselves amended Marx's own analysis by declaring that an ideology was, in fact, simply a view of the world adopted by a particular social class. While liberalism was a middle-class ideology, socialism was the ideology of the rising working class and conservatism was the ideology of the aristocracy and landed gentry. In the twentieth century, fascism became known as the ideology of the 'petite bourgeoisie' — members of the lower middle classes who earned their living independently. Ideologies had therefore become partial analyses of the world, proposing new social arrangements that would serve the interests of a particular class, and not merely the ruling class, as Marx had suggested.

Another definition of ideology is that it is a system of belief which is designed to maintain the status quo — a defensive view of the world which sees all alternatives as false and dangerous. Conservatism appears to fit well into this category, as does the modern world consensus that encompasses liberal democracy, individualism and free-market capitalism. This consensual, ideological view of the world is under threat from both environmentalism and religious fundamentalism, and in response asserts that its values are eternal and uncontestable. Ideology in this sense is a return to the Marxist perspective, in as much as the opponents of the dominant **Weltanschauung** (world-view) of the USA and its allies see it as a distorted vision of the world that is designed to maintain the dominant position of the 'rich club' of nations.

Key term

Weltanschauung

This German word translates literally as 'view of the world'. It refers to the way in which various belief systems or ideologies see the world. When there is a dominant *Weltanschauung*, all other ideologies are considered to be flawed. For example, present-day liberal capitalism sees the world as a huge market in which free enterprise should be allowed to operate and in which all individuals should be free to progress through their own efforts. It competes with an alternative belief that the less economically developed countries of the world are exploited by rich nations.

The nature of ideology

These competing definitions of ideology, although interesting, will not help to clarify the issues raised in this textbook. A more neutral and universal idea of the concept is needed in order to compare the various ideologies. Below is a description of ideology that can be applied to all the ideas that this book explores:

> Ideology incorporates a collection of principles, values and doctrines which are inter-locking, i.e. form a coherent whole.
> It includes a theory of society, with some explanation of the true nature of how people live in society and how society has developed.
> Ideologies that challenge the existing order offer a critique of existing society. Those that oppose change offer critiques of those movements that propose change.
> Ideologies develop a vision of how they believe future society should be. This may be a specific blueprint, or it could be a partial idea which includes generalised aims based on certain fixed principles.

This description of ideology may not be exhaustive and there may be others that are equally valid. It is possible, for example, to describe a belief system based on a single principle as an ideology. Thus libertarianism, which proposes absolute freedom, can be so described. There is also a looser definition, which may be better termed a 'philosophy'. A philosophy is a generalised way of looking at the world and its problems. It is therefore less rigorous than an ideology, which is more specific in its aims. Conservatism is often seen as a philosophy, not an ideology. For many, conservatism is a state of mind and a way of thinking about the world, rather than a formula for social transformation. However, for the purposes of this book ideology is defined according to the criteria given above.

At this stage, it is worth considering the distinction between utopianism and scientism. Utopianism refers to ideological thought which is based on a set of desirable outcomes, and not on any scientific or objective principles. Anarchism is often seen as utopian. Critics of such movements call them unrealistic, but their supporters argue that they are examples of purposeful idealism — the pursuit of desirable goals which will create a better society. Scientism, on the other hand, is based upon empirical, objective studies of history and society. Such movements either see the perfect society as an inevitable outcome of historical processes — e.g. Marxism — or they claim to have discovered truths about the nature of humankind and wish to construct a society that will allow the natural state of human nature and potential to develop.

Once you have read the descriptions of the main political movements and theories of the past 250 years or so, as they appear on the pages that follow, you can make up your own mind whether each ideology is utopian or scientific.

Chapter 1

Liberalism

Liberalism is a wide-ranging political movement which has its origins in the Enlightenment. Its central value is that individuals have a fundamental right to personal freedom. However, liberals accept that liberty entails responsibility. At its minimum, this responsibility implies that the actions of an individual should not harm others or curtail the individual's own freedom. Liberals support the existence of the state and its laws to enforce this kind of responsibility. The liberal state must be formed by popular consent and must be accountable to the people. This is to ensure that it does not curtail freedom without justification. The liberal state should be limited in its scope and only act in such a way as to advance freedom and opportunity. Liberals demonstrate strong attachments to equal rights for all groups, tolerance, diversity and equality of opportunity. More recently, they have also embraced the idea of social justice, accepting that people are naturally unequal but insisting that all should have equality of opportunity, and that wealth should not be achieved at the expense of the poorer members of society. In modern politics, liberalism can be compatible with both conservative and social democratic movements.

Introduction

It could be argued that liberalism has been the dominant ideology in Western society since the early part of the twentieth century. This is not to say that it has prevailed everywhere. It has been challenged and on occasions defeated by communists, socialists, fascists and conservatives. Nevertheless, it has always returned as the central element of political cultures in the West. Liberal *parties*, as such, may not have won elections or formed governments with any great regularity, but all mainstream parties in modern democracies have liberal values as part of their core identity. Conservative and social democratic parties, which tend to win most democratic elections, have come to accept many key liberal beliefs. It could be said, indeed, that liberalism has seeped into the social and political culture of all economically developed countries.

During the nineteenth century, liberalism did not enjoy such pre-eminence. Conservatives placed themselves in direct opposition to liberal values, seeing them as a threat to the preservation of order. Later, socialists associated liberalism with capitalism and so challenged it on the most fundamental grounds. Towards the end of the nineteenth century, liberalism began to transform itself into a **doctrine** which was far more wide ranging and able to answer the criticisms posed by both conservatives and socialists. To deal with conservative concerns about the creation of disorder by an individualistic society, liberals introduced the idea of social responsibility. In response to socialist claims that the philosophy entailed excessive inequality, liberals developed the principle of equality of opportunity. In this way, liberalism faced its challenges and absorbed criticisms. By the time the smoke of battle had cleared after the First World War, it was clear that the dominant values of liberalism would prevail in most economically developed, non-communist societies.

Key term

Doctrine

A doctrine is a strongly held single view or collection of connected views. It is less comprehensive than an ideology in that it does not encompass a complete vision of a desired society. The term suggests that those who hold doctrines adhere to them strongly and that their thoughts and actions are determined by them. For liberals, the desire for freedom in its various forms is a doctrine; for socialists, equality is a doctrine. Liberalism can be described as a doctrine in that it includes closely connected beliefs that all liberals believe in strongly.

The Enlightenment

The Enlightenment period, which roughly corresponds to the eighteenth century, may not have created liberalism, but it certainly made such a movement possible. The new philosophies of the period challenged existing assumptions about the nature of humankind and society, and made unprecedented assertions about the human condition. Among the most significant were the following:

➤ Each person is born a free, rational individual.
➤ An individual does not have to accept the judgement of rulers or the established churches to determine what is in his or her own best interest. Rather, each individual is the best judge of his or her own interests.

- An individual is not subject to forces beyond his or her control, including the will of God, but instead possesses free will.
- Society does not have a preordained order that consigns each person to a fixed status. Rather, every individual is free to find his or her own place in society.
- We are born fundamentally equal. Although we may have different powers and potential, we do inherit equal rights.

Today, we take such principles for granted. During the Enlightenment, however, these were truly revolutionary ideas that shook the Western world. A number of celebrated sources illustrate how dramatic these ideas were and how influential they proved to be. In 1689, at the dawn of the Enlightenment, the English philosopher John Locke (1632–1704) wrote in his *Two Treatises on Government*:

> The liberty of man in society is to be under no other legislative but that established
> by consent in the commonwealth, nor under the dominion of any will, or restraint of
> any law, but what the legislative shall enact, according to the true trust put in it.

Thus, in one statement, Locke dramatically rejects the idea of any form of government established without the expressed consent of the people.

Nearly a century later, the near-opening lines of Thomas Jefferson (1743–1826) in the 1776 American Declaration of Independence widened the debate. This statement established the rights of individuals and so, by implication, asserted the appropriate limits to government power:

> We hold these truths to be self-evident, that all men are created equal, that they are
> endowed by their Creator with certain inalienable rights, that among these are life,
> liberty and the pursuit of happiness.

The phrase 'the pursuit of happiness' implies that individuals are the only judge of what is best for them.

Jean-Jacques Rousseau (1712–78) had already argued that humankind was being unjustifiably controlled by social and political restraints. In the introduction to his 1762 book, *The Social Contract*, he declared:

> Man is born free, but is everywhere in chains.

The 'chains' to which he refers were not merely the restraints imposed by absolute rulers, but any restraint upon the exercise of an individual's rights. He also implies that **natural rights** (e.g. to freedom) exist for all.

What the Enlightenment did, therefore, was to open people's minds to new possibilities. It enabled political movements to challenge the existing order and to establish forms of government which would free humankind, rather than enslave it. It made individuals into citizens with rights, rather than subjects with only obligations to obey. It also freed people's minds, enabling them to accept that it was possible to hold different beliefs without necessarily threatening public order and security.

Key term

Natural rights

This concept was developed by philosophers in the seventeenth and eighteenth centuries. It asserts that all individuals are born with rights that are granted by God or nature. The main natural rights specified are life, liberty and the pursuit of happiness. The theory of natural rights implies that such rights may not be removed or reduced except by the consent of the individual. The English philosopher Thomas Hobbes (1588–1679) is often viewed as the first major theorist of natural rights, but the liberals who followed him (Hobbes was not a liberal), such as John Locke and Thomas Paine (1737–1809), are more closely associated with the concept.

Liberalism and capitalism

Just as liberalism was made *possible* by Enlightenment philosophy, so it became *necessary* in order to underpin the development of free-market **capitalism**. Towards the latter part of the eighteenth century, it was clear that a new economic order was emerging in the more developed parts of the world, mainly in western Europe. Fundamental economic changes were occurring as a result of the growth of international trade and the early stages of the industrial revolution. The old feudal order was crumbling and being replaced by a new system. This was spawning new social classes — independent farmers, free traders and merchants, industrialists and entrepreneurs, as well as workers who were free to seek employment by selling their labour to the highest bidder. The effect was the creation of a new dynamic economic structure, characterised by rapid growth and, above all, by freedom of the individual.

The most celebrated observer of the new capitalism was a Scottish economist, Adam Smith (1723–90). Smith's great work, *The Wealth of Nations*, was, by an interesting coincidence, published in the same year as the American Declaration of Independence — 1776. In it, he described how the new economic order was inhabited by individuals with free will, who would pursue their own self-interest as they saw fit. Far from resulting in chaos, the new free economy was forming a cohesiveness and a fresh order of its own. Through what he called the 'hidden hand', the development of free trade and unregulated business would act in the best interests of all. In essence, the 'hidden hand' would regulate the economy. Governments, he asserted, should be restricted to ensuring that all obey the law, and should steer clear of economic management.

Smith and the other advocates of free-market capitalism, such as David Ricardo (1772–1823), saw how vital it had become for individuals to consider themselves to be free, both in their pursuit of self-interest and from over-regulation by governments. The success of new free economies in creating wealth was a testament to how desirable such economic liberalism had become. In the early decades of the nineteenth century, however, liberalism was unable to dominate completely. The forces of conservatism and the interests of the traditional landed gentry opposed it ferociously. As the century wore on, conservatism lost its battle with economic liberalism, but a new adversary emerged to take its place. This was early socialism and later radical Marxism.

Key term

Capitalism

Capitalism is the name given to the economic system that emerged in Europe and spread to the developed world during the eighteenth and nineteenth centuries. It describes a system in which entrepreneurs take risks in organising production and extract a profit in return for the risks they take and for their organisational efforts. Under capitalism, goods, labour and finance are all exchanged between capitalists and consumers at values determined by free-market forces. Capitalism, liberals argue, requires a high degree of economic freedom for workers, consumers, financiers and entrepreneurs in order to operate effectively. Most of its aspects are criticised by socialists and anarchists. A more complete description is contained in the chapter on Marxism.

The development of the concept of liberty

The rationalism of the Enlightenment and the emergence of market capitalism both proved fertile ground for the growth of liberal ideas. One further element was needed in order for such ideas to become a complete philosophy. This was the concept of liberty. The way in which liberty (or freedom — the two terms are used here interchangeably) has been used by liberals is described in some detail below, but the term also has an important role in the development of liberalism itself.

French revolutionaries storm the Bastille in Paris, 1789

The two great events of early liberal history were the American (1775 onwards) and French (1789) revolutions. In both cases, the revolutionaries were inspired by a desire for freedom. The Americans sought refuge from the increasingly autocratic rule of the British Crown, while the French overturned the *ancien régime* in the hope of gaining freedom from undemocratic institutions. Most of us are familiar with the great battle cry of the French Revolution, 'Liberté, égalité, fraternité', which placed freedom as its first goal, as well as with the early words of the American Declaration of Independence (see p. 3). However, despite this, the freedom being promoted here was not quite what we would understand by the term today.

Events in America and France were based on what might be called 'revolutionary liberalism', which used the term freedom to mean escape from existing political authority and the establishment of a new government, a government by consent. The revolutionaries were, in fact, less concerned with individual liberty than with the freedom of the whole people — their freedom from oppression and arbitrary rule. The newly emerging societies of the 1770s and 1780s were not quite ready to deal with widespread individual freedom.

Freedom of the individual was a concept which was developed throughout the nineteenth century. It was the product of a new philosophy, often described as *classical liberalism*. As we have seen above, it became a necessary companion to the growth of free-market capitalism, but the idea of freedom of the individual was pre-eminent in liberalism for a relatively short time. It was not long before the dangers of excessive amounts of individual liberty were recognised and had to be confronted by liberals.

There were two main responses. First, liberals came to accept that freedom should not be exercised to the detriment of others in society, and that therefore the concept had to be combined with a sense of social responsibility. This can be described as a kind of social freedom, whereby individual liberty is exercised only in a socially responsible way. Second, liberals began to accept that there were two kinds of freedom — now commonly called *negative* and *positive* liberty. These are described fully below; it is sufficient to note here that negative liberty refers to the freedom of the individual from external restraints, while positive liberty refers to maximising the individual's choices and opportunities.

By the twentieth century, liberals had moved some distance from their early support for a more general concept of liberty. There had to be a balance between the rights of individuals in society, freedom should be exercised with a sense of social responsibility and governments needed to promote both positive and negative liberty. The idea of liberty had indeed come a long way from its first practical applications in France and America.

Core values of liberalism

Liberty/freedom
This is the central value for all liberals and therefore worthy of lengthy consideration. There are various different conceptions of liberty, all of which have been used by liberals at different times and in different circumstances. It bears repeating that, in this context, the terms liberty and freedom have essentially the same meaning. We can usefully divide the examination of liberty into three parts, as outlined below.

Political or revolutionary liberty
When the Scottish rebel William Wallace (1272–1305) cried the single word 'Freedom!' before his death on the scaffold in 1305 (at least according to Mel Gibson's film portrayal

of the character), he did not mean that the Scottish peasantry should become free from the government and laws of Scotland at the time, or free from the duties that they owed to their landlords. What his futile plea meant was that Scotland as a whole should be free from English domination. Wallace's use of the term expresses its principal meaning over the next 500 years. The only other context in which the term was used in this period was in circumstances where serfs, who were tied to the land and their feudal duties, or in some countries were even slaves, were granted their freedom. This did not imply that they should be 'free' as we understand the word today, but that they be released from their specific feudal or slave duties. They could then become wage earners or independent tradesmen.

As we have seen above, the freedom that the French and American revolutionaries sought was similar to Wallace's idea. For most of the early liberals, political freedom implied the freedom of a people to determine their own form of government and not to be ruled by any external power. This kind of freedom is also often known as *self-determination*. Throughout the nineteenth century, the word became the rallying cry of many independence movements throughout the Austro-Hungarian, Russian and Ottoman empires, as well as among German and Italian nationalist movements.

Although this particular meaning of freedom is no longer central to liberal thought, it remains true that one of the core values of liberal philosophy is that all peoples should be independent, should determine their own form of government and should be masters of their own national destiny.

Individual liberty

The transfer of emphasis among liberals from political to individual liberty occurred in the early part of the nineteenth century. Writing in 1820, French liberal Benjamin Constant (1767–1830) expressed the transition thus:

> The aim of the ancients was the sharing of social power among the citizens of the same fatherland; that is what they called liberty. The aim of the moderns is the enjoyment of security in private pleasures; and they call liberty the guarantees accorded by institutions to these pleasures...Individual liberty is, I repeat, the true modern liberty. Political liberty is its guarantee.
>
> From *Political Writings*, 1815

Before such thinkers as Constant, individual liberty, as a goal, had been the preserve of those philosophers who were considered to be exceptionally radical, for example Rousseau and the English anarchist William Godwin (1756–1836). From Constant's time onwards, however, it became clear to liberal thinkers that it was a practical aspiration.

The main enemies of liberty, in the view of early liberals, were over-powerful governments. Two main charges were laid against them. The first was that governments were too paternalistic, claiming to understand what was in people's best interests better than the people themselves. The second charge was that governments regulated the behaviour of individuals without just cause, in particular controlling their actions, even though those actions did not affect anybody else or threaten society. This effectively divides the idea of individual liberty into two categories.

First, the *utilitarian* tradition of liberalism held, as its fundamental belief, that each individual is the best judge of his or her own interests. For the celebrated English utilitarian Jeremy Bentham (1748–1832), the concept of freedom was relatively simple. As individuals, we are motivated to pursue pleasure and to avoid pain. In other words, we know what we wish to pursue and what we wish to avoid. For Bentham, being allowed to make those decisions for ourselves and to act on them was the essence of freedom. He argued that the role of government should not be to make those decisions for us, nor should government prevent us from following our own self-interest, unless, of course, in so doing we prevent others from pursuing theirs. Hence, the *enlightened pursuit of self-interest* became a central liberal idea and, of course, one which coexisted well with free-market capitalism.

Second, in England, a follower of Bentham, John Stuart Mill (1806–73), developed a view of 'true' freedom based on the absence of constraint — perhaps this is how most of us tend to perceive the concept. Mill divided our actions into two types. The first were *self-regarding actions,* i.e. those that do not affect other people. In Mill's day such actions would have been mainly those of religious observance and the development of beliefs and personal morality. In a modern context, they might include recreational drug use, smoking, drinking alcohol etc. The second type was *other-regarding actions* that do affect others adversely, such as assault or theft, but also negligent behaviour, cruelty and discrimination.

Mill's explanation of this principle of true freedom has become a motto which all liberals can follow:

> The sole end for which mankind are warranted, individually or collectively, in interfering with the liberty of action of any of their number, is self-protection. That is the only purpose for which power can be rightfully exercised over a member of a civilised society, against his will, is to prevent harm to others. His own good, either physical or moral, is not a sufficient warrant. He cannot rightfully be compelled to do or forbear because it will be better for him to do so, because it will make him happier, because, in the opinion of others, to do so would be wise or even right.
>
> From *On Liberty*, 1859

This famous passage encompasses both Bentham's idea of self-interested freedom and the classical view of liberty as the absence of unwarranted constraints.

Negative and positive liberty

The term 'negative liberty' was not used by Mill himself; the modern philosopher Isaiah Berlin (1909–97) coined the term a century later to describe Mill's view. By 'negative' he did not imply any criticism of the idea but rather that it referred to an absence of restraint. Berlin was concerned to differentiate between negative freedom and another kind of liberty which had been developed by liberals later in the nineteenth century (see Box 1.1).

Differences between negative and positive liberty

Two short passages reveal the differences between negative and positive liberty, as described by Isaiah Berlin:

> Liberty in this [negative] sense is simply the area within which a man can act unobstructed by others. If I am prevented by others from doing what I could otherwise do, I am to that degree unfree.

> The positive sense of the word liberty derives from the wish on the part of the individual to be his own master. I wish my life and decisions to depend on myself, not on external forces of whatever kind. I wish to be the instrument of my own, not of other men's acts of will. I wish to be a subject not an object.
>
> Both from *Two Concepts of Liberty*, 1969

We can trace the concept of positive liberty back to the English moral philosopher, T. H. Green (1836–82). Like Mill, Green did not use the term 'positive liberty', but his meaning was close to Berlin's definition. He rejected the classical liberal view of Mill and others that society is made up only of self-interested individuals. Instead, he saw society as 'organic' and its citizens as interdependent as well as independent. In other words, citizens are not merely motivated by self-interest but also by a desire to promote the common good.

It follows from this that individuals achieve self-fulfilment not merely through pursuing their own happiness, but by pursuing social goods such as the welfare of others. Green's freedom is positive in that we can achieve personal satisfaction by doing good for others as well as for ourselves.

A more modern conception of positive liberty is that there should be the widest possible degree of choice and opportunity for everybody. We can synthesise this with Green's view in that, given freedom and choice, we will exercise a sense of social responsibility by pursuing the common good. This does not make Green a socialist. He still believed that the state should promote individual liberty and that we pursue self-interest, but he asserted that freedom is not one-dimensional: it is both individual and social in nature.

Green's divergence from the traditional, classical liberal view of freedom opened the door for liberalism to expand its political horizons beyond individual freedom. His philosophy ushered in a new liberal age which was able to embrace equality of opportunity, state welfare provision and even redistribution of income from rich to poor.

Tolerance

The liberal love of tolerance flows directly from Mill's principles of individual liberty, but it predates him in liberal thought by over a century in the ideas of John Locke. Locke was almost exclusively concerned with religious tolerance, an idea that was relatively radical at the time he was writing. He drew his conclusions from one simple principle: 'That every man may enjoy the same rights that are granted to others.'

Political controversy over religious tolerance raged throughout the eighteenth century and into the nineteenth century. With the arrival of liberals such as Mill, however, the tolerance debate transcended religion and involved every sphere of life. It was in the field of freedom of expression that liberalism campaigned most strongly in the nineteenth century. Toleration of other people's beliefs, values, thoughts and faiths, and their right to express them openly, became one of liberalism's most cherished goals.

In the twentieth century, attention switched to public attitudes towards minority groups. In recent times, liberals have defended and campaigned for the rights of minorities such as gays and ethnic and religious groups and have opposed all forms of censorship in the media and the arts.

A well-known liberal expression, dating back to the French philosopher Voltaire (1694–1778), is: 'I detest what you say, but I shall defend to the death your right to say it.' To this, Mill added that to prevent the expression of different beliefs and faiths was an exercise in arrogance. How are we to know, he asked, that our views are correct and those of others are wrong? This principle, nevertheless, needs some qualification.

Liberals will tolerate different beliefs and views but assign limits to this tolerance. If the security of the state or the freedom of individuals is threatened, or if people are being incited to commit crimes, act in a violent way or discriminate against any group, freedom of expression should be curtailed. This brings us back to Mill's view of freedom. We should be free as long as our actions are self-regarding and do no harm to others. Words or actions that adversely affect others should not be tolerated.

Two further modern aspects of liberal tolerance should be considered. First, a typical liberal is sympathetic to the idea that individuals are influenced by their social and economic circumstances. In other words, we are not always responsible for our own actions. It follows that those who become involved in what is considered anti-social behaviour — notably crime, substance abuse and addiction or personal neglect — may do so as a consequence of social circumstances beyond their control. Thus, a liberal tends to be tolerant in his or her outlook and

John Stuart Mill, who saw freedom in terms of the absence of constraints

proposes measures to assist individuals in the reform of their behaviour, rather than merely punishing them.

Second, modern liberals have tended to demonstrate greater tolerance than most people over personal morality. On issues such as sexual mores, abortion, homosexuality, same-sex marriage and the like, liberals generally take the view that these are private matters, not the concern of the state or of others in society. Indeed, it is in this area that the divisions between modern conservatism and liberalism are most sharply drawn. Conservatives insist that there is no such thing as entirely private morality; immoral behaviour does threaten the fabric of society and so should be controlled.

Equal rights

Liberals disagree among themselves about the existence of natural rights. Locke and Paine certainly based their whole belief systems around their existence. Bentham and Mill, on the other hand, rejected natural rights theory. For them, freedom consisted of the natural inclination of humankind to pursue its own selfish interests. However, this disagreement disguises a principle held universally by all liberals — that we are all entitled to equal rights.

Those liberals who support the idea of natural rights have no difficulty in translating this into support for equal rights. After all, if we all enjoy rights granted to us by God or nature, it must be true that they are given on an equal basis. Other liberals adopt a purely rational position. They can see no reason for inequality. For them it is unnatural, the creation of men in history who have sought to exercise power over others. For a liberal, we are all created equal and so must enjoy equal rights.

However, we must be careful here. A belief in equal rights is not the same as a belief in equality in general. Most (though not all) liberals accept that we have different abilities and potentialities when we are born. What they seek is the equal right to reach our full potential and to seek self-fulfilment.

These positions lead to two further conclusions. First, all distinct groups in society are entitled to the same rights. In other words, discrimination against groups should be outlawed. This has led liberals to advance the causes of full rights for women, gays, the disabled and ethnic minorities. Second, we are all entitled to **equality of opportunity**. This second issue is explored below.

Equality of opportunity

The classical liberals of the nineteenth century proposed a society in which individuals were largely free from restraint and therefore free to succeed or fail, to grow rich or to remain poor, to choose their own occupation and lifestyle and to find their own road to self-fulfilment. However, this philosophy began to present problems for many liberals as the century wore on. It became clear that the doctrines of equal rights and individual liberty were conflicting with each other. Many members of society, through unfortunate circumstances of birth and through no fault of their own, were not blessed with equal opportunity to benefit from such a free society. Early social researchers, such as Charles Booth (1840–1916), revealed to a surprised world that there was such a thing as a cycle of deprivation, that poor families produced poor offspring and that there was little or nothing that could break this cycle.

John Stuart Mill himself, the great champion of individual liberty, late in his life came to accept this as a problem with his own philosophy. At the same time, the newly formed Liberal Party of Great Britain, led by William Gladstone (1809–98), espoused greater equality of opportunity as one of its goals. Thus, elementary education for all was introduced and entry into the professions — law, government and the army, for example — was opened to a wider spectrum of society. These were small advances in equality of opportunity but they indicated how liberal opinion was changing. The next great advance was promoted by William Beveridge (1879–1963), the creator of the welfare state. Beveridge proposed that the availability of welfare for all, notably education, healthcare and social security, would expand opportunity for all, no matter what their circumstances of birth.

After Beveridge, the cause of equality of opportunity was largely taken up in Britain by the Labour Party. From the 1960s, the introduction of comprehensive education and the expansion of higher education were the principal measures adopted, with the outlawing of discrimination against women, ethnic minorities and the disabled coming close behind. Indeed, at this time, the idea of equality of opportunity became part of the British political consensus, with all three main parties supporting, or claiming to support, the principle.

Key term

Equality of opportunity

This emerged as a political principle in the latter part of the nineteenth century. It recognises that some individuals are born with disadvantages which cannot be overcome by their own efforts. It is also a moral principle that suggests that all are entitled to equal life chances. Inequality can be justified, argue liberals and conservatives, provided all begin life with equal opportunities. Equality of opportunity is mainly promoted through universal education, but also implies the removal of artificial obstacles and other social problems which could hold some individuals back. In modern politics, all mainstream politicians and theorists accept it as a necessary feature of society, although liberals and socialists stress it most. It applies to class differences, gender issues and ethnic diversity.

So far we have concentrated on British liberalism, but the discussion would not be complete without reference to the US experience. In many ways the USA can be seen as the natural home of equality of opportunity and, indeed, some might say the whole of its society is based upon it. Education in the USA has long been supplied on a comprehensive basis and there are strong safeguards against discrimination both in the constitution and in the laws. The belief that every individual should have the opportunity to advance in life has become part of the so-called 'American Dream'. Indeed, as in the UK, it has become so much a part of the country's culture that it is no longer associated specifically with liberalism. This should not, however, disguise the fact that it emerged very clearly from the liberal tradition of which Thomas Jefferson, James Madison (1751–1836) and Alexander Hamilton (1755–1804) were founding members.

Pluralism

The term 'pluralism' relates to a modern conception of the truly liberal society. Indeed, the French philosopher Alexis de Tocqueville (1805–59) regarded pluralism as an essential requirement for true democracy. For Tocqueville, pluralism was characterised by a flourishing collection of groups to which people owed allegiance and in which they could freely participate. Such a healthy **civil society** would prevent the state from becoming too powerful. It would also act as a balance against the potential tyranny of rule by the numerical majority.

Tocqueville's vision of pluralism was based upon his observations of the USA in the 1830s, but it was not until the twentieth century that liberals in Europe became concerned with the positive potentialities of pluralist democracy and society in general. The modern conception of pluralism includes a number of aspects:

- The diversity of cultures, religions, ethnic groups and lifestyles in society are tolerated and the rights of such groups protected.
- The state tolerates the expression of a variety of beliefs, philosophies and political creeds, provided they do not threaten the peace and security of the country.
- People are used to participating freely in such groups.
- Groups have access to the political system and therefore the opportunity to influence policy-making.
- The existence of different cultures, values and belief systems helps to prevent domination of society by any single section of society.

In summary, for liberals a pluralist society enhances freedom, spreads opportunity widely and helps to control the power of the state.

Key term

Civil society

This expression refers to the wide variety of groups that flourish in pluralist societies. Individuals may be part of such groups naturally, or may choose to join them in order to achieve certain personal goals or aspirations. Families are included as part of civil society, but the term generally refers to such groups as political parties, pressure groups, religious organisations, voluntary groups and charities, trade unions and media organisations. A free and active civil society is now seen as vital to a healthy democracy. It ensures that people become actively involved in society; it can also help to act as a counterbalance to the power of the state.

Government by consent

One of the key elements of the Enlightenment was its questioning of the basis of political societies. Before rational thought was applied to this problem, principles such as the divine right of kings, the sanctity of obedience and the acceptance of the traditional basis of authority were used to explain the legitimacy of government. The new thinking challenged such legitimacy and searched for a new kind of political authority.

The seventeenth-century English philosophers Hobbes and Locke are widely acknowledged to have developed, between them, the concept of government by consent. Hobbes imagined a circumstance in which the people would come together in a free compact or agreement to set up a great power over them; this would bring about peace and security. This was not enough for Locke. First, his contract was to be real and not merely a notional device. Second, it would have to be constantly confirmed. This is how Locke described the original contract:

> And thus every man, by consenting with others to make one body politic under one government, puts himself under an obligation to every one of that society to submit to the determination of the majority.
>
> From *Two Treatises of Civil Government*, 1690

Nearly a century later, in 1787, the representatives of the newly-freed American people came together to make such a contract a reality. The preamble to the US constitution echoes Locke's description of political consent:

> We, the people of the United States, in order to form a more perfect union, establish justice, insure [original spelling] domestic tranquility, provide for the common defense, promote the general welfare, and secure the blessings of liberty to ourselves and our posterity, do ordain and establish this Constitution for the United States of America.

Two years later the French revolutionaries followed suit, although the government they established proved to be short-lived. For Locke, the original consent was assumed to be constantly renewed as long as future generations did not dissolve a government. Followers of Locke have argued that consent must be a more continuous process. It follows that by the term 'government by consent' liberals mean that the people should have regular opportunities to express their consent, or indeed to withhold it.

This means more than regular free elections. It implies the use of referendums when any major change to the power or system of government is proposed. On a more general level, we can say that the state must tolerate the free expression of public opinion, even if it challenges the basis of government. Should there be indications that the people, or at least the majority of them, wish to withdraw consent, the whole basis of government would need to be reconsidered.

On a global level, liberals insist that governments, at any time and in every place, should only be considered legitimate if the people have freely given their consent to the system of government. In a UK context, for example, the people of the Falkland Islands,

Gibraltar and Northern Ireland have all been offered the opportunity to vote in a plebiscite over whether they wish to remain under British rule. In each case, 'Yes' answers have been enough for liberals.

Limited government and constitutionalism

According to liberals, merely ensuring that government is established by consent is not a sufficient safeguard for the people. It is essential in the interests of liberty that government should operate within strict boundaries. If government is not limited, it is likely to encroach upon the freedom and the private lives of its citizens. Power is a dangerous thing and it must be controlled at all times.

Liberals also fear three other potential consequences of government:

- the exercise of arbitrary power, i.e. power that has no legitimate authority
- the tendency for power to become concentrated in too few hands
- that democratic systems may simply become the tyranny of the majority, to the detriment of legitimate minorities

Liberals offer a solution to all of these difficulties. This is the imposition of constitutional rule (see Box 1.2).

Box 1.2 A liberal constitution

- It is sovereign. Governments are strictly subject to its terms except in times of national emergency.
- It defines the limits to the jurisdiction of government. This prevents both arbitrary power and any drift towards increased state power.
- It defines the rights of the citizens, which is a further safeguard against encroachments by governments.
- It distributes power among different institutions of government. This prevents the concentration of power in too few hands.
- It includes special arrangements for the amendment of the constitution, ensuring that the citizens themselves are in control of the process. This prevents governments accumulating excessive power without popular consent.

By combining the doctrines of government by consent and constitutionalism, modern liberals have found a way of reconciling effective government with the rights and freedoms of both individuals and intermediate groups.

Justice

There are two aspects of this concept to consider. *Legal justice* consists of the equal application of the law to all citizens. Clearly, liberals have no difficulty in supporting this principle. It conforms to their attachment to equal rights. The idea of *social justice*, on the other hand, is more contentious.

Social justice is more closely associated with socialists than liberals. This is mainly because the achievement of a more just society usually requires the intervention of the state. Liberals have traditionally been suspicious of such intervention. Although late-nineteenth-century liberals endorsed the implementation of equality of opportunity — a key element in a just modern society — since then liberals have tended to accept that inequality is natural and, in a genuinely free society, social outcomes are all 'just'. Some contemporary liberals, however, have challenged this position.

Beveridge and others have concluded that deprivation of various kinds curtails freedom just as much as governments and their laws can. It has also been recognised that, even in a free-market system, excessive inequalities cannot be considered just. It may be acceptable to tolerate some degree of inequality in the free market, but not to the extent that the poorest members of society are seriously deprived. Many liberals therefore share with socialism a desire to redistribute some income from rich to poor. A liberal philosophy of social justice was offered by John Rawls (1921–2002). He took the view that some inequalities cannot be tolerated and that the state is therefore justified in intervening. His ideas are explored further below.

Of course, many modern liberals do not accept such intervention in the interests of social justice. They retain the classical, nineteenth-century view that inequalities are justified in the free market, being the result of each individual's own efforts and abilities. It is therefore not without some reservations that this kind of justice is stated as a core liberal value. Liberals would disagree among themselves on this point.

Types of liberalism

Early forms

The first true liberals did not call themselves 'liberals'. They tended to be referred to as 'radicals' or 'republicans', or sometimes even 'rationalists'. In retrospect, however, we may correctly describe them as early liberals. The main principle of the early liberal movement was natural rights. The champions of natural rights theory came from all parts of the Western world and included such historically significant figures as John Locke, Jean-Jacques Rousseau, Thomas Paine and Thomas Jefferson.

The emphasis on natural rights gave rise to the various practical developments given below:

- A government has no authority to encroach upon the rights of its people, unless the people expressly consent to sacrifice some of their rights to that government. Furthermore, even if individual rights have been sacrificed, people must retain the option of reclaiming them by dissolving the government.
- All are born with equal rights (although this perhaps excluded women at this early stage of liberal development). Governments should respect and promote equal rights.
- The most important right that nature grants to all, after the basic right to life, is the right to be free. Freedom in this context means the right to pursue one's own interests. Here again, governments must respect and protect the freedom of its citizens.

➤ The exercise of power without the expressed authority of the people cannot be justified since it denies fundamental rights.

These were revolutionary ideas and it is therefore no surprise that they gave rise to revolutions. The old world of hereditary rulers, strict social hierarchies and limited individual liberty was either swept away or dramatically reformed by these early radical thinkers.

Utilitarianism

The concept of 'utility' was developed by early economists in the late-eighteenth and early-nineteenth centuries. The term meant satisfaction or perhaps even happiness — whatever gave an individual pleasure. The utilitarians, led in Britain by Jeremy Bentham, believed it was possible to calculate how much utility each individual could derive from consuming certain goods, and that it was therefore also possible to calculate the total amount of utility a whole society was achieving. However, it was not for external powers to decide what gave people utility. Individuals were to decide what gave them more or less utility for themselves.

Jeremy Bentham, Britain's chief proponent of utilitarianism

The significance of this concept for economists of the period was that if there were free trade within and between countries and if each consumer were able to purchase whatever goods he or she liked within his or her income constraints, total utility in a society would be automatically maximised. Put another way, a free-market economy, inhabited by free individuals, would guarantee the common good.

The political utilitarians agreed, but added a further element. They admitted the possibility that governments could add to the total sum of utility by taking certain actions. Indeed, Bentham argued that all actions by government should be judged on the basis of a kind of algebra or calculus which would establish whether total utility would be increased or reduced. This implied two principles. First, that governments had to accept what people asserted would give them satisfaction, and second, that government should be limited to providing what the people as a whole preferred. The principle was famously summarised in the idea that governments should pursue 'the greatest good for the greatest number.'

Utilitarians can be described as liberals in that they accepted the freedom of individuals to determine their own best interests and insisted that the role of government should be limited. However, the liberals that followed them identified two main problems with utilitarianism. The first was that it took a simplistic view of what motivated individuals and what gave them pleasure. For example, the consumption of goods may give pleasure, but it is not as high a form of pleasure as, say, gaining a good education or appreciating the arts. The second objection was that the doctrine opened the door to excessive state intervention. As long as total social utility was increased, the utilitarians argued, the state could take positive action, but early liberals feared that any state activity would threaten the freedom of individuals.

Thus, utilitarianism declined in influence as the nineteenth century progressed. It was replaced in the world of radical politics by a purer form of liberalism known as classical liberalism.

Classical liberalism

The classical liberals were largely inspired by the dominant philosophy of John Stuart Mill, a disciple of Bentham, who took the philosophy of freedom to new heights. For those who later became known as classical liberals, the freedom of the individual was every-thing. This is how Mill described the scope of liberty:

> [Liberty] comprises first the inward domain of conscience in the most comprehensive sense; liberty of thought and feeling; absolute freedom of opinion and sentiment on all subjects, practical or speculative, scientific, moral or theological... Secondly the principle requires liberty of tastes and pursuits; of framing the plan of our life to suit our own character; of doing as we like... Thirdly from this liberty of each individual follows the liberty, within the same limits, of combination among individuals; freedom to unite, for any purpose not involving harm to others.
>
> From *On Liberty*, 1859

Today we talk of such freedoms as 'civil liberties' and summarise them as freedom of expression, thought, worship, association and movement.

It is important to understand why Mill and the other classical liberals worshipped liberty to the extent that they did. The early liberals derived freedom from natural rights; utilitarians saw freedom in terms of the ability to pursue one's own self-interest. For Mill, individual liberty was associated with higher ideals than these. He believed that freedom would maximise human progress by promoting innovation, creativity and self-fulfilment. It went hand in hand with the entrepreneurial spirit. This is what Mill had to say about his own utilitarian principles:

> I regard utility as the ultimate appeal on all ethical questions; but it must be utility in the largest sense, grounded on the permanent interests of a man as a progressive being.
>
> Ibid.

We should note here his use of the term 'progressive being'. Whereas Bentham largely saw self-interest and freedom in terms of the consumption of goods, Mill was interested in human progress. In other words, Mill saw humans as creative individuals, whereas the utilitarians saw them merely as consumers. Thus we can interpret the classical liberal idea of freedom as partly a matter of principle (Mill) and partly a matter of economic wellbeing (Bentham).

The concept of freedom naturally led to an interest in tolerance as a political virtue, i.e. **political tolerance**. Such a progression was utterly logical. The liberals' argument was that our own freedom depends upon all people enjoying the same freedom. In other words, if we expect others to respect our freedom, we must respect theirs. This principle is particularly relevant to freedom of expression, although Mill himself accepted that there were limits to free speech — our words must not be used to harm others or to incite other people to harming others. On the whole, however, we and the law should respect people's right to choose their own beliefs and values and to express them publicly. This same principle has been applied in order to guarantee civil liberties such as freedom of movement, freedom of association and freedom of worship. There is no reason, say liberals, why such freedoms should not be tolerated by the state.

Key term

Political tolerance

This principle was developed by liberals, notably Locke and Mill. It asserts that the state should tolerate all beliefs and activities which do no harm to the security and integrity of the state, and which do not result in harm to individuals or groups in that society. It mainly refers to freedom of religion, political belief, lifestyle and expression.

Nineteenth-century liberals were concerned by the dangers of rulers accumulating too much power. However, they did not see the growth of democracy as the answer to this. Indeed, classical liberals were opposed to the introduction of popular democracy. For them this meant majority rule and, as both Tocqueville and Mill remarked, this was the *tyranny of the majority.* For these liberals, universal suffrage was a dangerous idea. The numerical majority formed by the working class would permanently suppress minority groups. Many early liberals therefore supported the retention of the property qualification for voting so as to counterbalance the power of the majority. (Property owners were considered to be more tolerant and responsible in their outlook.)

As for the dangers of powerful government, liberals argued for a minimal state, to be granted only a narrow range of essential functions. The minimal state was to retain responsibility for maintaining order, security and peace in order to guarantee the protection of individual liberties and prevent the formation of monopolies. In a free-market economy, it was understood that some companies might be so successful and grow so large that they would be in a position to exploit both workers and consumers. It was a legitimate function of the state, therefore, to control such economic power. To this day such 'competition policy', as it is now known, has been supported by those who wish to see the deregulation of economic activity in other areas.

Box 1.3 summarises the main principles of classical liberals. It is worth adding that they subscribed to the core liberal value that government should only be established by consent, that it should be regulated by a binding constitution and that all citizens should enjoy the benefits of legal justice and equal rights.

> **Box 1.3** **The main principles of classical liberalism**

> ➤ Individual freedoms should flourish and be respected.
> ➤ The state should be limited to a minimum number of functions, largely confined to protecting people from each other, defending the nation and preventing the accumulation of economic and political power.
> ➤ There should be a tolerant society in which behaviour that was not harmful to others would be uncontrolled.
> ➤ The economy should be based on completely free markets, except where monopolies were developed.
> ➤ The state should be placed in the hands of a representative democracy.

One variation of classical liberalism is worthy of note: the Manchester School in England. It was led by two radical politicians, John Bright (1811–89) and Richard Cobden (1804–65). They concentrated on the issue of free trade, although Bright also supported full adult suffrage (unlike Mill). They believed that free trade — national and international — would mean cheap goods, especially food. This development would be the most effective way of improving the conditions of the working classes — more effective, indeed, than state-organised welfare. 'Manchesterism', therefore, looked at liberty from the point of view of the working classes, whereas the Millite liberals were associated with the property-owning and entrepreneurial middle classes. These ideas remain interesting today, as free trade has returned as a key issue in the modern world, receiving support from liberals and conservatives who consider the interests of Western consumers, and from radicals on the left who believe it can benefit poor countries suffering from excessive protectionism in world trade (see Box 1.4).

> **Box 1.4** **Contemporary neo-liberalism**

> During the late 1970s and in the 1980s interest in classical liberal ideas enjoyed a major revival. It was not a feature of liberal parties at the time, but of the new style of conservatism known as the 'New Right'. Indeed, Margaret Thatcher (1925–), the British champion of the New Right, was happy to admit that she was 'at heart' a classical liberal. Spurred on by liberal economists and philosophers such as Milton Friedman (1912–) and Friedrich Hayek (1899–1992), she and other disciples of the New Right, including US president Ronald Reagan (1911–2004), set about re-establishing free markets in both a domestic and a world setting.

> As a conservative development, the classical liberal revival is normally known as *neo-liberalism* to distinguish it from its nineteenth-century ancestor, but the philosophies of Mill and Bright and Cobden are echoed in this passage from Friedman's work:

>> Another essential part of economic freedom is freedom to use the resources we possess in accordance with our own values — freedom to enter any occupation, engage in any business enterprise, buy from and sell to anyone else, so long as we do so on a strictly voluntary basis and do not resort to force in order to coerce others.

>> From *Free to Choose*, 1980

We must be extremely careful not to imply that neo-liberalism and classical liberalism are the same thing. In terms of their beliefs about free trade they might be, but the New Right neo-liberals had no hesitation in accepting that the state should intervene in people's lives to maintain law and order and to enforce a particular view of personal morality. In other words, for the neo-liberals, the minimal state principle applied to economics but not to politics in general.

Social Darwinism and libertarianism

In 1859, at the height of the classical liberal era, Charles Darwin (1809–82) published his great work *On the Origin of the Species*. His theories of evolution shook the scientific world and had a dramatic impact on social theory.

A number of thinkers looked at Darwin's discoveries and immediately set about applying them to human society. Herbert Spencer (1820–93) was a leading thinker of a political movement which was later described as 'social Darwinism'. Spencer was already interested in the idea that social justice consists of individuals making whatever they can of their lives, provided (as other classical liberals had insisted) they do not interfere with the freedom of others. Since we are innately unequal in our abilities and our motivation, it is only natural that some will succeed and others will fail. Spencer used the term 'survival of the fittest' to describe this process, even before Darwin's theories were published.

Refining his theories in response to the Darwinian revolution, Spencer argued that it is those who adapt most appropriately to their social environment who will do best. Those who fail to adapt will inevitably suffer. He saw this as the natural order of things, just as it was among animal species. Samuel Smiles (1812–1904), a contemporary of Spencer, turned social Darwinism into a quasi-religion. In his best known work, *Self Help* (1859), he argued that it is within the capability of all individuals, including members of the working class, to improve themselves through diligent activity and a willingness to set up new economic ventures. Nobody should rely on others, charities or the state to support them. We succeed or fail according to our own efforts. Smiles made this high-minded exhortation:

> The healthy spirit of self help created amongst working people would, more than any other measure, serve to raise them as a class, and this, not by pulling down others, but by levelling them up to a higher and still advancing standard of religion, intelligence and virtue.

> From *Self Help*, 1859

The fact that *Self Help* sold over 150,000 copies, at a time when a minority could afford books and many were illiterate, bears testament to how strong the entrepreneurial spirit was in mid-nineteenth century England.

In the 1980s, when classical liberalism was enjoying a revival within the New Right movement, social Darwinism and libertarianism, its close associate, were also enjoying growing popularity. This revival was based on two main beliefs.

First, many conservative and neo-liberal thinkers took their support for free economic markets to extremes, proposing the complete removal of all state restrictions, in particular the removal of nearly all taxation. These followers of **libertarianism** even proposed that services such as education, law and order and healthcare should be transferred to the private sector and left to market forces. This was linked to social Darwinism, in that it implied the survival of the fittest. In a completely deregulated society, free rein would be given for able and dynamic individuals to succeed and, therefore, for those who are lazy and fail to adapt themselves to get what they deserve — very little.

Second, there was a growing belief that state welfare had become excessive. What the libertarians (and members of the New Right in general) called a *dependency culture* had developed, to the detriment of prosperity and human progress. Dependency culture suggested that many people had become used to relying heavily on state support, through social security benefits and the provision of 'free' services by the state. This was sapping people of their dynamism and motivation. Too many individuals, they argued, had grown used to contributing little to society so that growth, innovation and progress were stifled. They therefore proposed the removal of virtually all welfare services. As Samuel Smiles had argued over a century before, people should learn to stand on their own two feet. Furthermore, whatever the outcome of such a free society and however much economic inequality might result, natural justice would be considered to have been done.

Key term

Libertarianism

This term refers to an extreme form of liberalism. Libertarianism emerged in the latter part of the nineteenth century and has become more popular since the 1980s. Though they are ideologically closer to liberals, most modern libertarians have seen themselves as part of the conservative movement. They insist that the state is an unwarranted restriction on freedom and its functions should be reduced to a bare minimum. However, unlike anarchists, libertarians stop short of proposing the state's complete abolition. Certainly, they argue, the state should not interfere with economic and social affairs, nor should it become involved in matters of morality. Most social problems can be solved by the free market, even those concerning law and order. The state should therefore do little other than defend the people. Libertarianism's leading modern exponent has been the US philosopher Robert Nozick (1938–2002).

It is a strange irony that libertarianism, considered a 'right wing' ideology, is often also known as *anarcho-capitalism* and is therefore associated with the most left wing of all philosophies — anarchism. Political ideology appears, therefore, to have come full circle. Perhaps the leading modern exponent of libertarianism, or anarcho-capitalism, was the US philosopher Robert Nozick. Nozick argued for the near complete abolition of the state and its functions. This implied no taxation, no welfare and almost no laws restricting human behaviour. Rejecting Mill's principle that our freedoms should not interfere with the freedom of others, Nozick insisted that it was up to individuals to protect themselves from others. They should not rely on the state to do it for them. In other words, Nozick's ideal state was more minimal even than Mill's and Spencer's.

New liberalism

The term 'new liberalism' is potentially misleading. It does not refer to a contemporary movement. This 'new' philosophy was developed and so named around 1870, the purpose being to distinguish it from the dominant classical liberal form. The change in liberal philosophy occurred as a result of two developments, one philosophical, the other practical.

The new philosophical perspective was supplied in Britain by T. H. Green. Green accepted the liberal belief in the importance of individual ('negative') liberty, but made two observations that were to have a profound influence on the future of liberalism. The first was that we cannot consider ourselves to be completely free merely to pursue our own interests. We also have a social obligation to consider the needs and the welfare of others. Second, he described a further kind of freedom — what Berlin was to call 'positive' liberty a century later. This was freedom in the form of choice and opportunity, the chance to achieve **self-realisation**.

Key term

Self-realisation

Sometimes also known as 'self-fulfilment', this term describes a situation in which individuals (or sometimes groups) are able to achieve their own aspirations. It is related to the idea of positive liberty, suggesting that individuals obtain freedom by experiencing social conditions that allow them to fulfil their own hopes and goals.

On a more practical level, liberals had to come to terms with the fact that, as the nineteenth century wore on and capitalism and industrialisation intensified, many unpalatable social consequences were emerging. The conditions of the working classes showed few signs of improving, despite the fact that national prosperity, especially in Britain, was growing. Numerous social deprivations were coming to light, notably persistent illiteracy, poor health conditions, bad housing, and recurring unemployment causing economic insecurity. Many argued that these problems were the result of an excessively free market and a lack of positive intervention by the state. Allied to Green's identification of social responsibility as a vital human virtue, the revelation of widening inequality in society caused the liberal movement to re-examine its core beliefs. The result was new liberalism.

The fundamental belief upon which new liberalism was based was that the poorer sections of society were unable to benefit from the economic freedoms that the classical liberals had supported. Society had the potential to progress collectively, provided that all individuals were able to take advantage of their freedom. This implied intervention by the state to provide education in particular, but also a range of other welfare benefits, notably healthcare, pensions and housing. This would achieve two social objectives: greater equality of opportunity and a more humane society in which the benefits of progress would be spread more evenly. Green paid relatively little attention to the practicalities of such welfare. William Gladstone, the great liberal prime minister of the nineteenth century, did attempt to reduce inherited privilege and introduced primary education, but these developments were relatively modest. Gladstone, however, was followed by liberal thinkers and politicians who were prepared to act more decisively.

Elementary education was extended to all in 1901 and the Liberal administration of 1906–11, led by Herbert Asquith (1852–1928) and David Lloyd George (1863–1945), widened the process. It provided the first pensions and state-sponsored insurance schemes for unemployment and sickness. It was not yet a welfare state, but it was a major step in that direction. L. T. Hobhouse (1864–1929) and J. A. Hobson (1858–1940), two major liberal thinkers, argued aggressively that the state needed to take an increasingly active role in creating more social justice. This is how Hobhouse expressed the state's new role:

> Liberalism is now formally committed to a task which certainly involves a new conception of the State in its relation to the individual life and private enterprise... From the standpoint which best represents its continuity with earlier Liberalism, it appears as a fuller realisation of individual liberty contained in the provision of equal opportunities for self-development.

> From *The Crisis of Liberalism*, 1909

These developments brought liberalism a long way from its classical roots. The new liberals now saw the state as a vehicle for the enhancement of liberty rather than a threat to it. This was a different kind of freedom, effectively positive freedom, represented by equality of opportunity and the widening of choices for all. It was to be achieved by the use of general taxation to provide welfare services and to spread prosperity more widely. Hobson, who was close to the newly formed Labour Party in his views, even proposed some public ownership of major industries.

The problem for the liberal movement in Britain was that the Labour Party, which was formed in 1900, was moving in the same direction. Furthermore, Labour had no qualms about extending the role of the state. Many liberals remained concerned about state power, which inhibited freedom of action, so it was no surprise that Labour effectively annexed most of the new liberal philosophy.

Welfare (social) liberalism

As the liberal movement came to accept the expanded role of the state, it became clear that it needed to respond to the growing popular support for socialist initiatives. In the event, the final acceptance of the state as a vehicle for extending liberty was provided not by a philosopher or a politician, but by a senior civil servant, William Beveridge.

In the 1940s Beveridge was charged by the wartime coalition government with producing a blueprint for social policy after the war had ended. As a liberal, he needed to address the problem of how to propose large extensions to the role of the state without jeopardising people's liberties. He did this by formulating new conceptions of freedom. For Beveridge, such deprivations as poverty, unemployment and lack of education were curtailments of freedom as serious as laws and overbearing governments. By relieving the poorer and needier members of the population from these problems, liberty would be extended, not threatened. He was guided by a Liberal Party report of 1929 which had signalled a new attitude to the state. A key passage read as follows:

> Liberalism stands for liberty, but it is an error to think that a policy of liberty must always be negative, that the state can help liberty only by abstaining from action, that invariably men are freest when their Government does least.

Released from the obligation to limit state power, Beveridge was able to consider how an active state could extend freedom. This is how he expressed his fundamental beliefs:

> To my mind there are three things above all that every citizen of this country needs as conditions of a happy and useful life after the war. He needs freedom from want and fear of want, freedom from idleness and fear of idleness enforced by unemployment, freedom from war and fear of war.

From *Why I am a Liberal*, 1945

Postwar liberals, therefore, came to accept the welfare state that the Labour Government set up from 1945. Although this is seen as the jewel in the British socialist crown, it should be emphasised that it was inspired by a leading liberal figure, namely Beveridge. **Welfare**, especially education, extended equality of opportunity and expanded positive freedom.

Key term

Welfare

This concept was developed largely in the nineteenth century. It refers to the provision of services and subsidies to individuals and families to help provide them with an acceptable standard of living. Welfare involves the collection of funds — either through taxation or voluntary and charitable contributions — and their distribution in the form of money or services to those who are considered in need. In the case of the welfare state in Britain, some welfare is distributed to all, irrespective of their economic circumstances, e.g. education, state pensions and healthcare. Welfare usually includes provisions such as education, healthcare, pensions, subsidised housing, social services, benefits for the unemployed, disabled, long-term poor etc.

Meanwhile, another liberal, the economist John Maynard Keynes (1883–1946), felt able to justify extensions in the state's role on the grounds that economic stability could also enhance freedom. He argued that the state needed to engage in positive economic management in order to create an economic environment in which individuals would feel confident in their ability to engage in commercial and industrial enterprises, to pursue their careers with some confidence about the economic future, to enjoy their private property and to be released from excessive fear of unemployment (the last issue being echoed by Beveridge).

Most of the proposals of welfare liberalism were adopted by Labour governments and, to some degree, were also supported by the Conservatives, with the consequence that the 1950s and 1960s became known as the era of 'consensus' politics. This political consensus over welfare, economic management and equality of opportunity spread to the USA and elsewhere in Europe. There was a pattern of governments extending their role to create the social 'goods' that liberals had promoted. Sadly for the liberals, the consensus meant that they were often squeezed out of power by more successful socialist and conservative administrations. It would therefore be true to say that from about 1940 to 1970 liberalism had enormous success in terms of the propagation of its new social philosophies, but was unsuccessful in securing the election of liberal governments.

Contemporary liberalism

Recently, mainstream liberalism has spent much of its time on the fringes of the political arena. In most of the democratic world, governments have been largely dominated either by social democratic or neo-liberal conservative administrations. Liberals have occasionally found themselves in coalitions, for example in Germany, Holland, Japan and Scotland, but have failed to dominate political agendas. This is not to say that liberalism has been totally ineffective. Social democrats, in particular, have adopted many of the core values of liberalism. The US philosopher John Rawls provided a bridge between liberalism and social democracy by developing a theory of justice which combined individual liberty with the provision of social justice. His ideas are described further below (see pp. 32–33).

The most original aspects of contemporary liberalism perhaps lie in its proposals for political reforms. These conform to liberalism's core values. They are designed to protect individual liberties and to preserve the independence of minority groups. The political and constitutional reforms which liberals have supported in recent years include the following:

- decentralising power to regional and local government
- promoting stronger constitutional safeguards against governmental power
- increasing use of referendums to promote popular democracy
- strengthening legal safeguards for individual rights
- promoting freedom of information legislation
- safeguarding and extending the rights of women and minority groups

Box 1.5 Some major modern liberal principles and policies

➤ The defence and extension of individual and group rights, e.g. women's rights, and equality of treatment for ethnic minorities, gays and the disabled.

➤ Campaigns to extend both worker and consumer rights. Liberals recognise the dangers of excessive economic power being wielded by big business corporations.

➤ Concern for environmental protection.

➤ Policies to counteract the growth of the inequality which has resulted from neo-liberal, free-market measures introduced by New Right conservatives. In particular, liberals have increasingly proposed taxation and welfare policies to redistribute income to the poor.

➤ Efforts to reduce the causes of crime rather than simply relying on punishment, a reaction to hard-line law and order policies.

➤ Political reform designed to counteract the growing power of the centralised state.

A general overview of contemporary liberalism, therefore, would present the movement as engaging in the defence of groups and in the promotion of policies which have been ignored by other political movements. Put another way, contemporary liberalism can be seen as a reaction against the growth of both state power and the undesirable consequences of free markets.

Summary

Table 1.1 Summary of the principal forms of liberalism

Classical liberalism	New liberalism	Welfare liberalism	Contemporary liberalism
• Liberty of the individual	• Sense of social obligation	• State-sponsored welfare schemes	• Promotion of greater economic equality or justice
• Individuals free to pursue self-interest	• Promotion of positive liberty	• State management of the economy	• Political and constitutional reform to control state power
• Tolerance of different beliefs, religions and cultures	• Promotion of choice and opportunity	• Greater concentration on equality of opportunity	• More popular democracy
• Minimal government	• Equality of opportunity	• Freedom from social deprivation	• Decentralisation of government
• Free-market economy	• Limited welfare provision		• Environmentalism
• Representative democracy			• Defence of group rights
			• Promotion of worker and consumer rights
			• Tolerant social and law and order policies

Key liberal thinkers

John Locke (English, 1632–1704)

Locke predates the term 'liberal' and is therefore better known as the father of 'Whig' philosophy. He was part of the political movement which resulted in the Glorious

Revolution of 1688. This peaceful revolution replaced the Catholic James II with the Protestant William of Orange but, more importantly, established the sovereignty of parliament over law making.

Locke took as the basis of his philosophy the twin ideas of natural rights and natural laws. For Locke, government had to be established by consent, respect the natural rights of its citizens and govern according to natural laws. No government could claim its legitimacy either from God or from nature. The only political authority for rulers could come from the people. Such governments should be limited and must respect people's natural rights. He identified these rights as life, liberty, property ownership and the pursuit of happiness. Locke was one of the first philosophers to promote religious and political tolerance; natural law, for Locke, included such tolerance and dictated that man should take into consideration the interests of others when deciding how to act.

The key political concept of the 'social contract' was developed by Locke. Contract theory in politics insists that government should be established by a contract between the government and the governed. The government agrees to govern according to natural law and respect individual rights, while the people agree to accept the authority of the government and to obey its laws. Should the government not govern by natural law or should it abuse natural rights, the people should have the right to cancel the contract and dissolve the government. In practice, Locke proposed a system of constitutionally controlled monarchy, accountable to an elected representative parliament.

Locke can be seen as the earliest proponent of liberal ideas. His influence was felt a century later when both the French and American revolutionaries were chiefly inspired by his philosophy.

John Stuart Mill (British, 1806–73)

The son of the utilitarian philosopher James Mill, John Stuart Mill was a politician and social campaigner as well as a philosopher. He began his political life as a utilitarian, following the teaching of his father and Jeremy Bentham. He took as his starting point the idea that an individual is the best judge of his or her own interests and that no authority has the right to claim a superior knowledge of that individual's interests. However, he soon broke with the utilitarians, claiming that their philosophy was intolerant and inflexible. He also criticised utilitarians' proposals for state intervention in some circumstances to promote the common good; Mill, at least in his early life, saw state intervention as a threat to individual liberty. More importantly, he argued against the utilitarian view that the sole motivation of human beings was the pursuit of material pleasures, claiming that, on the contrary, there were higher goals such as learning and aesthetic appreciation. For Mill, liberty should be used to progress human civilisation, not just to enrich it. He famously expressed this in colourful language:

> ...better to be a human being dissatisfied than a pig satisfied; better to be Socrates dissatisfied than a fool satisfied.
>
> From *Utilitarianism*, 1871

Mill's main contribution to liberal theory was to define the limits of freedom. He divided actions that were *self-regarding* and that had no effect on others from those that were *other-regarding* and clearly did impinge on the freedom of others. For example, expressing religious or other beliefs publicly is self-regarding, whereas anti-social behaviour is other-regarding. Governments, therefore, should tolerate self-regarding behaviour but are justified in regulating other-regarding actions. This implies that governments should be limited in their jurisdiction. They should never curtail freedom of thought, religion or expression, nor should they regulate economic activity, other than that which oppresses people, for example monopoly power.

In other matters, Mill was an unusual mixture of radicalism and conservatism. As regards representative parliamentary democracy, which he supported, he hatched a scheme to grant different numbers of votes to people, depending on their level of education. The illiterate would have one vote, while those who could pass tests on political knowledge would have more. This conservative view contrasted with his campaign to extend women's rights, a crusade which he shared with his wife, Harriet Taylor, and his stepdaughter, Helen Taylor. In 1869 all three wrote an early feminist tract together entitled *The Subjection of Women*, which proposed that voting and other rights be granted equally to women.

Towards the end of his life, Mill did modify his views somewhat, accepting that members of the working class required some support from the state. An entirely free society could be unjust, he admitted, and some state interference to correct these injustices could be tolerated.

Mill was one of the greatest English political philosophers. His influence spread well beyond England and remains important today. French and American liberals followed his theories, modern neo-liberals remain inspired by his teachings and even Karl Marx (1818–83) respected his views on the benefits of individual liberty.

Herbert Spencer (British, 1820–1903)

A journalist and philosopher, Spencer wrote at a time when the English state was beginning to engage in an increasing degree of interference and regulation. The era of Mill's classical theories was coming to an end and new liberalism, inspired by Green and Gladstone (see below), was proposing the provision of equality of opportunity by the state.

For Spencer, human society was an evolving organism and therefore subject to natural laws of progress. However, he rejected the emerging notion, shared by new liberals and traditional conservatives, that society is organic and people are interdependent. Instead, Spencer believed that all individuals were free and independent of each other. Indeed, as in the animal kingdom, humankind was in competition for the scarce resources offered by the Earth. This is not to say that he advocated any actions being justified in order to secure an advantage over others; rather he accepted that, within the natural laws, humans are engaged in an economic struggle against each other. He did not suggest that those who are successful should be so at the expense of others. His argument was that those who adapt best to the changing economic environment will move forward, and those who fail to do so will fall back. The term *social Darwinism* has often been applied to these theories.

Spencer enjoyed widespread but brief popularity in the latter part of the nineteenth century. For most mainstream political thinkers, his beliefs and schemes were simply too extreme at a time when social welfare was becoming popular. In the 1980s and 1990s, however, there was a revival of interest in Spencer among Conservatives and libertarians. In particular, Spencer's opposition to state welfare (and the tax needed to finance it) has proved attractive to those who oppose the so-called 'dependency culture'.

Thomas Hill Green (British, 1836–82)

The moral philosopher T. H. Green (as he is more usually known) made two main contributions to liberal thought. The first was the proposition that we are not merely self-seeking individuals who have no responsibility for others. Rather, he insisted, we do have an obligation to care for the welfare of others. He argued that it is possible to enjoy our own liberty without losing a sense of social responsibility. The second was the concept of the *organic society* and its application to modern conditions. This was not a new concept. It had become a key part of nineteenth-century German political philosophy, upon which Green based his teaching. Its basic proposition was that society is not merely a collection of unrelated individuals, but a single entity, a living organism with a life of its own which exists above the consciousness of individuals. This implies that society can have a collective consciousness, dubbed *Volksgemeinschaft* by the Germans.

Green's views on freedom proved to be revolutionary for liberals, forming the basis of what became known as 'new liberalism'. He recognised two senses of the term freedom. One was that of external constraint, as propounded by J. S. Mill. The other was a positive sense of the term, referring to the ability to realise one's own aspirations — in other words, to achieve *self-realisation.* In a completely free society, with little or no state regulation, self-realisation would be unachievable for most people. Some state intervention was therefore required to promote positive liberty. In practice, Green proposed a narrow range of measures, mainly to reduce inherited privilege and to provide equality of opportunity through education.

At a time when liberalism was in danger of becoming discredited, Green saved the movement from political decline: had liberals continued to support free-market economics and to oppose state welfare, they would have been accused of promoting a heartless and amoral philosophy.

William Gladstone (British, 1809–98)

Gladstone was prime minister four times between 1868 and 1894. He was also, arguably, the founder of the modern Liberal Party. In many ways he was a conventional liberal in that he supported individual liberty, religious tolerance, free trade and independence for Ireland. He also believed that inequality was the natural state of humankind. He can be considered more a follower of Green's than Mill's brand of liberal thought.

In particular, he promoted the introduction of widespread elementary education with the Forster Education Act of 1870. This opened the way for education that was free of Church control. Under his ministries trade unions were granted more rights, voting was extended to virtually all adults, and the civil service, universities, the army and the legal system were all opened to wider recruitment. Gladstone attacked privilege wherever it appeared to be restricting opportunity and stifling enterprise.

We should not, however, think of Gladstone as a radical. His reforms were relatively modest and many cynics suggest he only adopted his liberal policies in order to attract votes from the newly enfranchised working class. Nevertheless, he was a key liberal figure in that he gave liberalism political coherence. Under Gladstone, liberalism at last achieved its maturity as an ideology.

William Beveridge (British, 1879–1963)

The great liberal prime minister David Lloyd George had already introduced a wide range of welfare services sponsored by the state by the time Beveridge produced his famous report in 1942. Unlike many earlier liberals, Beveridge did not fear the extension of state intervention in society. Nor was he overly concerned by the need to raise finance through taxation (National Insurance payments to be precise), although the idea that the state should take compulsory collections from working people would have been unthinkable for nineteenth-century liberals.

William Beveridge discusses his report at a press conference, 1942

Two main elements of Beveridge's philosophy enabled him to retain his liberal credentials. The first was his argument that liberals stand for social justice. It was clear that free-market capitalism could not deliver such justice. The Great Depression of the 1930s had created enormous hardship and resulted in millions of citizens relying on a minimal level of financial support. Inequality grew and so did inequality of opportunity.

The second was his attitude to freedom. He insisted that liberty was a 'good' which should be available equally to all. The existence of equal legal and political rights, however, was not enough for Beveridge. He believed that various kinds of deprivation were a curtailment to freedom. In particular, poverty and unemployment made the idea of equal rights an absurdity. Poor individuals could not be said to be free to enjoy their fair share of the country's prosperity. Health problems and lack of education similarly narrowed the range of opportunities available to the poor. In 1940 Beveridge addressed the Liberal Party annual conference, describing his new conception of freedom:

A starving man is not free, because, until he is fed, he cannot have a thought for anything but how to meet his urgent physical needs; he is reduced from a man to an animal. A man who dare not resent what he feels to be an injustice from an employer or a foreman, lest this condemn him to chronic unemployment, is not free.

Beveridge's place in the sun was short-lived. He served the wartime government and his report was so eagerly awaited that crowds queued for hours to obtain the first copies. Later, he was granted a peerage and had to watch from the House of Lords while his proposals were implemented — not by a Liberal administration, but by a radical Labour government. Although he spent the rest of his political career in relative obscurity, he remains the principal architect of Britain's much-admired welfare state. The idea that the state should organise a compulsory, publicly-funded system of education, healthcare, pensions, social security and unemployment insurance was more at home in socialist ideology than liberal, but Beveridge had at least succeeded in bringing liberalism to the forefront of British politics.

John Rawls (US, 1921–2002)

This enormously influential US philosopher formed a bridge between modern liberal and social democratic thought. His best known work is a weighty book entitled *A Theory of Justice*, which was published in 1972.

Rawls saw his main task as reconciling the firm liberal belief in freedom with the need to prevent excessive inequality in society. In tackling this, he addressed a problem faced by both liberals and socialists — that measures taken to reduce inequality, or to prevent inequality occurring in the first place, will inevitably involve a loss of liberty for some. For example, if income is to be more evenly spread, there must be higher taxation for the rich and lower for the poor. This clearly represents a loss of liberty. Taxpayers are no longer free to spend their income in the way they wish: the proportion taxed is spent on the individual's behalf by the state. Similarly, any attempt to manipulate wages to prevent poverty among low-paid workers interferes with labour markets and curtails the freedom of entrepreneurs to run their businesses as they wish.

Rawls tackles the problem logically and step by step. His objective is to reconcile individual liberty with social justice and to establish criteria under which inequality or state regulation may be tolerated. He uses a philosophical device, which he calls the *original position*, to develop his conclusions (see Box 1.6).

Box 1.6 Rawls's original position and 'veil of ignorance'

Rawls imagines humankind in the situation that would have existed before society came into being, that is, a natural state, which he terms the 'original position'. If people are to create a society from this state of nature, they need to decide how wealth and goods are to be distributed within society. However, Rawls places a condition upon them before they can make their decisions. People are placed behind what he calls a 'veil of ignorance'. By this he means that they do not know how successful or unsuccessful they are likely to be or where they will end up in the scale of wealth. Life becomes a kind of lottery for them. In these circumstances, he believes individuals would construct a society where the worst off would not be more deprived than they themselves would wish to be if they ended up at the bottom of the scale. They would probably create an unequal society, but one where there was a minimum acceptable standard of living. Nobody should be allowed so much wealth that it would make the worst off in society fall below this minimum.

Applying this philosophical position to the practical, modern world, he suggests that a just society will be one where inequalities do not mean that the worst off are deprived as a result of the wealth of others. If this undesirable position is likely to occur, Rawls argues, the state is justified in intervening in the interests of social justice.

This principle has acted as a guide for both liberals and social democrats who have struggled to determine how much inequality is acceptable.

Rawls's practical principles, in brief, are organised as follows:
- Individuals should be as free as possible.
- Such freedom should only be tolerated if it is compatible with freedom for all. In other words, liberty should not be enjoyed at the expense of the freedom of others.
- Inequalities have to be justified.
- An inequality can be justified if it increases the prosperity of society as a whole.
- An inequality cannot be justified if it results in the poorest in society being made worse off than they were before.

Thus, according to Rawls's 'difference principle', even large inequalities can be justified. Inequality is not an evil in itself, but it cannot be tolerated if it disadvantages those at the lowest point on the economic scale. Similarly, individual freedom cannot be considered to be universally good. It can only be allowed full rein if all are free and have a high enough standard of living to enjoy a reasonable amount of personal liberty.

Rawls's supporters claim that he has provided a firm philosophical justification for a society in which there can be a great deal of individualism and inequality, but within which there can also be said to be social justice and freedom. Cynics suggest his ideas are merely a fudged compromise between socialism and liberalism, but this has not prevented his popularity among politicians of the centre and the centre left. He could certainly count both Bill Clinton (1946–) and Tony Blair (1953–) among his political disciples.

Issues in liberalism

Democracy

Although liberalism is closely associated with the modern development of democracy and democratic institutions, there have been a number of problems in its relationship with democracy. Jean-Jacques Rousseau predicted many of these problems before democracy, as we know it today, had been developed. Rousseau saw democracy as being fundamentally majority rule. While this initially seems to be an acceptable form of government, he points out that there is a key difference between the will of the people, which is simply derived from their expressions of *self-interest*, and the general will, which is the *collective* expression of the common good.

In Rousseau's view, even if 99% of the people supported one course of action, it would not necessarily be for the common benefit if it were simply the sum of the self-interested motives of the individuals who formed the majority. In modern terms, we might say that Rousseau was showing a preference for consensus politics over simple majority rule. He therefore rejected democracy as a satisfactory system of government, except in the unusual circumstance that a small community of enlightened individuals take into account the interests of others as well as their own. Rousseau regretfully rejected democracy with these famous words:

> Were there a people of gods, their government would be democratic. So perfect a
> government is not for men.
> From The Social Contract, 1762

Since Rousseau, liberals have continued to be suspicious of democracy as majority rule, but for a different reason. It is perfectly acceptable to liberals that individuals pursue self-interest, and that they should use their participation in the political system (mainly by voting) to pursue that self-interest. What is not acceptable, however, is that the majority should govern at the expense of minorities, or of individual rights. Many instances of this happening can be found in places where direct forms of majority-based democracy exist, for example the persistent discrimination against the Catholic minority in Northern Ireland by Unionists, and the 2005 ban on hunting with dogs, which appears to persecute a minority pursuing a private pastime. Mill's theory of tolerance is relevant here, too — as long as we see hunting with dogs as a self-regarding action.

Democracy therefore emerged as a means by which people could be liberated and free to express their self-interested individualism, and yet excessive amounts of this can result in the oppression of individuals and minorities. This is often said by liberals to be the *paradox of democracy*. There is no guarantee that the majority is right, or that the outcome of majority rule will be just.

Nineteenth-century liberals were concerned by the *tyranny of the majority* and recommended a number of remedies. The most common was to retain the property qualification for voting so that the irresponsible majority would be denied political rights. Conservatives insisted that the monarchy and landed aristocracy would govern in the common interest rather than their own; liberals were sceptical of this, but nevertheless many of them believed that property owners would be responsible in their use of political power and not use it to oppress other classes.

Modern liberals could not accept this denial of voting rights to the majority and social and welfare liberals have been forced to accept considerable extensions in the role and power of the state during the last century. Democracy was essential to control state power, but simple majority rule remained dangerous. The solution was to be found largely by referring to the US experience:

➢ First, the sovereign constitution of the USA was constructed to protect the people against majority power. By carefully placing controls over governmental power, dividing power among different institutions and including guaranteed rights for individuals and groups, popular democracy could flourish. Inspired by the American experience, therefore, all modern liberals support **constitutionalism** and limited government to protect democracy.

➢ Second, the political structure of the USA has developed into a pluralist system. Groups have considerable access to decision-making institutions and have many legal safeguards to protect their rights. Perhaps the most important of these safeguards is freedom of expression and thought, ensuring that a wide variety of views and beliefs may flourish.

Key terms

Constitutionalism

This liberal-inspired principle asserts that modern states and governments must be controlled by a binding constitution which limits their powers and protects the rights of individuals and groups. It also insists that governments cannot set aside constitutional principles for their own purposes. It was first established in the early nineteenth century by the founding fathers of the USA and their first chief justice, John Marshall (1755–1835). Constitutionalism is weak in Britain since there is no binding, codified constitution, although there are constitutional principles by which government is guided.

By adding the ideas gained from the US experience to some of the core principles of the philosophy, we can summarise how modern liberals have been able to offer solutions to the dilemmas and paradoxes of democracy. This is shown in Box 1.7.

Box 1.7 The liberal answer to the paradox of democracy

➢ The basis of democracy must be government by consent.
➢ Government should be limited by a sovereign constitution.
➢ Individual and group rights must be protected.
➢ The political system should allow full access to all legal groups.
➢ There must be freedom of expression.
➢ Only where a fundamental issue concerning the jurisdiction and system of government arises should direct democracy (effectively a referendum) be used.
➢ Representative and responsible government is essential in ensuring moderate politics that will mediate between the majority and minorities.

The state

For much of its existence, liberalism has seen the state as a threat to individual liberty and the natural development of society. This was especially true during the classical period of the nineteenth century and the neo-liberal revival of the 1980s and 1990s.

Liberals' original fear of the state, as expressed by Mill in particular, was that it might seek to interfere with aspects of people's lives that were private. Mill also believed that intervention in economic markets would inhibit innovation, enterprise and dynamic progress. The earlier utilitarians had been concerned that government intervention should always consider the best interests of society as a whole, but classical liberals considered only the interests of individuals. For them, if individuals could flourish free of state interference, this would automatically create social progress.

Later in the nineteenth century, the more extreme followers of the classical tradition, often known as social Darwinists, emphasised the dangers of the state providing too much support for people who should take responsibility for their own welfare. Each individual, argued the likes of Smiles and Spencer, is the guardian of his or her own prosperity. He or she should not expect help from the state. They added that individual enterprise is vital if society is to progress successfully. More recently, in the 1980s, the 'excessive' provision of social welfare was seen to be creating a 'dependency culture'. Within this culture, individuals had grown used to relying on the state, so that private enterprise and hard work were stifled. The neo-liberals who opposed the dependency culture therefore proposed the abolition of some social benefits and a reduction in others. In both the UK and the USA, the frontiers of the state were, in Margaret Thatcher's words, 'rolled back'. By this time, however, traditional liberals were more concerned with social justice and so they had become more tolerant of state activism.

The welfare tradition of liberalism and the liberalism of Green, Gladstone, Lloyd George, Beveridge and Rawls saw the state as an ally rather than an enemy. Of course, all liberals will still seek to protect individual and group rights from the power of the state, but it is felt that, as long as this can be guaranteed, the state should be allowed to pursue liberal objectives. Equality of opportunity requires state intervention in the fields of education and welfare. The more recent pursuit of social justice, too, has implied the redistribution of income and wealth through state policies. The demand for economic stability, which Keynes saw as vital for the maintenance of individual economic enterprise, has meant that the state must intervene whenever the forces of the free market fail to ensure favourable conditions for that individualism.

In summary, therefore, the relationship between liberalism and the state has been a variable one. All liberals have a healthy fear of state power, but most liberals have come to accept the state for the benefits it can deliver.

Liberalism in the UK

Liberalism and the parties

Parties that have called themselves 'liberal' in the UK — the Liberal Party and later the Liberal Democrats — have had remarkably little electoral success since the 1920s. One might, therefore, be forgiven for thinking that liberalism as a political doctrine has been in decline. In fact, the reverse could be said to be true. Liberal ideas now form a large part of the political consensus. In a sense, all mainstream British parties are liberal parties.

The Labour Party in particular has been characterised by its liberal philosophy. Indeed, the moderate nature of British socialism is unique. Many socialists, especially on the European continent, have been notorious for their careless attitude to personal freedom in the pursuit of equality. Labour, in contrast, has always been careful to strike a balance between the two goals. The party was always committed to parliamentary democracy, but from the 1950s onwards it was also associated with pluralist politics and a determination to tolerate alternative doctrines to its own and even varied beliefs among its own members. Labour has also championed the causes of minorities and of civil liberties. In the 1960s and 1970s in particular, Labour governments presided over such liberal reforms as changes to laws on homosexuality, the legalisation of abortion, equal pay for women, the outlawing of racial discrimination and protection for workers against unfair dismissal. Some of these measures may have been proposed by Liberal politicians, but Labour administrations made them a reality.

The arrival of New Labour in the 1990s introduced more liberal values to the party. Under John Smith (1938–94) and Tony Blair, Labour accepted that the promotion of individualism should be given considerably more prominence, even at the expense of collectivism in some cases. Constitutional reform, a cherished goal of the Liberal Democrats, has formed a central feature of Labour policy. Devolution of power to Scotland and Wales, the incorporation of the European Convention on Human Rights into British law, the removal of most of the hereditary peers from the House of Lords and the introduction of proportional representation for several types of regional election are all liberal aspirations. This is not to say that New Labour is synonymous with liberalism. A number of its key policies have been heavily criticised for being distinctly illiberal, notably in the fields of law and order and security, but the basis of New Labour philosophy has its roots in liberal doctrine.

On a more fundamental level, the Labour Party has come to accept inequality as an inevitable consequence of free-market economics. Like liberals, New Labour believes that, as long as equality of opportunity can be promoted, people should be free to be unequal. The idea that equality can be imposed upon a society has been left far behind by British social democrats. Furthermore, the individual pursuit of self-interest, a throwback to utilitarian liberalism, is now tolerated and even encouraged.

The Scottish Parliament. Although implemented by Labour, devolution is inspired by liberal ideas

Classical liberalism and social Darwinism enjoyed a revival in the 1980s among New Right, neo-liberal conservatives, but this is not the only sense in which conservatism has been imbued with the liberal spirit. US conservatives, especially, follow doctrines such as limited and decentralised government, constitutionalism, civil rights and economic liberty. The UK Conservative Party has also come to accept the need to safeguard minority and individual rights.

Many small parties in the UK have also embraced liberal values. The Welsh and Scottish nationalists base their philosophy upon the principles of government by consent and the self-determination of national groups. These parties have also shown staunch support for human rights and the protection of minorities. Welfarism and equality of opportunity are also key elements in nationalist thinking (excepting, of course, the British National movement and extreme Northern Ireland unionists, who are decidedly illiberal).

Turning finally to the Liberal Democrats themselves, it is clear that liberal philosophy remains at the heart of the party. They place greater stress on state intervention, to create social and economic equality, and on social justice, in the form of the redistribution of income from rich to poor, than most liberals in the past, but individual liberty and tolerance still form their central philosophy.

Liberal democracy in the UK

Although the UK has no codified constitution — a key liberal demand — the story of the development of its political system has been that of the gradual evolution of a true liberal democracy. Without a recognisable constitution the system can never claim to be fully liberal in its inspiration, but it is now true that the vast majority of the UK's political arrangements have become entrenched in law. This may be seen as the next best thing to a real constitution. The 'liberal' elements of the UK political system can be summarised as follows:

- Elections are largely uncorrupted and virtually all adult citizens have the right to vote and stand for office.
- All legal political parties and pressure groups are free to operate within the political system.
- Government is permanently accountable to Parliament and to the people through general elections.
- Important constitutional changes are now subjected to popular referendum and therefore consent.
- National minorities have been granted a large amount of political independence.
- The Human Rights Act guarantees most individual rights.
- Parliament provides a powerful means by which individual grievances can be redressed.
- Parliament — both the Commons and the Lords — sees itself as a mediator between the interests of the majority and minorities.
- The law reflects a high degree of tolerance to minority groups.

➤ Equal legal and political rights are guaranteed.

➤ There is a wide variety of social rights accorded to minority groups, to workers and to consumers.

Of course, not all aspects of the political system are liberal:

➤ The sovereignty of Parliament always threatens individual liberties, especially as the executive branch is usually able to dominate the legislature.

➤ Much of the prime minister's power remains unchecked and the main electoral system is often considered to be unjust.

➤ A few unelected institutions have retained a limited political role — mainly the monarchy and the House of Lords — and many public officials are neither elected nor fully accountable to the public.

But despite these reservations, it would not be realistic to describe the UK political system as anything other than liberal in spirit.

Core British values

Finally, the question must be addressed as to whether British political and social culture is liberal in nature. The UK is certainly often praised for its tolerance towards a wide variety of beliefs and cultures. Despite racial tensions, most ethnic minorities live in peace alongside the indigenous population. Even some extreme beliefs — those of the British National Party, for example — are granted freedom of expression. Visitors to the country often speak of the atmosphere of freedom and tolerance that prevails in the UK.

Britain is also said to be notable for its sense of social and legal justice. It is open to question whether it is the mother of modern democracy (the USA and France perhaps have stronger claims), but the common law tradition, which embraces individual rights and protection from excessive state power, is certainly rooted in the UK.

The British media is remarkably free from state influence, as is the broadcasting establishment. Mill's insistence that all reasonable values and beliefs should be tolerated is enshrined in the long-held principles of freedom of speech and of the press. There is widespread artistic freedom and little sense that experimental ideas should be stifled. On the economic front, too, the UK has come (perhaps only recently) to embrace the free entrepreneurial spirit so beloved of nineteenth-century liberals. It is part of the British way of life for a host of intermediate groups to flourish, enabling most citizens to participate in political, social and community-based activities. In other words, the UK has a **pluralist** culture.

Key term

Pluralism

This term describes a society in which there is tolerance of many different beliefs, movements and faiths. It suggests a political system in which different political parties and pressure groups are free to operate and have access to decision-making processes. Modern liberal democracies are pluralist in nature, while totalitarian regimes inhibit or destroy pluralism.

There is a strong claim to be made that Britain is not just a liberal democracy, but also a liberal society. Neither conservatism nor socialism — both strong British traditions — have ever overshadowed the fundamentally liberal spirit of the country.

Exam focus

Using this chapter and other resources available to you, answer the following questions.

Short questions

Your answers should be about 300 words long.

1 Distinguish between the concepts of negative and positive liberty.
2 Why have liberals supported the idea of individual liberty?
3 Why do liberals support constitutionalism and consent?
4 What is a typical liberal attitude to equality?
5 What part has tolerance played in liberal doctrine?

Long questions

Your answers should be about 900 words long.

1 Why and how did classical liberalism become transformed into modern liberalism?
2 What form should a modern liberal state take in order to conform to the main principles of the movement?
3 In what ways is there a conflict between liberalism and democracy and how have liberals attempted to solve such conflicts?
4 How liberal is the UK's political system?
5 'All main UK political parties are now essentially liberal.' Discuss.

Further reading

Bellamy, R. (1992) *Liberalism and Modern Society: An Historical Argument*, Polity Press.
Gray, J. (1995) *Liberalism*, Open University Press.
Mill, J. S. *(1998) On Liberty*, Oxford University Press.

Chapter 2

Socialism

Socialism is a political movement, or collection of movements, which advances a number of criticisms of society, particularly the type of society that emerged with the onset of industrialisation and free-market capitalism from the latter part of the eighteenth century onwards. Socialism proposes that humans are naturally sociable, prefer to achieve goals collectively rather than individually and are content to cooperate with others to serve the common good. It also asserts that people are fundamentally of equal worth and should therefore have equal rights and equal opportunities. Extreme examples of socialism argue for total economic and social equality and common ownership of all means of production. More moderate forms of socialism accept less than full equality, replacing it with various ideas of social justice and partial common ownership of property. Modern socialists have accepted a variety of compromises between the pursuit of individual goals and the collective provision of welfare.

Introduction

It is worth beginning a review of this wide-ranging ideology with the words of Jean-Jacques Rousseau, written in 1755:

> The first man who, having enclosed a piece of ground, bethought himself of saying 'This is Mine', and found people simple enough to believe him, was the real founder of civil society. From how many crimes, wars and murders, from how many horrors and misfortunes might not any one have saved mankind, by pulling up the stakes, or filling up the ditch, and crying to his fellows: 'Beware of listening to this impostor; you are undone if you once forget that that the fruits of the earth belong to us all, and the earth itself to nobody.'
>
> From *A Discourse on the Origin of Inequality*

This is a useful point of departure for a number of reasons. First, and perhaps most importantly, it predates the onset of the Industrial Revolution and the advanced form of capitalism that resulted from it. It has often been argued that socialism should be seen as a reaction to capitalism, but it is clear from this passage that, at least on a philosophical level, a critique of private property and inequality already existed.

Second, it highlights one of the basic assumptions of all socialists: that private property is not natural, but a result of the pursuit of self-interest. Third, as Rousseau so colourfully asserts, many of the evils of modern society arise out of property and inequality. It follows that the replacement of private property by common ownership — the natural state of affairs — would alleviate most or all of these problems.

Jean-Jaques Rousseau connected social evils with private property

There is no doubt, however, that socialism as a political movement, rather than a collection of philosophical ideas, gained most of its momentum when it became clear that free-market capitalism was creating misery among the poorer elements of society. Furthermore, the gap between rich and poor grew alarmingly during the nineteenth century.

Early socialist ideas

Social anthropologists have discovered economically primitive tribal societies in various parts of the world which practice common ownership and egalitarianism, and there are many examples of small-scale experiments in socialism in Europe's history.

The English Levellers (also known as 'Diggers') mounted one of the first attempts at organised socialism. During the Civil War of the 1640s they flourished within the republican movement and were influential in the army of Oliver Cromwell (1599–1658). They set up a self-governing community, working land collectively and sharing out its produce on an equal basis. This was ridiculed by many and they were suppressed by Cromwell when it became apparent that they were becoming a dangerous force.

Their leader, Gerrard Winstanley (1609–76), based his ideas on a simple principle — that God had given the world and its fruits to all humankind, but that individuals had exercised greed in order to take as many of those fruits as possible at the expense of others. He described the position thus:

> And so, from the thief upon the highway to the king who sits upon the throne, do not everyone strive, either by force of arms or secret cheats, to get the possessions of the earth one from another, because they see their freedom lies in plenty, and their bondage lies in poverty.
>
> From *The Law of Freedom*, 1652

In this passage, Winstanley unwittingly foresaw the battle that was to come between liberal supporters of free-market capitalism and socialism. The advocates of capitalism argued that the pursuit of self-interest was the true nature of freedom. Winstanley agreed that this might be thought to be freedom, but it was not true freedom. For him, true freedom consisted of the pursuit of the common good and general equality.

Some rudimentary ideas about economic equality emerged during the French Revolution. The revolution was inspired by a desire to create equal rights, yet only a few saw equality as an economic and social ideal. The radical Gracchus Babeuf (1760–97) produced a pamphlet entitled the *Manifesto of the Equals*, which attracted the attention of the authorities. Apart from being extremely dangerous for the bourgeois class who had gained power in France, Babeuf's call for economic equality and common ownership of all property was simply too radical to be taken seriously at the time.

A similar fate awaited the radical ideas of the French **utopian** socialist Charles Fourier (1772–1837). The philosophy behind Fourier's scheme was similar to the kibbutz movement in Israel. He advocated setting up independent communities of nearly 2,000 people, in which all production would be undertaken on a communal basis. (Fourier resisted mass production, insisting that labour should be creative and based on craft skills.) Goods would be shared on an equal basis and all decisions would be made collectively. Had he not also argued for the abolition of marriage and the traditional family, proposing free love instead, his ideas might have been taken more seriously. Fourier was an early influence on all socialists and anarchists, to the extent that Karl Marx (1818–83) and other scientific socialists reserved a good deal of their writings for criticising this kind of idealistic socialism.

The British equivalent of Fourier was Robert Owen (1771–1858), who attempted to set up similar communities in America (but without the free-love element). Owen took the early principles of socialism a stage further by exploring the nature of human character. Like many anarchists, he believed that human nature could be moulded by society, and that nothing was fixed. It appeared logical, therefore, that if a perfect socialist community could be set up on strict principles of equality and community spirit, its people and their descendants would adopt these values as their own, quite naturally.

Key term

Utopianism

This is generally used as a critical term and has been applied to a number of political movements, including early socialism. The charge of utopianism usually implies that an ideology is not based on rational thought or scientific truths, but on hopes and aspirations alone. It also implies that the goals of such movements are unrealistic and cannot be achieved or sustained. Furthermore, many claim that utopians, such as socialists and anarchists, present their beliefs as rational and scientific, but are in fact deceiving themselves and their followers.

Owen and Fourier were both described as utopian in that their schemes were not based on any scientific study of society and economics, and the social and economic systems they proposed were impractical. The true reasons why the utopian socialists were unsuccessful were probably threefold:

➤ They predated the full development of capitalism. Instead of being a reaction to free-market capitalism, utopian socialism represented an alternative to the early growth of capitalism. In a contest between the dynamic new economic order and idealistic small-community socialism, capitalism was bound to win.

➤ The social evils of capitalism had not become apparent in the early part of the nineteenth century, which was when the utopian socialists were prominent. It was certainly true that agricultural and craft workers were being forced into factories and mines, but it was not yet clear how much social conflict this would create.

➤ The utopian socialists, including the later English socialist designer and craftsman William Morris (1834–96), were concerned by the onset of mass production, fearing it would drain working people of their creative instincts. They were, therefore, reactionaries, seeking to hold back the progress of industrialisation. This may have seemed a romantic ideal, but set against the unstoppable force of mass-production capitalism, which could produce cheap goods and provide large-scale employment, it was unlikely to gain many supporters — and in the event it never did.

Socialist reactions to capitalism

Socialism as an influential political movement can best be seen as a reaction to growing unrest over the course that free-market capitalism was taking. The most important reaction was undoubtedly that of Karl Marx, which is described fully in Chapter 5. Many other socialist movements were spawned as a direct result of the problems created by free-market capitalism. The nature of these problems provides a useful summary of nineteenth-century socialist issues (see Box 2.1).

Box 2.1 Key socialist criticisms of nineteenth-century capitalism

➤ The increasing division and specialisation of labour was creating an army of unskilled workers. Traditional skills were therefore in decline. There was also a marked fall in the number of independent peasants as agriculture became increasingly mechanised.

➤ Wages paid to the growing unskilled labour force were persistently low.

➤ Although capitalism was clearly creating great wealth, this was not being shared by the workers. The gap between rich and poor was steadily widening.

➤ When workers attempted to organise themselves to improve wages and/or working conditions, governments and employers refused to recognise their unions, and even outlawed them. Ruthless methods were used to break strikes.

➤ There were frequent slumps resulting in unemployment and falling wages.

➤ With the spread of urbanisation the living conditions of the working class became increasingly squalid. Bad housing, poor health and lack of education were particular problems.

Socialists fell into three main categories with regard to these issues:

1 **Scientific** socialists, of whom Marx was the most prominent, believed that it was in the nature of capitalism to exploit labour and create inequality. They argued that the problems were insolvable and that capitalism would have to be abolished completely, to be replaced by a compulsory and exclusively socialist society. This group was typically revolutionary in its methods, believing that the capitalist state would not relinquish its power through peaceful means.

2 Democratic, state socialists saw granting democratic rights to the working class as the answer. If workers could vote and gain office through socialist parties, the worker-dominated state could modify capitalism radically to alleviate the problems described in Box 2.1. This could be achieved by a combination of state control of industry, strong trade union rights and regulation of private enterprises.

3 A further category comprised a collection of socialist movements, which can be described loosely as 'cooperative'. These socialists proposed that the means of production — factories, land, mines, commerce and banking — should be brought directly under the control of workers and peasants, who would run them themselves, in their own interests, and would therefore create economic equality among themselves. The syndicalists, who proposed trade union control of all industry, were the most radical of this group of socialists.

Key term

Scientism

This term can be applied to a number of political ideologies that claim to be based upon scientific conclusions drawn from an objective and empirical study of history and society. In some ways, scientism stands as an opposite to utopianism. Many socialists — Marxists being a primary example — claim to be scientific in their beliefs and conclusions. They suggest that by understanding the fundamental nature of humankind, the meaning of historical change and the nature of contemporary society (especially capitalism), they can draw scientific conclusions about how society should be changed and ordered. Such thinkers claim that, because they use scientific methodology, their idealised society would be in accordance with natural circumstances and natural justice.

Social class under capitalism

For virtually all nineteenth-century socialists, the defining characteristic of capitalist society was its **class** structure. They saw class conflict as capitalism's main weakness and the ultimate cause of its demise. Marxist theory is the most important example of a class analysis of capitalism; indeed, for Marxists class conflict was the only significant aspect of capitalism.

The most radical socialists believed that the divergent interests of the working class and the bourgeois or entrepreneurial class could not be reconciled within capitalism.

For them, capitalism depended upon the exploitation of one class by another. Class conflict could therefore only be resolved by the victory of the working class and the introduction of a working-class state. There were many more moderate socialists who believed that the way forward lay in striking a better balance of economic power between the working class and the bourgeoisie. These socialists therefore campaigned initially for trade union rights, legislation to improve working conditions, enfranchisement for all adults and a state system of welfare and industrial regulation. The British Chartist movement of the 1830s and 1840s, for example, had these relatively limited aims.

The British socialist movement was especially moderate in its class outlook. Represented largely by the Labour Party, it suggested that the interests of the working class and the capitalist class could be reconciled within a democratic political system. Elsewhere in Europe, socialist parties were more radical and campaigned for a more permanent arrangement to protect the interests of the working class, especially state control of major industries and extensive rights for trade unions.

Key term

Social class

At its basic level, social class is a way of dividing society into economic and social groups. It has been used by historians, social theorists and political ideologues as a means of analysing society. The most important class analysis has come from socialists, especially Marxists. They believe that class distinctions are based on specific economic circumstances (e.g. whether one is a wage earner, capitalist, landlord, tenant etc.) and that they determine the character of society. For socialists, class conflict is the most basic problem of modern societies and needs to be resolved. Other political movements, including moderate socialists, have accepted that class divisions and conflicts are important, but hold that they are not necessarily crucial. Most contemporary social theorists argue that social class is declining in importance as a defining feature of society.

As the twentieth century progressed, however, the class divide began to abate. Growing affluence among the working classes and the establishment of effective welfare systems rendered the idea of class conflict an apparent anachronism. Many socialists accepted this reality and introduced both pluralism and individualism as core values of the movement. Others remained militant, with communist parties continuing to wield influence into the 1970s. But these radical groups became increasingly marginalised, and social theorists insisted that class divisions were decreasing in importance. Socialism was therefore forced to transform itself into a different movement altogether. At this stage, terms such as *democratic socialism* and *social democracy* began to be used instead of socialism to describe political movements on the left of Western politics.

Inequality

Socialism was not only a reaction to the growth of capitalism itself; it was also a response to the increasing levels of inequality emerging under capitalism. Different strands of the socialist movement can therefore be defined not only in their reaction to capitalism and class conflict, but also in their proposals to achieve social and economic equality.

Marxists and revolutionary socialists were unequivocal in their attitude to equality. For them, all humans were of equal worth and equally deserving of the rewards of their labour, both physical and mental. Less radical socialists, while abhorring inequality, recognised that our varying abilities and contributions to society might be recognised by differentials in rewards. Some, indeed, recognised the need for incentives to promote efficiency and effort.

Modern moderate socialism has gone a stage further than this. Social democrats accept that inequality is natural. They seek to ameliorate the effects of such inequality mainly in two ways. The first is to ensure that there is equality of opportunity — that all individuals are granted an equal chance to make the most of their abilities. The second is to examine the nature of inequality, judging what can be justified and what cannot. Put another way, these moderates have replaced the pursuit of equality, with the concept of *distributive justice.* This principle is discussed further on p. 51.

Core values of socialism

Equality

Although equality is seen as the central principle of socialism, it is not a simple issue and has created conflict both between socialists and adherents to other ideologies and within the socialist movement itself.

It is worth beginning with those aspects of equality upon which all socialists, or the vast majority of them, can agree. First, all socialists believe that we are all born with equal rights. Socialists share this belief with liberals. It suggests that we are created equal in terms of our right to both justice and access to power. Second, all socialists reject the idea that society has any kind of natural order. Instead, every individual has the potential to take up any position in society to which he or she may aspire. Third, all socialists believe in equality of opportunity. However unequal people may prove to be, all are entitled to the same life chances.

None of this is particularly contentious, which is why there is unity over these principles among socialists. When we look more deeply, however, fragmentation appears within the movement. Perhaps the issue over which there is most controversy is the extent to which *absolute equality* should be pursued. This principle is relatively simple — the resources of a society should be distributed equally throughout the community. Whatever contribution is made by an individual, he or she is entitled to an equal share of the rewards. Clearly this presents a number of problems. It eliminates the conventional incentives upon which a modern economy is said to rely and does not acknowledge the variety of contributions that each person makes. It can even be seen as fundamentally unjust, even though many socialists see it as the ultimate expression of social justice.

This problem with equality arises from two differing views of the nature of humankind. Some socialists believe we are all born with equal potential. In other words, we all have the potential to become equal. Others acknowledge that inequality is inevitable, that we have different abilities and potentialities, and that these should be recognised by differential rewards. One way to solve this conflict is to distribute property equally so that each individual has the same opportunity to make what they can of that property. Although this is feasible in peasant-based societies, it does not appear to be practical in modern industrial society. A further solution could be described as equal access to welfare. This accepts that rewards will be unequal, but asserts that certain basic services and a minimum quality of life should be available for all. In other words, there will be a standard of living below which nobody will be allowed to fall.

Box 2.2 Kinds of equality supported by socialists	
Equal rights	We are all entitled, as a right of birth, to be treated equally by the state and to exercise all our rights as equal citizens.
Equality of opportunity	We are all entitled to equal chances to make the best of our abilities. Positive steps should be taken to ensure equal opportunities. There should be no artificial barriers to the progress of any individual or group.
Equality of outcome	This is a principle held by more fundamentalist socialists. It proposes that rewards should be based on the value of each person's contribution. This will inevitably mean some inequality, as contributions are bound to vary in terms of both quality and quantity. It also implies that the differences in rewards will not be as considerable as they are in a free-market system.
Absolute equality	This is more extreme than equality of outcome. It suggests that all individuals will receive the same rewards, as long as they make a contribution that is to the best of their ability. It is the ultimate goal of Marxist communists and anarchists, but it is assumed that each individual will come to make a broadly equal contribution. Opponents see this as unreasonable utopianism.
Equality of welfare	This sees human society as inevitably unequal but argues that everyone should be entitled to an equal minimum standard of living, which can be ensured by the provision of state welfare.

Class conflict

All but the more moderate socialists see social class as a crucial aspect of society. It has been assumed by socialists that most people define their position in society in terms of their social class. This implies that they develop a sense of common interests and common purpose with other members of their class. Marx described this effect as 'class consciousness', but most socialists use the more moderate expression 'common class interest'. Thus, for example, the middle classes feel they have a strong common need to protect private property interests, to promote and protect business and to keep taxes as low as is reasonably possible. The working classes, on the other hand, are more concerned with welfare issues, sympathetic industrial relations, fair wages, good working conditions and policies that promote greater equality. These two sets of interests conflict with each other. Low taxation combined with high welfare expenditure is not feasible. The business classes normally oppose higher wages since it conflicts with the need to make profits and generate funds for further investment.

Box 2.3 gives the four main strands of socialist response to the problem of class conflict.

Box 2.3 Socialist solutions to class conflict

Revolutionary socialists, including Marxists, have argued that the conflict of interests simply cannot be resolved within the context of capitalism. Indeed, they argue that capitalism creates the conflict and that it will intensify as capitalism develops. The answer, therefore, has to be the destruction of capitalism itself and its replacement by a socialist order that will eliminate class conflict altogether.

Non-revolutionary socialists, such as state socialists, have simply sought to form governments that will operate largely in the interests of the working class. Such a working-class state might abolish or dramatically modify capitalism, and would certainly introduce a high degree of economic and social equality. The most common form of socialist system which has been promoted by such socialists is one in which most production and distribution is organised by a central state.

Democratic socialists have also sought to modify capitalism, but have stopped short of creating a working-class state. They have instead introduced extensive controls over capitalism, some state intervention in industry and commerce and high levels of state-sponsored welfare provision. The postwar Labour government (1945–51) in the UK and the modern Swedish state provide examples of how democratic socialism can work. Class conflict is suppressed as the state is seen as a relatively neutral arbiter between conflicting class interests.

Social democracy, the dominant form of socialism in Europe since the 1980s, downplays the importance of class. Indeed, many social democrats effectively ignore class as a social or economic phenomenon. The state, therefore, can simply work in the broad national interest, seeking a consensus which is not based on class at all. The apparent fragmentation of the class system and an increase in general affluence have contributed to a decline in the importance of perceptions of class conflict.

In many ways, therefore, changing attitudes to class and class conflict have defined the ways in which socialism has evolved from its predominantly revolutionary character in the nineteenth century to the moderate forms which have proliferated and are now current throughout the developed world. Many commentators, mostly on the left of politics, have suggested that movements that no longer analyse society in terms of class interest should not be described as socialist. New Labour in the UK would certainly fall into this category.

Social justice

Social justice is a difficult concept, not least because it is claimed as a virtue by most mainstream political movements, from Marxism through to contemporary neo-liberalism. The issue to concentrate on here is what meaning the term has for a typical socialist.

This can be simplified if we reduce our discussion to the issue of how the rewards which the economy generates (effectively the national output) should be distributed. Two further questions arise from this.

First, there is the question of what method should be used to distribute the rewards. Marxists and other revolutionary socialists insist that capitalism can never produce a just distribution. They argue that this is because the system contains inequality within its own mechanism. If we attempt to retain capitalism but remove inequality from it, capitalism as a system simply will not work. Capitalism, they assert, relies upon incentives and inequality for its dynamic nature. Therefore, capitalism must be abolished. In its place, some form of rational distribution of rewards should be organised by the state.

More moderate socialists have suggested that social justice can be achieved under capitalism, although different degrees of modification have been proposed by different branches of socialism. Essentially, these proposals have concentrated upon measures such as interference with the wage system to create less inequality (for example, minimum wage legislation), granting significant trade union rights to allow workers to negotiate for more justice, the use of taxation and welfare to redistribute wealth and income from the rich to the poor, and the traditional theme of equality of opportunity. Distribution of rewards is therefore fundamentally determined by the market forces of capitalism, but with the state intervening to a greater or lesser extent to promote social justice.

Second, there is the question of what constitutes a just distribution. Perhaps the best known formula for a just distribution was provided by Karl Marx:

> When labour is no longer just a means of keeping alive but has itself become a vital need; when the all-round development of individuals has also increased their productive powers and all the springs of cooperative wealth flow more abundantly — only then can society wholly cross the narrow horizon of bourgeois right and inscribe on its banner: **from each according to his abilities, to each according to his needs**.
>
> From *Critique of the Gotha programme*, 1875 (my bold)

There are a number of problems with this apparently simple idea. Marxism itself, of course, has now been discredited. Marx himself also admitted — in the quotation above

— that such equality requires 'abundant wealth' and the elimination of scarcity. Many argue that scarcity will never be eliminated, so society will always have to accept some forms of competition for scarce resources. Furthermore, the principle of absolute equality of rewards has been seen as hopelessly utopian and ignores the basic human drive to progress by accumulating more income and wealth.

Most socialists have been forced to find more complex formulae for distributing wealth. Under a state socialist system, it is possible to organise affairs so that each receives rewards according to the *value of his or her contribution*. This creates some incentives and seems to be naturally just. The problem with this, however, is that it still entails the destruction of free-market capitalism and its replacement by a system of distribution which is bound to be subjective and open to dispute.

Those more moderate socialists who have reached an accommodation with capitalism have had an even more difficult task in defining social justice. They have sought to achieve what has become known as **distributive justice**, and have had to face the issue of how much inequality can be tolerated.

Key term

Distributive justice

This term refers to any conception of justice that seeks to establish a fair and just principle for how rewards should be distributed within a society. It is mainly associated with modern social democracy and especially the US philosopher John Rawls.

Perhaps the simplest conception has been provided by welfare socialists. They seek to establish a minimum standard of living, below which nobody should be allowed to fall. This almost certainly involves considerable redistribution of income from rich to poor through taxation and welfare. Above this base level, there will be inequality within market capitalism. However, as long as workers have strong trade unions and legal protections and there is equality of opportunity, mainly involving education and training, the outcome of capitalism can be seen as 'just'. The Labour government that came to power in Britain in 1945 and produced the welfare state was based upon these principles.

More recently, social democratic forms of socialism have come to regard inequality as inevitable. They have agreed that there must be a minimum standard of living for all, but that modern society must tolerate considerable incentives in order to ensure dynamic wealth creation. Although the philosopher John Rawls is chiefly associated with liberalism, he did provide a formula of social justice for these moderate socialists which has become widely acceptable:

I shall now state in a provisional form the two principles of justice;

First: each person is to have an equal right to the most extensive basic liberty compatible with a similar liberty for all.

Second: social and economic inequalities are to be arranged so that they are (a) both reasonably expected to be to everyone's advantage, and (b) attached to positions and offices open to all.

From *A Theory of Justice*, 1972

Put another way, Rawls is saying that inequalities are natural and somewhat desirable, but that they must be justified by existing within a just society. For him, a just society provides freedom, equality of opportunity, no barriers to individual advancement and, above all, prevents anybody enriching themselves at the expense of the poorest members of society.

Summarising the socialist attitude to social justice is a difficult task because the concept has evolved so much since its earliest origins. We can, however, make one key generalisation. This is that all socialists, however extreme or moderate, believe that the outcome of a completely free-market system of capitalism cannot be just. They therefore propose some form of intervention to create more just outcomes.

Equality of opportunity

Closely allied to social justice is equality of opportunity. This has already been described as a principle in the previous chapter on liberalism (pp. 11–13). The difference between a liberal and a socialist attitude is subtle and not extensive, but there are some differences in emphasis.

Before examining the principle within modern socialism, it should be stressed that revolutionary and state socialists have a specific idea of equality of opportunity. For them, equality and equality of opportunity are essentially the same thing. Once a socially just society is established, with the equal distribution of rewards and common ownership of industry, land and so on, all its members will automatically be equal and have equal access to what society offers. Those who accept the maintenance of capitalism in some form, however, do not see equality and equality of opportunity as coterminous.

First, all socialists tend to emphasise the belief that people who live in deprived circumstances do not have equal opportunities. This is not merely a question of education. Socialists believe that there is generalised discrimination against those who come from poorer backgrounds. If living standards can be raised for all, there will also be more opportunities for all.

Second, socialists believe that there are social forces which operate against the interests of some sections of society. In the fields of higher education, the professions, government and business in general, there remains a certain degree of class-based bias which discriminates in subtle ways against those who come from less-privileged backgrounds. Equality of opportunity therefore demands that such institutions must make themselves open to a wider social spectrum. Members of the middle classes still seem to have advantages in a number of walks of life, especially in university education. Socialists seek to break this cycle of discrimination, either by **positive discrimination** or by introducing laws and codes of practice which outlaw social discrimination.

Third, modern social democrats, along with liberals, have sought to open up opportunities for a wider section of the community to become involved in business and so secure for themselves a greater share of society's wealth.

Key term

Positive discrimination

Known as 'affirmative action' in the USA, this term arises from the belief that some sections of society, mainly women and members of ethnic minorities, suffer systematic discrimination. This applies mostly to employment, but also to education and government. In order to counter this apparently unfair treatment, many propose positive discrimination. This gives a positive advantage to such groups in the form of minimum quotas which must be met when people are being recruited or promoted in an organisation. This counterbalances the suspected discrimination and so recreates equality of opportunity. Critics argue that positive discrimination is in itself unfair, as it discriminates against the majority. There are also fears that people who are not suitable will advance simply because they are members of one of the favoured groups.

Collectivism

The term collectivism refers to two main ideas. The first is that people usually prefer to achieve goals collectively rather than independently. The second, and more fundamental, is that action taken by people in organised groups is likely to be more effective than the sum of many individual actions. These ideas stem from the socialist view of human nature, which is that man is a social animal who prefers to live in social groups than alone.

Of course, the degree to which society should be organised on the basis of collectivism varies between different branches of socialism. Marxists and state socialists have proposed that a centralised state should be the vehicle for collective action, organising all or most production and distribution. Socialists who accept some degree of free-market capitalism have promoted collectivism alongside individualism.

Socialist collectivism became the norm for socialists throughout Europe after the Second World War. The collectivist arrangements introduced even came to be accepted by non-socialist governments, albeit reluctantly. Since the 1980s, however, the focus of socialism, and the political consensus in general, has moved away from collectivist ideas. They became discredited in economically developed countries since they appeared to be holding back economic progress, stifling individual enterprise and suppressing individual instincts. As collectivism drifted out of favour, most socialists responded by placing less emphasis on the principle.

Perhaps the clearest way of demonstrating the nature of socialist collectivism is by showing how collectivism has worked in a variety of social contexts and by contrasting it with the individualist approach. This can be seen in Table 2.1.

Table 2.1 Collectivism and individualism

Context	Collectivist solution	Individualist solution
Industrial relations	Most workers are organised in strong trade unions with bargaining rights.	Free labour markets exist with weak or non-existing unions. Wages and working conditions are determined solely by market forces.
Healthcare	A national health service provides free care according to need and is paid for by general taxation.	Individuals are responsible for their own health provision, probably through insurance.
Housing	Housing is available from local government, subsidised through taxation.	Widespread private home ownership exists.
Key industries	Large industries are nationalised — i.e. brought under government control — so that they operate in the national interest.	All industry and commerce are privately owned.
Education	State education is available to all.	Individuals must buy education privately, possibly with state financial support.

Common ownership

A feature of socialism which is closely related to collectivism is common ownership of the means of production and distribution. Indeed, common ownership is a form of collectivism. It is perhaps the oldest socialist idea, since it predates the onset of capitalism.

Some socialists have claimed that common ownership of property is a Christian principle, pointing out Christ's insistence that his followers pool their resources and share them out equally. There have been many movements throughout history — mostly among the poor peasantry — that have demanded the seizure of land and its transfer to a communal system of production. In England, the Levellers (or Diggers) purchased tracts of land in the south of England and began to farm collectively with the equal distribution of output. It was the development of capitalism, however, which brought about a more complex set of ideas relating to the evils of **private property** and the virtues of common ownership.

As with most socialist principles, there is a great deal of variation in thought in this area. Before looking at common ownership itself, it is useful to consider the variety of reasons why socialists have objected to private property. These have included the following:

> The Earth is given to humankind in general. No individual has the right to claim that any part of it belongs to him or herself.

> Claiming private property deprives someone else of its use.

- Property gives rise to inequality, especially between those who have and those who lack property.
- Ownership of property, particularly land and capital goods, gives rise to the exploitation by property owners of those who lack property.

By contrast, common ownership can give rise to a number of good outcomes, including:

- The possibility of imposing economic equality, as described above.
- Since many socialists see collectivism as natural, common ownership creates, or recreates, a natural state of society.
- It is possible to direct commonly owned property to serve the interests of the whole community, not just those of fortunate owners of property.

Key term

Private property

It is important not to confuse the term 'private property' with the term 'private possessions'. This is especially true in the context of socialist thought. Socialists distinguish between possessions, such as houses, clothes, personal items etc., and property, which is used in the process of production. Property in this latter sense includes farm and building land, factories, mines, machinery, retail outlets, banks and so on. The crucial distinction is that 'property' can be used to exploit workers and consumers and to promote inequality. Possessions, on the other hand, are simply those goods which we consider our own, and which are not involved in production.

Among socialists, the value of common ownership, along with equality, social justice and collectivism, has certainly declined in the modern age. The failure of the socialist 'experiments' that were introduced in the USSR, China, Cuba and much of eastern Europe during the twentieth century served to destroy faith in the idea of common ownership by the state (on behalf of the people). Socialists have therefore tended to modify their attitude to common ownership, seeing it as a complement to private property rather than a replacement for it.

Some socialists have argued that soviet-style socialism failed not as a result of common ownership, but because it was based on the centralised state. Syndicalists, for example, have proposed that property should be owned collectively by groups of workers, not by the state. In other words, the workers in each industry should become the collective owners of their own enterprises. This is similar to the cooperative ideal common in continental Europe, whereby independent producers own their own property, but then pool their output and sell it collectively. Such producer cooperatives collectively own the distributional elements of their activities. Similarly, in some parts of Europe, worker cooperatives own individual companies collectively and distribute profits among themselves. In England, a system of consumer cooperatives was developed in the 1840s and has flourished ever since. Under this system, retail businesses are effectively owned in common by the consumers, who then have access to cheap goods.

In recent times, democratic socialists and social democrats have retained some elements of common ownership, organised by the state, but have also encouraged free enterprise when this is seen as the best method of wealth creation and distribution.

Table 2.2 summarises the ways in which different branches of the socialist movement have made use of common ownership.

Table 2.2 Socialism and common ownership

Branch of socialism	Form of common ownership
Marxism	All property is held in common. There is no private enterprise.
State socialism	All means of production and distribution are publicly owned and run by the state. Possibly some small private enterprise is allowed.
Syndicalism	Industries are owned and run collectively by their own workers.
Cooperative movement	Groups of producers distribute their goods in common. Worker cooperatives are owned by their own workers. Retail cooperatives are owned in common by consumers.
Democratic socialism	Welfare organisations, such as for health and education, are publicly owned and state controlled. Some large strategic industries are publicly owned (i.e. nationalised) and run for the public good.
Social democracy (and New Labour)	Welfare services remain publicly owned. Very few enterprises are nationalised.

We can now see that the story of socialism in the modern age is one in which there has been a decline in common ownership as part of the central belief system. The success of private enterprise in creating wealth and promoting innovation has made it difficult for socialists to argue that common ownership is successful or desirable.

Types of socialism

Primitive socialism

Primitive socialism can be defined as those forms of the philosophy that existed before the onset of capitalism in the late eighteenth century. Perhaps the best known of these was the imaginary world described by Thomas More (1478–1535) in his *Utopia*, written in 1516. More imagined an island where there was no money or private property and where everybody received goods according to their needs. It was described as a utopia in that it presupposed the elimination of greed and competitiveness. It was, of course, just a fictional creation, but it is possible that More's work inspired a number of social-ists who were to follow much later.

In Gerrard Winstanley's Leveller movement in England in the 1640s and 1650s, in partic-ular, can be found echoes of More's *Utopia*. Winstanley raged against inequality and the iniquities of greed and private property. He believed that the world had become corrupted because people thought that 'their freedom lies in plenty and their bondage lies in poverty', and so sought to take each others' possessions (from *The Law of Freedom*, 1652). The answer for Winstanley and his followers was to abolish private property, work the land cooperatively and distribute its output equally. In this project, all men (women were excluded from equal rights) would have an equal say in the running of the common property.

Winstanley's movement was crushed by Cromwell and early socialism disappeared until the French Revolution, when some of the rebels hoped to use the upheaval as an opportunity to campaign for economic as well as political equality. These opportunists were also suppressed. The French Revolution was essentially a bourgeois enterprise; the idea that the working classes should be emancipated could not be tolerated. It was another 30 years or so before socialism became a significant movement. Indeed, the term 'socialism' itself does not seem to have existed before the 1830s.

Utopian socialism

The first recognisable socialists came to be known as 'utopian' for a number of reasons. First, they lacked scientific rigour. Second, their ideas were seen as impractical at best, eccentric at worst. Third, the ideas were based on an intensely optimistic and romantic view of the natural state of humankind. All utopians appeared to desire a return to a simpler form of production and social order. In other words, they were reacting violently to the growing problems associated with industrialisation and mass production by attempting to roll back progress. Three prominent utopians are worth describing at this point.

Charles Fourier was an eccentric French social theorist who briefly attracted a following but was ultimately thought to be too outlandish to be taken seriously. This is not to say he was not influential. Marx himself, for example, admitted to drawing some inspiration from his ideas.

Fourier proposed that society should be organised in small communes, which he called 'phalanxes'. Each commune was to be characterised by the complete freedom of individuals, common ownership of all property, communal possession of children and women (he believed in free love) and the opportunity for each individual to pursue his or her own creative instincts. There was to be no money and no system of exchange. Everyone would draw from the common stock of goods according to need. Leaving aside his more radical moral and social views, the economic system that Fourier devised bore a remarkable resemblance to Marx's view of **communism**, described several decades later.

Robert Owen began his career as an industrialist and therefore as a capitalist employer. However, he felt a deep sympathy for the plight of poor workers and so set up New Lanark Mills. There the workers received decent wages, company housing, subsidised goods and a rudimentary level of education and healthcare. In many ways, Owen created a miniature welfare state.

Later in life he became more radical in his beliefs, and certainly more anti-capitalist, setting up a number of small communes with common ownership and equal distribution of goods. He even exported his plans to the USA, setting up an experimental society there known as New Harmony. His system became known as cooperativism and was an influence on the direction of socialism in the UK. Owen was neither a revolutionary nor a scientific socialist. He expected that, once his communities became well known, society would naturally follow him and a cooperative world composed of free communes would be established.

William Morris connected social ills with the denial of creativity

William Morris was well known as both an interior designer and as one of the founder members of the Arts and Crafts movement that sought to combine art and craftsmanship in furniture, fabrics and architecture. Industrialisation, Morris argued, had drained the creative instinct from workers and had exploited them. In his view, mass production and the factory system reduced workers to machines, alienated them from the product of their labour, brutalised them as human beings and held them in abject poverty. He therefore promoted a twofold attack on capitalist organisation.

First, mass production was to be replaced by creative work, based on both skills and artistic instincts. Second, workers were to be organised into communes or cooperatives in which the rewards of their creative labour were to be shared equally. Goods produced in this way would be sold according to the work and skill which had gone into making them, rather than on their exchange value in free markets.

Key term

Communism

This term refers to any social system that is based upon small, independent communities; it is derived from the French word 'commune', which means a small village community. Communists propose not only communal living, but also the abolition of systems of money, exchange and competition. Instead, goods are to be produced on a cooperative basis and income distributed equally within the commune. Government of the commune is usually based on direct democracy. The idea of the commune has been shared by utopian socialists, Marxists and anarchists.

All three utopian socialists described above had a common desire to hold back the progress of capitalism and industrialisation. It was this unrealistic aspiration that was their undoing. Those forms of socialism that proved to be successful accepted that economic progress was a fact of life and would have to be accommodated.

Marxism

The Marxist form of socialism and communism is covered in Chapter 5. However, a brief description is useful in order to place it within the context of the wider socialist movement.

Marx and his close associate Friedrich Engels (1820–95) were among the first social-ists to recognise the importance of class conflict in their critique of capitalism. They saw the working class as the only revolutionary class because it was suffering such intense exploitation. Marx and Engels also sought to move socialism away from its utopian roots. They did not merely see a socialist order as a desirable answer to the evils of capitalism: for them socialism, and later communism, were the inevitable consequences of the growing crisis of capitalism. Socialism was therefore a natural development of society, not a political ideology.

They made two further major contributions to socialist thought. First, they were unashamed revolutionaries. They rejected any notion that socialism could be brought about peacefully and/or democratically. Capitalism would have to be smashed by the exploited working class. Second, they understood that industrialisation and mass production were here to stay. A socialist society would have to come to terms with that fact.

Finally, we can compare Marxism with the growing state socialist movements of the nineteenth century. The Marxist idea that a new socialist order should be organised by the centralised state was shared by socialists throughout France, Germany and much of industrially developed Europe. Many socialists and anarchists in the later nineteenth century proposed the creation of small, independent communities. However, Marx and Engels saw this kind of communism historically, as a later phase of human development. After capitalism, the state would be needed to build socialism. Too much freedom and independence would place the achievements of the **revolution** in jeopardy.

Key term

Revolution
This term refers to a circumstance where there is a complete (usually sudden) transformation of the whole nature of society. Revolutions are often violent, as in the case of the French (1789) and Russian (1917) revolutions, but are not necessarily so. It is possible to have peaceful revolutions, such as the 'velvet revolution' in the former state of Czechoslovakia around 1990, when the communist system was replaced — without bloodshed — by free-market capitalism and liberal democracy.

Revolutionary socialism

Marxism is, of course, a form of revolutionary socialism. However, in the nineteenth and twentieth centuries there were revolutionary socialist movements that were not completely based on the writings of Marx and Engels.

In France, Auguste Blanqui (1805–81) formed a small socialist party of conspirators and agitators, which he hoped would bring down the capitalist state and replace it with a permanent workers' government. In England, H. M. Hyndman (1842–1921) formed the short-lived Social Democratic Foundation in 1884, an organisation dedicated to the destruction of the bourgeois state by revolution or other means. These two movements were remarkably unsuccessful. They lacked the scientific rigour of Marxism and their ideas on what could replace a capitalist order proved to be too unspecific.

In practice, the most successful revolutionary socialists have been inspired by Marxism. In Cuba, Fidel Castro (1927–) took control after a short guerrilla war in 1959 and set up a centralised socialist state that still endures. Although he drew most of his support from the Soviet Union, Castro was not strictly a Marxist. He did not share Marx's view that the socialist state would ultimately 'wither away' and be replaced by a communist order. However, he did set up an all-powerful state to administer production and distribution and to impose social and economic equality upon Cuban society. Similar regimes were set up, with varying degrees of permanence, in places such as Vietnam, North Korea and a number of former African colonies, e.g. Mozambique and Tanzania.

Fabianism and evolutionary socialism

The Fabian Society was established in Britain in 1884, the product of a group of socialist intellectuals. Notable founders included the playwright George Bernard Shaw (1856–1950), the novelist H. G. Wells (1866–1946) and the academics Sidney (1859–1947) and Beatrice Webb (1858–1943). (The latter couple went on to found the London School of Economics.) All were influenced by Marx, but did not accept his revolutionary theories.

The society was named after the Roman general Fabius, who was said to have won his battles through a gradual war of attrition rather than a single decisive blow against his enemy. This was a conscious indication that the Fabians were opposed to revolution, expecting instead that socialism would come about through a long-term, gradual process. They also developed the idea of the *inevitability of gradualism* (see Box 2.4).

Box 2.4 The inevitability of gradualism

This doctrine encompassed two main ideas. The first was that socialism would be the inevitable outcome of the development of capitalism. As capitalist enterprises grew and began to dominate the economy, it would become necessary for the state to bring them under its control to ensure that they operated in the public interest. The Fabians believed that working-class demands for social justice and greater equality would become irresistible. The numerical advantage enjoyed by the working class would make the democratic establishment of a socialist state a natural consequence. The second idea was the belief that the transition to socialism would be gradual. The working class would not be ready to administer a socialist state, but would require the leadership of its intellectual superiors. Only when the working classes had become fully educated and informed would they be capable of taking over government. At the same time, it would not be practical to replace all capitalist institutions at once. Socialism would have to be established through a gradual, step-by-step process.

Over the years (it still exists as an instrument of debate and education among social democrats and as a think-tank associated with New Labour), the Fabian Society has become more moderate in its outlook. It has had a profound influence upon the British Labour Party (many of whose members have also been Fabians). The society helped to ensure that British socialism remained a moderate, non-revolutionary movement. It also brought a strongly middle-class, intellectual element into the Labour Party.

In the UK and elsewhere in Europe, the early part of the twentieth century saw the development of an evolutionary form of socialism which rejected the radical, revolutionary nature of Marxism exemplified by Vladimir Ilyich Lenin (1870–1924) and the Russian Bolsheviks. Its leader was Eduard Bernstein (1850–1932).

Eduard Bernstein, who favoured gradualism over revolution

Bernstein argued that capitalism was not going to collapse of its own accord and nor was revolution the way to get rid of it. Like the Fabians, he recommended a gradualist approach and, in so doing, set the tone for mainstream, non-Marxist socialism during the early part of the twentieth century. Socialists, he argued, should not rely upon a revolution created by an alienated and exploited working class. Instead, socialists should adopt a variety of tactics, including the following:

➢ setting up political parties that would seek representation in parliaments
➢ working with trade unions to improve wages and working conditions
➢ pursuing welfare and social justice through democratic means
➢ advocating state control of major industries in order that they be run in the interests of workers and the community in general

Bernstein, his close associate Karl Kautsky (1850–1938) and socialist parties all over Europe entered into a struggle against the Marxists, who were insistent that revolution was the only way to introduce socialism.

Syndicalism

While groups such as the Fabians and evolutionary socialists proposed an alternative to revolutionary Marxism, a different form of socialism was also gaining ground. This became known as syndicalism, a term derived from the French word *syndicat,* meaning trade union.

The syndicalists, who thrived around the turn of the nineteenth century, advocated subversive or outright revolutionary activity by groups of workers, directed specifically at capitalist enterprises. Their objective was that workers would eventually take over their own industries and run them for their common benefit. The bourgeois state would then collapse as the capitalist system which supported it fell into the hands of the working class.

The syndicalists were notorious for their violent methods, especially those promoted by the Frenchman Georges Sorel (1847–1922). Sorel believed that working men formed a heroic class and that their capacity for social solidarity was forged in their struggle against capitalism and the exploitation which it imposed on them. By taking decisive action, the working class would simultaneously defeat capitalism and create new bonds of cooperation and equality. Trade unions provided an ideal structure for this form of socialism, as they were potentially internally democratic and self-governing and gave their members equal status.

Unfortunately for the syndicalist movement, it became closely associated with the fascist ideology which was gaining ground in Italy and Germany. Benito Mussolini (1883–1945) in particular admired syndicalism for its organisation and heroism and used some of its principles in setting up a fascist 'corporate state'. This connection doomed syndicalism to obscurity as its fascist associations alienated most members of the working class. A moderate form of syndicalism, known as 'guild socialism', gained some followers in Britain in the 1930s, but this too had withered away by the 1940s.

Democratic socialism and British Labourism

The British Labour Party was founded at the beginning of the twentieth century. Although technically a product of the trade union movement, its roots lay in a more complex set of influences (see Table 2.3). At first it competed with a party known as the *Independent Labour Party (ILP)*, which was a radical but gradualist movement of the kind that Bernstein had advocated. However, the Labour Party soon won the struggle for dominance of the left in British politics and the ILP drifted into obscurity.

Table 2.3 **Influences on the British Labour Party**

Influence	Manifestations
Trade unionism	British trade unionists are usually moderate, preferring to rely upon collective bargaining, welfare systems and legal rights for workers rather than radical socialism. However, the objective of bringing major industries under state control (nationalisation) was mainly advocated by union leaderships.
Fabianism	This provided the middle-class intellectual element of Labour, concentrating on social justice through the redistribution of income, equality of opportunity and state controls over capitalism.
Nonconformist Christianity	This tradition saw socialism as an ethical issue, based on the idea of a sense of community. It therefore advocated socialist objectives through local government and the formation of consumer cooperatives.
Utopian socialism	Welfare and the welfare state was a key element in this tradition. It stressed the importance of skills training and education to raise the fortunes of the working class. The idea of worker cooperatives was also part of the utopian philosophy, although they failed to achieve popularity or economic success.
Liberalism	The close link between the British Labour movement and liberalism was apparent through the first half of the twentieth century. The liberal wing of Labour therefore promoted the causes of equal rights for individuals and minorities, as well as insisting on parliamentary democracy as the main vehicle for reform.

British socialism, usually known as 'democratic socialism', has a particular character, largely because of the varied nature of its origins and the fact that it was not heavily influenced by Marxism or other movements that based their ideas on the notion of class conflict. European socialists in the modern era have tended to see their role in terms of government on behalf of the working class in order to provide balance with the economic power of the capitalist middle classes. British Labour, on the other hand, while recognising the importance of class differences, has always understood that it would only be electable if it governed in the national, rather than narrow class, interest. In other words, the party has believed that it is possible to serve the interests of both major classes in society.

British socialism has therefore been a relatively moderate movement that has pursued social justice without jeopardising the achievements of market capitalism. A review of its main policies and methods illustrates this. Between 1945, when the first Labour government with an overall majority was elected, and 1979, when the traditional party lost power for the last time, Labour based its socialism on the following principles:

1 Total defence of the parliamentary system of government.
2 The pursuit of equal rights and equality of opportunity.
3 The state control of large strategic interests in order to prevent capitalist monopolies working against the public interest, and to run them instead in the interests of the community and of their own employees. This was known as nationalisation.
4 The provision of a welfare state, with compulsory contributions from all those in work and their employers, and services or benefits provided free on demand for all those in need. This included pensions, healthcare, education and various social security benefits.
5 A range of personal services provided by local government, such as subsidised housing, social services and public health measures.
6 The redistribution of some income through the tax and welfare system.
7 The defence of powerful trade unions and workers' rights in order to promote justice in the workplace between employers and employees.

Traditional Labour policies implied that an accommodation could be reached between free-market capitalism and a just society. European socialists, on the other hand, have tended to oppose capitalism and propose its replacement by some form of state planning. Labour did flirt with the idea of centralised planning in the 1970s and early 1980s, but, true to its moderate roots, it rejected it, preferring instead the maintenance of a mixed economy.

New Labour and modern social democracy

The success of the free-market capitalist, neo-liberal reforms that swept the economically developed world in the 1980s, together with the end of the Cold War and the dismantling of soviet-style socialism, saw the demise of traditional socialism virtually everywhere. Socialist parties throughout Europe went into decline and then transformed themselves into moderate, quasi-liberal reforming parties. They accepted the capitalist system as inevitable and campaigned instead for more social justice, the protection of workers' rights and controls designed to prevent large-scale corporations from exploiting consumers and their own employees. In the UK, this process was seen in its most dramatic and celebrated form in the creation of New Labour as a force for **social democracy** in the UK.

Key term

Social democracy

This term has been used in so many different ways that it scarcely retains any meaning. In the nineteenth and early twentieth century, it was used by revolutionary as well as evolutionary socialists. In the second half of the twentieth century, it came to mean a moderate form of socialism committed to democratic methods and a pluralist political system. Its current usage implies a movement in the centre of the political spectrum that takes a social perspective on many issues and mediates between the demands of individualism and those of the community as a whole.

Arguably New Labour is not a form of socialism at all. Indeed, members of the party today rarely use the term 'socialism' for fear of appearing to be anti-modernist or of frightening the electorate. Despite this, New Labour is included in this chapter for two reasons. First, it still can lay some claims to being a socialist-based movement. Second, it does not belong in any other chapter in this book: it is not liberal nor, despite critical claims to the contrary, is it conservative in nature.

It is now well documented how Labour veered sharply to a left-wing socialist position in the 1980s and, as a result, fell foul of an electorate which was ready for the free-market, individualist policies of Margaret Thatcher. Under three successive leaders, Neil Kinnock (1942–), John Smith and Tony Blair, Labour reinvented itself to the extent that it added the term 'New' to its title. **Clause IV**, which stated the party's socialist intentions, was radically amended and the socialist old guard was marginalised.

Key term

Clause IV

This feature of Labour's history has always assumed iconic status in that it was said to encompass the basis of the party's claim to socialism. Part of the party's constitution, which was first written in 1918, Clause IV was included in the section dealing with the party's political objectives. Its most important clause stated that the party was committed to:

> secure for the workers by hand or brain the full fruits of their industry and the most equitable distribution thereof that may be possible upon the basis of common ownership of the means of production, distribution and exchange and the best obtainable system of popular administration and control of each industry or service.

When John Smith and Tony Blair transformed the party into 'New Labour', it was clear that the clause did not reflect modern conditions. It was a key moment when, in 1995, the party agreed to drop the old Clause IV and to replace it with a vaguer commitment to social justice. Labour's traditional claim to be an old style socialist party was, by that single act, finally laid to rest.

The creation of New Labour was effectively a response to the post-Thatcher consensus which had dominated Britain from the mid-1980s onwards and which had spread to the USA and most of the rest of Europe. The end of the Cold War and the demise of socialism in the communist-bloc countries after 1989 also contributed to the defeat of traditional forms of socialism. All over the developed world, socialist parties were restyling themselves as moderate, social democratic parties.

The main elements of the post-Thatcher consensus and New Labour's reaction to it are given in Table 2.4.

Table 2.4 New Labour and the post-Thatcher consensus

Consensus issues	New Labour response
A belief that free markets are the best way of creating wealth and economic progress	Accepting free markets, but control of monopoly power through state regulation
Competition is a useful device for promoting efficiency and innovation	Promoting competition, even within public service institutions such as hospitals and schools
People prefer to own their own homes	Accepting the decline of subsidised rented housing supplied by local government
Privatisation of major industries	Accepting privatisation, but also introducing partnerships between public and private sectors
Withdrawing the state from economic management	No attempt to exercise active control over the economy but introducing measures to ensure stability and discipline in monetary control and the public finances
Weakening the power of trade unions and freeing up labour markets in general	Not restoring union powers but strengthening the individual rights of workers, mainly through the Social Chapter of the European Union and the national minimum wage
Inequality is a natural and just consequence of free markets	Accepting inequality, but establishing a minimum standard of living below which nobody should be allowed to fall
High taxation is unjust and inhibits wealth creation and economic growth	Taxation has drifted up, but taxes on income have been held down and business taxes have been reduced
High levels of social security benefits are a disincentive to work and create a 'dependency culture'	Social security benefits should be targeted at the most needy to ensure a decent standard of living for all, and at those who are working, are seeking work, or are unable to work

We can see from the table above that many of the key values and institutions of socialism have largely disappeared under New Labour. It would be wrong, however, to suggest that Labour has moved away from its socialist roots completely. Indeed, there are some examples of New Labour initiatives which could be said to have advanced the cause of socialism.

In particular, Labour has retained the essentials of the welfare state, perhaps the jewel in the crown of British socialism. All sizeable employers and all those in work must contribute to the welfare state. Its provisions remain, on the whole, free at the point of delivery according to need. It is true that some charges have crept in, notably tuition fees for higher education and a range of medical charges, but the welfare state in general is totally funded by taxation. It is still the main vehicle for equality of opportunity and poverty control. Furthermore, education has been stressed as the most effective way of widening opportunity for all.

There has been an extensive programme of poverty reduction too. Measures such as the national minimum wage, tax credits for working individuals and families, targeted benefits for pensioners and poor families and a new 10% tax band for those on low incomes have all been introduced to take people out of the poverty trap.

New Labour has accepted inequality and understands its role in creating incentives that promote a healthy and dynamic business environment. However, it also recognises the phenomenon it has dubbed **social exclusion**. This refers to a section of society whose members remain so deprived that they are effectively excluded from mainstream society. The problems of the socially excluded tend to be multiple, and can include poverty, low educational attainment, bad housing, crime, poor parenting, drug addiction etc. The state therefore needs a multi-institutional approach to social exclusion policy.

Key term

Social exclusion

This term was created by New Labour and refers to those groups in society who suffer multiple deprivation and therefore do not enjoy the usual rewards, choices and opportunities. They are therefore socially excluded. Social and economic policy should be directed at such groups.

New Labour has virtually abandoned its attachment to a class analysis of society. It accepts that we see ourselves mainly as individuals, pursuing our own goals, and that we do not identify strongly with a social class, although we may be members of smaller groups such as religions, campaign groups, sectional interest groups and so on. This carries the danger that society may lose its cohesion as a result of too much individualism. Concern about this is shared by modern liberals and progressive, social conservatives.

The nearest thing New Labour has to an all-embracing term that addresses this concern is 'communitarianism'. However, this term should be used carefully. It has been used to denote forms of communism and anarchism that propose the establishment of small-scale, autonomous communities. In the context of New Labour, communitarianism is a very different concept. It accepts that society is basically individualist in nature, but also recognises an obligation to maintain the integrity of the community as a social entity. Instead of using the state as the chief method of retaining this community, individuals are expected to take responsibility for maintaining society. This implies taking an active role in the political process, in the promotion of community spirit, in caring for those less fortunate and in caring for the environment. To a large extent it is envisaged that such active citizenship should take place at a local level. It also implies that if citizens enjoy the rights bestowed on them by the state then they must accept responsibilities for the whole community. The extracts in Box 2.5 demonstrate how Tony Blair expressed the communitarian ideals of New Labour, as the party completed its second term of office.

Box 2.5 **Combining an individualistic society with traditional social democratic aims**

These extracts are taken from Tony Blair's keynote speech to the Institute for Public Policy Research in October 2004.

> The vision of a true opportunity society replacing the traditional welfare state can be realised only if we deepen the changes we have made to the country and have the courage to see them through.

> But now, on the foundations of economic stability and record investment, the third term vision has to be to alter fundamentally the contract between citizen and state at the heart of the twentieth-century settlement; to move from a welfare state that relieves poverty and provides basic services to one which offers high-quality services and the opportunity for all to fulfil their potential to the full.

> The values which animated those great reformers of the 1940s — Beveridge, Attlee and Bevan — are our values: equity, solidarity, a society of mutual obligation; the condition of the poor and less advantaged, the test of humanity and decency of the nation at large. Yet the institutions they created 60 years ago were rooted in social conditions and assumptions radically different to those of today.

> There is a vast agenda of change to bring about…all of it based on a belief that today people want the power to change their lives in their own hands, not those of an old-fashioned state and government. All of it pervaded by a strong commitment to the values of social justice, equality and opportunity for all.

Socialism today

It is clear that in the economically developed world the traditional form of socialism is largely a thing of the past. There are some factions and individuals, such as Tony Benn (1925–) and George Galloway (1949–) in the UK, who still believe that socialism can be applied to modern society, but they represent small minorities. In other parts of the world, however, recognisable forms of socialism survive.

Cuba is perhaps the prime example of this. Under Fidel Castro, the country has retained a socialist system since 1959. The state controls most of the means of production and distribution and there is a high degree of economic equality. Great emphasis is placed upon the education and health systems, which are famous for their high quality. In a 1968 speech, Castro set out his vision of socialism:

It is clear that capitalism has to be pulled out by the roots. We cannot encourage or even permit selfish attitudes among men. If we don't want man to be guided by the instinct of selfishness, of individuality; by the wolf, the beast instinct; man as the enemy of man, the exploiter of man, the setter of snares for other men. The concept of socialism and communism, the concept of a higher society, implies a man devoid of those feelings; a man who has overcome such instincts at any cost; placing, above everything, his sense of solidarity and brotherhood among men.

China, on the other hand, has abandoned its socialist structure and is gradually encouraging private enterprise and accepting the inequality that inevitably follows. In Africa, a number of quasi-socialist regimes still exist, notably in Zimbabwe and Tanzania, but they have been undermined by the policies of the International Monetary Fund and the World Bank. These organisations have insisted that, in return for loans and aid, these states must dismantle their socialist systems and introduce free-market policies. It remains to be seen whether such developments can bring these countries significant economic growth or whether there will be a return to socialist ideals if free-market systems fail.

Elsewhere, socialism remains in retreat, being replaced either by neo-liberal, conservative administrations as in France and Italy, or by moderate forms of social democracy as in the UK and Germany. Many argue that socialism was a historical phenomenon that belonged to a specific period in the development of capitalism. The current age is often described as the post-industrial or post-capitalist era, in which individualism is firmly established, it is accepted that governments must take active steps to regulate free-market capitalism without controlling it, and most of the infamous evils of industrial society have been reduced. The US philosopher Francis Fukuyama (1952–) has argued that there is now no place for ideologies such as socialism. History has perhaps moved on and the socialist era may be finally over.

Key socialist thinkers

Charles Fourier (French, 1772–1837)

Although his early brand of socialism was short-lived and did not attract a wide following, Fourier is nonetheless an important figure in the history of the ideology. Marx and Engels clearly thought him significant since they spent a good deal of time refuting his utopian socialist ideas. Marx's description of communism, the ultimate goal of his type of scientific socialism, owed much to the community-based ideas of Fourier.

Fourier saw socialism as a means by which people could rekindle the community spirit that had been threatened by the growth of capitalism. His schemes may have been eccentric, but he did understand that socialism is about fellow feeling and social responsibility. He believed that industrialisation was perhaps the worst evil of capitalism in that it drained workers of their creative abilities and drove them into competition with each other. He insisted that in free, small-scale communities, where everybody was guaranteed a minimum standard of living, children were well educated and everybody was well housed, the genuine human spirit could be released. Fourier had an intensely optimistic view of the potentiality of human nature to create genuine, cooperative communities.

Fourier therefore represents a particular kind of utopian socialism — one that is less concerned with great issues such as class conflict, exploitation and the evils of private property, but rather sees socialism as literally 'social' in nature. It is a tradition that has been followed by such disparate figures as the Victorian designer and craftsman William Morris and the twentieth-century novelist George Orwell (1903–50).

Robert Owen (Welsh, 1771–1858)

Owen has sometimes been called the father of British socialism. This is perhaps an exaggeration, but it is true that he had an immense influence on the movement. He is known as a utopian, but can be described as an ethical or even Christian socialist too. He did not share the class conflict analysis of the Marxists and other revolutionaries, nor did he advocate a state-sponsored system of common ownership. Owen's socialism was, like Fourier's, of a humanist kind, based on compassion, altruism and social responsibility.

Robert Owen is best remembered for his cooperative theories

He set up an experimental ethical capitalist enterprise at New Lanark in Scotland and another experimental community in New Harmony, USA. Neither was especially successful and he was much criticised for his unrealistic schemes, which were based on an over-optimistic view of human nature. He believed that capitalists could be persuaded to adopt a more humanitarian approach to their workers, and that the workers themselves could be turned into creative, enlightened individuals through education and welfare.

It is not, however, for his experiments that Owen is celebrated and revered but for his contribution to the cooperative movement. At New Harmony he set up a cooperative organisation where workers could produce goods on a collective basis and share out the proceeds on the basis of need. The community could operate successfully within a capitalist environment by removing the exploitation of both workers and consumers that the system produces. Owen's principle was a simple one. Capitalism exploits consumers and workers because they are powerless individuals. If both groups can come together as cooperative organisations, they can counterbalance the power of capitalist enterprises. He did not, therefore, advocate the destruction of capitalism, but merely a redressing of the balance of power *within* capitalism. This turned Owen into the champion of both the growing trade union movement and the developing British cooperative movement, which was first set up in Rochdale in 1844.

British cooperative societies have taken the form of consumer organisations selling food, other products, and a variety of services, such as insurance, to consumers at low prices. They have achieved this by cutting out most of the distribution chain and by using their collective market power to obtain low wholesale prices. They exist to this day, albeit in a modified form. Members of these societies still elect representatives to Labour Party committees and to the party's annual conference.

Like most of the British Labour movement, Owen represents a complete antidote to the revolutionary, Marxist forms of socialism popular at the time in mainland Europe. He understood that capitalism would probably survive, and that therefore the most effective response to its evils was to modify its operation and empower the working class, rather than engage in a futile attempt to destroy it.

Auguste Blanqui (French, 1805–81)

In contrast to Robert Owen, a moderate exponent of socialism, stands the notorious, French revolutionary figure of Auguste Blanqui, a man famous for having spent half his life in various prisons. Like Marx, Blanqui saw society in terms of class conflict. The solution to the exploitation of the working class was to rise up, destroy the capitalist system and the state that supported it, and replace it with a workers' state.

Blanqui represented an uncompromising kind of socialism, implacable in its opposition to capitalism. He was even more revolutionary in his outlook 'than Marx and his followers. He advocated conspiratorial methods among his own followers and set up clubs and societies among intellectuals, students and workers, which were dedicated to revolution and the undermining of the state. Although he stood for election to the French Assembly, he did not approve of parliamentary methods and took advantage of any insurrection that might break out. He was a leading figure in the 1848 revolution in France and in the uprising of 1871 known as the Paris Commune.

In some ways, Blanqui was a similar socialist to Marx, but he had no scientific theory of history and did not attempt a thorough explanation of the true nature of capitalism. He was an emotional socialist who cared only for the emancipation of the downtrodden working class.

Karl Marx (German, 1818–83)

Chapter 5 of this book covers Marxism, but Marx's place in the socialist pantheon should be established here too. Marx was the pre-eminent scientific socialist of his day. He was, indeed, the first of the scientific socialists, yet his theories were derived from a variety of sources. His understanding of the nature of capitalism came largely from liberal economists such as David Ricardo, his theories of history were derived from the philosophy of social progress espoused by Friedrich Hegel (1770–1831), and his revolutionary fervour came from figures such as Blanqui. The result, however, bore little resemblance to any of these origins.

After a career as a political agitator and journalist, Marx settled in England. He spent more than 20 years there, effectively in exile, as he was a wanted man in many parts of Europe. His description of capitalism was the result of his own observations of England at the height of the Industrial Revolution. He received help from his lifelong friend and benefactor, Friedrich Engels, who ran his own business and so had an intimate knowledge of capitalism in action.

Marx's socialism was both scientific and idealistic. Although he developed a huge and impressive theory of historical development, his ideas were ultimately based upon a view of the nature of humankind that many have criticised. For Marx, work represents the essence of the human spirit; it is an individual's life force and gives life meaning. His whole theory of human development rested on this assumption. Marx believed alienation was the key feature of capitalism which would ultimately bring the system down. By robbing workers of their own labour, capitalism was sowing the seeds of its own destruction. This is a critical idea, since it gives rise to the concept that a socialist revolution is, effectively, inevitable. Thus, socialism was not merely an aspiration but the logical outcome of fully-developed capitalism.

The idea that socialism is inevitable was shared by the Fabians, but, unlike them, Marx believed that it would not be the outcome of a gradual process, but would result from a hammer blow struck by the revolutionary working class. This was the inevitable revolution.

Marx's critics focus on his assertions about the nature of humankind. He did not allow for the modification of capitalism which would allow individuals to achieve self-development, even though they might continue to sell their labour in order to live.

Eduard Bernstein (German, 1850–1932)

Bernstein began his active political career as a Marxist sympathiser, but towards the latter part of the nineteenth century he began to lose faith in the ideology and developed a new form of socialism. This would ultimately form the main opposition to classical Marxism during a period when the capitalist structure wobbled and almost collapsed in the early part of the twentieth century. The Marxists turned their fury upon Bernstein, seeing him as a traitor to the cause of socialism. His ideas were branded **revisionism**, the worst kind of insult within the revolutionary socialist world. Bernstein's theories, however, came to dominate European socialism, while Marxism turned into a distinct movement far removed from socialist principles. As such, many argued, Marxism became merely a distortion of socialism.

Key term

Revisionism

This term is most commonly used by Marxists to describe, in pejorative terms, the ideas of those followers who have distorted Marxist theory to such an extent that they can no longer be described as socialists at all. Eduard Bernstein was perhaps the most notorious of the Marxist revisionists. The term has also been used by other movements to describe anyone who moves too far away from orthodox beliefs. Anthony Crosland (1918–77) (see below) was often described as a revisionist in the context of orthodox Labour Party policies in the 1970s.

Bernstein was one of the most important early exponents of what became known as *social democracy*. He rejected Marx's assertions that class conflict would intensify, that this would culminate in revolution and that revolution would usher in a worker's state. He argued instead that socialist principles would be best advanced through democratic, parliamentary means. Furthermore, he rejected the notion that inequality and exploitation would inevitably worsen under capitalism. Within a democratic framework, he asserted, the interest of the working class would receive a fair hearing and capitalism would respond favourably. The appropriate role of socialists should therefore be to form democratic parties, to seek election to power and then to implement reforms in the interests of the working class. Such reforms would include welfare systems, trade union rights and equality of opportunity for all.

Bernstein's brand of socialism successfully opposed Marxism and social democratic parties sprang up all over Europe (the British Labour Party can be counted as one of these). As communism became a distinct ideology, separate from socialism, the Bernstein position became the heart of non-Marxist socialism.

Anthony Crosland (English, 1918–77)

Crosland's best known work, *The Future of Socialism*, which was published in 1956, can be seen as the beginning of a process of change in the Labour Party and, consequently, in British socialism; this came to its logical conclusion with the emergence of New Labour in the 1990s. Just as Bernstein was called a revisionist by the Marxists, Crosland was a Labour revisionist.

In particular, Crosland attacked the view that the most effective way of achieving socialist aims was through the **nationalisation** of major elements of the economy. He argued that capitalism should be allowed to flourish as long as it created wealth effectively and did not exploit workers in the way that nineteenth-century capitalism had undoubtedly done. Under certain circumstances he accepted that nationalisation might be appropriate, as might worker cooperatives, but alongside these two forms of common ownership capitalism would play a leading role. He rejected the idea of centralised state planning, which was gaining favour within the Labour Party in the 1950s and 1960s.

Crosland rejected a wholly class-based analysis of society, arguing that this was outdated in a world that was, in fact, becoming more pluralist and diverse. Furthermore, the working classes themselves were becoming more affluent, so state intervention to create more equality was no longer so necessary.

In essence, Crosland saw socialism as a collection of values rather than as a slavish attachment to a set of institutions. Labour had overemphasised the importance of trade unions, state-run industries and taxation at the expense of its general values. For Crosland, socialism referred to ideas such as social justice, equality of opportunity and greater social equality. As capitalism generated increasing amounts of wealth, it was the role of socialists (or social democrats as we now call exponents of this philosophy) to redirect this wealth downward through taxation and welfare. Crosland wanted to see an end to poverty, poor health provision and lack of education by harnessing the wealth of capitalism, not by taking capitalism over.

Crosland provoked a furious debate within Labour circles that was mirrored within the European socialist movement. In 1959, for example, the German social democrats revoked their Marxist roots and declared a set of principles remarkably similar to those of Crosland. While traditional socialists remained committed to common ownership of the means of production, state planning, powerful trade unions and income equality, the more moderate social democrats were becoming less dogmatic, more tolerant and pluralist in their views and much more accepting of free-market capitalism. The Crosland style of socialism won its final victory when Tony Blair announced that New Labour had arrived and that, as a party, it could occupy the central ground in British and, ultimately, European politics.

Key term

Nationalisation

This refers to a device associated with socialism throughout Europe after the Second World War. It involved taking large private enterprises into public ownership. It was also a way of bringing large monopolies under control. The state ran nationalised industries on behalf of the community as a whole. Most of the industries that were nationalised were public utilities, such as gas, electricity, public transport and telecommunications. Some industries producing basic commodities such as coal, iron and steel were also taken into public ownership. These nationalised industries were able to keep prices down since there was no profit motive, and they were able to provide more employment than the private sector. They ran services which might normally be deemed unprofitable and so would have been abandoned by the private sector. Nationalisation became a central part of European socialism, but fell into disrepute; most nationalised industries were privatised in the 1980s and 1990s.

Tony Benn (English, 1925–)

Benn comes from a socialist tradition which can be described as ethical or even Christian. He believes that the principal messages of Christ were equality and brotherhood. Christ condemned the pursuit of wealth and the inequalities that existed even in ancient times. Benn argues that inequality is unethical and must therefore be drastically reduced.

Benn's book, *Arguments for Socialism* (1980), can be seen as a somewhat belated answer to Crosland's 1956 work. In it, he asserted that it was large-scale, monopoly capitalism which was preventing the more even distribution of wealth. Capitalism, he claimed — in direct contradiction of Crosland — would never accept higher taxation as a means of redistributing income. Public ownership of all major industries (what he called the 'commanding heights') was essential, argued Benn, if economic equality was to be achieved.

Benn advocated centralised state planning as a way of running the economy in the interests of the whole community, not just the wealthy few. Production and distribution should be controlled by the state and not left to free markets, he argued. Public ownership and planning, in particular, could eliminate unemployment forever. Permanent full employment and economic equality were, for Benn, both desirable and feasible.

It would be wrong, however, to suggest that Benn was advocating a soviet-style socialist workers' state. He has always been a vehement advocate of parliamentary democracy and an opponent of dangerous concentrations of power. Yes, the state should be the vehicle for socialist aspirations, but it should be a highly democratic state firmly in the hands of ordinary working people, not in the hands of a political elite. If Crosland can be described as a *social democrat*, Benn can be termed a *democratic socialist*. When asked whether socialists would relinquish power if defeated in an election and allow the achievements of the movement to be dismantled, Benn has always claimed that socialism would never lose power. Once people experienced a truly democratic socialist state, they would not go back voluntarily.

Today, Bennite socialism has become marginalised and defeated by the moderate form of social democracy that has taken over Labour. Benn is perhaps the last exponent of traditional socialism in the UK and perhaps even in Europe as a whole.

Issues in socialism

The role of revolution

For much of the nineteenth century, divisions within the socialist movement centred largely on the need for, and role of, revolution. Revolutionary socialists, such as Marx and Blanqui, insisted that there could be no compromise with capitalism and the bourgeois state that supported it. They both believed that capitalism would defend itself against socialist attack, so it was almost inevitable that revolution would be violent and bloody. They rejected any notion that socialism could be achieved through peaceful, democratic means. This view was based on the assumption that the state was the agent of capitalism, even though it gave the appearance of democracy and pluralism. Some extremist revolutionaries, such as the Bolshevik Leon Trotsky (1879–1940), went so far as to suggest that the experience of revolution was an important element in the creation of the socialist spirit among the working class.

Of course, revolution need not be violent. The term itself can simply mean the complete transformation of society, and this can be by peaceful means. The English socialist H. M. Hyndman, for example, entertained the possibility that capitalism would simply give up under constant attacks by socialists. Indeed, Hyndman's mentor, Marx, admitted that there was a possibility that a socialist state could be established by parliamentary means, but only in Britain where the political system was least class dominated.

Ranged against the revolutionary socialists were those who believed that socialism could come about by peaceful and gradual means; they became known collectively as *evolutionary* socialists. To some extent, their beliefs were based on the assumption that, when popular democracy was established, the numerical superiority of the working class would simply vote socialism into power. It was evolutionary socialists such as the Fabians and the revisionists, led by Bernstein, who represented the principal opposition to revolutionary socialism. The Fabians saw socialism as the inevitable outcome of capitalism, largely on the grounds that the evils thrown up by capitalism would become intolerable and all sections of British society would come to realise that socialism was the only answer to these evils. The role of socialists, therefore, was to bide their time, to educate all classes in socialist truths and to wait for the right moment to dismantle capitalism. Named after Fabius, a cautious Roman general, the society's motto includes this exhortation to its followers:

> For the right moment you must wait, as Fabius did most patiently, when warring against Hannibal, though many censured his delays.

Meanwhile, Bernstein, at the end of the nineteenth and beginning of the twentieth centuries, echoed the Fabian non-revolutionary methodology. In his case, he believed that socialism — albeit a more moderate form than that inspired by Marx — could be brought about by purely democratic means.

In the twentieth century, revolutionary and non-revolutionary socialism divided along Marxist and non-Marxist lines. The Marxists remained almost exclusively revolutionary until after the Second World War, when a movement known as *Eurocommunism* emerged. This short-lived philosophy suggested that Marxist-style communism could be brought about within a liberal democratic environment. Eurocommunists made some progress in France, Italy and Germany during the 1960s and 1970s, but their gains were modest and had withered away by the 1980s. Meanwhile, the non-Marxist socialists were making more significant progress within western European democracies. Restyling themselves democratic socialists, they fully favoured liberal democratic methods and gradually modified their principles to support a milder form of socialism. This was essential in order to make socialist parties an electable proposition in increasingly affluent societies.

Thus, revolutionary socialism virtually disappeared as a movement after the Second World War. With the exception of a number of quasi-anarchist groups of the 1960s, nearly all socialists — both Marxist and non-Marxist — came to accept that the possibility of revolution had all but disappeared, at least in the affluent West.

The state
The issue of the appropriate role of the state in a socialist society has divided socialists to a much greater extent than the role of revolution. At one end of the spectrum lie the Marxists, whose ultimate goal is the disappearance of the state, while at the other end are hard-line state socialists who see the centralised state as the ultimate vehicle for, and expression of, all socialist ideals and objectives. Between the two exists a wide variety of attitudes. These are explored in detail below as well as in Table 2.5.

Marxism

Marx saw the state as an expression of class rule. The old bourgeois state had to be removed and replaced by a workers' state, a phase known as the *dictatorship of the proletariat.* The role of this socialist state was to dismantle the capitalist edifice, create a socialist society under the auspices of a central state, engage in propaganda, effect the re-education and socialisation of the people to establish socialist consciousness, and finally to create a classless society where the state was unnecessary and could wither away. Thus, the socialist state was to be the architect of its own death. Engels put the death of the state in these terms:

> The proletariat seizes political power and turns the means of production into state property. But, in doing this, it abolishes itself as a proletariat, abolishes all class distinctions and class antagonisms, abolishes also the state as state... government of persons is replaced by the administration of things.
>
> From *Socialism, Utopian and Scientific*, 1892

Utopian socialism

Utopian socialists like Fourier and Owen did not see the state as a vehicle for socialism. For them, relatively small-scale, cooperative communities were the way forward in promoting socialist values. Fourier believed that the whole population could come to live in small communities so that the state, in a similar manner to Marx's belief, would become irrelevant and unnecessary. Owen did not see the state as irrelevant, but believed that its role should be minimal and confined to security, defence and the organisation of exchange between communities. The utopian socialists underestimated the extent to which the state was entrenched in modern society and were unrealistic in their belief that small communities could provide all the social and economic needs of the population.

State socialism

The extensive state socialist movements of the nineteenth century saw the central state as playing a major role in achieving socialist ends. Henri de Saint-Simon (1760–1825), who is often associated with the early utopians as well, proposed a state that would govern in the interests of all, not merely the wealthy few, and would take special care to advance the interests of the deserving poor. However, Saint-Simon's state was not to be a great economic institution that would control industry and commerce. Instead it was to be a regulatory body, consisting of the 'great and the good' in society, such as intellectuals, scientists and industrialists. The state would control capitalism so that it created more equality and advanced to the benefit of all.

Auguste Blanqui represented a more orthodox kind of state socialism. For him, the central state was to take over complete control of the means of production and distribution. In this way, complete equality of outcome could be achieved. The state would not be democratic in the traditional sense, but would be run on behalf of the working class. For Blanqui and similar state socialists, the idea of self-governing communities was hopelessly utopian. Social solidarity and economic equality could only be guaranteed if the state became the sole vehicle of common ownership of the means of production and distribution.

Fabianism

The Fabians also demonstrated faith in the state's ability to create socialism, but there were two important distinctions between them and hard-line state socialists. First, they were insistent that the state should be fully democratic. This assumed, of course, that the people of Britain would voluntarily vote for socialism (something Tony Benn asserted later in the twentieth century). Sidney and Beatrice Webb — two of the movement's founders — argued that as long as people were educated in socialist principles, they would be willing to vote consistently for a socialist society. The second distinction was that the Fabians saw local government as an appropriate vehicle for socialism.

Municipal socialism was indeed popular at the end of the nineteenth century. This was the theory that some socialist goals, including subsidised housing, public healthcare and education provision, could best be achieved at local level. Ironically, it was a Conservative mayor of Birmingham, Joseph Chamberlain (1836–1914), who pioneered such plans. The attraction of socialism at local level lay in the fact that, by bringing government close to the people, it could also be more democratically based.

Democratic socialism

Like the Fabians, and as their description suggests, this group were convinced democrats. Their position was less clear as to the role of the state in socialist society. In general, they believed that the state had a role, and that the private sector could coexist with it. There should be some kind of state-run welfare system, of course, and taxation would serve to redistribute income.

Public ownership of industry, however, posed a problem. In simple terms, democratic socialists have argued that all major and strategic industries should be under state control to ensure that they serve the community and not merely their owners. By insisting on a democratic political system, state control of these industries effectively becomes *popular* control. Industries that supply consumer goods, on the other hand, can be left to the free market. The thinking behind this is that, as long as consumers are left with free choices, they will regulate such industries themselves. As for the workers, strong trade unions and employment rights would help prevent exploitation.

Democratic socialists also support state planning. Outside the free market, the state should play some role in planning the output of important goods and services. This is based on the principle that economic development should be carried out in the interests of the community and not merely left to the random, irrational outcomes of a market-based system. Again, democracy would ensure state planning came under popular control.

Social democracy and New Labour

Social democracy entailed a dramatic change in attitude to the role of the state. Control of virtually all industry has been removed from the state and placed into the private sector. There is now a consensus among members of the centre left that individualism should be allowed to flourish, and that excessive state power threatens individualism.

The transfer of large sections of industry from state control to the private sector ('privatisation') in the 1980s has been accepted by social democrats and New Labour in the UK. This development has not, however, spelled the end of state involvement. In place of the *'provider state'*, social democrats have introduced the *'regulatory state'*. This state does not control industry and commerce, but does insist on methods of regulation to ensure that the public interest is served. Large utility industries, in particular, have to accept some degree of control over profits, pricing and supply policies.

As well as accepting privatisation, social democrats have supported relatively low levels of personal and corporate taxation, devices which have been used by socialists to redistribute income. Instead of redistribution, therefore, the state has largely been confined to protecting the interests of the poorest sections of society and, where possible, to reducing poverty. Welfare systems have remained a legitimate aspect of state activity, but in general inequality is tolerated.

Perhaps the most important role of the state for social democrats has been to guarantee equality of opportunity. State education lies at the centre of this objective, but state interference and regulation is also tolerated in the interests of broadening and increasing opportunities.

Capitalism

A historical analysis of socialism can be undertaken by considering its changing attitude towards capitalism. Indeed, it is often suggested that socialism, since its origination, has been fundamentally a series of reactions against capitalism.

The early socialists, of course, did not attack capitalism head on, but instead offered alternatives which they assumed workers would adopt. The small-community socialism of Owen and Fourier was one such alternative. Saint-Simon, too, did not propose to dismantle capitalism, but rather to control it through an aristocracy of intellectuals, managers and other experts.

The Marxists and fundamentalist socialists, however, did work for the total destruction of the capitalist system. They argued that it was fundamentally exploitative and that the interests of its two great classes could not be reconciled. The Marxists in particular viewed capitalism as an all-pervasive system of production relations that dominated the state, politics, religion, ideology and society as a whole. Those non-Marxist socialists who adopted a less radical view of capitalism nonetheless asserted that equality and social justice could never be achieved within a capitalist context.

In the twentieth century, socialists began to adopt a less radical approach to capitalism. They saw signs that the interests of the working class were being considered by both capitalist enterprises and the state. Trade unions were allowed to be established, wages rose and welfare systems were introduced. Perhaps, they suggested, socialism and capitalism could reach an accommodation. As long as the state ensured that there was oversight of capitalism, and as long as key enterprises and welfare systems remained under state control, there was no reason why socialist values could not coexist with some kind of capitalist organisation.

When democratic socialism was further modified into contemporary social democracy, capitalism and socialism finally became compatible. Two key events in this development were the declaration by the German Social Democratic Party at Bad Godesberg in 1959 that there was no longer a need to destroy capitalism, and the abandonment of Clause IV of the Labour Party Constitution in 1995. Modern social democrats now accept that capitalism is the most effective way of creating wealth. The inequality that results is an acceptable outcome, and it is the role of social democrats to reduce its negative effects.

Table 2.5 compares the attitudes of different groups of socialists towards a range of themes.

Is British Labour still a socialist party?

Although most left-wing critics of New Labour assert that the party has departed from socialism completely, there are some legitimate claims that it remains, at least in spirit, a fundamentally socialist-inspired party. Few would suggest it is actually socialist as such, but the question is whether it still retains some elements of socialism. The main evidence in favour of this lies in the following:

Socialist features of New Labour
- The party remains committed to the reduction of poverty.
- Social exclusion policy is attempting to create greater social equality.
- The principles of the welfare state have been preserved.
- There is some regulation of large-scale industries in the public interest.
- The Labour government signed the European Social Chapter, which extends considerable employment rights to all workers.
- The rhetoric of New Labour is that the wealth being created in society should be spread more widely.
- The emphasis on education aims to widen opportunity.

On the other hand, there is considerable justification for the view that New Labour has departed utterly from socialism. The principal elements that support this are the following:

New Labour's non-socialist features
- The goal of common ownership of the means of production was abandoned when Clause IV was amended.
- The party leaders, and Tony Blair in particular, have praised the virtues of individualism above collectivism.

Table 2.5 Thematic comparison of socialist forms

Theme	Marxism and revolutionary socialism	Democratic socialism	Social democracy
Capitalism	It must be completely dismantled and replaced by full-scale common ownership	It must be severely modified; ownership of the means of production to be shared between the state and private enterprise	Enterprise mostly private, with large-scale industry regulated, but not run by the state; limited state ownership
Equality	Absolute economic equality should be pursued, with minimal inequalities to create incentives; rewards must be based on need, not contribution	A high degree of equality should exist, but rewards to be distributed on the basis of the value of one's contribution, not merely on the basis of need	Inequality is the natural result of free markets and can be justified; however, a minimum standard of living for all to be guaranteed, with some mild redistribution of income
The state	The state to be a workers' state, not necessarily democratic; all production and distribution to be under state control; Marxists aim to create conditions where the state can wither away; non-Marxists see the state as a permanent institution	The state to be democratic and largely pluralist in nature, with the assumption that a democratic state would also be just in its outcomes; large scale production to be state run	Promotes a pluralist, liberal democracy; the state should not organise production and distribution, but should regulate it to some extent in the national interest and the interests of the less well off
Freedom	Individual freedom seen as a bourgeois concept; collective freedom to be created through equality	Individual liberty to be preserved as long as it does not conflict with socialist objectives	Individual liberty and individualism are to be preserved and guaranteed almost without qualification
Social class	Society is understood in terms of class and class interest; revolutionary socialists seek a state organised exclusively in the interest of the working class; Marxists seek an ultimately classless society	Adopts a class analysis of society; a socialist order would aim to reduce class conflict but balance power in favour of the working class	Social democrats do not analyse society in class terms; they see society as pluralist and class as having reduced importance; the state to be inclusive, protecting and advancing the interests of all groups
Collectivism	A totally collectivist perspective; all important economic and social activities to be collective	A largely collectivist outlook; however, individualism can flourish alongside important collectivist institutions	On the whole, individuals prefer to pursue their own goals; collectivism largely limited to the welfare state and other public services

- The party accepts that a considerable degree of economic inequality is acceptable.
- New Labour has failed to restore the power of trade unions, thus weakening the position of the organised working class against capitalist enterprise.
- Some of Labour's traditional social-ist policies have been lost, notably progressive taxation to redistribute income, subsidised council housing, free higher education and generous state pensions.

Students demonstrate against tuition fees, which were introduced by Labour

Socialism and liberalism

Equality

There is considerable overlap between the enduring principles of liberalism and those of socialism. This is especially true of their respective attitudes towards equality. Both traditions have insisted upon the primacy of equal rights and equality of opportunity. Of course, for radical socialists, especially Marxists, these concepts could not be held by capitalists. The socialist movement in general, however, has always seen the creation of this kind of equality as one of its goals.

A useful start in a comparison of socialist and liberal attitudes towards the issue of equality is to consider the perspectives of two radical authorities, that of Marx for extreme socialism and that of Robert Nozick for extreme liberalism:

> ...from each according to his abilities, to each according to his needs.
>
> Karl Marx, *Critique of the Gotha Programme*, 1875

> ...from each according to what he chooses to do, to each according to what he makes for himself.
>
> Robert Nozick, *Anarchy, State and Utopia*, 1974

However, when we make more general comparisons between the two ideologies on the issue of equality, we run into some difficulties. Fundamentally, liberals believe that humans are naturally unequal, whereas socialists have argued that the inequality we observe in society is artificial and the product of an unjust society. Thus, while liberals argue that a free society is one where people are 'free to be unequal', socialists seek to create conditions where greater equality can be achieved. In other words, socialists are more optimistic that every individual is capable of becoming equal, as long as he or she has equality of opportunity and society is organised on a just basis. However, when we consider the mildest form of socialism, as represented by New Labour, it is questionable whether there is any real distinction between its outlook and that of liberalism.

Rawls may provide a possible path through this difficulty of uniting both approaches. He suggests:

> All social values — liberty and opportunity, income and wealth, and the bases of self-respect — are to be distributed equally **unless an unequal distribution of any, or all, of these values is to everyone's advantage**.
>
> From *A Theory of Justice*, 1972 (my bold)

This formula appears to be a way of reconciling the socialist insistence on equality and the liberal response that this would be artificial and an infringement on liberty. It is also something of a throwback to utilitarian theory. If inequality can be seen to be for the 'greatest good of the greatest number', and if it does not make the poorest in society any poorer, inequality can be just. When we add that both traditions can agree on equal rights and equality of opportunity, we may have discovered the essence of liberal social democracy.

It should not be forgotten, however, that fundamental socialists still object to inequality, even when it appears to result in greater general prosperity. For them, this is a matter of principle. At the same time, those who are more radical in their liberal outlook still argue that the inequalities thrown up by a free society are all just.

Freedom

The charge which is most often levied by liberals against socialism is that as an ideology it entails the curtailment of liberty. If liberty is fundamental to human existence, attempts to pursue greater equality represent an affront to human dignity.

We can start by turning the discussion round and asking what socialists believe about freedom. Marx provides a critique of the traditional liberal view of freedom, claiming that it is really an illusion:

> In theory, therefore, individuals appear to have greater freedom under the rule of the bourgeoisie than before, in reality of course they are less free, because they are more subject to the **power of things**.
>
> From *The German Ideology*, 1845 (my bold)

By 'the power of things', Marx meant that individuals were subjected to economic forces beyond their control. They believed they were free because they could sell their labour to the highest bidder and were not subject to undue restrictions on their lives. But the fact was they were not free to decide *not* to sell their labour at all. They had lost control of their life essence — their own labour.

Yet as capitalism began to modify itself, as workers became free to form trade unions and as working-class parties were formed to represent them, the Marxist view began to appear overcritical. Attention among socialists turned to the charge that freedom itself was unevenly distributed in society. For those with control over their own lives, those who were born with greater opportunities and those with comfortable incomes, there was clearly more *positive* liberty available. The poorer sections of the community, by contrast, were less free, because they had less income, were subject to more social problems and enjoyed a narrower range of opportunities. Twentieth-century socialists therefore argued that the expansion of opportunities and the provision of welfare, together with some redistribution of income from rich to poor, would result in a more even distribution of freedom. In this sense they followed the philosophy of William Beveridge) who, though a liberal, had suggested that social evils were as great a curtailment of freedom as government and its laws.

When liberals and conservatives complained that the expansion of state power after the Second World War was becoming a threat to liberty, the socialist response, typified by Tony Benn, was 'whose liberty'? The liberty of entrepreneurs and the wealthy may indeed have been narrowing as the state redistributed some of their income, but the liberty of the majority was being expanded.

Turning back to the liberal perspective, however, problems remain. Attempts to create greater economic equality, which means redistributing income and wealth through taxation and welfare, inevitably curtail freedom. This is specifically the freedom to spend one's income as one wishes. There is an additional danger that a society in which there is excessive equality would lack incentives and so progress would be held up; this view stretches back to the beliefs of John Stuart Mill. Inheritance tax, capital gains tax and corporate taxes are all relevant in this context.

Although the liberal suspicion of measures to create economic equality is most at home in the USA, it remains a strong instinct among neo-liberals in the British Conservative Party and a right-wing faction of the Liberal Democrat Party. Mainstream liberals throughout Europe, however, have tended to move towards the social democrat position.

This view is close to Rawls's philosophy. His idea of distributive justice protects the concept of individual liberty, but accepts that the economic liberty of some may reduce the economic liberty of others. Therefore, general liberty remains intact, but economic liberty becomes negotiable. On rational grounds, most liberals and moderate social democrats now accept that the main objective of a liberal society is to be just in terms of the distribution of both goods and freedom.

Exam focus

Using this chapter and other resources available to you, answer the following questions.

Short questions

Your answers should be about 300 words long.

1 Distinguish between revolutionary and evolutionary socialism.

2 What does a socialist mean by the term 'equality'?

3 Distinguish between democratic socialism and social democracy.
4 How do socialists view social class?
5 What is meant by the term collectivism?
6 Distinguish between a socialist and a liberal view of equality.
7 How do socialists reconcile equality and freedom?

Long questions

Your answers should be about 900 words long.

1 'Socialists have disagreed over means more than ends.' To what extent is this true?
2 'Socialism is best defined in terms of its changing attitude to capitalism.' Explain and discuss this statement.
3 How have socialists disagreed over the role of the state?
4 In what ways has British socialism differed from forms of socialism seen elsewhere?
5 Distinguish between Marxism and other forms of socialism.

Further reading

Benn, T. (1980) *Arguments for Socialism*, Penguin Books.
Berki, R. N. (1975) *Socialism*, Everyman.
Crick, B. (1987) *Socialism,* Open University Press.
Harrington, M. (1993) *Socialism Past and Future*, Pluto Press.
Pimlot, B. (ed.) (1984) *Fabian Essays in Socialist Thought*, Heinemann.
Sassoon, D. (1997) *One Hundred Years of Socialism*, New Press.
Wright, A. (1987) *Socialisms; Theories and Practices*, Oxford University Press.

Chapter 3

Conservatism

Conservatism is a political tradition that contains both constant and variable principles. A conservative in politics is one who resists the dominance of fixed political doctrines and ideologies. Conservatism prefers the status quo as long as there are no compelling reasons for radical change. When change is needed, conservatives prefer reform to radical transformation or revolution. The nature of conservative thinking depends upon the dominant political ideas of any age or situation; it is in this sense that its principles are variable. The enduring principles of most conservative movements include respect for tradition, a preference for what *is* over what *might be* and a tendency towards empiricism — basing future action on experience of the past — rather than fixed principles as a guide to action. Conservative views on the nature of society vary, but all conservatives support individualism, i.e. the pursuit of individual goals and fulfilment. Traditions are important to conservatives because they preserve links with the past, which provide a sense of security. Conservatives are pragmatic, not judging political action on the basis of specific principles, but on what is preferable and acceptable to the people at any given time and under those particular circumstances. Above all, conservatives believe that good social order and security are the most basic of human needs. Order is seen as more important than ideas such as freedom, rights and equality.

Introduction

The doctrine of conservatism is perhaps one of the most difficult to pin down. This is because conservatism is, by its nature, a reactionary movement. Its character depends upon what it is reacting against at any particular time. For example, during much of the nineteenth century, conservatism appeared as an antidote to the individualist liberalism that had become dominant in the USA and Europe. By the second half of the twentieth century, conservatives were principally concerned with the progress of socialism. In both cases, the nature of the conservative reaction inevitably varied. In contrast to liberalism, conservatives stressed the collective, organic nature of society. By the 1980s, when collectivist forms of socialism had become popular, conservatives such as Margaret Thatcher were stressing the importance of individualism.

Conservatism has, however, included a number of constant and enduring principles. These provide a degree of continuity which enables us to differentiate between conservatism and other political movements. Nationalism, opposition to rigid ideology, respect for traditions and a paternalistic view of democracy are all examples of conservative constants.

We must be careful to distinguish between conservatism as a specifically political movement, and a mere state of mind. We often speak of people having conservative tastes in fashion, the arts, food and design. These are merely personal attributes and do not necessarily relate to political principles. We can, also, identify conservative elements in *any* political movement. For example, Stalinism is often described as a conservative form of communism, and Tony Blair and his close followers are characterised as conservatives within the New Labour movement. This chapter is not concerned with these two types of conservatism, but with a political tradition that has enduring political significance.

One final word of caution: the British Conservative Party is not the same thing as conservatism in general. Naturally most members of the party have been conservatives, but the party has experienced many changes in character and has contained many individuals whose views have been considered un-conservative in nature. Conservatism is an international phenomenon with varying characteristics in different parts of the world. For example, US conservatism tends to have a strong religious element, French conservatives are intensely nationalist, while British conservatives have often been liberal in their outlook. We are therefore justified in considering national variations in conservatism, and should beware of identifying the tradition too closely with particular parties.

The origins of conservatism

The basic nature of conservatism depends upon its reaction to other ideologies. Its origins can therefore be identified in the origins of ideology itself. This approach places the dawning of conservatism, as we understand it today, in the latter part of the eighteenth century. Before that, there were no true ideological movements for it to react against.

The period roughly corresponding to the eighteenth century is now known as the 'Age of Reason' or the 'Enlightenment'. It was an age when many previously held certainties were being challenged by new rational modes of thought. The Enlightenment spread through virtually all aspects of human existence: not only religion, ethics and politics were affected, but also the physical sciences, mathematics, the arts and architecture.

Names that are familiar to us today were part of this dramatic new age — Isaac Newton (1642–1727) in science, Wolfgang Amadeus Mozart (1756–91) in music, Robert Adam (1728–92) in architecture and Jean-Jacques Rousseau in philosophy.

In terms of the development of conservatism, however, developments in philosophy, ideology, religion and politics are the most significant. It is useful to consider the ways in which new thinking affected these four fields.

Philosophy

As early as the seventeenth century, René Descartes (1596–1650) proposed that man was capable of rational thought and indeed was capable of leading a life based on reason. It had previously been taken for granted that man was driven by his physical appetites and emotions. Descartes's proposition had a profound influence on political and religious thought, both of which had been based on the pre-Cartesian view of man. Thinkers such as John Locke, Immanuel Kant (1724–1804) and Jean-Jacques Rousseau converted these rationalistic ideas into political principles, structures and aspirations.

Ideology

Several prominent ideologies owe their conception to Enlightenment thinking. Liberalism and socialism, in particular, were the products of the belief that society and politics could be ordered in a rational way so as to produce predictable and desirable outcomes. Marxism, anarchism and even early feminism can be included among those ideologies which were made possible by rationalism.

Religion

Roman Catholicism had dominated religious thought in Europe for many centuries before the Enlightenment. Leaving aside purely spiritual matters, Roman Catholic Christianity incorporated ideas such as obedience, divine authority, hierarchy and, perhaps above all, the fundamental belief that humankind carried the burden of original sin. This last principle was to become a key aspect of conservative thought in the nineteenth century. Original sin proposes a pessimistic view of human nature, suggesting that each of us is born with a flawed personality and is incapable of throwing this off completely, however well we try to lead our lives.

Rationalism rejected this notion and asserted that human beings are able to order their lives on a moral, rational basis. Enlightenment thought also challenged the traditional, purely spiritual authority of the Roman Catholic Church in general. It opened the door to radical ideas such as free will and individualism and a generally more optimistic view of human nature. The new religious movements that emerged in the sixteenth century became known collectively as Protestantism. To some extent, Protestantism can be seen as a rational form of Christianity. It was strongly linked to liberalism and capitalism, which were both born out of Enlightenment thought. By the eighteenth century, the Protestant creed in various forms had become dominant in northern Europe, significantly in those areas where the Industrial Revolution was also dawning.

In discarding the previously unquestioned ideas that human society naturally falls into an ordered hierarchy and that the traditional authority of monarch and church should be obeyed in all circumstances, political thought and spiritual life were liberated.

Politics

The practical application of the new philosophies and religious thinking arrived in two main stages. The first was the challenge to the traditional or divine authority of absolute monarchy. This occurred as early as the 1640s with the English Civil War, but achieved more permanent forms in the French and American revolutions at the end of the eighteenth century. The second stage was the creation of representative forms of government to replace monarchical authority. Principles such as government by consent, constitutional government, individual rights and, eventually, universal suffrage naturally followed.

Reaction

So radical was the nature of Enlightenment thinking that it was almost inevitable there would be a reaction. It was the representatives of the social class whose power was threatened by the new order — the aristocracy and landed gentry — who led the way. They owed their economic and political power to the Church and monarchy. When these institutions were threatened, so too was their social dominance.

The conservative reaction, however, was not only self-interested and defensive. As we shall see below, there were principled and pragmatic objections to the new philosophies. It was these empirical and moral objections that created modern conservatism.

Class and conservatism

As is shown above, conservatism, at least in the nineteenth and first half of the twentieth centuries, was associated with class interest. As the Industrial Revolution gathered pace and the economic power of the new capitalist middle classes grew, the landed classes found their position increasingly threatened. Conservatives therefore found themselves in the position of 'conserving' the interests of a particular class. As it became clear that this was merely a cynical exercise in self-interest, conservatives had to develop a more rigorous and justifiable theory of class. Furthermore, the power of the aristocratic ruling class needed more justification than mere tradition. It was the great **Tory** prime minister, Benjamin Disraeli (1804–81), who expressed this most successfully, developing a quasi-political theory of class known as *neo-feudalism*. Since the original feudal system had maintained an ordered society for centuries, it was therefore logical that a modern structured class system could continue to maintain that sense of order.

Key terms

Tory and Toryism

The expression 'Tory' originated in Ireland. It was a term of abuse for a certain type of travelling vagabond or criminal. The early Whigs in England in the late seventeenth century adopted it to describe the royalists, their political opponents. It came into common usage in the nineteenth century as a description of conservatives in general and thus began to lose most of its negative implications.

Today, 'Tory' can have three meanings. First, it is often used, especially by journalists, to refer to any member of the Conservative Party. Second, it can have negative connotations when used by those from the political left. In this sense it suggests a politician who is excessively right wing and out of touch. Third, it can refer to a traditional conservative, as opposed to a modern neo-liberal or neo-conservative. The term Toryism describes the brand of conservatism a traditional conservative would adhere to: one-nationism, inclusiveness, consensus politics and pragmatism.

Disraeli observed that by the 1860s it had become clear that contemporary societies were divided into three great classes. The working class consisted mainly of producers. They could not be expected to exercise power directly, although certainly their interests had to be expressed and represented. The capitalist and commercial classes were the main wealth creators. They could not be entrusted with power since they were self-interested and could not be relied upon to consider the national interest. The landed and aristocrat class was a special case. It enjoyed great privileges and always had done. However, its position now had to be justified; it could not rule simply because it had always done so. It had to accept responsibilities if it were to enjoy privileges. The principle that responsibility comes with power became known as *noblesse oblige*.

Benjamin Disraeli, for whom the power of the aristocracy brought with it a duty of responsibility

Despite this analysis, Disraeli insisted that the traditional ruling class still had a key role to play in politics. Traditional conservatives continued to support this view right up to the 1960s. The great 'father' of English conservatism, Edmund Burke (1729–97), argued that the power of the ruling class could be justified on a number of grounds:

➤ The traditional ruling class enjoyed great wealth and had no pressing need to toil for a living, so therefore it could govern the country in a disinterested way. The middle and working classes would govern in a self-interested way since they had so much to gain or lose.

➤ Having governed the country for centuries, the landed class of gentry and aristocracy had accumulated the wisdom of the past. In other words, the ability to govern well was passed down from one generation to the next, each generation learning from the past and adding something to it.

➤ In a spiritual way, the ruling class was seen by conservatives as superior to all others. Its wisdom would enable it to understand best how to preserve and increase the welfare of the people. This notion came to be described — often by its opponents — as the exercise of *paternalism*.

For a century after Disraeli, conservatism continued to cling on to ruling-class philosophy, gradually accepting popular democracy and that the authority to govern had to be earned by election.

Class, however, remained an important issue. Conservative movements throughout Europe and the USA became vehicles for the demands of any class with a vested interest in the status quo, or at least with a reason to oppose the new ideologies. Thus, farming groups, especially the small peasant class on both sides of the Atlantic, have tended to be conservative, as have small business owners in general. In Britain, the middle classes have traditionally been conservative, especially those engaged in private enterprise. They hold an interest in the maintenance of order and oppose any ideological change, such as socialism, which would threaten their position in society and politics.

The main practical way in which the conservative attachment to the middle classes in the twentieth century manifested itself was in the movement's support for free-market capitalism. While socialists were arguing for increased state involvement in redistributing income from rich to poor, and liberals supported state welfare provision, conservatives usually opposed excessive state activity. This of course suited the middle-class preference for lower taxation and the free operation of capitalism.

By the 1970s, it was clear throughout the more prosperous Western countries that class divisions were breaking down. People had become less concerned with collective class interests and more interested in their own individual progression. This posed a problem for conservatism since it had always presented itself as a class-based movement. It was, therefore, at this time that New Right conservatism emerged as a new philosophy of individualism, led by Margaret Thatcher and Ronald Reagan. The relationship between conservatism and class had finally ended.

Conservatism and ideology

As we have seen above, conservatism would probably not need to exist if political ideologies did not exist. Ideologies, by their nature, propose social change. Conservatives are fundamentally opposed to such change when it has not arisen out of natural forces. When change is created by political action motivated by ideological beliefs, conservatives become suspicious and usually hostile towards it.

In opposing ideological change, conservatism has changed its own character in order to provide an effective opposition. The following examples illustrate this:

1 The arrival of liberalism in the nineteenth century gave rise to the protection of individual liberty, human rights, representative democracy and minimal interference by government in the economy or welfare issues. Conservatives responded by stressing the importance of social unity and the need for welfare to combat the

divisive effects of free-market individualism. In Britain, this was promoted by Disraeli and became known as *one-nation conservatism*.

2 With the emergence of socialism as the main opponent of liberalism in the twentieth century, conservatives changed their philosophy. They sought alternatives to the collectivist and egalitarian aspirations of the socialists and thus became the champions of private enterprise and individualism. Excessive action by the state was regarded suspiciously and usually opposed.

3 When fascism began to spread between the world wars, conservatives were at first at a loss as to how to react. This was compounded by the fact that fascism tended to appeal to the same groups in society as conservatism — peasants, small business owners and elements of the disaffected, anti-socialist working class. Once the true nature of fascism was revealed, however, conservatives such as Winston Churchill (1874–1965) began to stress the importance of individual liberty, democracy and firm limits to the activities of the state. In other words, they became more liberal in character.

4 More recently, progressive liberalism has come to the fore. This philosophy supports individual liberty, moral and social diversity and some mild redistribution of income and wealth from rich to poor. In the USA, however, conservatism has developed a more authoritarian position on morality and law and order issues in reaction to this permissive philosophy. In many cases, the quest for a more moral society and the restoration of traditional values has given rise to a religious element in conservatism.

Conservatism has often been described as chameleon-like in that it changes its characteristics as its political environment changes. Its objection to ideology and ideological change, however, runs deeper than this, and is further examined later in this chapter.

Core values of conservatism

Conservatism, then, altered its character in the face of two kinds of challenge — that of supporting the dominant social class in any particular age and that of responding to the emergence of new, popular ideologies. This has resulted in considerable variation in the nature of the philosophy. However, conservatism does have enduring values and these are discussed below.

Human nature

Perhaps the most fundamental value of conservatism is its belief about basic human nature. This is more pessimistic in attitude than that of most other ideologies, notably liberalism and socialism. It is demonstrated by the following examples:

➤ The deepest conservatives take the Roman Catholic view that humankind is born with original sin and must therefore remain severely flawed in character. However much individuals try, they will be unable to achieve perfection. Ideologies such as socialism and anarchism have argued that individuals can be moulded by a just society into more perfect creatures. Not so, say such conservatives, who regard these ideologies as impractical and utopian. The religious nature of modern US conservatism has seen a restoration of this fundamentalist view.

➤ Individuals are not driven by reason, as Enlightenment thinkers had asserted, but by basic appetites. These include the desire for physical prosperity, for property, for power and to avoid deprivation. The implication is that individuals cannot generally be trusted with government since they will simply use it for their own ends rather than for the welfare of the whole community.

➤ Human nature is not a constant, but is always changing as the nature of society itself changes. The conservative philosopher Karl Popper (1902–94), for example, criticised all ideologies on the grounds that they have been based on a fixed view of human nature. This was, for him, an error which invalidated all ideologies. Thus, there may be periods when people mostly crave freedom and the pursuit of individualism, while at other times they may be fearful and crave security and welfare.

➤ It is a conservative tradition to see people as, on the whole, untrustworthy, self-seeking and generally feckless. This leads to the conclusion that humankind is sorely in need of firm government. This should not be government by dictators, who may too easily rise to power since people are readily persuaded by populist figures. Rather, it should be government by benevolent rulers, who need to be firm, but who have the people's general interests at heart. As Edmund Burke observed in the eighteenth century, the relationship between government and the people should be similar to that between a parent and a child. This view is often referred to as **paternalism**.

➤ We are, say conservatives, basically individuals who are more concerned with our own welfare than that of the community as a whole. As Margaret Thatcher famously asserted in a 1984 television interview: 'There are individuals and there are families. There is no such thing as society.'

Key term

Paternalism

Paternalism is a style of politics usually associated with conservatives, though this is not necessarily always the case. The concept suggests that those who govern claim superior knowledge and judgement over those who are governed. Rulers therefore believe that they understand what is best for the people to a greater extent than the people do themselves. A paternalist may well oppose democracy on the grounds that people will make poor judgements compared to their political masters. The paternalist model derives from the relationship between a parent and a child. This means that it can have positive implications, in that a paternalistic ruler would normally have the best interests of the people at heart, just as parents care for their children. Although mid-nineteenth-century conservatives, such as Peel and Disraeli, adopted a paternalistic approach to politics, in modern political life it has mostly been rejected in favour of popular democracy, whereby the people have a major input into the decisions which affect them.

The conservative view of human nature has a number of implications, for example in the field of law and order. The causes of crime and disorder, conservatives believe, lie with the individual. Indeed, some have argued that criminal behaviour is the product of humankind's inherent sinfulness. This directly opposes the more liberal view that it is the result of economic and social deprivation. The practical application of these beliefs therefore involves exemplary punishment rather than social remedies.

A further consequence of this conservative philosophy concerns the nature of government. If there is an excess of popular democracy, the country is likely to be poorly governed. As long ago as the 1870s, Disraeli advocated that conservatives accept the need for universal suffrage, but this did not imply that people could be completely trusted with government. The conservative view of representation is that governments should not slavishly follow the fluctuating desires and demands of the people, but should use their wise judgement to serve the best interests of the whole community. In a modern context, this is reflected in the conservative suspicion of the referendum as a governing mechanism. (The British Conservative Party, however, has supported the use of referendums in some circumstances, such as possible approval for a European Union constitution in 2005 — a typical example of conservative pragmatism.)

A more dramatic example of the conservative view of human nature can be found in Margaret Thatcher's policies of the 1980s. She sought to unlock what she saw as humankind's natural desire to be free of the shackles of government (for example, in the form of personal taxation), to pursue individual goals and to compete freely with others in search of prosperity. Her pursuit of free-market policies certainly seemed to tap into the fundamental desires of many people for individualism. Of course, critics have suggested that what she did was to suppress community spirit and the desire for social justice, pandering to those who could benefit from free-market economics and ignoring those who were not in a position to take advantage of it.

Order

In the most basic terms, it could be said that liberals see humankind's most fundamental need, after food, clothing and shelter, as individual freedom. Socialists and anarchists, on the other hand, stress humankind's social nature and its preference for the collective rather than individual pursuit of goals. The conservative view is clear and stands in opposition to these beliefs. Conservatives affirm that humankind's most basic need is for order and security.

We can trace this key aspect of conservative philosophy to two English thinkers, Hobbes and Burke. Thomas Hobbes, writing shortly after the end of the English Civil War in 1651, examined humankind's basic predicament. On the one hand, individuals have a desire to be free and to exercise all their rights. On the other hand, individuals are intensely competitive and self-seeking. This would, if allowed to flourish, lead to an intolerable situation. Life, he famously argued, would become 'nasty, brutish and short' (*Leviathan*, 1651). In practice, people would consider themselves to be in competition with every other person and therefore live in fear of the results of that restless society. Hobbes believed that, faced with such a dilemma, humankind would choose to sacrifice much of its freedom and rights in favour of a secure existence. The only way to ensure this was to allow an absolute ruler to govern and protect us from each other.

Ever since Hobbes, conservatives have preferred strong government and have tended to favour the community's need for security over the rights of individuals. Again, we see this philosophy most clearly in the conservative attitude to law and order and its reluctance to champion the cause of civil liberties.

Edmund Burke's great work, *Reflections on the Revolution in France*, was written in 1790, one year after the French had dismissed their monarchy and at a time when there was growing hysteria in England over whether revolution would cross the Channel. Starting as a vehement criticism of the actions of the revolutionaries, the book turned into a general manual of conservatism. Above all, Burke's *Reflections* is a plea for the preservation of order and gradual reform as opposed to the disorder that results from revolutionary change. The French Revolution sacrificed order and security in order to impose abstract theories which were premature, unnecessary and not generally supported by the majority of the people. Since Burke, conservatives have always erred on the side of caution and preserving order — until Margaret Thatcher, that is.

Edmund Burke, the 'father' of conservatism

Peter Newark's Historical Pictures

Tradition and preservation

Conservatives' preference for the preservation of tradition is closely related to their desire for public order. When we refer to tradition in this context, we mean both traditional *institutions*, such as the monarchy, established Church and political constitution, as well as traditional *values*, such as the preservation of marriage and the importance of the nuclear family, religion and established morality. Again, this is an attitude that traces back to Burke.

The greatest crime of the French revolutionaries, according to Burke, was to abandon traditional forms of authority that had stood the test of time. This is summarised in his ringing criticism that 'No generation should ever be so rash as to consider itself superior to its predecessors' (*Reflections on the Revolution in France*, 1790). The fact that values and institutions have survived, argue conservatives in general, is a testament to their quality. Furthermore, they carry the accumulated wisdom of the past and should therefore be respected. In a similar way, traditions bring to contemporary society some of the best aspects of past societies. How people thought and behaved in the past can inform current generations. Thus, the nineteenth-century poet and philosopher G. K. Chesterton (1874–1936) called tradition the 'democracy of the dead', because it allows the wisdom of previous generations to be involved in the activities of current society.

Burke also praised traditions for their ability to provide continuity between the past and present. They give a sense of security and help to prevent violent transformations in society. He described tradition as:

> a partnership...between those who are living, those who are dead and those who are to be born.
> From *Reflections on the Revolution in France*, 1790

A typical example concerns the monarchy. Elected governments, political ideologies and social change may come and go, but if the monarchy endures in its traditional form the people will retain a sense of security and continuity amid the turmoil. Conservatives take a similar view of traditional morality based around the family. This helps each new generation hold onto a lasting set of values in an ever-changing world, giving them a sense of security which they can pass on to the next generation.

Allied to their theories of tradition, conservatives believe that when institutions and values have proved useful in promoting order and stability in the past, they should be preserved. It is irresponsible, they argue, to reject them for the sake of ideological principles or new theories. This is not, however, a recipe for 'no change'. Rather, it is a tendency to conserve what is seen to be good and to reform what proves to be undesirable.

Despite this, modern British conservatism has largely ignored the importance of tradition, especially since the 1980s. It has embraced new social theories, such as economic monetarism, privatisation and opposition to the dependency culture, and has attacked some traditional institutions, such as the civil service, the Church of England, the legal establishment and the long-standing practices of the financial centre in London. There is still evidence, however, of strong support for traditional institutions and values in US and French conservatism, which have proved resistant to 'excessive' social reform.

Inequality

Until the eighteenth century, the idea that humankind is naturally divided into a hierarchy — that we are born into unequal circumstances, with the few privileged at the top of the hierarchy and the many inferiors at the bottom — was taken as natural and inevitable.

Conservatives gradually modified their view of the natural structure of society during the nineteenth and twentieth centuries. It was becoming clear that society was more fluid than it had ever been and that people had begun to view themselves as individuals rather than as members of a social class (which would give them little chance to progress). By the 1980s, conservatives had abandoned their views of a hierarchical society, but held on to the belief that individuals are unequal in terms of their abilities and potentialities. This is a view shared by both conservatives and liberals.

In particular, conservatives have emphasised their belief in natural inequality in response to socialist ideas. The socialist objective of creating more social and economic equality is seen by conservatives as a completely artificial aspiration, unnatural to society. Furthermore, they suggest that inequality is a positive aspect of society since it creates competition and dynamism.

Pragmatism

It would be entirely wrong to suggest that conservatism is a doctrine of 'no change', or that it treats its own principles as eternal and fixed. Conservatives are, above all, pragmatists. Michael Oakeshott (1901–90), a leading conservative philosopher of modern times, particularly advocated a pragmatic approach. He asserted that politics should be 'a conversation, not an argument' (*On Being Conservative*, 1962). What he meant was that political action should never be the result of conflict over political dogmas and theories. Instead, it should be the result of a more gentle relationship between government and the governed. The good conservative politician should engage in a relationship with the people which would allow him or her to reach decisions based on the 'intimations and traditions' of the community.

Pragmatism implies a flexible approach to politics: an understanding of what is best for people, what is acceptable to them and what will preserve a stable society. It is also a rejection of the politics of strongly-held ideology and of a dogmatic approach to decision-making. Perhaps the most striking example of pragmatism occurred in the 1950s. A series of moderate Conservative governments in the UK was confronted with a number of radical reforms which had been implemented by the Labour governments of 1945–51. Should the Conservatives cancel the widespread nationalisation of major industries, dismantle the newly created welfare state and remove freshly granted powers from local government? In principle, the party was opposed to the reforms, but it had to recognise that they were both popular and seemingly successful. It therefore reached a pragmatic decision to retain Labour's radical initiatives.

Individualism

This is perhaps the most difficult conservative principle to define. It has lost much of its distinctiveness since it is a value which is now shared with liberals, most European democratic parties, both Republicans and Democrats in the USA and the British Labour Party. There is also a problem in distinguishing individualism from individual liberty. Although the ideas are linked, they are not necessarily the same concept and represent distinct political traditions.

Individual liberty, a fundamentally liberal principle, concerns mainly an absence of external restraint. It refers to the extent to which our activities, as individuals or groups, may be constrained by laws, customs or a moral code. Prominent examples of individual liberty in Western democracies are the right to freedom of worship, thought and expression, freedom of movement and freedom to associate in whatever law-abiding group we wish. Individualism is a more positive concept and refers to choice, opportunity and self-fulfilment.

Conservative individualism has two main elements. First, it suggests that each individual and household should be presented with the widest possible range of choices and opportunities. The state should restrict such choices as little as possible. This provides a link with liberal freedom, but conservative individualism is distinguished from it in that the state can *enhance and facilitate* choice and opportunity. In other words, the state can play a positive rather than a negative role. Second, individualism implies a sense of privacy. There are many areas where interference by the state may be seen as legitimate — for example, in the fields of law and order, national defence and management of the currency — but there is also an extensive private sphere. For conservatives, private life is not the concern of the state. Matters such as operating private businesses, religious belief, enjoyment of property and family-expenditure decisions are not normally to be interfered with by government. Therefore, it is part of the essence of conservatism that a strong barrier should be preserved between the *public* and *private* or *individual* spheres.

There is one further important implication of the conservative support for individualism. For conservatives, individualism can best flourish in a stable social, moral and economic environment. The continuity provided by morality, law and order and traditions provides the necessary scenery in which individuals can play their roles securely. Indeed, in many circumstances, the excessive exercise of individual liberties, as advocated by pure liberals, threatens individualism. A society that allows too much personal freedom may threaten its own security and stability. Given the choice between a free society and a collectively secure society in which individuals can flourish, conservatives usually favour the latter.

Michael Oakeshott describes such a society as *nomocratic*, i.e. one where people enjoy shared morality, values and beliefs, thus creating fertile ground for individualism. This, he continues, is preferable to a restless society which is always pursuing utopian goals — he critically refers to this as a *teleocratic* society. The analogy Oakeshott used in *On Being Conservative* (1962) was that of a ship adrift in an open sea. The ship had no port of departure and no destination, but was constantly faced by crises and dangers which had to be dealt with by its officers. So it is with society, he argued. In the following passage from the work, he expresses the conservative view that society should not be driven towards a preferred goal and that government should confine itself to preventing social conflict:

> Government, then, as the conservative in this matter understands it, does not begin with a vision of another, different and better world, but with the observation of the self-government practised even by men of passion in the conduct of their enterprises; it begins in the informal adjustments of interests to one another which are designed to release those who are apt to collide from the mutual frustration of a collision.

Oakeshott's phrase, 'the mutual frustration of a collision', is a telling one for conservatives and sums up why order is so vital for them. Without order, we are liable to be constantly thwarted in our endeavours by conflict with others. For some extreme liberals and New Right conservatives, conflict can be a creative force. For traditional conservatives, however, it is seen as destructive.

Property

For much of the nineteenth century, conservatives (then usually referred to as 'Tories') feared the rise of the property-owning middle classes. This was mainly because they believed the middle classes would sweep away traditional authority by using their vast economic wealth to wield political power. The Whig Party was seen at that time as the promoter of capitalist property. Following the Disraelian era of the 1860s and 1870s, however, the British Tories (who were in the process of turning themselves into the Conservative Party) accepted that they too must incorporate the interests of property owners. Similar stories were unfolding in the rest of Europe and the USA. As the growing property-owning classes required a political force to hold back the rise of working-class movements, mainly socialism, conservatism became a fundamentally middle-class tradition.

The defence of property has included opposition to the introduction of common ownership (i.e. nationalisation), resistance to high property taxes (e.g. Margaret Thatcher attempted to replace local property rates with a non-property-based poll tax in 1988) and heavy stress on law and order since high crime levels tend mostly to affect private property. In much of Europe, conservative parties also took up the cause of small farmers and business owners. Here again, it was socialist modes of thinking that threatened their enjoyment of their own property.

Perhaps the clearest example of conservative support for private property comes from Margaret Thatcher's time in office. In the early 1980s, shortly after coming to power, she announced an initiative known as the 'right to buy', whereby tenants in council-owned housing would be given the opportunity to purchase their own homes on preferential terms. She saw this as part of a new 'property and share-owning democracy' in the UK. She believed that owning property or shares in businesses (widespread privatisation of nationalised industries gave people the opportunity to buy shares at discounted prices) would give people a stake in society and thus promote a sense of responsibility. This has become a key element in the conservative attitude to property. It was opposed by socialists in the UK, who were strongly attached to collective ownership of low-cost housing. However, ultimately the popularity of the policy went a long way to eroding socialist elements in the Labour Party. Attachment to private property rights, in other words, became part of a new British consensus.

Opposition to ideology

As has been seen, conservatism changes its character according to the dominant ideology it is resisting at any given time. However, the movement's opposition to ideologies in general runs deeper than merely a suspicion of radical change. It has a number of different aspects:

➤ Oakeshott's view, described above, that societies should not be directed towards specific social goals has implications for anti-ideology. Most ideologies propose an ideal form of society and are dedicated to working towards it. This is seen by conservatives as contrived and artificial; it flies in the face of both tradition and the need for social stability. They derive no sense of social progress from it. However, this is not to say that conservatives oppose social improvement. On the contrary, they believe that this is a worthwhile goal, but it should be pursued, they argue, in accordance with the emotions and traditions of the people, not according to an abstract set of political principles.

➤ Ideological change is normally radical in nature. As far back as Burke's opposition to the actions of the French revolutionaries, conservatives have resisted rapid forms of social revolution or transformation. Reforms, when clearly necessary and desirable, should be gentle and should be carried out with continuity in mind. Burke's warning has remained relevant to conservatives:

> [revolutionaries] despise experience as the wisdom of unlettered men, and, as for the rest, they have wrought underground a mine that will blow up, at one grand explosion, all examples of antiquity, all precedents, charters and acts of parliament.
>
> From *Reflections on the Revolution in France*, 1790

➤ Excessive attachments to ideologies may result in tyranny. There are two main reasons for this. First, ideological leaders tend to become totalitarian in their ruthless pursuit of political goals. Burke observed this in the French revolutionaries; since then, movements such as fascism, communism and even radical feminism have suffered the same fate. Indeed, ideas alone can be tyrannical in nature (a concept which has come to be known as Jacobinism, after Robespierre's revolutionary party in France). The so-called political correctness proposed by militant feminists is seen by conservatism as a form of Jacobinism. Second, the revolutionary change which often results from ideology sweeps away traditional authority and stability, resulting in disorder at best, and anarchy at worst.

➤ Ideologies have a fixed view of human nature; indeed, several are actually based on such an assumption. Conservatives see human nature as fickle, non-rational and changeable. This makes all fixed political principles fundamentally flawed. The academic conservative Karl Popper further suggested that ideological movements, far from being based on human nature, actually influence human nature. They are not scientific in nature, therefore, but are manipulative. It follows that they create artificial societies and so are doomed to fail. For Popper, the Marxist-inspired communist regimes were a classic example of this. Ideas such as equality and common ownership of property, which communists imposed on their states, were not natural to human nature, so therefore they could not hope to endure.

Scepticism and empiricism

This review of core ideas can be summarised by returning to the typical conservative political state of mind. First, conservatives are, by nature, sceptical of most fixed political principles. As the modern conservative politician Michael Portillo (1953–) stated in a 1996 television interview:

> If there were no political nostrums [i.e. fixed beliefs], there would be no need for conservatism.

In fact, conservatives tend to be suspicious of the activity of politics in general. For them it should be a limited activity since they doubt how effective it can, or ought, to be. Another modern British conservative, Lord Hailsham (1907–2001), has gone as far as to say that:

> The man who puts politics before his family is not fit to be called a civilised human being.
> From *The Case for Conservatism*, 1947

For many traditional conservatives, it is the main role of their philosophy to express reservations and doubts about all political movements.

Second, conservatives are usually empiricists. Empiricism involves judging current actions against the experience of the past. Respect for tradition, pragmatism and suspicion of the new and the untried are all aspects of this empirical approach. The wise politician, it is suggested, builds on the wisdom of the past and is informed by that past. This is a preference for the known (what has gone before) over the unknown (what may be in the future). This view follows Chesterton's concept of the 'democracy of the dead' and respects Burke's plea not to believe that the current generation is wiser than those which have gone before. Critics see this as permanently looking backwards, but conservatives respond by pointing out how much that is positive has been achieved in the past, from which we can still learn.

Box 3.1 gives quotations on some key traditional conservative ideas.

Box 3.1 **Some key traditional conservative ideas**

'The Tory Party has three great objects...to maintain the institutions of the country...to uphold the Empire of England...and to elevate the condition of the people...'
Benjamin Disraeli, 1872 speech

'Scepticism and empiricism are the foundations of Conservatism.'

'The Tory Party has emotions, but no doctrine.'
Both from Ian Gilmour, *The Body Politic*, 1969

'Moderation is indispensable if passionate men are to escape being locked in an encounter of mutual frustration...'
From Michael Oakeshott, *On being Conservative*, 1962

'If the main strength of Conservatism is adaptability, its main enemy is ideology.'
From Francis Pym, *The Politics of Consent*, 1984

Types of conservatism

Early conservatism

At the beginning of this chapter, we placed the origins of conservatism at the end of the eighteenth century. The term 'conservatism' itself is probably of French origin, referring to the reaction against the ideals of the French Revolution; at that stage, it represented a movement that hoped to restore the traditional authority of the monarchy and the Church. In the early days of the USA, the conservative elements among the founding fathers wished to see the retention of central authority and the political power of the propertied classes. In England, conservatism was known as Toryism. Its main concern was to hold back the rise of liberal ideas which prompted such fearful developments as constitutional reform and free-trade policies.

It is tempting, therefore, to see the origins of conservatism in reactionary ideas, and thereby to view it as a wholly negative philosophy. Certainly, there was a powerful conservative movement in the first half of the nineteenth century which challenged all the main ideas of the Enlightenment. Conservatism stood for romantic ideals in preference to rationalism. Politics was seen largely in terms of paternalism and judgement, rather than rational thought and democratic fervour. There were desperate appeals to retain the authority of the Church, the aristocracy and the monarchy.

It was Sir Robert Peel (1788–1850), widely known as the founder of the British Conservative Party, who understood that conservatism would not survive with such a negative philosophy.

The Peelites

Peel recognised that if reform and change were both inevitable and desirable, it was pointless for conservatives to resist it. In his widely acclaimed *Tamworth Manifesto* of 1834, he insisted that conservatism had to become a pragmatic, rather than a reactionary, movement. By then Parliament had been reformed and there were proposals to introduce free trade in place of the protectionism that served the interests of the great landowners rather than the common people. He urged his party to embrace these changes and to move on to new concerns.

In effect, it was Peel who enabled the British conservative movement to ally itself to free-market capitalism and so gain the support of the growing middle classes. Peelite conservatism was, therefore, pragmatic, tied to capitalism, protective of property rights and fundamentally middle class in nature. For many of its followers, the movement remained basically Peelite up until the radical reforms introduced by Margaret Thatcher.

One-nationism

After Peel, the next great conservative leader was Benjamin Disraeli. Like Peel, he was a pragmatist and, as such, dealt with the threat posed by the rise of the working classes and their main political tradition — socialism. While Peel had recognised the importance of taking up the cause of the middle class, Disraeli had to decide where to take his party in relation to the working class.

Perhaps Disraeli's main contribution to conservatism — not only in Britain, but also in the rest of Europe and the USA — were his theories about the organic nature of society. What capitalism was doing, he argued, was to create a society of individuals at the expense of a general sense of social responsibility. In other words, the country was in danger of losing its sense of community (what German conservatives were calling *Volksgemeinschaft* — a common feeling of national identity). People who were too busy pursuing their own selfish ends were liable to lose a strong sense of nation and society.

At the same time, the effect of free-market capitalism, which Peelite conservatives had supported, was dividing the country into distinctive groups — the prosperous few and the many poor. Disraeli described this growing phenomenon as *two nations.* It was a recipe for revolution since it created class conflict. It was the role of conservatives, Disraeli insisted, to unite the nation and create *one nation.* In order to do this, government should cease to rule in the interests of only one class and, instead, care for the welfare of all classes. R. A. Butler (1902–82), a 'one-nation Tory' and government minister of the 1950s and 1960s, admitted still to be inspired by Disraeli nearly 100 years later. He said in 1954:

> Underlying all our differences there should be fundamental unity — the very antithesis of class war — bringing together what Disraeli called the Two Nations into a single social entity.

So Disraelian, one-nation Toryism was a type of conservatism which had as its core aim the unity of the people and the avoidance of social conflict. This was a theme taken up by continental European conservatives at the same time. In Germany in the 1870s, for example, Otto von Bismarck (1815–98) was preaching a similar message to his people.

According to Disraeli, national unity was to be provided by four main forces. These were constitutional unity of the UK (he opposed Irish independence, for example), the maintenance of great traditions around which people could unite, the encouragement of patriotism and the provision of welfare for the poor to prevent excessive inequality and therefore conflict.

One-nation conservatism survives to this day. It formed a powerful opposition from *within* the Conservative Party to Margaret Thatcher's radicalism in the 1980s. Figures such as Michael Heseltine (1933–), Kenneth Clarke (1940–), Ian Gilmour (1920–) and Francis Pym (1922–), collectively and disparagingly known to Thatcher's supporters as 'wets', all claimed to be social unifiers. They criticised the new individualist and free-market policies of the Thatcher era. These new ideas within conservatism were once again, they argued, threatening to divide Britain into two nations — the haves and have-nots. Ultimately, the one-nation group lost the argument and their own positions in the party. It nevertheless remains as a significant minority within the Conservative Party; now often known as 'social' conservatives, the group continues to resist the movement to the right in British conservatism. In the USA, 'progressive' conservative members of the Republican Party have, by contrast, been completely routed and have moved to the Democratic Party.

The nationalist-authoritarian right

There is a long tradition in Europe of a type of conservatism often characterised as 'ultra right' and, in its most extreme form, even quasi-fascist. A typical example has been the National Front movement in France, led by Jean-Marie Le Pen (1928–), but there have also been popular movements in Austria, Russia, Serbia, Denmark and even in the Netherlands (which has one of the most liberal reputations of the continent).

Ultra conservatives are radical nationalists, placing the national interest above all other considerations. As one would expect, they oppose the activities of the European Union and international organisations in general, and are extremely resistant to immigration into their countries. It would be wrong to characterise this group as 'racist' in outlook, but they certainly do oppose multiculturalism, preferring a 'monoculture' where all citizens are expected to adopt the dominant domestic culture.

It would also be mistaken to describe them as fascists. While they do propose an extremely authoritarian form of state in terms of law and order, morality and national security, they are democrats and support a pluralist society where different groups can be allowed to flourish as long as they do not threaten the national culture or public order. They tend to support free-market economics, insisting that the state, although strong, should be limited to matters of order and security, not industrial and commercial activity.

Few British conservatives have conformed to this model. Enoch Powell (1912–98), a leading politician of the 1960s and 1970s, perhaps came closest to doing so. He was noted for his opposition to immigration on the grounds that it would lead to excessive conflict (he claimed his policy was not racially based), his reaction against the growth of moral permissiveness in the 1960s and his championing of free-market economics (this was well before Margaret Thatcher reintroduced them). Arguably, the emergence of the UK Independence Party (UKIP) in the early years of the twenty-first century marks something of a revival of this political tradition. Although opposition to European integration is the UKIP's emblematic policy, there is no doubt that the party contains many authoritarian-conservative politicians.

The New Right

It is important at this stage to be clear about what is meant by the term 'New Right'. It was coined in the USA to describe a new wing of the Republican Party, represented by Ronald Reagan's presidency, and was imported into the UK to describe the wing of the Conservative Party that gathered around the leadership of Margaret Thatcher. Although it was described as 'new', its main ideas were not new at all. They were, in fact, a revival of a number of past political traditions including classical liberalism, populism, Whiggism and conservatism itself. What was 'new' was that these different strands of thought were brought together into one political movement. In addition, many of the ideas of the New Right were new to the British Conservative Party.

The movement has also been described as 'Thatcherism' or 'Reaganism', or sometimes a blend of 'neo-liberalism' and 'neo-conservatism'. All these terms may prove to be misleading so, for the purposes of this book, it will be referred to as the 'New Right'. A second potential confusion arises from the identification of the sources of the movement. It was certainly not developed by Thatcher and Reagan. They were merely the dominant political leaders who were able to put its principles into practice. Our search for its origins are best centred on the USA.

The 'Chicago School' of economists was led by Milton Friedman, who is still seen as the leading figure of the New Right. His great work, *Capitalism and Freedom* (1962), has become something of a bible for New Right thinkers. The Chicago School argued that the rise of socialist thinking had resulted in excessive interference by the state in the workings of the economy. This was holding back progress, stifling enterprise and curtailing individual freedom. Friedman believed that the loss of economic freedom involved in state planning and control would eventually lead to a wider loss of political freedom.

Meanwhile, in Europe, Friedrich von Hayek, the Austrian philosopher, was becoming widely read in conservative circles, notably by Margaret Thatcher and her close adviser, Keith Joseph (1918–94). Like Friedman, Hayek saw the future dangers of the growth of socialism; the pair effectively founded the Chicago School in the 1950s. Hayek's major work, *The Road to Serfdom,* written in 1944, assumed a similar role to that of Friedman's *Capitalism and Freedom* as a source of New Right thinking. For Hayek, the casualty of socialism was individualism and the inevitable result of its progress was a form of totalitarianism. Both the growing power of the state and the influence of organised labour, in the form of trade unions, were identified as vehicles for this new totalitarianism.

Margaret Thatcher, British Prime Minister 1979–90

It existed in full form in the Soviet Union, but Hayek warned that similar states could develop in the West. If we are ever to doubt Hayek's influence we should note the words of Margaret Thatcher in her 1995 memoirs, *The Downing Street Years*:

> The most powerful critique of socialist planning and the socialist state which I read and to which I have returned so often since is F. A. Hayek's *The Road to Serfdom*.

A third key figure of the New Right was Robert Nozick of the USA, whose obsessions with individual liberty and the evils of the strong state are sometimes described as 'anarcho-capitalism'. Nozick had a major influence on US Republicanism at a time when the party was moving towards an anti-government position. Indeed, Ronald Reagan, in his 1981 inauguration speech, expressed the view that 'government is not the solution to our problems, government *is* the problem'. Thatcher was also prone to describing her policies as 'rolling back the frontiers of the state'. Perhaps Nozick's quasi-anarchist views represent the extreme of the New Right in that he proposed the withdrawal of the state from nearly all activities. Most New Right conservatives limit their anti-state views to the economic sphere.

So the New Right, unlike conservatism in general, does have strong philosophical roots, running through Hayek, Friedman and Nozick. It also draws inspiration from a number of other political traditions. Some of these are described briefly below.

Classical liberalism

This nineteenth-century movement was closely associated with the growth of free-market capitalism. Classical liberals began by supporting extensive individual freedom. This was carried forward into advocating a minimal state, free economic markets, a competitive society and the absence of state-organised welfare. Classical liberals believed strongly in self-responsibility: that individuals should not expect to be cradled by the state but instead must accept that their life circumstances are under their own control. The New Right did not accept the whole of classical liberal philosophy. For the New Right, freedom was to be extended in the economic sphere, rather than in society in general.

Neo-classical economics

The economics of Alfred Marshall (1842–1924) in the early twentieth century were known as neo-classical because they were an adaptation of the economic theories from a century before. In short, this kind of economics included two main propositions. The first was that the state should intervene solely to control the currency and public finances so as to maintain stability (effectively to avoid excessive price inflation). The second asserted that the economy contained internal mechanisms which would always bring it back to full employment and growth. This automatic stabilising system relied upon the state not interfering.

In the 1980s, conservatives rediscovered neo-classical economics and renamed them *monetarism*. Edward Heath (1916–) had a brief and unsuccessful flirtation with monetarism when he was prime minister at the start of the 1970s, but it was Margaret Thatcher who was the first to dare to experiment with it, when she was faced with a severely depressed British economy in the early 1980s. She argued that high inflation and unemployment resulted from an excess of government intervention, not a lack of it. She refused to intervene and the economy recovered, albeit temporarily. The USA under Ronald Reagan followed suit with the same results. The one-nation conservatives who had opposed such audacity went into retreat and the New Right was well and truly established.

Populism

This political tradition is largely American and French in origin. It is a philosophy and style of politics that is centred on the potential of individuals to succeed as a result of their own efforts. It appeals to individuals who earn their living independently, without the support either of the state or powerful economic interests. It therefore finds supporters among groups such as small independent farmers, shopkeepers, tradespeople and entrepreneurs who run their own small businesses (groups Marx described as the 'petite bourgeoisie'). Populists are suspicious of the power of the state, oppose personal and corporate taxation, seek to control the power of both trade unions and big business and are intensely nationalistic in their outlook. Certainly, it was these petite bourgeois groups that formed the bedrock of support for Margaret Thatcher's brand of conservatism in the 1980s.

Right-wing nationalism

The New Right took the traditional conservative philosophy of nationalism and raised it to new heights. As a movement, the New Right was faced by the challenges of both globalisation and the advance of European integration. Its UK supporters reacted strongly by asserting national interests in the face of these threats to the autonomy of nation-states everywhere. Their nationalism was inevitably defensive and, at its extreme, became somewhat xenophobic in nature.

The issue of Europe created a dilemma for the New Right. On the one hand, a single European market with no trade barriers was consistent with its attachment to the importance of free markets. On the other hand, integration threatened the nation's political independence. Ultimately, it was this latter political consideration that won the day, but not before the Conservative Party in the UK had torn itself apart over the issue.

Neo-conservatism

Although the New Right has been suspicious of state power, it has become equally concerned by the potential social disorder resulting from increased freedom, permissiveness, lack of social responsibility and challenges to authority from alienated sections of society. It has therefore adapted aspects of the origins of conservatism (hence the term *neo-conservative)* to the modern world. Just as Burke stressed the need for good order and took a paternalistic view of the role of the state, so too has the New Right. A strong stance on law and order issues, attempts to restore traditional values and morality and a firm position on national security have therefore been adopted.

Putting together the *neo-liberal* position on the economy and welfare and the *neo-conservative* stance on law and order, moral values and national security gives a useful summary of New Right philosophy.

Contemporary US conservatism

The rise of the New Right in the USA largely coincided with the movement's success in the UK. Its origins, however, are different. In the USA there was no perceived threat from socialism, as was experienced by British conservatives. It is true that the role of the federal government had expanded considerably in the 1960s and that there was a conservative reaction against this, beginning with the 1968–74 presidency of Richard Nixon (1913–94), but socialism and the expanded state were not the main enemies. For US conservatives, the principal adversary was 'progressive liberalism'.

Classical liberalism and populism had always been important features of US Republicanism, but in the 1980s a new feature emerged. This was a moralistic, religious element. Many of society's problems, especially rising crime rates, public disorder and family breakdown, were blamed on the excessively liberal and permissive culture of the 1960s. The growth of religious observance — mainly Christian — gathered pace in the USA in the 1980s and 1990s. This gave rise to an increasingly moralistic outlook and a stern defence of traditional family values, as well as opposition to feminism and its objectives, such as equal opportunities and abortion on demand. Christianity and a moralistic interpretation of its teachings were now part of the US 'way of life', claimed conservatives. The traditional love of individual liberty in the USA did not, for them, extend to private morality. This was because private moral permissiveness, they suggested, ultimately led to public disorder.

The rise of the 'religious right', represented largely by a movement known as the *Moral Majority,* coincided with the triumph of the USA and its allies in the Cold War. For US conservatives, this was a victory not just for US economic and military prowess, but also for its traditional values.

The challenge of Islamic fundamentalism has reinforced this belief further and added a new dimension. Traditionally, US conservatives have been isolationist in global terms. They have been reluctant to support foreign adventures and have believed that it is up to other nations to defend their own interests. The Cold War victory and the fundamentalist threat have resulted in a new proactive, interventionist attitude to world affairs. The term *New World Order* was coined in 1990 by James Baker (1930–), then Republican secretary of state under President George Bush Senior (1924–). It suggested two main propositions. First, that there was now only one world power able to maintain peace — the USA. The second proposition — essentially conservative in outlook — was that traditional US values were superior to those of other cultures and were, therefore, exportable all over the world. In short, the long-term creation of a stable world order depended on widespread acceptance of those values.

The main elements of contemporary US conservatism can be summarised as follows:
> a religious and moralistic attitude to social issues
> opposition to socially progressive ideas
> deep suspicion of centralised state power
> an attachment to pluralist, decentralised democracy
> classical liberal economic views
> a fixed view of US culture and a sense of its superiority
> a desire to spread US influence and values globally

Continental European conservatism

It would be a mistake to make too many generalisations about conservatism in Europe outside of the UK. Nevertheless, there are some elements that help to distinguish it from the British tradition.

First, continental conservatives tend to be more nationalistic in their outlook. French Gaullism is a good example. Inspired by President Charles de Gaulle (1890–1970), Gaullists believe that French national interests are absolutely paramount. This results in French refusal to cooperate fully with international organisations and a monocultural outlook. Like US conservatives, the French are intensely patriotic, especially about French social and political values. They argue that all citizens should support these values.

Second, it is generally true that continental conservatives are less suspicious of state power than their British and US counterparts. They have largely accepted that the state is crucial in maintaining social, political and economic stability. This is probably the result of the greater tendency to revolutionary activity that exists in European countries. The UK and the USA have not come under serious internal threat for more than 200 years. This is not the case in continental Europe: most countries there have turbulent pasts. The interwar fascist regimes are well known. It should also be noted that France suffered violent changes of government as recently as 1958 and 1969; Italy has endured frequent and rapid changes of government since 1945; the Spanish and Portuguese democracies are still in their infancy and Greece was under military rule as recently as the 1970s. For conservatives in these states, liberalism and socialism represent instability. By contrast, the state provides order and security — classical conservative goals.

Third, there is a much stronger element of populism among such conservatives. Many European states have large and influential agricultural sectors. Farmers (especially small, independent farmers, still often described as 'peasants') are well known for their conservative outlook, as, typically, are small-scale entrepreneurs and the inhabitants of the many thousands of small towns characteristic of continental Europe. Conservatives have appealed successfully to these groups by promoting their independence, adopting agriculture-friendly policies and defending rural causes in preference to metropolitan values. The concerns of the UK's Countryside Alliance — pro-hunting, protectionism against foreign competition, better transport facilities, opposition to excessive environmental interference and low taxes, for example — are typical of conservatism in much of the rest of Europe. It is no coincidence that the cross-national conservative group in the European Parliament has adopted the collective name European Peoples Parties.

Social and liberal conservatism

Although the New Right has dominated conservative parties in the USA and Europe, there remains a faction in the conservative movement which is more liberal and progressive in its outlook. Its members call themselves 'social conservatives'. In the UK, these conservatives still describe themselves as 'one-nationists' in that they see many problems arising from the individualistic society which has been created by neo-liberal policies and values. They support the notion of an *organic society* in which people have a sense of responsibility for each other, not just for themselves. They accept that the growing economic inequality which has been the outcome of neo-liberalism is a threat to the unity of society. Although they support free-market economics, as all conservatives do, social conservatives admit the need for the state to intervene to create greater social equality and equality of opportunity.

These conservatives have strongly opposed the cultural values of the New Right. They support a multicultural society, with cultural diversity, tolerance and equality of opportunity for all groups. In this respect, they sometimes class themselves as the 'liberal' wing of the Conservative Party. They have supported causes such as women's equality, gay rights, racial harmony and liberal solutions to the economic and social causes of crime.

Since losing his seat in 1997, Michael Portillo has embraced social conservatism

Typically — although not in all cases — social conservatives downplay the importance of nationalism. While supporting national unity and patriotism, together with the retention of traditional institutions, they accept the internationalisation of the world. European integration, for example, is seen as inevitable and therefore to be embraced rather than resisted.

Are social conservatives actually conservatives? Michael Portillo, a leading British exponent of social conservatism and a convert from the New Right (although still a Eurosceptic), claims that they are. They remain pragmatic and empirical in their outlook. They can support all the virtues of Disraelian Toryism as well as subscribing to traditional values. Where they differ from conservatives is in their refusal to be reactionary; rather, they accept social and cultural change where it has occurred naturally.

Contemporary conservatism

On a global scale, conservatism has become a fragmented movement. There are considerable differences between US Republicanism and continental European conservatism. US conservatism has come to dominate US politics and now commands the active support of over half the population. In Europe, by contrast, conservatives have been forced to compete against powerful liberal and social democrat parties. Meanwhile, British conservatism in the 1990s and early twenty-first century became fractured, uncertain about its future role and therefore unpopular.

Conservatives in the USA and Europe had hoped that a new political consensus would grow up around US neo-conservative ideas. In the USA, there has certainly been a widespread movement in the direction of a more moral and social conservatism allied to free-market economic theories, but as yet this has not been extensively exported to Europe. But there have been signs that such 'ultra conservatism', as it can be described, is beginning to take root elsewhere.

As well as these developments, many members of the British right — including UKIP — and US Republicans wish to take the New Right agenda even further. They challenge the desirability of state activities such as welfare, industrial relations, consumer and environmental protection and support for industrial development. They propose lower taxation and public expenditure to create a freer environment for enterprise, self-responsibility and prosperity. They accept that this will lead to an even more unequal society, but argue that this a worthwhile price to pay for economic success for the majority.

Others, who see themselves as the heirs of one-nation Toryism, hope to reinforce the new consensus. They believe that conservatism can still succeed by stressing order, stability and sound management by government — in other words, traditional conservative values.

Key conservative thinkers

Edmund Burke (Irish, 1729–97)

Burke is often described as the father of conservatism and, although he did not coin the term, his best known work, *Reflections on the Revolution in France,* is certainly one of the first great conservative texts. Burke was born in Ireland and became an MP at Westminster. Confusingly, he described himself as a Whig and associated with other well-known Whigs of his day. His thinking, however, was predominantly conservative. Equally confusingly, he was a supporter of the US revolutionaries and spoke for them in Parliament. He believed that the USA had been hopelessly misgoverned by Britain and that the actions of the republicans were therefore justified. The French Revolution, however, provoked his utter disapproval and prompted him to develop his conservative philosophy.

Burke opposed all rational ways of thinking about political and social issues. Action, he asserted, must always be based on practical experience. Furthermore, it should never threaten the security of a society. 'Good order is the foundation of all good things,' Burke declared; it is the most important good that mankind can enjoy (*Reflections on the Revolution in France*, 1790). He berated the French revolutionaries on the grounds that they had not just threatened order — they had actually thrown society into the melting pot and attempted to reform it along rational lines. In the colourful passage from *Reflections* quoted below, Burke likens the state to a parent and subjects to its children. He expresses horror at the way the children of France have treated their parent:

> We are taught to look with horror on those children of their country who are prompt rashly to hack that aged parent in pieces, and put him into a kettle of magicians in hopes that, by poisonous weeds and wild incantations, they may regenerate the parental constitution, and renovate their father's life.

The 'kettle of magicians' undoubtedly refers to the philosophers of the Enlightenment who were proposing a 'renovation' of society along the lines of rational principles.

For Burke, and for all those conservatives who have followed him, social and political change should be undertaken with great caution, and only with reference to the experience of the past and the traditions of the people. Tradition was a key element in society for Burke. He described it as a 'partnership' between 'those who are living, those who are dead and those who are to be born' (*Reflections on the Revolution in France*, 1790). Tradition therefore provided continuity from the past into the future. Furthermore, Burke believed that society was an organic, living thing and as such constantly developing naturally. It was not for humankind to interfere with nature on the excuse that it was attempting to improve it.

Burke is also famous for his view on the nature of representation. The electorate, he announced, should not vote for an MP and then expect him to do its bidding. Instead, it should elect him to use his judgement on its behalf. This extremely conservative view of representation was the result of Burke's fear that politics might become nothing more than a struggle between warring factions and interests. Politics should be a measured activity, based on pragmatism, knowledge of the past and good judgement. In this view he was following the teaching of one of his US associates, James Madison (1751–1836), who attempted to build a constitution for the USA which would not require party activity. Both Burke and Madison were, of course, to be disappointed in this respect.

Although Burke has often been accused of an inconsistent approach to political philosophy, there is a detectable thread that connects his ideas. The development of Burkean conservatism is illustrated in Box 3.2.

Box 3.2 Key elements of Burke's political philosophy

➢ The most important quality of any society is order.

➢ The people have an obligation to obey the state as long as it provides them with order.

➢ The affairs of the state should be conducted on the basis of measured judgement and consideration of past experience, not on the basis of abstract theories and principles.

➢ Traditions and traditional institutions are key factors in the preservation of order and continuity.

➢ Change in society should only be undertaken when it becomes clear that the existing order is untenable.

Benjamin Disraeli (British, 1804–81)

Disraeli was prime minister twice and, along with his Liberal Party counterpart, William Gladstone, dominated late-Victorian British politics. He rivals his predecessor, Robert Peel, in being credited as the founder of the Conservative Party. Disraeli wrote and worked at a time when there was real danger of social conflict breaking out in Britain. In other words, the greatest of all conservative objectives — the maintenance of order — was threatened.

He saw that Britain was in danger of becoming effectively 'two nations', divided into the rich and the poor. As capitalism flourished, the plight of the working classes and the unemployed worsened. It was for conservatives, or 'Tories' as Disraeli's followers were usually known, to take a paternalistic view and intervene on behalf of the downtrodden masses. Disraeli knew that if the Tories did not take up the cause of the poor, the socialists would. As representatives of the aristocracy and landed gentry, Disraeli believed that conservatives could play a dispassionate, neutral role in the struggle between labour and capitalism. Furthermore, the traditional wealth and privilege which the ruling class enjoyed in society also carried with it responsibility — that of preserving the welfare of the people. The term *noblesse oblige* has often been applied to this concept of the social obligation of the wealthy. Its modern equivalent suggests that those who benefit most from the fruits of capitalism have an obligation to consider the plight of the less fortunate. It is an appeal against a totally self-interested form of economic life (see Box 3.3).

Box 3.3 Disraeli and noblesse oblige

In 1882 Disraeli described the principle that the landed class should care for the people:

> What is the fundamental principle of the feudal system gentlemen? It is that the tenure of property shall be the performance of its duties. Why, when William the Conqueror carved out parts of the land and introduced the feudal system, he said to the recipient, 'You shall have the estate, but you shall do something for it; you shall feed the poor; you shall endow the Church; you shall defend the land in case of war; and you shall execute justice and maintain truth to the poor for nothing'.

Disraeli and his Tory, one-nation followers sought to preserve national unity by stressing the importance of the great traditional institutions of the country, the Church of England, the monarchy and the Empire, allegiances to which all classes could subscribe. By granting the franchise to a wide section of the population, he believed that people would feel they had a greater stake in their own society.

Many conservatives to this day follow Disraelian principles, albeit updated to suit modern conditions; they are still often described as one-nation Tories. Prominent contemporary examples include Michael Heseltine and Kenneth Clarke. They support tradition, promote policies that unite rather than divide the nation, and wish to see political actions that create **inclusiveness**.

Key term

Inclusiveness

This concept is associated mainly with liberalism, but is also supported by moderate, one-nation conservatives. It suggests that all sections of the community should be included in decision-making, the enjoyment of rights and in the rewards that society has to offer. Put another way, it implies that no legal groups should be *excluded* from opportunities or from full participation in society on an equal basis.

Michael Oakeshott (British, 1901–90)

Perhaps Oakeshott's main contribution to conservative thought was to suggest that politics should not have any fixed goals or sense of specific direction. In *On Being Conservative* (1962), he likened the state to a ship afloat on a boundless sea with no origin and no destination (see p. 97). The role of government, which commands the ship, should simply be to keep it on an even keel and care for the welfare of its passengers. The state, therefore, should be governed on a pragmatic basis, taking into account the traditions and 'intimations' of the people. By intimations, Oakeshott meant the general way in which people wish the affairs of state to be run. He was insistent that political action based on fixed theories and principles leads to conflict and takes too little account of the wishes of the people.

In a sense, Oakeshott's philosophy is simple. Governments should merely govern, and that means doing what *is* right for the people, not what politicians think *ought* to be right for the people. This is how he sums up his view:

> The office of government is not to impose other beliefs and activities upon its subjects, not to tutor or educate them, not to make them better or happier in another way, not to direct them, to galvinize them into action, to lead them or co-ordinate their activities so that no occasion of conflict can occur; the office of government is merely to rule.
>
> From *On Being Conservative*, 1962

In some ways, Oakeshott's philosophy can be seen as a bridge between traditional and New Right, neo-liberal conservatism. In line with traditional conservative thinking, he sees government as a pragmatic activity, free of ideological content. On the other hand, he wishes government to be a limited activity. This is linked with the New Right, which prefers that government disengages from regulation and so restores widespread freedom of action to its citizens.

Karl Popper (Austrian/British, 1902–94)

Sir Karl Popper began life as an Austrian, but fled from Nazi persecution and became a British citizen in 1945. He is mainly known for his opposition to totalitarianism, and was particularly critical of extreme examples of socialism. He based his opposition on what he saw as their flawed view of human nature; in line with other conservatives, he believed that human nature is not a fixed aspect of society, but the product of historical change. Those ideologies that viewed human nature as fixed were therefore in error.

Popper argued that scientific enquiry is based upon the assumption that what has always happened in the past (if it is observed often enough) will continue to happen in the future. He saw this as potentially mistaken. There is no guarantee that what has been happening will continue to happen. Scientific method, therefore, is about proving things to be wrong, rather than confirming that they are right. He called the process of discovering errors in prediction *falsification*. This theory can also be applied to political action.

We cannot truly predict what will happen in the future, Popper asserted. Human nature and human society are constantly evolving, so society in the past is never like society in the future. For that reason, political theories based on scientific explanations of history and society cannot be proved. They are all utopian in nature. This leads to a rejection of both Marxist and socialist claims that their philosophies are scientific.

In practice, Popper's philosophy suggests that no one has a valid claim to understanding what is best for society in the future. All that politicians can do is attempt to achieve what appears to be in the best interests of the people at any given time. It would be an error for them to claim that they are always right. It follows that good government must be open to criticism and must be removable by the people if it is not acting in their interests. Popper called this the *open society*. Conservative followers of Popper have used his philosophy to demonstrate the flaws in all ideologies and to justify a pragmatic outlook in politics.

Keith Joseph (British, 1918–94)

Together with Margaret Thatcher, Keith Joseph founded the Centre for Policy Studies in 1975. This think-tank was to become the driving force behind the dramatic change that took place within British, US and European conservatism in the 1980s and 1990s. Indeed, although neo-liberal conservatism became known as 'Thatcherism', it was Joseph who was the ideological inspiration behind it.

Joseph began with the assertion that deprivation in society was inherited from one generation to the next. He called this the 'cycle of deprivation', claiming it was not caused by lack of action by the state, but by too much action. The state was creating a *dependency culture* in which families had no incentive to better themselves because they had grown used to relying on the state. The answer, therefore, was to create a freer economic society which would produce more wealth — wealth which would trickle down to all parts of society and so benefit everybody.

Joseph became the main architect of the 1980s programme of liberalising the British state. This involved privatising major industries, reducing the power of trade unions, reducing personal and corporate taxation, deregulating financial markets to make more capital available and reducing the scope of the welfare state, especially social security benefits. When recession struck the UK in the early 1980s, it was Joseph who encouraged Thatcher not to intervene, as so many of her predecessors had done, and to withdraw from economic management and allow the slump to work its natural way through. Many other conservatives lost their nerve, but Joseph and Thatcher stuck to their guns. When the economy eventually recovered of its own accord, Joseph's ideas were vindicated.

In areas of government such as law and order, immigration and social policy, Joseph was a traditional conservative, but his economic ideas were a throwback to classical liberalism, as he and Thatcher freely admitted. His was a new kind of economic conservatism, dedicated to the free market rather than to state management.

Pat Buchanan (US, 1938–)

Buchanan is one of the most prominent members of the US conservative right (which is seen as more extreme than its British counterpart). He has unsuccessfully challenged for the Republican nomination as presidential candidate and he has also stood for the presidency itself. Although Buchanan attracted the votes of 3 million Americans, he has never looked likely to win office. Nevertheless, his relative success in garnering support has had some influence in shifting the Republican Party to the right.

Like many other neo-conservatives, Buchanan was influenced by the philosopher Leo Strauss (1899–1973), who called for the moral regeneration of the USA and a new sense of shared values, based on a traditional form of Christianity. Strauss saw the world as being divided sharply into good and evil. US citizens must, he insisted, be firmly on the side of good.

Buchanan is the founder of a campaigning organisation known as the *American Cause*. The 1993 mission statement of the American Cause reveals its aims:

> Our mission is to advance and promote traditional American values that are rooted in the conservative principles of national sovereignty, economic patriotism, limited government and individual freedom.

We can certainly recognise limited government and individual freedom as being major features of the conservative New Right, but the inclusion of national sovereignty and economic patriotism demands some explanation. National sovereignty implies that Buchanan's brand of conservatism is determined to protect US interests. It is, in effect, a charter for isolationism, denying that the USA has any global responsibilities or that it should be influenced by any other power or organisation. Certainly, George W. Bush's (1946–) refusal to cooperate with international agreements on global warming and nuclear weapons control are examples of this position.

Economic patriotism is connected to the idea of national sovereignty. It asserts that the USA should be concerned only with its own economic interests. The benefit of world trade is not a consideration. Buchanan has therefore campaigned to protect US industry from competition through the use of tariffs and subsidies. For him, the employment of US citizens is of greater importance than the long-term benefits of international trade. There are echoes of this attitude in the British New Right's opposition to further European economic integration and its suspicion of international trade organisations.

Buchanan and his followers wish to see strict controls over immigration into the USA. They oppose multiculturalism, arguing that there should be one dominant culture in the USA and that all citizens should adopt it. Both these positions are shared by the right wing of the British Conservative Party.

The principal distinction between Buchanan's brand of conservatism and its counterpart in the UK and the rest of Europe concerns religion. For him, religion cannot be separated from politics, and morality is strictly based on a traditional brand of fundamentalist Christianity. European conservatives support the maintenance of traditional values too, but this support has not necessarily been based specifically upon religion. This type of conservatism, which is based on Christian values but is not overtly or exclusively religious, is often described as **Christian democracy**.

Key term

Christian democracy

This term refers to a European form of conservatism originally inspired by Christian values; its religious content has since declined. It is similar to the one-nation, social conservatism that flourished in the UK in the 1950s, 1960s and 1970s. Christian democrats support market capitalism, but believe its aim should not be merely personal gain. Its wealth should be spread more evenly, to the benefit of the whole community. The state is therefore justified in intervening to create more social justice and alleviate deprivation. Tony Blair has often been seen as a kind of Christian democrat, rather than a socialist.

The conservatism of Pat Buchanan and others like him somewhat echoes that of early-twentieth-century Republicanism. Indeed, it is so historical in its outlook that it has been described as *paleoconservatism*, a term implying that its views are truly ancient in their origins. Nevertheless, it has gained adherents in recent years, especially after the 9/11 terrorist attack.

Issues in conservatism

Conservatism as an ideology

In essence, the term 'ideology' implies a strong sense of progress towards a specific set of social goals. Ideologies have fixed principles that are coherent and interlocking. They make assumptions about the nature of humankind and develop theories about the true nature of society. Furthermore, ideologies are consistent in their belief systems.

We can now examine the extent to which conservatism conforms to this definition. Traditional conservatism certainly has no sense of progress. Indeed, Michael Oakeshott specified that true conservatism should avoid adopting any sense of direction. On the other hand, the New Right, as defined by Keith Joseph and Margaret Thatcher, certainly did envisage the creation of a society of free individuals, with wide access to ownership of property and shares in industry and in which each individual was responsible for his or her own welfare.

Similarly, traditional conservatives have tended to avoid adopting fixed principles and have opposed political movements based on such fixed principles. Conservatism has often been described as chameleon-like in that it changes its appearance according to the dominant political environment at any given time. In the nineteenth century, when liberalism was its main opponent, conservatism adopted an organic vision of society, seeing it as a living entity and expecting people to demonstrate a sense of responsibility towards each other. When socialism came to the fore, however, conservatives changed course and began to emphasise the virtues of free markets and individualism to combat collectivist ideals. Such an adaptable movement certainly cannot be described as ideological in nature.

Once again, however, the New Right does not conform. It adopted some fixed ideas which could be described as ideological in nature. In particular, monetarism became its political dogma. This was the belief that the state should confine itself to controlling the currency and public finances rather than attempting to regulate the whole economy. Furthermore, these conservatives, also known as neo-liberals, were inflexible in their attitudes to taxation and welfare, believing both to be barriers to economic progress. There is, perhaps, a case for arguing that the anti-state position of New Right conservatives is an ideological position in that it suggests a fixed view that society will flourish only if it is free of government regulation.

This evidence appears to lead to the conclusion that, while traditional conservatism is very much a state of mind, and a broad and flexible philosophy, the more modern forms of the movement have become ideological in character. The conservative state of mind is to prefer order to liberty, to be suspicious of radical change and to prefer what is known from the past to what is unknown in the future. The New Right, in contrast, has been a radical movement; its adherents have been prepared to reject the past in favour of the pursuit of New Right doctrines.

The paradox of the New Right

The New Right has often been characterised as a synthesis between neo-liberalism and neo-conservatism. This gives rise to an apparently contradictory attitude towards the role of the state.

The neo-liberal aspect of the movement proposes the restoration of free markets, without interference from the state. This echoes the classical liberal era of the nineteenth century. Margaret Thatcher was content to describe herself as a classical liberal at heart and famously claimed that 'there is no such thing as society'. What she meant was that she viewed society as a collection of individuals, not as an organic whole. Taxation and welfare were to be reduced in order to create more individual incentives. The so-called 'nanny state' was blamed for sapping society of its dynamism, for reducing the economic freedom which was necessary for wealth creation and for granting excessive amounts of power to organised labour. As far back as 1968, Margaret Thatcher expressed distaste for the role of the state in a speech she gave to a Conservative Party conference:

> What we need now is a far greater degree of personal responsibility and decision, far more independence from the government and a comparative reduction in the role of government.

All these ideas would have been at home in the middle of the nineteenth century, when free-market capitalism was at its height and at its least regulated. Friedrich Hayek and Milton Friedman, both members of the Chicago School of economics, were the inspiration behind the restoration of classical liberal values. Both these philosophers argued that a lack of economic freedom would entail a loss of political freedom in general. In other words, the heavily regulated and partly government-controlled states run by socialist governments could never be described as 'free' because individuals were not free to pursue their own economic goals.

The main criticism faced by these neo-liberals was that the excessive amounts of freedom and the inequality it generated would threaten the unity of society. The New Right responded by developing a set of policies which became known as 'neo-conservatism'. Recognising that order in society might be threatened by an excess of freedom in the economic sphere, the New Right has emphasised personal morality. It has been relatively intolerant of lifestyles considered to be outside of the 'norm', such as homosexuality. Several attempts have been made (with little success, it has to be said) to return to basic values, for example the nuclear family, traditional education methods and patriotism. This echoes the principle, dating back to Burke, that respect for traditions stabilises society.

The second strand of neo-conservatism concerns law and order. Again, more traditional methods have been supported, notably the use of prison sentences as a deterrent, a hard line on youth crime and extended powers for an expanded police force.

Conservatives have always accused those on the left of politics of lacking patriotism and paying too little attention to the UK's best interests. With European integration uppermost in their minds, members of the the New Right have stressed national sovereignty and the need to preserve the unity of the UK. They have opposed political integration in Europe and devolution on the grounds that they threaten to remove national sovereignty either upwards to Brussels or downwards to Scotland and Wales. The New Right sees the **nation-state** as the fundamental political community and will resist any threat to its independence.

Key term

Nation-state

This term combines the concepts of nation and state. The *nation* is considered the natural basis for any political community. It is seen, by both conservatives and many liberals, as the most significant binding force for a society since it comprises a people's common circumstances of birth and experience. The *state* is a political entity. It is the territory within which a single centre of sovereignty can be identified. When the nation is also a state, and the state is based on the identity of a nation, this is a nation-state — the most common form of political society.

Finally, the neo-conservative wing of modern conservatism has been concerned with the effects of immigration and increasing cultural diversity. Again, diversity is seen as a threat to the unity of a community. The neo-conservative answer is to limit immigration and to insist that all sections of the community learn to conform to a common set of British values.

It should be noted that the British New Right's attitude to the European Union is itself something of a paradox. The movement's neo-liberalism leads it to support the idea of a completely free European market; free trade has always been a goal of economic liberals. On the other hand, the political integration of Europe threatens the integrity of the nation-state and so has been opposed.

Although the blending of neo-liberalism and neo-conservatism in the New Right emerged largely in the UK, it is also a feature of contemporary US conservatism. There, neo-conservative features are underpinned by a strong attachment to fundamentalist religious belief, especially Christianity. Indeed, much of the US style of religion is highly conservative in nature. This has led to a harder line on moral issues, especially abortion and homosexuality.

Table 3.1 summarises the neo-liberal and neo-conservative strands of the New Right.

Table 3.1 Summary of the two strands of the New Right

Neo-liberalism	Neo-conservatism
UK • Restoration of free labour, product and financial markets wherever possible • Minimal role for the state in regulating commerce and industry • Minimal state role in regulating the economy • Taxation to be kept to a minimum, especially income and corporate taxes • Belief that welfare is a disincentive to work and enterprise, and therefore should be kept to a minimum • Support for a free market in Europe **USA** As above, plus: • Preference for power to be reserved for individual states, not federal government	**UK** • Traditional position on morality and lifestyles • Authoritarian stance on law and order issues • Heavy emphasis on national self-interest and patriotism • Opposition to excessive immigration and cultural diversity • Opposition to European political integration **USA** As above, plus: • Strong religious element to moral and social issues • Insistence on protection for US industry from foreign competition

Conservatism in the UK

The crisis of conservatism

In the UK, conservatism has endured a politically difficult period since 1992. To some extent, this is the result of the aftermath of Margaret Thatcher's fall from power in 1990, a blow from which the movement has not fully recovered. In particular, conservatives have been uncertain whether to carry the Thatcher reforms still further or to propose a period of consolidation. Her long political shadow continues to cause controversy. The Conservative Party itself has suffered from a combination of weak leadership, internal divisions and a loss of economic direction, while the wider conservative movement faces longer-term difficulties which have become so marked that the situation may be described as a crisis.

As a philosophy, conservatism has invariably been a reaction against ideological tendencies which have threatened the order and unity of society and which have been based on apparently 'false' assumptions and principles. In the post-Thatcher era, however, it could be said that a political consensus has descended upon the UK (and indeed the rest of western Europe). This consensus has been based upon the neo-liberal and neo-conservative principles described above. In some ways, therefore, it could be said that modern conservatism has become the victim of its own success. Its ideas have dominated the political culture to such an extent that conservatism has nothing to react against. At the same time, there are no new political movements threatening the existing order. New Labour and the contemporary Liberal Democrats in the UK may wish to change the emphasis of public policy, but they propose no radical reforms.

Conservatism has also suffered from the legacy of the 1980s — that of being seen as a movement which lacks compassion and which has failed to adjust to the changing social and cultural structure of the UK. Some critics have suggested that the movement has not been true to the traditional principles put forward by the likes of Michael Oakeshott and even Benjamin Disraeli — it has failed to consider the welfare of the whole country and has, instead, concentrated on the interests of one section of the community. There have been many who have benefited from the neo-liberal reforms of the Thatcher era — the business classes, property owners, middle-income families and the like — but there are also many who have suffered, for example those who rely on welfare, lone parents, deprived ethnic minorities and alienated youths living in depressed regions of the country.

Despite these criticisms, conservatism has not come under serious attack from either the left or the right of British politics. Instead, its philosophy and policies have been absorbed by other political parties. The Conservative Party has tried to respond by supporting multiculturalism and inclusiveness, and by adopting a more compassionate approach to deprived sections of the community, but these causes have already been taken up by liberals and social democrats. They do not represent a distinctive position for conservatives.

The one political stance which does single out modern conservatives as radically different is their attitude to European integration. They have been hampered in this area by internal divisions, and many see their position of supporting a single, free European market while opposing any political integration as illogical, as we have seen above. However, Euroscepticism does resonate with the British people and has been a potential touchstone for a conservative revival. However, on this issue the Conservative Party has been effectively outflanked by the Labour Party. Labour has insisted that any future progress towards integration — mainly entry into the single currency and adoption of a European constitution — should be put to the British people in referendums, thereby taking the whole issue of Europe effectively out of the arena of party politics.

It may be that the UK Conservative Party and the wider conservative movement will suffer the same fate as liberalism did in the 60 years after the First World War. In that period, liberal principles were absorbed by the Conservative and Labour Parties, and liberalism, as a distinctive movement, was squeezed out of the political arena. The Liberal Party found itself in a political wilderness from which it did not emerge until the 1980s. The current Conservative Party is seeking to present itself as the best manager of the post-Thatcher consensus, but perhaps the days of the party being seen as the 'natural party of government' are over.

The issue of Europe has taken a back seat under Michael Howard's (1941–) leadership

The impact of Thatcher

Margaret Thatcher became leader of the Conservative Party in 1975. She was a relatively little-known politician at the time, and in many ways a compromise candidate since the party could not agree on any of the more conventional candidates for the office. The party was taking a further chance since it was not clear at that time whether a woman was electable. It is often claimed that the party chose her as a short-term leader while it searched for someone more suitable to fight the 1979 election. Whatever the party's motives were in electing her, there were few clues to the ideological position she was to take up later. Having said that, her close association with Keith Joseph (see p. 114) should have been an indication that she was going to support neo-liberal policies.

She began her premiership cautiously. In this she had little choice, having inherited a front bench full of natural enemies and a country in the grip of economic recession. Over the next few years, however, she replaced most of her opponents with allies and, at the same time, the economy began to recover. She ruffled feathers by insisting that her government would not attempt to 'spend its way out of the recession' — that is, borrow large amounts of money to subsidise failing industries and create jobs artificially. Her neo-liberal instincts, reinforced by Joseph's economic philosophy, told her that if government held on and refused to intervene, the economy would naturally pick up. Traditional conservatives, who were associated with the Keynesian idea that aggressive economic action by government was needed to cure recession, found themselves marginalised and many left the government. The first impact of Thatcher, therefore, was that in times of economic difficulty, governments should do less, not more. This policy was described as **laissez faire**.

Buoyed up by the success of her economic policies, Thatcher turned to the issue of trade union power. Again, traditionalists warned her against confrontation. They saw the unions as an entrenched and vital part of the economic structure. Attacking them was seen as a radical and dangerous undertaking. But Thatcher once more won her battle with the doubters and embarked on a series of measures to reduce the legal and economic power of the unions. This was the beginning of a series of actions against British institutions. She later turned her attention to the civil service, local government and the financial institutions of the city, reducing their influence and subjecting them to competitive forces. Once again, we can see how her radicalism enabled her to challenge established traditions and the institutions that underpinned them.

Key term

Laissez faire

This is a nineteenth-century expression, literally meaning 'let them act', which is associated with classical liberalism. It refers to the government policy of not intervening in economic activity, but allowing economic forces to work naturally. The policy assumes that the operation of free markets, without state regulation or any external interference, will create wealth effectively and so benefit the whole community.

The privatisation of major industries was part of her general commitment to 'rolling back the frontiers of the state'. This marked the end of the type of conservatism, dating back to Harold Macmillan (1894–1986) in the 1950s, which accepted the state as a vehicle for providing stability and serving the interests of the community as a whole. The conservative support for the welfare state itself was also shaken under Thatcher. While she preserved the state health and education systems, her governments reduced the size and scope of social security benefits and the old age pension.

Thus, the traditional conservative tendency to paternalism was eroded. The Disraelian view that it was the duty of conservatives to care for the welfare of the people was being replaced by an insistence that individuals should be responsible for their own welfare. Thatcher's attack on the dependency culture flew directly in the face of the traditional Tory sense of social responsibility and its vision of the organic society. For Thatcher, society was made up of self-interested individuals and it was the role of government to provide the conditions where such an individualist community could flourish.

We can see that the impact of Thatcherism and the New Right was considerable and the challenges it posed to traditional conservatism were numerous. These are summarised in Box 3.4.

Box 3.4 Thatcher's challenges to traditional conservatism

➢ Society is made up of free individuals; it is not organic.
➢ Excessive interference by the state is counterproductive, holds back economic progress and inhibits the development of a sense of self-responsibility.
➢ Traditional institutions may be challenged if they can be shown to be holding back progress.

➢ Conservative paternalism denies the individual spirit of enterprise and self-responsibility and so should be curbed.

➢ Individuals prefer to be granted freedom rather than to rely upon the support of the state.

➢ Radical government can improve society and does not necessarily create unexpected consequences.

➢ A slavish attachment to traditional modes of thinking prevents original solutions to society's problems.

Conservatism and liberalism

Individualism

What is the difference between the liberal conception of freedom and the conservative notion of individualism? On a simple level, liberal freedom is essentially negative: it proposes a society where there is a minimum of restrictions on the actions of individuals. Conservative individualism, on the other hand, is more akin to positive liberty. It entails the provision of opportunities and choices for individuals and families and the ability of people to achieve their own goals without hindrance. The difference, however, may be more complex in reality.

Individualism is perhaps best viewed as a reaction against collectivism. It is based on the belief that people prefer to achieve their goals individually and not collectively, as socialists insist. Conservatives therefore argue that they have a duty to create the conditions in which such individualism can flourish. This involves economic certainty and stability, low levels of taxation, the protection of private property, low crime rates and a secure international environment. The state has a duty to produce these conditions, but its role should end there. It should not interfere in people's lives directly.

Liberals who promote freedom are also suspicious of state interference, but they concentrate on the need for individuals to enjoy their private lives and to have their rights protected. This kind of free society can, in theory, flourish even in a situation where collectivism is a common method of achieving social goals. This means that, for liberals, there need be no contradiction between a welfare state and a free society. Put another way, freedom requires that the state should guarantee its people's liberties, whereas individualism requires that the state create a stable environment in which people can pursue their own goals. Individualism opposes the idea that the state can achieve goals which individuals could achieve for themselves. Liberals believe freedom need not be compromised by state involvement in society.

One final observation can help to distinguish between the two concepts. A conservative will accept that the state might be justified in curtailing some freedom in society if it can promote individualism by doing so. For example, it may be necessary to reduce the scope of civil liberties in the interests of crime reduction, perhaps by granting extensive powers to the police. Reducing crime in this way might encourage people to feel more secure to enjoy their property and to engage in new economic ventures. Similarly, by removing some of the legal rights and freedoms of workers, entrepreneurs may feel encouraged to employ more labour and so create more wealth to the benefit of all. Box 3.5 summarises these arguments.

Box 3.5 Liberal freedom and conservative individualism

At first, these terms seem to be almost identical. Both liberals and conservatives extol the virtues of a free society and tend to be suspicious of the role of the state. However, the concepts do have distinct meanings.

For a liberal, freedom mainly means the absence of restriction. We are free if nobody controls our ability to say what we like, go where we wish and worship whatever gods we may choose. We are also free if the state does not restrict our ability to engage in economic enterprise and does not place too many regulations on our activities.

Individualism is more closely associated with conservatism. The term refers to the ability of the individual to be able to pursue his or her own happiness, to make free choices and to be presented with a wide range of opportunities. It implies too that we will be secure enough to enjoy whatever wealth and property we may possess. Individualism in this sense could only flourish in a society in which each person is free to pursue his or her own goals and is not forced to accept the collective goals of a society. It is therefore associated with free enterprise, the encouragement of the private sector, low taxation, a favourable environment for property owners and minimal regulation of business activities. To secure such freedom necessitates a heavy emphasis on national defence, law and order and property rights.

The main conflict between the two concepts lies in the contrast between the liberal belief that the individual will flourish most successfully in a free society, whereas conservatives typically believe that the individual most needs a secure society. Nevertheless, both philosophies agree that the state should be organised to promote the interests of individuals and individual self-fulfilment; it is about the means to achieve these ends that they disagree.

Property and rights

It is perhaps in their attitudes to private property that conservatives and liberals agree to the greatest extent. When we consider the more general field of rights, however, there are critical points of difference.

The right to private property is one of the original beliefs of liberalism. Figures such as John Locke, Thomas Jefferson and Thomas Paine all saw the possession and enjoyment of property as a basic human right. They believed that the possession of property and wealth is the natural outcome of an individual's pursuit of his or her own interests. This has always remained a liberal aspiration. Liberals are not collectivist by nature and see private property as one of the most important aspects of the individual's fulfilled life.

Conservatism, too, has always been committed to property rights, but for different reasons. For conservatives, property ownership promotes social stability. Those who own property will have a stronger sense of responsibility and will have a vested interest in the preservation of order. It follows from this that all conservatives see the protection of property, both from criminal behaviour and from encroachments by government, as a priority of the state.

The preservation of rights and the guarantee of legal and political equality are fundamental liberal principles. There are very few circumstances in which liberals will accept any compromise in their defence of rights. Conservatives, too, accept that rights are worthy of protection, especially in modern constitutional democracies. There are, however, circumstances in which a conservative would abandon this commitment. Conservatives insist that the community as a whole has rights, not just individuals. There will be occasions when the rights of individuals conflict with the rights of the community. When this happens, the conservative tendency is to consider the community first.

This is most clearly seen in the field of crime. While suspected criminals may expect rights to protect them from injustice, the community also has a right to be protected from criminals. In practice, this might mean that conservatives would support the right of property owners to protect their property over and above the criminal's right to be protected from injury. The clearest example of the conflict between conservative and liberal views concerns the issue of terrorism. While liberals say our rights cannot be sacrificed even in the interests of anti-terrorism measures, conservatives argue that we must be prepared to sacrifice some individual rights in the interests of our security. In short, this means that conservatives revere property and community rights, but their commitment to the rights of individuals remains relatively fragile.

Exam focus

Using this chapter and other resources available to you, answer the following questions.

Short questions
Your answers should be about 300 words long.
1 What is a typical conservative attitude to human nature?
2 Why do conservatives emphasise property rights?
3 What do conservatives mean by individualism?
4 Why do conservatives support tradition?
5 What is meant by the term neo-liberalism?
6 What is one-nation conservatism?
7 Why do conservatives oppose ideology?

Long questions
Your answers should be about 900 words long.
1 'Conservatism is more a state of mind than an ideology.' Discuss.

2 To what extent have conservatives preferred pragmatism and empiricism to political principles?

3 Is conservatism a coherent philosophy?

4 To what extent was the New Right a departure from traditional conservative values?

5 Is the British Conservative Party still essentially Thatcherite in character?

Further reading

Burke, E. (1999) *Reflections on the Revolution in France*, Oxford University Press.

Gray, J. and Willetts, D. (1997) *Is Conservatism Dead?*, Profile Books.

Green, D. (1987) *The New Right*, Prentice Hall/Harvester Wheatsheaf.

Honderich, T. (2005) *Conservatism*, Pluto Press.

O'Sullivan, N. (1976) *Conservatism*, Everyman.

Scruton, R. (2001) *The Meaning of Conservatism*, Macmillan.

Chapter 4

Nationalism

Nationalism is a collective emotion felt by groups of people who consider themselves to have common circumstances of birth. Its origins lie in the desire of some eighteenth- and nineteenth-century peoples to create a solid and enduring basis for the formation of a political community. As the nationalist spirit of common identity developed in Europe, it became popular to associate national identity with a need for government by consent. By setting up its own government, it was believed, a nation could confirm its separate identity. When nationalism developed further political aspirations, it became a specifically political movement. The objectives of political forms of nationalism have varied a great deal and have included: a need to protect the nation from conquest or domination by other peoples; a desire to unite a people, thus creating a nation-state as a political reality; a desire for independence of a people; a desire to conquer and/or dominate weaker nations; or simply a desire to protect a threatened culture. Nationalism has been associated with a number of other political movements, notably fascism, liberalism and conservatism. In each case, the dominant values of the political movement in question have been underpinned by the synthesis of political and national aspirations.

Introduction

It is useful to start a discussion of nationalism with an extract from Bernard Crick's (1929–) famous work, *In Defence of Politics*, which was published in 1962. This is how he expresses the power of nationalist sentiment:

> Nationalism is at this time perhaps the most compelling of all motives that can lead men to abandon or to scorn politics. Every feeling of human generosity is stirred by

the struggle of an oppressed people to be free. And nothing can argue people who feel themselves to be a nation out of the belief that they are a nation; and that if they are to be oppressed, it is better to be oppressed by their own people than by foreigners.

On this evidence, political movements described as 'nationalist' appear to be straightforward. Nationalists are evidently people who have a strong attachment to the nation of which they are part. Nationalism is therefore an emotion felt by such people. This is clearly true, but it tells us little of nationalism as a specifically *political* movement.

The early development of modern nationalism is relatively easy to follow. At the end of the Enlightenment period, there was a need to create a basis for the legitimate establishment of new states or new forms of government to replace monarchical authority. If communities were to come together and freely consent to place themselves under a government, there was a need to define such communities. The most obvious solution was to identify *national* groupings and to agree that each nation should have the right to set up its own state and government. Napoleon Bonaparte (1769–1821) believed that France had achieved this after the 1789 revolution, and he hoped to establish the principle for all the aspiring states of Europe.

However, there are a number of problems in following the later development of various types of nationalism. Individuals express their support for, or even love of, their national identity in a number of different ways. For some, nationalism implies a sense of superiority over other nations; for others, it expresses a desire to be free of domination by people of another nation or nations. In some cases, nationalism seeks to unite a people who have become divided by historical circumstances; in other cases, the term may mean nothing more than pride in one's cultural identity and a desire to protect that identity.

Further difficulties arise when we attempt to place nationalism within a conventional political spectrum. It can be an extremely right-wing movement, as was the case with fascism, but there have been left-wing nationalists too, for example a number of independence movements in Africa and South America. At a more moderate level, there have been liberal nationalists who combine national aspirations with a democratic spirit. Nationalism is also one of the core values of traditional conservatism. In this context, it does not necessarily relate to a desire to conquer other nations, to create an empire or even to demonstrate a people's superiority, but rather represents a means by which a people can develop a strong sense of unity for the sake of order and security.

Peter Newark's Historical Pictures

Napoleon, emperor of the new nation-state of France 1804–15

Finally, there are problems in distinguishing between nations and races, between nations and states and between nationalism and patriotism. There are even controversies about precisely what constitutes a nation. Are the citizens of the USA a nation, for example? Is the term 'Nation of Islam' anything more than a rallying cry for alienated ethnic groups? Are Jews a nation or followers of a religion? Is there a worthwhile meaning of the term 'British', when most people from the UK prefer to describe themselves as English, Welsh, Scottish, Irish or even Asian?

To find a way through this apparent maze, three objectives must be achieved. The first is to identify some values that can unite *all* nationalists. The second is to develop a way of categorising different kinds of nationalism effectively. Finally, nationalism must be distinguished from other movements based on different forms of popular allegiance.

Nations and states

Nations

It is important to define what constitutes a nation and to contrast this with the meaning of the term *state*. It remains true that most nations have formed a state, and that most states are constituted from one dominant nation, but it is important to make some distinctions.

A nation can be defined as a group of people who consider themselves to have common circumstances of birth. These common circumstances are strong enough for them to adopt collective goals based on their national identity. Nationalism is therefore an emotional phenomenon felt by a people. It may be that others will dispute whether such a group constitutes a nation, but this is less important than the fact that the people believe themselves to be a nation. In other words, a nation may be an objective reality or a subjective emotion.

There are a number of typical circumstances of birth which may give rise to nationhood. In some cases a nation may exhibit more than one at any given time. The scheme shown in Table 4.1 suggests the various criteria and offers some examples. These appear to be fairly clear, but many problems in defining nations remain. For example, is the USA a nation? It certainly tends to call itself a nation and it works hard to create a national identity, even though its people come from a wide variety of ethnic and cultural backgrounds. The key here is whether the dominant US culture is strong enough. Is Britain a nation? The Scots and Welsh would usually disagree, but there remains a strong sense of British national culture. Finally, and perhaps most controversially, are the Arabs a nation? They have a common ancestor in Abraham, but also exhibit a wide variety of cultural identities from the Bedouin in the desert to the city dwellers of Dubai or Beirut. Repeated attempts to unite the Arab peoples (a movement known as 'Pan-Arabism'), most recently by President Nasser (1918–70) of Egypt in the 1960s, have all failed because internal divisions have proved insurmountable.

Table 4.1 What constitutes a nation?

Circumstance	Example	Commentary
Single common ancestor	Jewish nation (not necessarily Israel)	Jews share Abraham as a common ancestor with the Arabs, but claim a later division between the two nations.
Common historical experience	England	The Scots, Irish and Welsh consider themselves to have different histories and so are separate nations.
Common culture	Germany	The German people became divided but were reunited by Otto von Bismarck in 1871.
Ethnic identity	China	Although there are different racial groups in China, there is an overarching Chinese ethnic identity.
Geographical separation	Malta	The Maltese are an island people with a strong national identity.
Religion	Tibet	The Tibetan people, now subsumed into China, all owe allegiance to a single religious leader — the Dalai Lama — who defines their identity.
Attachment to territory	France	Although the borders of France have changed frequently, there is a strong sense of 'France' as an historical reality.
Language	Wales	The Welsh (although not the whole nation) see their cultural identity in terms of their language and the culture it carries with it.

What matters most in political terms is not whether we accept objective tests of nationhood, but whether a people consider themselves to be a nation. The Chinese are an example of this. Divided into several ethnic groups, they all owe a strong allegiance to China as a single identity. The Italians, on the other hand, are less sure of nationhood and the Lombard (or Northern) League has been established, suggesting that Italy is an artificial creation dating back only to the 1860s. Unlike the Welsh, many Italians do not believe that a common language necessarily conveys nationhood.

States

A state is a political reality. It either exists or it does not. In contrast to the concept of nation, it does not convey a people's state of mind or emotion. Of course, there are national groupings that aspire to statehood, such as the Palestinians or the Basques of northern Spain and southwest France, but until that aspiration is realised no state actually exists. Nations, on the other hand, can certainly exist even when there is no state representing them.

A state is a defined territory within which there is a centre of sovereignty which is, more or less, in control of that territory. The German sociologist Max Weber (1864–1920) went further, defining a state as a territory within which a central body claims the legitimate use of violence (normally merely meaning force). However, we are not concerned here with whether a state is legitimate, or its borders disputed. What is important is that we can identify political institutions that control the people within a territory. Similarly, the issue is not whether a state is democratic. Even a totalitarian regime, where the people are kept in a state of fear or enforced obedience — for example, the Iraq of Saddam Hussein (1937–) — is still a state. Possibly the easiest way of defining a state is to give as examples all those countries that are members of the United Nations (UN) — perhaps the only member of the UN whose status as a state remains disputed is Palestine.

There is also a phenomenon known as the 'failed state'. This is a territory where there are no political institutions which can claim to control that territory effectively. Afghanistan has often been termed a failed state, since much of the country has been controlled by warlords. The same analysis has been applied to such countries as Sudan and Ethiopia, where civil wars have raged for many years and the recognised 'state', in each case, has appeared to be at the point of collapse.

The advent of nation-states

The most commonly acknowledged origin of the merging of the concepts of nation and state is the French Revolution. This is because three processes occurred at the same time as a result of the revolution. First, the old state (the *ancien régime*) was dissolved and a new state established. Second, it was declared that the French people were collectively free and had established the right to **self-determination**; the nation was therefore acknowledged to be the basis of the new political community. Third, the new political community was to guarantee individual rights. It was assumed that a state based on the nation would ensure the maintenance of such rights. Thus, the modern concepts of the state and the nation were brought together for the first time in history (see Box 4.1).

Box 4.1 **Articles 2 and 3 of the Declaration of the Rights of Man and Citizen by the French National Assembly, 1789**

2 The aim of all political association is the preservation of the natural and imprescriptible rights of man. Those rights are liberty, property, security, and resistance to oppression.

3 The principle of all sovereignty resides essentially in the nation. No body or individual may exercise any authority which does not proceed directly from the nation.

Napoleon Bonaparte, who ultimately became emperor of this new nation-state, saw it as a model that the rest of the world could follow. However, for the next 100 years the development of the nation-state as the accepted pattern for a political community was a painful one. Imperial powers, such as the Ottomans and the Austro-Hungarian emperors, denied the right of statehood to many nations. During the same period, peoples who had been divided into imperial territories, kingdoms, principalities and duchies, such as the Germans, Poles, Italians, Hungarians and Serbs, sought independent status. These peoples hoped — as the French had in 1789 — to rid themselves of oppressive, autocratic regimes, and to replace them with democratic institutions based on national sovereignty.

Key term

Self-determination

This term refers to a principle associated with the concept of the nation-state. It suggests that a people who have a just claim to nationhood should be granted the right to form their own government and to determine for themselves the manner in which they are governed. It also implies that a people cannot hope to claim freedom in general unless they are free to set up their own political institutions.

However, the leaders who gathered at Versailles to negotiate a peace treaty at the end of the First World War sought to establish the nation-state as a fundamental right of all peoples. President Woodrow Wilson (1856–1924) of the USA persuaded the victorious allies to declare that all nations had a right to statehood. Two great empires — the Ottoman and Austro-Hungarian — were therefore dissolved and a number of new nation-states came into existence. Of course, this did not mean that the European powers would relinquish their imperial possessions outside Europe and the Middle East. The issue of the nationalist aspirations of overseas colonies in places such as Africa and the Far East would not be settled until after the Second World War.

Races and nations

The relationship between the concepts of race and nation often causes confusion. This is not surprising since many nations consider themselves to be a race. This can certainly be said of the Japanese, Jews, Thais and Malays. In general terms, however, a race is not necessarily a nation and, furthermore, nations can contain more than one racial grouping, as is the case with the Chinese and, indeed, the English. The term **culture** helps little as it refers neither to race nor nationhood. Yet we do often refer to 'national' or 'racial' cultures.

Key term

Culture

This is a difficult concept to summarise. It refers mainly to the dominant historical experience, traditions, values and attitudes shared by a people who consider themselves to have a common identity. At its most basic level, it includes an identifiable 'way of life', artistic activities such as music, literature, dance and costume, and it can encompass national myths and legends (the Knights of the Round Table in England, for example). Language is a key feature, since it is through language that cultural attitudes and identities are passed down from one generation to the next. At a deeper level, however, culture refers to commonly held attitudes about a people's past, present and future aspirations. It may, in a few cases, also refer to a kind of civilisation, which implies the special qualities a people may have, such as organisation, intellect, and artistic or military prowess. This latter sense is especially associated with fascism and other right-wing nationalist movements.

The relationship becomes even more confusing when considering the attitude of extreme right-wing fascist or quasi-fascist movements. The synthesis of race and nation can be seen in the German idea of *volk*. Johann Fichte (1762–1814), perhaps the chief original architect of German nationalism, saw his people as a *volk* in that they were a close-knit culture, based on a narrow racial grouping, which had formed a superior culture and civilisation in the Middle Ages. He believed that the German people, scattered throughout central Europe, retained both their racial and national (or *volkisch*) identity. This identity was rekindled by the Nazis in the 1930s with dramatic consequences. In Britain, Oswald Mosley (1896–1980) propagated a similar belief about the British race, although his argument was not that the British had been scattered, but that they had been subverted by capitalist exploitation and weak, liberal democratic politicians.

The idea that common blood ties make up a nation can give rise to a number of problems. It can promote a sense of exclusiveness so that those who cannot demonstrate a blood connection may be excluded from society. This occurred in Nazi Germany and under the apartheid regime in South Africa. It has also been an important factor in intertribal warfare in Africa, where in some parts attempts at total genocide have been made in an attempt to create racially pure nations.

In an even more sinister way, it has led to ideas of racial — and therefore national — superiority. This arises from a social Darwinist view of the world, according to which different races are in a struggle for superiority against each other. It has led to quasi-scientific racialist beliefs that a nation can only retain its strength and superiority if it can maintain racial purity. Again, many German Nazis accepted this 'scientific' analysis.

Race as a basis for nationhood should generally be treated with great caution. It is clearly an important factor in some parts of the world, but it is only one of several components of nationalism. Furthermore, the synthesis of race and nation has often led to distorted and dangerous views of the world, based on partial truth and dubious science.

Globalisation, European integration and nation-states

The process of globalisation has been seen as a long-term threat to the future of nation-states. The increasing level of interdependence between states, together with the fact that many global problems do not recognise national borders, has led to a belief that the division of government into many different states is becoming an irrelevance.

As the world moves increasingly towards free trade, the existence of global, rather than national, markets has rendered national governments powerless to control economic forces. Indeed, a good deal of control over trade has now passed to international bodies such as the International Monetary Fund (IMF) and the World Trade Organisation (WTO). The internationalisation of financial markets, too, has marginalised the role of national banking institutions. Similarly, environmental issues do not respect national borders. The control of emissions, the health of the seas, the protection of endangered species and so on are all international problems. Even separate cultural identities are now threatened by the globalisation of culture and the influence of the internet.

Many liberals welcome these developments. They see globalisation as an opportunity to restore the importance of regional and local government, which they consider to be more democratic and directly accountable to the people. The power of nation-states is often seen by liberals as a threat to democracy and human rights. By reducing their power, globalisation will empower individuals, giving them the potential to be free citizens of the world and not merely subjects of nation-states. This is not to say that liberals would abolish the nation-state altogether; indeed, it was the liberal spirit that first breathed life into the concept of the nation-state. It is simply that liberals favour the dissipation of power into different levels of government, from local to national level.

Conservatives, on the other hand, are staunch defenders of nation-states. They fear the accumulation of power in **supranational** bodies such as the IMF, the WTO and the European Union (EU). They see democracy in terms of the nation, which is the natural unit of government. They also place greater emphasis upon the importance of the nation as an organic body that represents the culture of its people and its collective identity.

Key term

Supranationalism

This term refers to a process whereby decision-making power passes upward from national level to institutions that stand above the nation. Supranational organisations, such as the EU Commission, the European Court of Justice and the World Trade Organisation, look beyond national interests and pursue the interests of groups of nations instead. The principle means that individual nation-states accept decisions made by supranational bodies as binding upon them.

The development of the EU perhaps represents the greatest threat to the institution of the independent nation-state. The champions of European integration argue that economic and political independence must inevitably decline. However, the founder of the European Community — the French socialist Jean Monnet (1888–1979) — did not foresee the demise of the nation-state. Rather, he saw the long-term future of Europe as a single economic and political entity within which national cultures would still exist. For him, the idea of the nation was fundamentally cultural in nature. It could, therefore, survive the inevitable drift towards supranationalism in other spheres. Put another way, those who support European integration are happy to weaken individual *states*, but wish to preserve *national* identities.

Core values of nationalism

Self-determination

It has become a general principle of democratic politics that a people have the fundamental right to determine how they are governed. This idea, proposed in the late
seventeenth century by John Locke, has been enshrined in countless constitutional
documents and international agreements. The concept of self-determination, however,
contains a problem within itself: that is, what constitutes a 'people'? In other words,
how are we to divide humankind into natural units which will express their self-determination? The answer most commonly offered is that the nation is the most natural
unit, and so it has proved to be.

The origins and aspirations of nationalism based on this principle have varied
according to the circumstances preventing self-determination. In other words, for what
different reasons have national groupings been denied self-determination? These can
be classified as follows:

1 *Imperialism*

   Peoples who have found themselves subject to government by a foreign power will
   wish to throw off their subjugation and form their own sovereign state. The long
   struggle for independence from Britain by Indian nationalists and the nineteenth-
   century nationalist movements in the Ottoman and Austro-Hungarian empires are
   good examples.

2 *Sovereignty*

   There have been national groupings which have enjoyed a degree
   of self-government, but this has
   fallen short of full sovereignty.
   In these cases, nationalists have
   simply wished to establish full
   sovereign, independent powers.
   Examples include Irish nationalism (in both the south and the
   north), Catalonian nationalism in
   Spain, Québecois nationalism in
   Canada and Chechen nationalism
   within the Russian Federation.

Chechen women protest against Russian invasion in
Grozny, 1994

3 *Oppression*

   Peoples who have been subsumed into a larger oppressive regime may seek self-
   determination in order to escape from that oppression. The African National Council
   (ANC) in South Africa was a classic case of this occurring; other examples include
   the Kurds in the Middle East and the Tibetans who were annexed by a repressive
   communist regime in China.

4 *Diaspora*

National groupings that are scattered and subject to rule by many different states are said to have suffered diaspora. In such circumstances, a nationalist movement may seek to achieve statehood both to unite such a people and to achieve self-determination. The Jews in Israel are perhaps the clearest example, with Palestinians and some other Arab groupings finding themselves in a similar position.

5 *External threat*

This concerns nations that do enjoy their own sovereignty but are in danger of losing it as a result of annexation. Nationalist movements may spring up as a defensive force to guard against the impending loss of self-determination. Poland has experienced this kind of nationalist surge a number of times in its troubled history, as it has been constantly threatened from both east and west by Russia and Germany respectively; Israel has experienced this as a result of threats from neighbouring Arab states; Korea has responded to threats in this way, historically from Japan.

The desire for self-determination is clearly a strong one. It is therefore unsurprising that an equally strong phenomenon — national sentiment — should have become firmly attached to it. This is how the historian Hans Kohn (1891–1971) expressed the inexorable desire of nations to become states:

> The condition of statehood need not be present when a nationality originates; but in such a case it is always the memory of a past state and the aspiration towards state-hood that characterises nationalities in the period of nationalism.
>
> From *The Idea of Nationalism*, 1962

It is therefore hardly surprising, if we accept Kohn's assertion, that we have seen so many armed struggles involving nationalists who wish to establish statehood.

Organic society

The concept of nationalism presupposes that a people's common sense of nationality will bring them together into a single entity that will stand above the individual and have a kind of life of its own. This suggests that we all have at least two identities. One is as a sovereign individual; in this case we expect to enjoy rights, liberties and a private sphere of existence. The other is as a member of a nation; in this case we have a higher allegiance, which may, from time to time, transcend our individual identity.

One example of this is times of war. For better or worse, most individuals accept that when their nation is at war they should expect to make some personal sacrifices for the good of the nation as a whole. In extreme cases, individuals may lay down their lives for the national good. Another, more general example is the tendency to feel strong emotional attachments to national symbols and to become extremely patriotic at times of national sporting rivalry, such as during football World Cups and the Olympic Games.

Clearly there are strong emotions at work when the national interest is at stake. This suggests that we are bound together by ties which rival those of families, friendships and occupational units. This sense of 'oneness' is often described as the *organic society.* On the whole, this concept is seen as a conservative idea. Certainly, it was largely developed by conservative thinkers such as the German philosopher Friedrich Hegel and his fellow-German contemporary, the nationalist Johann Gottfried von Herder (1744–1803). Herder saw the world as being divided up into national cultures, each one of which formed an organic whole. For Hegel, the organic society was more an expression of what he called 'universal will' — that is, a people bound together by a common sense of themselves as a single entity, whether or not this was nationalist in nature. Put in more simple terms, the philosophies of Herder and Hegel suggest that we are bound together by forces which are the result of history, traditions and shared values. The German word **gemeinschaft** expresses this idea better than any English term. Clearly these binding factors are most likely to be found among national groupings.

Key term

Gemeinschaft

In a political context, this term refers to the collection of factors which help to make a people think of themselves as a single, separate community. These may include language, history, traditions, institutions and national symbols. The nearest English expression might be 'a common sense of shared identity', but the German word is perhaps stronger.

Although conservative in origin, the idea of the organic society has come to be shared by liberals — certainly since the end of the nineteenth century, when the Hegelian philosophy of T. H. Green became influential — and even by modern social democrats. As the socialist analysis of a society based on class conflict has declined, a new social perspective has arisen. Social democrats have adopted a more individualistic view of the world, but have also promoted the concept of communitarianism, which is similar to the philosophy of the organic society.

The most extreme example of the synthesis between organic society theory and nationalism has been found in fascism. Indeed, Benito Mussolini went a step further by developing the concept of nation into a myth, a creation which would inspire the Italian people to perform great deeds. Furthermore, all individual aspirations were to be sacrificed to the interests of the nation. This is how Mussolini expressed these ideas in 1922, at the dawn of his regime:

> We have created a myth. The myth is a faith, a passion. It is not necessary for it to be a reality. It is a reality in the sense that that it is a stimulus, is hope, is faith, is courage. Our myth is the nation, our myth is the greatness of the nation. And to this myth, this greatness, which we want to translate into a total reality, we subordinate everything else.
>
> From *The Political and Social Doctrine of Fascism*

Interestingly, and unlike German fascism, this Italian brand of radical nationalism sought to create a sense of national feeling where none existed, or at least where it was relatively weak. This is a more active form of nationalism, which leads its people, rather than follows them.

Whichever ideology embraces nationalism as part of its philosophy, all nationalists accept a general sense of the organic society. For some (e.g. fascists) it is stronger than for others (e.g. liberals), but it is present in all forms of nationalism.

Independence

Although achieving independence from other states is a core value of nationalists, there are some exceptions to this, three examples of which can be found in the UK.

The Welsh are the clearest example. Although some Welsh nationalists do support complete independence from the UK, on the whole the movement exists largely to defend the Welsh culture from dominance by England. The idea of a sovereign Welsh state is supported by a very small group. Most Welsh nationalists simply want to be recognised as a separate culture. Similarly, the Unionists in Northern Ireland wish to remain firmly within the UK. Indeed, their desire to maintain the link with the UK is the reason they exist as a political force. However, there is a sense in which Unionism is a nationalist grouping. Like the Welsh, Unionists seek to defend their own brand of Protestant/ Irish/British culture, mainly against the influence of Irish Catholicism.

Lastly, English nationalism is a small movement with virtually no political manifestation. However, as a cultural idea, English nationalism does exist in the minds of its people. Part of the nationalist aspirations of the English is to maintain the United Kingdom of England, Scotland, Wales and Northern Ireland (which is dominated by the English in demographic and economic terms). The desire to separate England from the others and create a new independent state is virtually non-existent.

Having identified these exceptions, we can nevertheless assert that nationalist movements generally seek total political independence. We have already seen that this is particularly important when nations are ruled by imperialist powers. It also applies to nations that feel threatened by other nations or states, for example, Israel, Cyprus and several of the Balkan nations. It can be important too in relation to supranational bodies, such as the EU. Many nationalists in Europe oppose further political integration on the grounds that this will threaten national independence. In a less specific sense, but no less powerful for that, many of the poorest nations of the world seek to assert their independence from what they see as the imperialism of international bodies. Thus, the World Bank, the International Monetary Fund and the World Trade Organisation are seen as threats to national independence because their policies demand a large degree of economic control. States such as Venezuela, for example, have sought to free themselves from these kind of strictures. More radical nationalist movements see the USA as being behind such economic imperialism. Nationalist aspirations of this kind can be found throughout Africa (e.g. Tanzania), South America (e.g. Argentina) and Asia (e.g. Indonesia).

Types of nationalism

Liberal nationalism

Although it is arguably the case that a form of cultural nationalism based in Germany predated the French Revolution, it is generally accepted that the earliest effective form of nationalism was linked to the Enlightenment, the development of natural rights theory and the advent of liberalism.

The influence of the Enlightenment led nationalists to believe that the nation-state was the ultimate expression of rational government. Until the nineteenth century, most states owed their existence merely to historical circumstances — they were derived from territories that had been governed by ruling families for centuries. They had originally come into existence through conquest and thereafter the descendants of those original conquerors (although succession was often disputed) continued to rule. Subject peoples accepted this situation, partly out of fear of the disorder which might result if absolute rulers were removed, partly out of respect for tradition and partly out of the absence of any alternative theory of government. Rationalist philosophy provided a new justification for government, an important factor of which was that the natural division of the world into nations could be replicated in sovereign states corresponding to those nations.

The philosophy of natural rights concluded that absolute rulers had denied such rights in the interests of state security. If the rights of individuals were to be restored, there needed to be a contract whereby the people agreed to sacrifice some of their natural rights to government. The seventeenth-century philosopher Thomas Hobbes had argued that this sacrifice of rights could be made to any ruler who could guarantee order. However, this was not enough for early liberals. Government needed a stronger basis for its legitimacy than merely the ability to keep the peace, and the modern state needed a firmer basis for its authority. By combining the state with the national identity, these liberals provided such a basis. If the state represented the nation, the social contract became acceptable. Rights could be sacrificed to the manifestation of the nation — the nation-state — in a way that they could not be to an 'external' ruler who did not embody the nation. Thus, the great King Louis XIV of France (1638–1715) was able to declare 'L'état, c'est moi' ('I am the state'), but he could never have justifiably claimed 'La France, c'est moi.'

Liberalism demanded simply that every individual should be free, but this could be extended to include the assertion that every nation should be free. If a nation were not free, the individuals who comprised it would also not be free. The freedom of nations and the freedom of individuals were therefore inextricably linked. This is how the nineteenth-century Italian nationalist Giuseppe Mazzini (1805–72) expressed the idea of liberation from autocratic government:

> Young Italy recognises therefore the universal association of the peoples as the ultimate aim of the endeavours of all free men. Before they can become members of the great association it is necessary that they should have a separate existence, name

and power. Every people is therefore bound to constitute itself a nation before it can occupy itself with the question of humanity.

Quoted in Elie Kedourie, *Nationalism*, 1966

Ever since, liberal nationalists have demanded that every recognisable nation has the right to freedom from subjection to the rule of other nations and states. This demand has manifested itself in a variety of circumstances, examples of which are shown in Table 4.2.

Table 4.2 Examples of liberal nationalism

Movement	Circumstances
Mazzini's 'Young Italy' movement	Established in the 1860s, this was a movement to unite Italian peoples who lived in separate states, some of which were subject to 'foreign' rule. The movement believed that the establishment of an Italian republican state would bring democracy and freedom with it.
Irish nationalism	In the nineteenth and twentieth centuries, this movement sought to separate the Irish people from British rule. The movement was also republican in character.
Scottish nationalism	In the second half of the twentieth century, this movement grew in the belief that the self-determination of the Scots was essential if true democracy were to be established.
Czech nationalism	Having been subjected to the hegemony of the Soviet Union, the Czechs seized the opportunity to establish their independence, individual liberties and democratic rule when the Union began to collapse in 1990.

Conservative nationalism

For much of the nineteenth century, conservatives were suspicious of liberal nationalism. They feared that it would lead to the destruction of traditional forms of authority and would therefore threaten order. It implied the demise of imperial power and the risk of civil war in those countries that were multinational in character. However, as more nation-states became established, conservatives began to understand that nationalism could become a force for order rather than disorder.

In this belief, conservative nationalists were inspired by the work of Johann Fichte, for whom the concept of the nation was a cultural idea. Peoples were bound together by their traditions and a common sense of their own history. This united them in a manner more powerful than anything a government could engender. While liberals saw nationalism as a way of creating and maintaining individual and collective liberty, for conservatives nationalism was a means by which societies could be held together.

The binding effect of nationalism could serve two main purposes. The first was to prevent social conflict. This was the motivation behind the nationalism of Benjamin Disraeli in Britain. He understood the dangers that free-market capitalism and the class conflict resulting from it could bring. One of these was the disintegration of society. By appealing to the nationalist instincts of the people, however, social conflict could be prevented. This theme was taken up much later by Margaret Thatcher, who was faced with the class conflict created by her neo-liberal policies of the 1980s. By arguing that her radical reforms served the national interest, and by resisting the increasing forces of European integration, she was able to unite the majority of the nation at a time when class conflict was growing.

The predominantly German form of conservative nationalism, represented by Fichte, and later by Otto von Bismarck as well as Giuseppe Garibaldi (1807–82) in Italy, concentrated more on the development of the nation and the achievement of its historical destiny. Progress depended on national unity. Without it, society would drift aimlessly and without spirit. Of course, as time went by, this conservative form of nationalism was to become more radical in Germany and Italy and contributed to the rise of fascism. The most sinister aspect of this transformation occurred when the fascists saw national destiny in terms of national superiority and the defeat of weaker nations. An exaggerated sense of national superiority of this kind has come to be described as **chauvinism**.

Conservative nationalism can also be defensive in nature. This occurs when a national identity is perceived to be under threat (even if that threat is illusory). In a British context, the rise of the UK Independence Party (UKIP) can be seen as a typical example. For UKIP, the threat to British national identity is posed by European integration. On a much bigger scale, there has been a recent emergence of Hindu nationalism in India in response to the perceived threat both from Islamic culture and from modernisation.

Key term

Chauvinism

Originally a French term, chauvinism refers to a sense of national superiority. It is associated with conservative nationalism, which regards such a sense of superiority as a means of uniting the people. Chauvinism can be displayed in an exaggerated sense of patriotism or as *jingoism*, a slavish, emotional attachment to nationalist symbols such as flags, anthems and mythology.

Right-wing nationalism

Right-wing nationalism includes those forms of nationalism that have gone beyond the type favoured by conservatism. For conservative nationalists, the doctrine's purpose was to maintain order and unity. Right-wing nationalists have developed ideas that are more active and purposeful than those of the conservatives. Some examples are given below.

Imperialism

Some nationalist movements have been overtly imperialist in nature, considering the creation of empires as a key element in the national interest and destiny. During the nineteenth and early twentieth centuries, France, Britain, Belgium, Germany and Holland all displayed imperialist motives. The competition for overseas possessions which resulted can be seen both as a Darwinian struggle for superiority and as a pursuit of national economic interests. In the 1930s, Japanese nationalists wanted to create a Pacific empire for themselves, while the Soviet Union demonstrated imperialist tendencies through most of the twentieth century.

Expansionism

A similar concept to imperialism, expansionism refers to a nation's tendency to expand its territory into neighbouring countries or to exercise political hegemony over them. In recent times, Serbia, Russia and China have all shown a desire to expand their influence over a whole region.

Xenophobia

Xenophobia is the instinct typical of right-wing nationalists to be suspicious of foreigners and to attempt to maintain the exclusiveness of the home nation. It manifests itself in resistance to immigration and, in some more sinister cases, in attempts to impose racial and cultural uniformity. Right-wing movements of this type have been most evident in recent times in France (the National Front movement of Jean-Marie Le Pen), Austria (the Freedom Party) and Holland (the anti-immigration party of Pym Fortuyn(1951–2002)).

Cultural nationalism and volkism

Cultural nationalism often does not include a desire for national independence, but rather a sense of national pride in a distinctive culture and a wish to free that culture from the **hegemony** of a more dominant neighbour. The classic example of this is Welsh nationalism. Based on an attachment to the Welsh language and the Welsh culture of art, poetry, music and nonconformist religion, this kind of nationalism is a reaction against the domination of the much stronger English culture (see Box 4.2).

Box 4.2 *An appeal to a people with a common language*

The Finnish nationalist Adolf Arvidsson (1791–1858) made this appeal to his people in the early nineteenth century in the hope that they would throw off the hegemony of the Swedish-speaking minority:

> When the language of its forefathers is lost, a nation, too, is lost and perishes. All speaking the same tongue naturally forms an indivisible whole; they are bound together internally by ties of mind and soul, mightier and firmer than every external bond. For language forms the spiritual, and land the material, boundaries of mankind; but the former is the stronger, because the spirit means more than material.

Such sentiments could apply to many cultural nationalist movements and were adopted by Julius Nyerere (1922–99), the great African nationalist, in his nation-building efforts.

Rather than striving for independence, Welsh nationalists have campaigned for the teaching of their language in schools, its use in public affairs and the preservation of Welsh literature. Although there is a weak sense of a separate Welsh history, including some struggles against English rule during the early Middle Ages, there is no history of distinct Welsh political institutions (in contrast to Scotland, for example). Thus, Plaid

Cymru — the Welsh nationalist party — is more interested in limited autonomy than full sovereign powers. There are Welsh separatists, but they are very much a minority. Movements similar to Welsh nationalism exist in Catalonia in Spain, in parts of the Italian Tyrol region and in French Brittany.

Key term

Hegemony

This term has a special meaning for Marxists of the Frankfurt School, but in the context of nationalism it refers to the domination of one culture over another. This may have political and economic significance, as in the case of the hegemony of the USSR over much of Eastern Europe, but it is often confined simply to dominant values, traditions, language, media and artistic pursuits. It does not necessarily mean complete political control, but rather irresistible domination. The great powers have often exerted hegemony over whole regions, e.g. the USA in South America and France in north Africa.

Volkism is a more powerful, and in some cases ominous, form of cultural nationalism. The type of cultural nationalism found in Wales is largely benign and non-violent, whereas volkism is radical and can lead to armed struggle. It is mostly associated with Johann Fichte, who identified the German people as a classic example of *volk*. By this he meant a people closely bound together by a common culture, language, religion, history and mythology. There is also an element of territorial possession associated with volkism. Peoples claim a historical attachment to land, sometimes associated with past conquest of that territory. In some cases, this might become a romantic ideal, a desire either to retain the traditional territory or to regain possession of it after losing it historically. Fichte, for example, believed that the German people had long been deprived of their ancestral lands. In this sense, both the Germans and the Jews could be said to have a *volkisch* identity. Zionism is a movement that seeks to restore and retain the historical (and indeed religious) claim of the Jews to the land of Israel.

The idea of *volk*, in the sense of pursuing a historical destiny, reached its height in Nazi Germany. The Nazis, however, added racial exclusivity and superiority to the concept of *volk*. This created an organic and radical form of nationalism that provided justification for conquest and expansionism. (This was known as Lebensraum — the right of a superior people to annexe additional territory occupied by inferior peoples.)

Post-colonial nationalism

It is not surprising that many examples of nationalist movements are found in countries that have struggled against colonial rule. When a subject people is fighting for its independence (and when it has achieved that independence), there is an overwhelming need to promote social unity. A strong sense of national identity can provide this. In Africa, where such post-colonial nationalist movements have proliferated, an additional problem has been the existence of tribal loyalties that cut across national identity.

The need to create unity is one of the factors which has led to regimes in such countries becoming highly authoritarian in nature. Were newly-independent states to be pluralistic and intensely democratic in character, there would be a danger that the state would fall apart under the strain of internal conflict. The plight of countries such as Uganda, Sudan and Ethiopia, all brought to the edge of ruin by civil war, bears testimony to this problem. By contrast, in Zimbabwe, Robert Mugabe (1925–) — a nationalist freedom fighter — has suppressed tribal rivalry through repressive political methods. Similarly, Julius Nyerere in Tanzania united his country by turning it into a one-party state, although his personal instincts were democratic in nature.

Post-colonial nationalism and anti-colonial nationalism, therefore, are often highly autocratic; many of the examples shown in Table 4.3 are of this type.

Table 4.3 Anti-colonial and post-colonial nationalist movements

Country	Leader(s)	Characteristics
China (1911–49)	Sun Yat Sen (1866–1925) Chiang Kai Shek (1887–1975)	Quasi-democratic
Vietnam (1950s–1970s)	Ho Chi Minh (1890–1969)	One-party communist
Cuba (1959–)	Fidel Castro (1927–)	One-party socialist
Ghana (1960s–1970s)	Joshua Nkrumah (1909–72)	Quasi-democratic
India (until 1947)	Jawaharlal Nehru (1889–1964) Mohammed Ali Jinnah (1876–1948)	Democratic/socialist
Congo (1960s)	Patrice Lumumba (1925–61)	Autocratic
Zimbabwe (1979–)	Robert Mugabe (1925–)	Quasi-democratic/autocratic

Post-colonial nationalist movements have often been socialist. This is the result of a specific set of circumstances and another type of nationalism, which is described below.

Socialist nationalism

Some nationalists — usually in states which were former colonies — adopted socialism or Marxism as a means of promoting both economic development and independence from world trading systems.

This was done despite the fact that socialism and nationalism are not natural bedfellows. In socialist theory, it is class solidarity which, it is hoped, will replace capitalist individualism. Marxists in particular viewed nationalism as a form of false consciousness, promoted by the bourgeois ruling class to bring together the working classes in the interests of capitalism and to divert their consciousness away from revolutionary activities. It is therefore surprising to find a number of modern nationalists who have also been socialists.

In many cases, the nationalist leaders in question began their freedom fighting activities as socialists or communists. This was true of Ho Chi Minh in Vietnam, Fidel Castro in Cuba and Robert Mugabe in Zimbabwe. It was therefore not surprising that they should synthesise their original socialism with the nationalist desire for independence and self-determination. In fact, a symbiotic relationship developed between nationalism and socialism: nationalism benefits from the imposition of socialism since this enables the country to avoid domination by external capitalist powers. This is most evident in Cuba, where the need to escape from the economic hegemony of the neighbouring USA required that the people of the island should reject free-market capitalism. At the same time, nationalism can assist the building of socialism by creating a sense of solidarity and national purpose. Finally, the social equality which socialism can bring creates a sense of unity through justice.

Racialism

In those states where the basis of nationhood is founded on ethnic identity, there is a synthesis between racialism and nationalism. In extreme cases, such as Nazi Germany, the two concepts can become virtually synonymous. In theory, there need be nothing sinister about such a relationship, but in practice many nations based on race have also adopted a Darwinist view of the world.

The philosophers of racialism who inspired Adolf Hitler (1889–1945), such as Count Gobineau (1816–82) and Houston Chamberlain (1855–1927), adopted a world view which suggested that races are arranged in a hierarchy, with Teutonic (German/Aryan) peoples at the apex of this system and various inferior peoples of Asia and Africa at the bottom. In the great struggles for superiority, those nations that demonstrated the strongest sense of unity and purpose would prevail. What would give them such strength of will? Racial theorists often suggested that it was the purity of the nation's bloodline which would be the decisive factor. Note that **racialism** should not be confused with **racism**. The distinction is explained below.

Key terms

Racism and racialism

These terms are certainly contentious in terms of their meanings. For the purposes of this book, however, racism is taken to mean a generalised sense of racial discrimination, prejudice and antagonism; racialism, on the other hand, can mean any form of scientific or quasi-scientific theory about race, the relationship between races and the history of racial development. Thus, those who routinely attack members of ethnic minorities, are prejudiced against them or who discriminate against them in the fields of work and education could be called racists. The theorists who underpinned Nazi theory, however, were racialists.

There have, of course, been a number of race-based national movements which have not engaged in a Darwinian struggle. In Africa, for example, many nationalists have proposed the restructuring of the continent into 'natural' countries based on ethnic groupings. However, there remains a sense of unity within Africa, suggesting that all racial units should be treated as equal. The desire of the Organisation for African Unity

(OAU) to recreate independent nations is based on aspirations for mutual respect and peaceful coexistence. Similarly, movements which have sought to unite ethnic groupings, such as Pan-Arabism (aiming to unite all Arab peoples) and Pan-Slavism (aiming to unite the Slavic race) may have proposed racial exclusivity and unity, but included no special sense of superiority.

These different types of nationalism are summarised in Table 4.4.

Table 4.4 Summary of types of nationalism

Type	Examples	Main characteristics
Liberal nationalism	• 'Young Italy' • Scotland • Ireland	Desire for self-determination; creation of democracy; creation or preservation of liberty
Conservative nationalism	• Traditional British conservatism • French Gaullism	Determination to preserve the national interest; nationalism used as a means of retaining social unity; historically imperialist
Right-wing nationalism	• Fascism • French National Front	Xenophobic; sense of national superiority; expansionist; totalitarian
Post-colonial nationalism	• Tanzania • Nigeria • Singapore	Often socialist, usually autocratic regimes; emphasis on national unity; economic self-sufficiency
Socialist nationalism	• Cuba • Zimbabwe	One-party, powerful centralised state; opposition to foreign investment; desire for industrialisation
Racialist nationalism	• Nazism • South African apartheid regime	Sense of racial superiority and racial exclusivity; expansionist; desire to unify the racial group into one state
Cultural nationalism	• Hindu nationalism in India • Wales	Desire to protect a cultural tradition under threat from another culture; usually politically moderate

Key nationalist thinkers

Johann Gottfried von Herder (German, 1744–1803)

Herder represents a kind of romantic nationalism which stands in opposition to the rational and liberal forms inspired by Jean-Jacques Rousseau, Napoleon Bonaparte and, later, John Stuart Mill. His conception of nationalism was based upon culture, and especially language.

In a Europe where various nationalities were mixed up in a patchwork of different states (especially in the region now called Germany), Herder sought to discover how peoples could extricate themselves from circumstances that tend to suppress traditional culture. Historically, civilisations that had retained their own particular culture, and had successfully guarded it against adulteration by other cultures, had retained their own identity and, in doing so, had become dominant.

Since Herder asserted that language was the main vehicle by which culture was transported from one generation to the next, nationality itself could be defined in terms of language. This is how Herder expressed his love of language:

> Has a nation anything dearer than the speech of its fathers? In its speech resides its whole thought-domain, its tradition, history, religion, and basis of life, all its heart and soul. To deprive a people of its own speech is to deprive it of its one eternal good... As God tolerates all the different languages in the world, so also should a ruler not only tolerate but honour the various languages of his peoples... The best culture of a people cannot be expressed through a foreign language.
>
> From *Materials for the Philosophy of the History of Mankind*, 1784

Although Herder was something of a cultural nationalist, it would be wrong to ascribe any of the later German nationalist tradition to him. German nationalism might be concerned with the restoration and preservation of culture, but it was also associated with state power. In other words, the will of the nation was to be expressed through the German state. Herder was less concerned with politics and more interested in the independence of cultures from domination by other peoples. His philosophy therefore had more in common with later Welsh, English and Italian nationalism, which were based upon language, culture and history. Although twentieth-century fascists drew some inspiration from Herder's thought, this was a distortion of his beliefs. He was a vehement opponent of all forms of tyranny and did not accept that nations were based on racial distinctions.

Giuseppe Mazzini (Italian, 1805–72)

In 1831, Mazzini founded a revolutionary nationalist movement known as 'Young Italy'. Like Herder, he was a romantic figure who saw nationalism in terms of brotherhood and comradeship, the ultimate expression of social solidarity. He linked the idea of uniting the disparate Italian peoples into a free nation with the right to self-determination and liberation from oppressive regimes. He was, in short, a liberal-republican nationalist, the ultimate symbol of the unity of freedom and self-determination. Although principally associated with Italy, he proposed that Europe as a whole should be divided into 12 nation-states, each of which was to be based on a dominant cultural grouping.

The purpose of nationalism and self-determination, Mazzini argued, was to ensure social progress. He likened the division of peoples into natural national groupings to the division of labour under capitalism. Once peoples were free from subjection to tyrannical foreign powers, they would be able to develop their own cultures and experience true liberty.

Mazzini's brand of nationalism became a popular model for other movements that spread through Europe in the nineteenth century, especially among the subject peoples of the Austro-Hungarian Empire. He was also one of the founders of the principle of guerrilla warfare, whereby small conspiratorial groups operated in secret to strike blows against repressive powers, reducing their will to govern and undermining their authority. By waging a war of attrition, the dominating power would ultimately be toppled. Mazzini therefore became an inspiration for later nationalist movements in regions such as Indochina, South America and Cuba.

Charles de Gaulle (French, 1890–1970)

De Gaulle led the free French forces against Germany during the Second World War. After the war, he remained on the fringes of French politics until 1958, when a major political crisis struck the country. The French colonies in Algeria and Indochina were in revolt and the government seemed unable to quell the rebellions. Army leaders in France appeared to be on the point of provoking a coup d'état against the tottering French state. The political leadership of France was therefore forced to ask de Gaulle, a figure who enjoyed the same kind of esteem as Churchill in the UK, to form a new government. De Gaulle agreed and took over, writing a new constitution that granted him extensive powers as president and ushered in the fifth French Republic.

De Gaulle was, above all, a French nationalist. His philosophy, which became known as the *politics of grandeur*, was based upon the principle of national self-interest. He sought to reconstruct the French economy so that the country could enjoy greater independence. He pursued an independent foreign policy, withdrawing from NATO in 1966 and maintaining an independent nuclear capability. In the early 1960s, he vetoed the UK's entry into the European Community on the grounds that it represented a threat to French interests. His nationalist credentials were enhanced when he openly supported a movement campaigning for the independence of French-speaking Quebec from Canada.

His brand of nationalism was the pursuit of national independence from growing international forces. The term globalisation was not widely used when de Gaulle was alive, but he certainly wished to maintain an independent status for his people. He refused to accept the dominance of either the USA or the USSR over world affairs. By courting the friendship of China, parts of the Arab world and various other nationalist movements in Africa and Asia, he was able to maintain France's unique position.

Widespread political unrest in France among students and workers and the rejection of his proposed amendments to the French constitution led de Gaulle to resign in 1968 and to retire from politics the following year.

Julius Nyerere (Tanzanian, 1922–99)

The nationalism of Nyerere was typical of a number of African post-independence movements. It synthesised independence, language and socialism as a means of uniting a people and maintaining its autonomy.

Nyerere was the first elected president of Tanzania, a country that was severely divided along tribal and linguistic lines, but which had been artificially thrown together as a single colonial state under British rule. The principle of using common language to unite the people was described by Nyerere as *ujamaa*, which literally means 'family bond'. He believed he could forge a new nation by insisting that the members of all tribes, who had their own languages, speak a common tongue. This left the problem of how to ensure that, having rid themselves of their former colonial masters, the Tanzanians would not fall prey to the **economic imperialism** of multinational companies and the richer trading states.

Julius Nyerere, president of Tanzania 1964–85

Key term

Economic imperialism

We usually associate colonisation with political and/or military control, and the removal of political sovereignty from a country. Economic imperialism, on the other hand, occurs even when states have their own political independence. Richer countries may continue to exercise decisive influence by forcing other states to be dependent on trade, penetrating them with large corporations and creating large quantities of debt. The USA in particular is often accused of exercising economic imperialism over poor states.

Nyerere developed a socialist, self-sufficient system which he hoped would reduce the need to become economically dependent on the outside world. Unfortunately, the imposition of socialism proved to be unsuccessful. Tanzania became extremely poor and unrest grew. Although Nyerere created a one-party dictatorship, he could not quell the opposition. In 1985, he bowed to the inevitable and resigned as president. During this period, many similar states went through much the same process. Socialist nationalism was failing everywhere and free-market policies had to be introduced.

Issues in nationalism

Conservative and liberal nationalism

The principal question to be asked here is: do these two traditions have anything significant in common, or are they completely different ideologies? It is possible to identify both similarities and differences.

The first feature which both have in common is an overarching aspiration to unite a people who believe that they share a common national identity. Both movements tend to stress characteristics such as common history and traditions, language and culture.

For liberal nationalists, who are invariably struggling against some kind of oppression or foreign hegemony, the need for unity is essential if the people are to throw off the controlling power and thereby restore collective and individual liberty. Mazzini, in nineteenth-century Italy, believed that this meant developing collective, national, revolutionary fervour. In Ireland, a small revolutionary group, Sinn Fein, dedicated itself to armed struggle, but the main thrust of the movement was cultural in nature. Modern Scottish nationalism, on the other hand, is almost exclusively peaceful and dedicated to working through the existing parliamentary system of the UK. It emphasises Scottish history and the traditional Scottish institutions around which the people can unite. The problem for Scottish nationalism was how to place concerted political pressure on Westminster to achieve its aims.

Conservative nationalists have stressed similar symbols of unity. However, the purposes of this type of nationalism are different. On the whole, conservative nationalists operate within a national state which already exists and already enjoys independence. The main purpose is therefore to maintain a sense of unity, which may be under threat. For Disraeli, in the late nineteenth century, the threat to unity was social conflict, mainly between classes. For the French under de Gaulle and his Gaullist descendants, the threat has been mainly from international organisations, such as the European Community and US-dominated institutions.

A second common feature is that both liberals and conservatives — including as disparate a group as Rousseau, Mazzini, Bismarck and the Palestinian nationalist Yasser Arafat (1929–2004) — have asserted that all nations have the right to form their own sovereign state, based largely on nationality.

A third common feature is a concern to unify a people who have become scattered. Such movements can be fundamentally liberal in nature (e.g. nineteenth-century Italy and the Jewish nation in the twentieth century), but can also be conservative (e.g. Bismarck's Germany and some contemporary Islamic 'nationalists'). These movements differ in that the liberal examples seek to emphasise freedom and democracy, whereas the conservative ones stress an organic, common cultural identity.

Notwithstanding the features they have in common, the two types of movement manifest themselves in different ways. At the centre of this distinction lies their differing political attitude towards freedom. For liberals, liberty remains paramount. The purpose of the nation and national independence is to safeguard the freedom of the individual citizen. For conservatives, on the other hand, order and unity stand above individual liberty as the key political objective.

It is normally the case that conservative nationalism is defensive in nature, whereas liberals usually have positive aspirations. Conservatives often emphasise the threats assailing national independence and unity.

Table 4.5 Similarities and distinctions between liberal and conservative nationalism

Common features
Desire to unite a people around national traditions, identity and institutions
Commitment to the nation-state concept
Need to unite peoples of common national identity who have been dispersed

Differences
Conservatives are often defensive while liberals are aspirational
Liberals are concerned with freedom while conservatives seek unity
Liberals tend to stress institutions and democracy while conservatives emphasise common cultural identity

These may come from excessive immigration, political and military encroachments by a neighbouring power or threats of internal disintegration. Liberals, by contrast, are usually concerned with establishing a state where none exists, or with asserting the right to independence of a national group that exists within a state. This implies that, once a liberal nationalist movement has achieved its primary objective, it will cease to be a major political force. This was certainly true after Ireland became independent from Britain in 1921 and once India achieved its freedom from the British Empire (although there has been a recent rise in Hindu nationalism there, as a reaction against Islamic activism).

Nationalism and racialism

It is usually wrong, and sometimes dangerous, to confuse nationalism with racialism. Of course, some nationalist movements have been racialist in character. Nazism is the clearest example (although its racial content was not part of its original appeal to the German people). Another example is the white nationalism of the South African apartheid regime. This movement based its beliefs on the principles that different races could not coexist in the same society and that white races were superior to others. It is also true that many nationalist movements have had a racial element, even if they have not been dominated by racialism. This has certainly been the case in China, Israel and many parts of Africa. The link between nationalism and racialism is not surprising: race is a powerful unifying force, and many assume that nations are derived from ethnic distinctions.

The truth is, however, that most large nations are multiracial in their origins. We only have to think of the USA, Russia, the UK, Australia, Canada and Brazil — the largest and most powerful states or nations in the world — to appreciate this. All of these countries are multiracial in character and tend to draw strength from this. Admittedly confusion may be caused by the relationship between nation, culture and race. In all of the above examples, there is certainly a discernible common culture. This characteristic — often represented by language — is usually based upon the culture of one dominant race. For example, the USA, Canada and Australia, all former British colonies, can be said to be based on Anglo-Saxon culture; Brazil's character is dominated by its Portuguese features, and Russia is essentially Slavic in nature. But this does not mean that **race** and **nation** are synonymous in such cases. Indeed, as time passes, the influence of the dominant culture, and therefore of the dominant race, may weaken.

Right-wing movements, such as the British National Party and the French National Front, continue to emphasis race as the key element in national identity, but the forces of liberalism are ranged against this view. Liberals hold that national culture is a pluralist concept, a synthesis of different traditions which is constantly evolving. The conservative view of race and nation seeks to preserve exclusivity and so opposes the assimilation of different ethnic identities. However, for conservatives, common national identity is based largely on the development of a single culture rather than on racial purity.

This is not to say that racialism should be ignored in studies of nationalism. Indeed, racialism and racial perspectives on the world can be key elements in preventing nationalism from taking hold. In Cyprus, for example, campaigners for the creation of a single Cypriot nation-state have been constantly thwarted by Greek and Turkish racialism. Similar problems have occurred in states such as Iraq and Sri Lanka. In summary, therefore, any study of nationalism must take race into account, but it would be a mistake to identify race as the key element in the development of modern nationalism.

Key terms

Race and nation

The term race refers to a grouping of people based on common ancestry and distinctive racial features, including skin colour and other physical characteristics. The origins of racial distinctions predate the existence of states and so cannot be seen as a political concept. Nations, on the other hand, are based on a people's perception of itself. National identity arises from a variety of common historical circumstances, including history, traditions, culture, language, religion and geographical separateness. Racial distinctions are only one of many factors which might separate one national identity from another.

Is the nation-state in decline?

Many modern historians and international relations experts suspect that the nation-state, as a particular political form, is in decline. It must be remembered that the concept is only just over 200 years old. In the context of human history, therefore, the nation-state could be seen as a temporary phenomenon.

The main reason why analysts suggest that the nation-state may be in decline is the development of globalisation. This is because globalisation threatens the basic functions of the state. Let us assume that these are to:

➢ maintain law and order within the territory
➢ secure the state against external threats
➢ develop and maintain useful relations with other states
➢ regulate the currency, the operation of markets and the economy in general
➢ maintain the general welfare of its people
➢ promote economic and social progress
➢ protect and improve the physical environment of the country

Bear in mind that these are basic functions. There are clearly other roles played by states, but these vary from state to state and are not usually fundamental activities. We can see how three general world developments have affected these functions:

1 Many of the problems which the nation-state must deal with have become supranational in character. Markets are increasingly international, crime operates across countries, environmental problems do not recognise national boundaries, individual states find it difficult to defend themselves against terrorism and economies in general have become more interdependent.

2 The rapid and extensive increase in international communication, e.g. the internet, and the widespread use of English, may be creating an international culture.

3 Partly because of the development of supranationalism, there has been a huge increase in the power and influence of international organisations, notably the European Union, the World Trade Organisation, the World Bank and the International Monetary Fund.

Therefore, if the nation-state is indeed becoming weaker and less relevant to world problems, it follows that it may well decline in importance and, ultimately, even cease to exist.

On the other hand, there are some reasons for believing that nation-states will endure. If we see the nation as a fundamentally cultural concept, there may be a reaction against the processes described above. Put another way, just as nineteenth- and twentieth-century liberal nationalism was largely a reaction against the imperialism of the great powers, so modern cultural nationalism may rebel against the effects of globalisation and the economic imperialism of supranational organisations. If national identity remains a strong enough human emotion, it may well triumph over historical forces.

Nationalism in the UK

The UK is a multi-national state in that it is a single sovereign state with a unitary government, but contains within it several different countries and nationalities. None of these constituent countries, however, enjoys any sovereignty: the UK is not a federal system like that in Germany. Of course, many other countries have strong regional cultures within them, for example Spain, Italy and Belgium, but these are not individual countries as such. The nearest thing to the British experience is perhaps Switzerland, where peoples of French, German and Italian origin enjoy partial self-rule.

The UK is unusual in another way, too. The types of nationalism which have flourished there have been different from each other in character. The way in which they have pursued their goals has therefore varied considerably (see Table 4.5).

Scottish nationalism

The principal aim of Scottish nationalism is political independence, either in the fullest sense of the word — i.e. separate statehood — or partially, through a federal system which would grant the country a limited degree of sovereignty. There have been a number of aspirations and grievances which have caused an upsurge in Scottish nationalism since the 1960s. These have included:

➤ a strong sense of Scottish history, much of which had been characterised by English domination
➤ the sense that the human and physical resources of Scotland have been consistently plundered by the dominant English
➤ the long history of separate Scottish institutions, such as the Church, universities, the school and examination system, the legal system and tradition, and sporting

institutions, but no independent Scottish control over these since the 1707 Act of Union abolished the Scottish Parliament

➤ a history of strong attachments and alliances with mainland Europe; in some ways, the Scots have felt themselves more continental than the English

➤ a growing belief that an independent Scottish political system would be more democratic and accountable, prompted by increasing disillusion with politics in Westminster

➤ as the British economy in general appeared to be stagnating in the 1960s and 1970s, many argued that an independent Scottish economy could be more dynamic

These beliefs add up to a clear example of a form of liberal nationalism. The Scots have sought both self-determination and a superior democracy. They have wanted control of their own resources and their own government. The devolution settlement of 1998 went some way to satisfying their desire for political autonomy, but, in truth, the powers which were transferred were disappointing for the nationalists.

Welsh nationalism

Unlike the Scots, the Welsh have no tradition of separateness and few distinctive political institutions. However, they have enjoyed a specific culture which is different from the dominant English culture. This is not to say that the majority of the Welsh have supported the nationalist cause. Most see themselves as members of a region of the UK with its own special character, but not distinct enough to suggest political independence.

It is true that a few extreme nationalists in Wales do want full independence, but for most members of the movement the concern is that Welsh culture is being swamped by the dominance of England, and may soon disappear. Language is the touchstone issue for Welsh nationalists. Should Welsh speaking disappear, they argue, the rest of the culture will soon go with it.

Welsh nationalism has therefore been a cultural form of nationalism, seeking a degree of autonomous control over cultural institutions, but not general independence. The Welsh Assembly that was established in 1998 has some control over education, the arts, sporting activities and the promotion of the Welsh language, as well as some responsibility for agricultural and industrial development, and sees itself as the guardian of a distinctive Welsh culture. This has little in common with the aggressive, radical form of cultural nationalism, or volkism, which arose in Nazi Germany. The Welsh are not concerned with national rivalry or expansion: their nationalism is defensive.

Ulster Unionism

Another form of cultural nationalism can be found in Northern Ireland. There, radical unionism is a synthesis of Ulster (not Irish) nationalism, British nationalism (the Unionists demonstrate a staunch loyalty to the Crown) and Protestantism. It would be wrong to describe Ulster Unionists simply as radical British nationalists; they also feel themselves to be Irish in character, and although they support the jurisdiction of the Queen, they harbour a deep suspicion of British government.

The political aspirations of the Unionists have been to ensure that their kind of culture is defended in Northern Ireland, both from English and Irish Catholic cultural domination. Even more than that of the Welsh, therefore, Ulster Unionism is a defensive form of nationalism. Unionists would ideally like a degree of autonomy for Northern Ireland with its own political institutions, but also a guarantee that the British will defend them from Irish domination. Failing such partial independence, however, they are content to place themselves under the protection of the Crown.

We should perhaps avoid describing Ulster Unionism as a form of nationalism *per se*, but rather as a blend of two brands of nationalism. Thus, in part, Unionists see themselves as loyal Britons, but they are also Northern Irish. They remain determined to protect both these identities for themselves.

Irish republicanism

Once Ireland had achieved its independence from Britain in 1921, Irish nationalism retreated largely into Northern Ireland, where it continued to struggle for the unification of all Ireland. In this respect, it became a republican movement. Irish republicanism has been represented by a radical wing — Sinn Fein — and a more moderate group of nationalists who formed the Social and Democratic Labour Party (SDLP).

Sinn Fein and the radical republicans synthesise nationalism with a degree of socialism. This arises from the belief that Britain was a colonial exploiter of Ireland and that it was the indigenous Irish Catholic population who were the main victims of this exploitation. Certainly, the followers of republicanism were drawn largely from the Catholic working class. By throwing off British rule and uniting the Irish peoples, radical republicans also hoped to emancipate the working class. Moderate Irish nationalism, represented by the SDLP, can be seen as a more liberal movement, appealing to all classes and to those who have no special religious conviction. Both movements could be said to be cultural in nature, too. Irish national pride is based upon its language (Gaelic), its rich literary tradition, its distinctive music and sport and shared

A Sinn Fein march

historical experience. Thus, the Irish can be seen as a classic *volk*, with a strong attachment to their own exclusive territory.

British nationalism

During the latter part of the twentieth century, a new nationalist movement emerged in the UK. Of an extremely right-wing character, it has been largely defensive in nature and can be seen as a reaction to a number of developments, including:

> the increase in immigration and the creation of large ethnic minority populations in British cities

> disillusionment with national politics in general

> the increasing influence of Europe

> a feeling that the UK is in long-term decline, having enjoyed a largely glorious history

> discontent among alienated groups in some regions who have not shared in the increasing general prosperity

The main standard-bearer of this movement has been the British National Party (BNP), which has enjoyed a steady growth of members in the early twenty-first century. The BNP seeks to restore British 'greatness' and opposes the apparent dilution of the traditional national identity by growing multiculturalism and the decentralisation of government. The party has a distinctly racial character, denying that it is overtly racist but admitting that it wishes to stem the flow of immigration and to 'encourage' peoples of 'non-British' races to return to their countries of origin.

The mission statement of the BNP, part of which is shown in Box 4.4, reveals its attitudes.

Box 4.4 Extracts from the BNP mission statement

The British National Party exists to secure a future for the indigenous peoples of these islands in the North Atlantic which have been our homeland for millennia. We use the term indigenous to describe the people whose ancestors were the earliest settlers here after the last great Ice Age and which have been complemented by the historic migrations from mainland Europe. The migrations of the Celts, Anglo-Saxons, Danes, Norse and closely related peoples have been, over the past few thousand years, instrumental in defining the character of our family of nations...

...The rich legacy of tradition, legend, myth and very real wealth of landscape and man-made structures is one of our island's richest treasures. The men and women of the British National Party are motivated by love and admiration of the outpouring of culture, art, literature and the pattern of living through the ages that has left its mark on our very landscape. We value the folkways and customs which have been passed down through countless generations. We enthuse with pride at the marvels of architecture and engineering that have been completed on these islands since the construction of the great megaliths 7,000 years ago.

These emotions should not be confused with **patriotism**. The British are known for their patriotism, but this does not denote the kind of outlook demonstrated by the BNP.

Such emotions should also be distinguished from English nationalism. Arguably, there is no such thing as English nationalism, and if it does exist, it is not right wing in nature. English nationalism would imply a desire to break away from the UK, relinquishing historic links with Wales, Scotland and Northern Ireland. This is certainly not a significant political aspiration among the English. The nearest English people come to such nationalism is during sporting events, mainly football and rugby. (Bizarrely, the 'English' cricket team is drawn from any part of the UK and has been captained by both a Welshman and a Scot in the past.)

Key term

Patriotism

This term is usually used to describe an exaggerated love and support for one's own state and the national culture. It is not a political phenomenon (although political leaders may use it for their own purposes, especially in times of armed conflict) and it does not have specific political aspirations. Nationalism, with which it is sometimes confused, does, on the other hand, have such objectives. A 'patriot' is one who loves his or her country and is willing to make sacrifices for it.

It is therefore useful to accept that there is such a thing as English patriotism (British patriotism is rarer and weaker), but there is effectively no significant degree of English nationalism. The defence of the culture, which goes hand in hand with opposition to European integration, refers to British, rather than English culture.

Nationalism and British conservatism

Traditionally, and certainly as far back as the leadership of Benjamin Disraeli in the 1870s, the British Conservative Party has been intensely nationalist in character. Furthermore, until the 1960s it was also linked to a strong sense of imperialism.

Conservative nationalism served three purposes. First, it encompassed a pride in, and support for, traditional institutions such as the monarchy and the Anglican Church. Second, it promoted a sense of national unity in a country where class distinctions have been traditionally significant and divisive. Third, the determination to retain the integrity of the UK was seen as vital to economic wellbeing.

The relationship between nationalism and the Conservative Party was highly successful. One of the main reasons why so many members of the working class consistently voted Conservative was a belief that the party was best equipped to protect the national interest and preserve UK's position in the world.

In the 1980s, however, the nationalist element of British conservatism changed character. The New Right, led by Margaret Thatcher, cared less for tradition and more for national interest. This manifested itself in opposition to European integration. As the 1980s progressed, conservative nationalism became xenophobic, campaigning increasingly for the retention of political independence in the face of European integration and globalisation. There was also a growing disquiet within the conservative movement about the effects on the British identity of large-scale immigration. The emergence of the UK Independence Party represents a culmination in the growth of this kind of defensive and isolationist nationalism.

Table 4.5 Summary of nationalism in the UK

Type	Political movement	Main characteristics and aspirations
Liberal nationalism	Scottish nationalists	Independence for Scotland
	Moderate Irish nationalism	Equal status in Northern Ireland for Protestants Possible future unity with the rest of Ireland
Cultural nationalism	Welsh nationalism (Plaid Cymru)	Greater political autonomy Defence of Welsh language and culture
	Ulster Unionism	Defence of the culture against Irish Catholic culture Some autonomy under the British Crown
Socialist nationalism	Radical Irish republicanism	Unity of Ireland Largely in the interests of the Irish working classes
Conservative nationalism	Conservative Party and UK Independence Party (UKIP)	Opposition to European integration Reduction in immigration Determination to maintain the territorial integrity of the UK Encouragement of patriotism
Right-wing nationalism	British National Party (BNP)	End of immigration and some repatriation of past immigrants Opposition to European Union Restoration of strong British industrial base

Exam focus

Using this chapter and other resources available to you, answer the following questions.

Short questions

Your answers should be about 300 words long.

1 Distinguish between a state and a nation.
2 Distinguish between racialism and nationalism.
3 Explain the concept of the nation-state.
4 What is meant by the term volkism?
5 Distinguish between liberal and conservative nationalism.

Your answers should be about 900 words long.

1 Is nationalism necessarily right-wing?
2 'Nationalism cannot be described as a single political ideology.' Explain and discuss.
3 In what senses is it a mistake to identify a single form of British nationalism?
4 'There is Scottish nationalism, Welsh nationalism, British nationalism and Irish nationalism, but no English nationalism.' Discuss.

Further reading

Alter, P. (1989) *Nationalism*, Hodder Arnold.

Guibernau i Berdun, M. Montserrat (1996) *Nationalisms*, Polity Press.

Hastings, A. (1997) *The Construction of Nationhood*, Cambridge University Press.

Hobsbawn, E. (1990) *Nations and Nationalism since 1780*, Cambridge University Press.

Kedourie, E. (1985) *Nationalism*, Hutchinson.

Smith, A. D. (2001) *Nationalism: Theory, Ideology, History*, Polity Press.

Chapter 5

Marxism

Marxism refers to a movement, or series of movements, which owe their existence and take their main beliefs from the work of Karl Marx. All Marxists share the same interpretation of history, the same way of analysing society, a similar critique of capitalism and propose revolutionary change to bring about a society where there will be both freedom and equality, where private property will cease to exist and, ultimately, where the state will become redundant.

Since Marx's death, there have been a number of different movements that have all claimed to be Marxist, but which have taken different paths towards the ideal society proposed by Marx. The Russian Bolsheviks, who created the first successful communist revolution, claimed to be the purest of Marxists, but there have been significant variations on Marxism, such as in China, independence movements in poor countries, South and Central America, and western European working-class and intellectual movements. The failure of so-called communist regimes and the victory of democratic capitalism in the Cold War led to a dramatic decline in the popularity and application of Marxist ideas, but they remain a major influence on socialism.

Introduction

There is a great deal of confusion concerning the relationship between Marxism, socialism and communism. This needs to be clarified before proceeding. The term 'communism' predates Marx himself by several decades. It was used by a variety of movements in the nineteenth and twentieth centuries to denote the revolutionary idea that society should be based on small communities; indeed, the term is derived from the French word *commune*, meaning a small village or community. In the middle of the nineteenth century, it was popularly used by both anarchists and socialists.

Marx himself used the term communism to describe the type of society he believed human civilisation was inevitably moving towards. For him this did not necessarily mean small communities, but rather a society in which there would be no state and all goods would be freely distributed among the population according to need. Marx and his followers are therefore often described as 'communists'. It is not necessary, however, to be a Marxist in order to be a communist: the countries that based themselves on Marx's teachings after 1917 are described as 'communist' too. This is somewhat misleading. None of these countries ever achieved communism, or anything like it. They were described as communist because they claimed to be moving towards communism.

Similarly, Marx is often described as a socialist, in particular a revolutionary socialist. This is accurate if socialism is considered to be a social system in which goods are distributed on an equal basis and in which the state organises this process. If there were no state, socialism would effectively be anarchism or communism. Marx argued that, after the anti-capitalist revolution, societies would and should adopt socialism as their system. This was to be an interim stage before communism could be achieved — in other words, before the state could safely 'wither away' without jeopardising equality. This principle was reflected in the names adopted by a number of Marxist-inspired states. Most famously, the USSR stood for the Union of Soviet *Socialist* Republics, implying that the country was in its interim phase and would move eventually to communism.

It is possible, therefore, to describe Marxism as either communism or socialism, or even both. To avoid confusion, however, it is probably best to describe all those forms of revolutionary socialism and communism which have claimed to follow Marx's teachings as Marxist.

Marxism is unique among the ideologies included in this book in that it takes its name from a single individual. Of course, there have been many individuals and movements which have adapted Marxism in various ways, but as long as they claim to base their ideas upon those of Marx, we can describe them as Marxist. In a way, this makes the study of Marxism fairly straightforward. If we know and understand the works of Marx, it could be argued, we understand Marxism, just as Muslims or Christians may describe their religions in terms of the teachings of Mohammed and Christ respectively. On the whole this is a fair statement. However, the variety of ways in which Marxism has been adapted, interpreted and applied must form part of the study of Marxism too.

The rise of socialism
As capitalism and industrialisation gathered pace in the first part of the nineteenth century, they brought with them a political movement which responded to the social evils and the conflicts they were beginning to cause. This was socialism. It took a number of

forms; some examples of early socialism were relatively mild and peaceful, notably the Chartist movement in Britain, which pressed for the regulation of wages and working hours, better conditions, more protection and, above all, votes for working people. Others were essentially 'ethical' or Christian, for example the beliefs of Henri de Saint-Simon in France and Robert Owen in Britain. Their brand of socialism did not make fundamental challenges to capitalism, but instead proposed more welfare and fair wages for workers, provided either by the state (Saint-Simon's theory) or by capitalists themselves (Owen's theory).

A third type of socialism to emerge was revolutionary in nature. These socialists believed that capitalism at that time was incapable of mere reform. It had to be abolished and replaced by a radically different economic and social arrangement. Capitalism itself was inevitably exploitative: it was impossible to maintain capitalism without exploitation. Karl Marx was part of this third tradition and became its leading exponent.

By 1848, when many regimes in Europe were threatened by nationalist, democratic or socialist revolutionary activity, socialism was reaching maturity as an ideology. Marx and his radical colleagues were convinced by the experience of 1848 (when most of the revolutionaries were crushed) that capitalism would have to be brought down by violent revolution, and that the working classes must unite to bring this about. Marx's battle cry in the *Communist Manifesto* of that year — 'Workers of the world unite! You have nothing to lose but your chains!' — was an acceptance that it was to be revolution or nothing.

Hegelian philosophy

Marx's theories were derived from those of Friedrich Hegel, whose work dominated European philosophy for much of the nineteenth century, especially in his native Germany. Hegel's ideas are extremely difficult and complex, but can be successfully distilled into some basic principles that influenced Marx.

The dialectic

Hegel did not see history as a series of unrelated events, but as a logical progression. Each historical age was a development from its predecessor. He deduced that historical progress occurred as the result of a process which can be described as *dialectic* in nature. Dialectic in this context literally means that a proposition is confronted by its own opposite, resulting in a new truth. Thus, each social circumstance will eventually evolve into another when it comes into conflict with its own opposite.

Consciousness and alienation

The dialectic can be explained in more concrete terms. At its height, an age displays a high degree of harmony in which the collective 'Mind' or consciousness of the people corresponds accurately with the reality of the world. People experience the world in an objective way and so do not feel *alienated*. Alienation occurs when people's perception of the world is generally different from the way the world actually is. When this state of affairs occurs, people feel alienated from the world they inhabit.

No age, however, remains in a state of harmony. As the world changes, collective consciousness evolves and moves away from the old perceptions, and therefore no longer corresponds with reality. This leads to alienation and social breakdown and conflict. An example of this is the height of Ancient Greek civilisation. This highly successful society began to break down when its great philosophers — Socrates (?470–399 BC), Plato (?427–?347 BC) and Aristotle (384–322 BC), for example — began to present new perceptions of the world that challenged existing consciousness. Such conflicts result in major social change and a new civilisation — a fresh collective consciousness — emerges. Thus, a new, higher form of harmony is born.

Destination of society

Crucially, Hegel believed that human society was moving towards a destination. This was a society in which there would be no alienation and where the dialectic process would finally end. It was a state of perfect 'Freedom' in which people would have the same *collective* consciousness of the world as every *individual's* consciousness. It was a collective form of freedom, rather than the individual liberty which liberals were concerned with at the time. This is a difficult concept which was shared by many conservatives and liberals during the nineteenth century. Put simply, it means that the will of each individual does not conflict with the collective will of all. Social conflict thus ends and nobody feels constricted by the rest of society.

Hegel eventually became controversial as a result of his assertion that the Prussian state of the early nineteenth century had achieved this ultimate Freedom. The combination of capitalism with a constitutional, limited monarchy and the imposition of the rule of law had for him created a state where there was indeed no social alienation.

Hegel's influence on Marx

Hegel's followers divided into 'right Hegelians', conservative nationalists who accepted Hegel's propositions at face value, and 'left Hegelians', who supported his general philosophy but argued with its ultimate conclusions. Marx was one of the 'left' Hegelians and a follower of the radical Ludwig Feuerbach (1804–72). Marx proposed two major modifications of Hegel's philosophy. First, the process of historical change took place within the real world of economics and economic relationships, rather than within human consciousness. Second, history has one further stage to reach. This final stage would be post-capitalist; private property and the state would be abolished, and humankind's freedom and personal creativity would be restored.

Those aspects of Hegel's philosophy which particularly influenced Marx, and indeed political philosophy in general, can be summarised as follows:

1 Although Marx made fundamental modifications to Hegel's ideas, he shared his belief that history moves forward in an objectively determined manner. In other words, history can be studied scientifically.

2 The concept of alienation was crucial to Marx. He applied this idea to the state of the working class under capitalism. Workers find that the division of labour, the wage system which exploits them, and the product of their own labour are all alien to them. The world which they inhabit confronts them in a hostile way. This creates the critical conflict within capitalism which ultimately will destroy it.

3 The social phenomenon of consciousness — described by Hegel as 'Mind' — plays a key role in Marx's philosophy. This describes a collective way of viewing the world. Marx often spoke of 'false consciousness', by which he meant a distorted view of the world that prevents social progress and promotes the domination by the ruling class. By contrast, consciousness can be positive if it is a true reflection of the world.

Marx the revolutionary

Marx began his political career as a student of German philosophy, along with his life-long friend and collaborator, Friedrich Engels. He chiefly engaged himself in three activities. He was a journalist and editor of left-wing newspapers, a writer on revolutionary philosophy and a participant in a variety of revolutionary movements throughout Europe. Indeed, the term 'revolutionary' was how Marx preferred to be described. Unsurprisingly, his activities drew him to the attention of the authorities and he spent a good deal of his adult life in exile. He lived in London, then a haven for a variety of political radicals from all over Europe, for the last 20 years or so of his life, and most of his important work was written there.

Karl Marx's revolutionary activities led to his exile

Illustrated London News

During the 1840s he became increasingly radical and convinced of the need for a working-class revolution. He was anxious that revolutionary movements were being diverted away from true socialist objectives, and became increasingly radical in his ideas. When revolutionary activity erupted in Europe in 1848, he and Engels rushed out the famous *Communist Manifesto*. This document revealed the truly radical nature of their beliefs. The manifesto urged the working class not to be limited in its aims, but to strike a decisive blow against capitalism and the ruling class which was maintaining it.

The 1848 revolutions were crushed and ultimately failed to advance socialist ideals significantly, so it became clear that a long-term campaign against capitalism was needed. Marx continued to encourage movements which he considered to be genuinely socialist and to warn against those which were making fatal compromises with capitalism. When the Paris Commune was established in 1870, on the whole along Marxist lines, he and Engels believed the communist revolution had finally arrived. When the Commune was crushed after only a brief existence, Marx was once again disappointed, admitting that he had underestimated capitalism's determination to survive.

When Marx died in 1883, his dreams and predictions of the final revolution were still to be realised. His words on his funeral monument in London reveal his attitude to his own political life:

> The philosophers have only interpreted the world in various ways; the point, however, is to change it.

In the event, it was for others to take up Marx's revolutionary banner. Marx knew that, despite all his scientific theories of history, and despite the apparent certainty of his prediction that capitalism was doomed, it was up to the revolutionary forces of the working class to usher in the new age of socialism and, finally, communism.

Core Marxist ideas

The dialectic and theory of history

Marx's theory of history is crucial to understanding his analysis of the future demise of capitalism. Marx saw history as moving in a specific direction and he shared Hegel's view that the progress of history was characterised by regular processes. However, Marx rooted his historical theory in the real world of economics, rather than the world of ideas, as Hegel had done. His theory of history is often described as *dialectic materialism*, based on *economic determinism*.

Marx analysed every age in terms of its dominant economic relations. All other aspects of society — religion, philosophy, ideology, culture and politics — are merely reflections of economic realities. The nature of economic relations is determined by how the means of production are owned, who owns them, how people are employed and what their relationship is to the means of production. For example, under the feudal system, land was owned by the monarch and was leased to a hierarchy of nobles, feudal lords, tenants, subtenants and, finally, serfs. The relationships between these different levels of feudal society determined the political system of monarchy and aristocracy, and were underpinned by Roman Catholicism. The Roman Church was also organised on hierarchical lines and its teachings emphasised authority, obedience and acceptance of one's position in life, however lowly. 'Blessed are the poor' and 'blessed are the meek', Christ had preached.

Under capitalism, the dominant economic relationship is between the capitalists themselves, who own all the means of production, and the proletariat (workers), who exchange their labour for money wages and who own none of the means of production. This relationship gives rise to a corresponding political system (representative democracy), religious tradition (Protestantism) and dominant ideology (based on liberalism).

Whereas Hegel observed that each age begins to change as new ideas challenge the dominant collective consciousness, Marx believed that the dialectic process occurs within the key economic relationships. Marx asserted that in every age there is an exploited class and that the nature of this exploitation always tends to intensify. Under capitalism, therefore, the working class is exploited by the economic system. As the capitalist system developed (faster than any previous system, Marx noted), the exploitation of the working class would grow more marked. This would inevitably lead to conflict, which would eventually bring down the whole structure.

Marx argued that every age progresses in the same fundamental manner. It followed, then, that capitalism would go the way of all past ages. It would create the seeds of its own destruction — an exploited, and therefore revolutionary, working class. As occurred in all other ages, the process would usher in a new age, a new harmony and, eventually, a new dialectic conflict. However, Marx believed that the age that succeeded capitalism would signal the end of historical change and the victory of socialism and communism. The communist age, he confidently claimed, would be like no other, since it would not contain any of the destructive forces (*contradictions*, as he usually described them) which had characterised all other epochs.

Social class

Marx had a specific understanding of the nature of social class and class structure. Contemporary sociologists have defined class largely in terms of occupation, lifestyle and, to a lesser extent, income. For Marx, however, class was defined in terms of a group's relationship to the means of production. For example, a peasant paid rent to a landlord, but did not own the land. These two facts defined the peasant's relationship to the land and therefore his social class. Indeed, the entire class system under feudalism could be understood in terms of land tenure.

Under capitalism, the **bourgeoisie** and the **proletariat** were the two key social classes. The bourgeoisie was the class which owned the means of production. The proletariat, Marx's term for the industrial working class, owned none of the means of production. Although there were other classes in nineteenth-century industrial society, notably the petite bourgeoisie of independent craftsmen, shopkeepers and professionals, *rentiers* (landlords) and peasants, the fundamental relationship was between bourgeoisie and proletariat.

Key terms

Bourgeoisie and proletariat

Marx defined class in terms of the economic position which people held in the structure of economic relations. It was not a distinction of income, lifestyle or even occupation. Classes were defined in terms of their relationship to the means of production. The bourgeoisie was a small class which owned all the means of production — factories, workshops, mines, etc. This class also included their 'servants', such as professionals, managers and government officials. Those who did not own the means of production and were forced to sell their labour for money wages were the proletariat. The proletariat only included industrial workers; peasants, who worked on the land, were considered to be individuals rather than a cohesive social group. As capitalism developed, Marx argued, virtually everybody would be sucked into one of these two classes, bourgeoisie or proletariat — a process known as class polarisation.

For Marx, every society could only be accurately understood by reference to its class system. He identified a number of characteristics common to class systems throughout history: there is always a major ruling class and a major exploited class, there is an insoluble conflict between the interests of the two great classes, and ultimately the exploited class will understand its true position and will attempt to overthrow the ruling class. He summarised this theory in the *Communist Manifesto*: 'The history of all hitherto existing societies is the history of class struggle.'

For Marx, a further crucial aspect of class was the concept of *class consciousness*. Classes are not revolutionary, Marx argued, until they become self-conscious. This entails two developments. First, its members understand that they are part of the same class with the same class interest. This creates the possibility of class solidarity and therefore collective action. Second, in its mature stage, a class comes to understand where its true interests lie. For the exploited class, this consists of the complete overthrow of the existing order. At this point, a class — or at least a part of it, comprised of its leading, most conscious members — becomes revolutionary. The process is reinforced by the fact that *class polarisation* also occurs. This is a process whereby the minor classes in a society become sucked into the two great classes. Most members of the peasantry and petite bourgeoisie, Marx confidently predicted, would therefore be forced to become members of the great industrial army of the proletariat.

The reason the proletariat could not recognise its own interests Marx admitted, was that the ruling class controls the dominant ideology in every age. This ideology tends to distort reality and prevents the exploited class becoming conscious of its true position and its true interests. Only the experience of intensified exploitation creates class consciousness — with help from philosophers such as Marx, of course.

After revolution, at every stage of history, the new age sees the fortunes of the classes reversed. The exploited class becomes the ruling class and oppresses the former ruling class. Only when the process of revolutionary change is complete can a new age emerge, with a new set of productive relations and a new class system. Crucially, however, the proletarian revolution will be the last. The reason why this dialectic process of history will end is that post-capitalist society will be classless in nature. The imposition of collective ownership of the means of production, together with the equal distribution of income and wealth, will end class-based society. Society will therefore be classless. This is because if everyone has the same relationship to the means of production, there are no class distinctions — effectively, society will contain only one class. Thus, there will be no class conflict (see Box 5.1).

Box 5.1 The end of class conflict

Capitalism is characterised by Marx in terms of class conflict. However, Marx predicted that, as revolution neared, the class system would begin to break up. He described this process in the *Communist Manifesto* of 1848:

Finally, in times when the class struggle nears the decisive hour, the process of dissolution going on within the ruling class, in fact within the whole range of old society, assumes such a violent, glaring character, that a small section of ruling class cuts itself adrift, and joins the revolutionary class, the class that holds the future in its hands.

Box 5.2 summarises Marx's position on class, specifically in relation to the development of capitalism.

Box 5.2 Class in the capitalist age

The class structure of capitalism is determined by the productive relations of the system.

∀

The key relationship is that between bourgeoisie and proletariat.

∀

As exploitation intensifies, leading members of the proletariat become more class conscious.

∀

Class polarisation occurs, increasing the size of the exploited proletariat.

∀

Social conflict intensifies as class consciousness grows.

∀

The proletariat overthrows capitalism and the rule of the bourgeoisie.

∀

There is an interim period, known as the dictatorship of the proletariat, in which socialism is built.

∀

Ultimately, a classless society will emerge — the end of the dialectic process of history.

The role of the state

As with class, Marx insisted that the nature of a political state cannot be understood except in terms of the system of productive relations and the class structure of the age. In other words, states have always been mere reflections of economic power. He sometimes referred to the state as the 'management committee of the ruling class'. Its role was always to underpin the dominant position of the ruling class, to oppress all those who might challenge the existing order and to control the dominant ideology which seeks to disguise the true nature of productive relations, thereby distorting conscious-ness and preventing class conflict.

This view is relatively easy to accept when analysing feudal society for example. The monarchy and aristocracy formed the state and few would argue that these elements also controlled the means of production — land. Under capitalism, the position became more complex, especially as representative democracy started to emerge in Marx's lifetime. The advent of elections and the spread of voting rights called into question the idea that the bourgeoisie controlled the state. Marx had two main answers to this. First, he argued that the political power of elected bodies — e.g. parliaments — is illusory. True political power lies with the permanent apparatus of the state — the bureaucracy, legal system, forces of security and law and order, and so on. Second, the political parties which were fighting out elections were not revolutionary in nature. By supporting or compromising with capitalism, the political parties were also agents of the ruling class, whether consciously or unconsciously. Offering a choice between parties at elections appears to place the state into the hands of the electorate, but this is only an illusion of choice (a common complaint in the UK to this day). For Marx, only revolutionary parties were independent of the ruling class and the state and therefore capable of challenging the existing order.

Marx and his followers accepted the need to retain the state after revolution. It would remain the agent of the ruling class, but the new ruling class would, of course, be the proletariat. Its role would be to suppress capitalism, preventing any chance of its re-emergence. At the same time, this dictatorship of the proletariat would be building socialism. Once a truly classless society had been established, the role of the political state would cease to exist and it would, in Marx's famous expression, 'wither away'.

The nature of capitalism

Marx spent much of his political life observing and describing the true nature of capitalism. For him, it was different from all past systems of productive relations. It was more dynamic and more exploitative than any system that had gone before (see Box 5.3). The reasons Marx gave for the rapid success and growth of capitalism mark him out as a great economist as well as a philosopher and revolutionary. It is not necessary to be a radical socialist to accept his analysis of nineteenth-century capitalism. The key aspects which he identified were as follows:

> It was a system based upon individual self-interest. This was a powerful force and gave capitalism its drive. Marx was a student of the liberal economists of the late eighteenth and early nineteenth centuries, notably Adam Smith, David Ricardo and John Stuart Mill. They recognised that capitalism was based on the free interaction of producers and workers, sellers and buyers. As all these agents operated in their own interests, there was a natural drive towards both efficiency and growth. Marx agreed with their conclusions, although, of course, he did not accept their assertions that capitalism could operate to the benefit of all.

➢ Capitalism was based on the use of capital — the energy systems, plants, machinery and technology which gave industry its productive potential. Unlike land, capital could be constantly increased and improved.

➢ Capitalism combined this capital with labour power in a unique way. First, it reduced labour to the same status as capital. It dehumanised workers, turning them into objects whose productive output could be purchased for money. Second, it drained human labour of its creativity, forcing workers to undertake mechanical, repetitive work, just as machines did. Indeed, labour became dependent on machines rather than the other way round.

➢ Most importantly, capitalism extracted what Marx called *surplus value* from workers. In short, this meant that workers were paid only a fraction of the value of what they produced. No matter how productive labour was, it would be paid only subsistence (i.e. minimum) wages. Thus, as capitalist enterprises become more efficient and productive, the amount of surplus value would simply mount up. The surplus value, controlled by the capitalist owners, would be ploughed back into the creation of more capital, which would in turn become more productive and extract yet more surplus value.

Clearly this is no longer an accurate description of capitalism in the economically developed world (although socialists argue that some of the essential elements are still present). However, many might still claim this to be an image of capitalist production in less economically developed countries.

Box 5.3 The exploitation of labour

This is Marx's description of how human labour is exploited under capitalism. It is taken from an article in the *Reinische Zeitung*, written in 1849:

> The labourer receives means of subsistence in exchange for his labour-power; but the capitalist receives in exchange for his means of subsistence, labour, the productive activity of the worker, the creative force by which the worker not only replaces what he consumes, but also gives to the accumulated labour a greater value than it previously possessed... But it is just this noble reproductive power that the worker surrenders to the capitalist in exchange for means of subsistence received. Consequently he has lost it for himself.

The development of capitalism

Marx was relatively specific about how he believed capitalism would develop from the middle of the nineteenth century and this analysis formed the basis of his theories. Marx undoubtedly provides the first example of political philosophy and sociology being based upon such empirical research.

At its height, Marx saw capitalism as the most dynamic economic system that had ever existed. The secret of the system's success was its use of **surplus value**. Capitalism produces enormous amounts of surplus value, i.e. resources which are generated well above what is needed to meet the basic needs of the community. Historically, economic systems had failed to produce such surpluses and so their development had been extremely slow. Capitalism was able to reinvest surplus value into the creation of more and more capital. This was the reason for both the quantity of capital — e.g. machines, buildings, transport, mines — and its quality — e.g. new technology.

Key term

Surplus value

We might simply describe this concept as 'profit', but Marx preferred not to use that expression. He saw surplus value as the portion of workers' *time* at work which was taken over by the capitalist. To describe this surplus as profit reduced it merely to money; instead, Marx saw it as labour being 'stolen'. Workers are paid considerably less than the value of the hours they work, so that some of the working day does not belong to them and the value of their product is then used by capitalism to exploit those same workers. This occurs when workers are so poorly paid that they cannot afford to purchase what they produce. Furthermore, for Marx labour represents an individual's 'life essence'. If it is converted into mere surplus value for capitalism, an individual is robbed of much of that essence.

The problem for capitalism, Marx asserted, was how it used its own rapid development. Naturally, profit would be reinvested to make the system more productive. This might be acceptable if the additional wealth created were to be distributed throughout the population, but capitalism, Marx observed, succeeded in keeping wages at 'subsistence level': in other words, just enough to maintain life. It did this by creating a system in which workers were forced to compete with each other for scarce employment. If wages rose, capitalists would lay off workers, thus creating unemployment and weakening the workers' bargaining power. Workers therefore accept lower wages in return for work. At the same time, an army of unemployed, semi-employed and seasonally employed labour (including women, a subject later taken up by socialist-feminists) would be retained to create competition in the workforce.

Thus, capitalism generated increasing amounts of wealth but did not use it to improve the conditions of the working class; instead, the working class was kept in a state of poverty. At first, capitalism's insatiable appetite for new workers was met by draining the population from the countryside and recruiting women and children. Hoards of workers migrated into the growing industrial towns and cities, creating squalor, deprivation, disease and extensive social problems. The gap between the living standards of the bourgeoisie and the proletariat steadily widened and increasing numbers of formerly independent tradespeople and agricultural workers were sucked into the ranks of the unskilled and semi-skilled working class.

Initially, this growing inequality would not create a problem for capitalists, but problems would emerge later. Since capitalism avoided paying workers more than the means of their own subsistence, as the system became increasingly productive capitalists would experience difficulty in finding markets for their own products. The bourgeoisie itself could not continue to consume all the surplus product, so there would be periods of overproduction. Workers would be laid off and economic slumps would result. Wages would then fall and some workers would be re-employed, ending the slump, but another economic crisis would always be just round the corner. These fluctuations, Marx predicted, would become increasingly dramatic and destabilising.

The next stage in the development of capitalism would be rivalry between capitalist nations as they competed for scarce world markets. The scramble for colonial possessions among developed countries in the second part of the nineteenth century was part of this process. Imperial competition would result in armed conflict, and Marx certainly saw the 1870–71 Franco–Prussian war in these terms. Although the First World War took place long after Marx's death, he would have analysed the conflict as being between advanced capitalist nations essentially fighting for economic dominance over ever scarcer markets.

At the same time as this international rivalry, conflict between the classes would intensify. The exploitation of the proletariat would become greater and more apparent. Workers, who were increasingly affected by urban deprivation, slumps and depressed wages, would develop class consciousness. At the centre of such consciousness would lie **alienation** — an increasing dislocation between the workers' view of the world and the reality of that world. As a result, trade unions would be formed and these would become increasingly militant. Strikes, demonstrations and even revolutionary activity would follow. Indeed, the wave of revolutions that swept Europe in 1848, and which encouraged Marx and Engels to publish the *Communist Manifesto*, were interpreted as manifestations of growing working-class consciousness.

Key term

Alienation

The full explanation of Marx's analysis of alienation (which he derived largely from Hegel's philosophy) is exceedingly complex. However, it can be considered in simpler terms in relation to the late stages of capitalism. Workers, Marx argued, become alienated in three main ways. First, they are separated from their own labour by the fact that they are forced to sell that labour for money wages. Second, their own workplace is physically alien to them; they become mere accessories to machinery and the production process. Third, the product of their labour, their output, has little or nothing to do with that labour. They do not see their output as a whole — it is often a small part of the production process, owing to the division of labour — nor can they buy most of the objects they help to make.

Marx was convinced capitalism would ultimately collapse, brought down by revolutionary activity. The intensification of the exploitation of the working class made it inevitable that it would become a revolutionary class. This is how Marx described the end of capitalism:

The antagonism between the proletariat and the bourgeoisie is a class struggle, whose most complete expression is complete revolution. It is astonishing, moreover, that a society founded on the opposition of classes should end in a brutal contradiction, in a hand-to-hand struggle, as its last act.

From *The Poverty of Philosophy*, 1847

Marx's description of how he saw capitalism developing and in the end collapsing can be summarised as follows:

1 Capitalism develops and becomes highly productive.
2 The surpluses being generated are reinvested to make capitalism even more productive.
3 The working class grows in size and class polarisation occurs.
4 Capitalism begins to overproduce and economic slumps become regular.
5 Inequality, alienation and socialist consciousness grow among the working class.
6 Rivalry between capitalist countries intensifies resulting in wars and imperial competition.
7 The class consciousness among the proletariat grows and becomes revolutionary, at which point the working class brings capitalism to an end.

Revolution

The most controversial element of Marx's philosophy was his apparent prediction that capitalism would *inevitably* be brought down by a violent revolution. Furthermore, this would occur in those countries where capitalism was at its most advanced stage. This is controversial for two main reasons. The first is that the earliest (some argue the only) Marxist revolution occurred in Russia, which was certainly not an advanced capitalist country. Second, revolutions did not occur in advanced capitalist countries such as Britain, Germany and France. If this element of Marx's analysis was wrong, it is argued, his whole theory must be flawed.

The idea that historical change is created largely by the actions of social revolutionaries is known as **voluntarism**, whereas those who suggest that historical forces are outside our control are usually known as **determinists**.

Key terms

Voluntarism and determinism

These two terms represent alternative analyses of historical development. Voluntarism suggests that people make history and that historical change is not inevitable, but the result of social movements created by people. Determinism suggests that we are slaves to the forces of history, which are out of our control. Major historical changes, therefore, are inevitable. Although most analysts argue that Marx was a determinist, it is more likely that he was a mixture of the two. In other words, he believed that the conditions for change will inevitably arise, but it is up to the actions of men to turn those conditions into tangible reality.

Marx found evidence for the inevitability of revolution in a number of observations. Most importantly he observed that every age — i.e. every historical economic system — had contained the seeds of its own destruction, which would grow, create conflict and ultimately destroy the very system which had spawned them. Capitalism was no exception to this law of historical materialism. Marx saw revolution as the inevitable result of the progress of capitalism. Because capitalism was the most developed of all systems in history, it would produce the most exploited and therefore the most revolutionary class in history. Finally, Marx claimed that this final revolution would be underpinned by the influence of philosophers (like himself) who would break away from the ruling class — their natural home — and join the socialist movement.

Furthermore, argued Marx, the revolution would probably be violent. The capitalist state was founded upon violence and it would defend itself with violence. Only in Britain, he suggested, might there be a peaceful, democratic transition to socialism. This was because Britain had the most genuinely open democratic system, which might allow for representation of the working class. In this respect, Marx found himself in agreement with the Fabian Society, which was founded in 1884, a year after Marx's death.

Why then did revolution not occur as Marx apparently predicted? There have been a number of explanations. These are outlined in Box 5.4.

Box 5.4 Why was there no Marxist revolution?

➤ The principal explanation is that Marx's whole analysis was flawed. There are no fixed laws of historical development and therefore no inevitable end to the capitalist era. The twentieth-century conservative philosopher Karl Popper was a leading exponent of this view.

➤ The Frankfurt School of Marxists, which flourished between the world wars, accepted that socialist revolution would not occur. They believed that capitalism would survive, although some of them, such as Herbert Marcuse (1898–1979), argued that the new exploited class was made up of manipulated consumers rather than alienated workers.

➤ The Italian communist Antonio Gramsci (1891–1937) argued that capitalism came to understand its own inherent weaknesses and was therefore able to control its own development. It introduced welfare systems and popular democracy, and permitted the formation of free trade unions to prevent the development of revolutionary socialism.

➤ A plausible analysis suggests Marx was right in that the conditions for revolution did indeed come about much as he had described, but the working class simply failed to topple capitalism, which was more entrenched than expected. After the First World War, there were certainly a number of attempted revolutions, for example, in Germany, Hungary and Italy, as well as in Russia. However, in every case except Russia the revolutions were put down.

➤ Accepting that revolution will not occur in developed economies, some modern Marxists, such as Frantz Fanon (1925–61), have transferred Marxist analysis to a global scale. They suggest that peasants and workers in less economically developed countries are the current exploited class and that the capitalist world as a whole is their exploiter. The conditions for revolution will arise, but only in such countries.

It must be remembered, however, that there *was* a revolution — that which occurred in Russia in 1917. The Bolsheviks, who led the revolution, followed Marxist analysis closely. It is therefore important to examine how Marx saw the development of society after the revolution.

The dictatorship of the proletariat

Marx did not suggest that society could move directly from revolution to communism. There would, he insisted, need to be a transition period known as the socialist phase or, more commonly, the *dictatorship of the proletariat*.

The dictatorship of the proletariat occurs as the product of historical progress. In every age, Marx argued, there will be a ruling class which will control the state and oppress other classes. Once the bourgeoisie has been toppled, therefore, only the proletariat can play the role of the ruling class. This interim phase has a key role to play in the creation of a communist society. Although leading members of the proletariat (the so-called *vanguard*) might be ready to move towards the purest form of socialism — communism — most of the new society would not. There would therefore have to be a period of preparation, carried out by the dictatorship of the proletariat. This would include the following:

➤ All private property would be abolished.
➤ In its place the state would take over control of all the means of production and distribution.
➤ Rewards would be distributed on the basis of 'from each according to his ability, to each according to his contribution'.
➤ There would be no capitalist forms of enterprise, although the state would offer limited incentives to boost production.
➤ Information would be controlled by the state to prevent the possibility that bourgeois modes of thought might be restored.
➤ Individuals attempting to recreate capitalist enterprise or propagate bourgeois modes of thought would be suppressed.
➤ Consistent attempts would be made by the state to raise the consciousness of the people to pure socialism.
➤ Although the usual liberal concept of freedom and democracy would be absent, the creation of social equality would effectively liberate the people.
➤ Ultimately, a classless society would be built, the necessary condition for the end of the socialist state.

Marx gives us few clues as to how long the dictatorship of the proletariat would last. He simply asserted that it would be over when the last remnants of capitalism and bourgeois consciousness had disappeared.

In Russia, under the leadership of Vladimir Lenin and Joseph Stalin (1879–1953), the essential features of the dictatorship of the proletariat were put in place. Arguably the 'dictatorship' element was carried to extremes, and certainly the charges that a new ruling class of party bureaucrats replaced the bourgeoisie can be justified. However, it has to be said that Stalin recognised that the oppressive state could not be dismantled as long as the Soviet Union was surrounded by a hostile capitalist world (something for which Marx had not allowed, since he assumed revolution would spread rapidly). Whatever an accurate analysis of the Soviet dictatorship may be, Marx described the circumstances under which it would be replaced by the final stage of history.

The withering away of the state and communism

According to Marx, the state is an instrument of class rule. If, therefore, a classless society is created under socialism, there would no longer be any need for the state. Having completed its task of building socialism and preventing capitalism from restoring itself, the institutions of the state would simply cease to function. Marx used the term 'withering away' to suggest that the state would simply have no more functions, rather than a conscious process of abolition. The transition to communism would therefore be far from instant. Indeed, in some of his writings Marx suggests a two-stage movement. In the first phase each worker would receive rewards according to the differential value of his or her contribution. This recognises that workers have unequal powers and skills, and so receive unequal rewards. In the second, or 'higher', phase, the inequalities between contributions would no longer be recognised and every individual would receive rewards according to need, not contribution (see Box 5.5). This implies complete equality.

> ### Box 5.5 The final transition to communism
>
> In the 1875 *Critique of the Gotha Programme*, a rejection of the anarchist experiments then taking place on the Swiss–French border, Marx presented this colourful description of the transition to communism:
>
>> In the higher phase of communist society, when the enslaving subordination of the individual to division of labour, and with it the antithesis between mental and physical labour, has vanished; when labour is no longer merely a means of life but has become life's principal need; when the productive forces have also increased with the all-round development of the individual, and all the springs of co-operative wealth flow more abundantly – only then will it be possible completely to transcend the narrow outlook of bourgeois right and only then will society be able to inscribe on its banners: From each according to his ability, to each according to his needs!

It is possible to piece together how Marx envisaged communist society from elsewhere in his writings. It would be a period of total equality, but other features would also be important, including the following:

➤ It would be a time of plenty. Presumably this was necessary to avoid competition for scarce resources.

➤ There would be no money as labour and goods would never be exchanged.

➤ All production would be placed into a central pool.

- Individuals would draw goods and services from the central pool according to need alone.
- The division of labour would be abolished. Labour would be unspecialised and each individual would freely choose what kind of work he or she would undertake.
- The creative aspect of work would be restored.
- There might be some organisational bodies, but the political state would not exist.
- There would be no laws since social consciousness would prevent the possibility of any deviant behaviour.

This vision, close to the ideas of anarchists such as Peter Kropotkin (1842–1921) and Mikhail Bakunin (1814–76), has been denounced as a utopian dream. Its critics argue that it implies a hopelessly over-optimistic view of human nature and is simply impracticable.

Marxism in practice

The Russian Revolution

Marx insisted that revolution would only occur in advanced capitalist countries. The Russia of 1917 certainly did not fit this description. It was largely agricultural and only a small proportion of the population were industrial workers and could therefore be described as the 'proletariat'. Yet Lenin, who led the Bolshevik Party which created the revolution, claimed that Russia could conform to classic Marxist ideology.

Lenin's theory of the late imperialist phase of capitalism suggested that the richer and more developed capitalist states would exploit less economically developed countries. Russia was one of the potentially exploited countries. The revolution could, therefore, emancipate the country before it became exploited. Furthermore, Russia contained two exploited classes — the growing proletariat and the peasantry. An alliance of these two classes could build a revolutionary force and begin to construct socialism within the context of a modified dictatorship of the proletariat.

Lenin's main opponents within the Marxist movement were the Mensheviks. They proposed that communists should cooperate with democratic parties to bring about a democratic bourgeois state. This would assist in the development of the economy and then build socialism within the growing proletariat. In

Vladimir Ilyich Lenin harangues Russia's embryonic proletariat

other words, they wished to remain faithful to Marx's original analysis of historical development. Lenin, however, was adamant that Russia was in danger of falling into capitalism, from which it might not emerge. He therefore proposed a pre-emptive strike. There was, effectively, chaos in Russia in 1917, as a result of the effects of war, economic crisis and growing unrest among the working class. This led to the overthrow of the tsar in February of that year. If the Bolsheviks seized the moment, they would be able to control the future development of the country.

Lenin's success in first overthrowing the embryonic democratic state, and then bringing post-revolutionary government under Bolshevik control, led, however, to a crisis. Who was to run the new state? The industrial proletariat was clearly not prepared to take over this huge country. At the same time, the Russian economy was in tatters. Soon the euphoria of revolution and the redistribution of property to the state and the people began to wear off. Before he had time to build a socialist state along Marxist lines, Lenin grew ill, and died in 1924. It was left to Stalin to construct the Soviet Union.

The Soviet Union and Eastern Europe

Lenin and Stalin set about constructing the dictatorship of the proletariat along the lines of Marx's theories. However, they faced two major problems. The first was that the industrial proletariat was underdeveloped and the majority of the population were peasants largely demanding their own land. Second, the country was surrounded by hostile capitalist powers.

Stalin dealt with the problem of the peasantry by turning them into industrial workers. The peasants were not granted their own land. Instead, farms were amalgamated and turned into collectives, with the peasants becoming wage earners — effectively, members of the classic proletariat. Stalin addressed the problem of the hostile capitalist world by cutting off the Soviet Union and instituting an oppressive regime in which information was controlled by the state. The people were subjected to constant socialist propaganda, were unable to travel and were told nothing about the capitalist world, except criticisms.

Stalin claimed to be building socialism from the bottom, completely recreating society along socialist lines. There had to be a repressive regime in order to achieve this, since he constantly feared attempts by the capitalist world to subvert his revolution. The Soviet Union was to be a model of how socialism could be created. When Stalin was able to extend the hegemony of the USSR into Eastern Europe after the Second World War, this model was exported to countries such as Poland, Hungary, Czechoslovakia, East Germany, Romania and Bulgaria.

The great Soviet experiment failed. It was unable to deliver economic prosperity, it could not deal with the implacable hostility of the capitalist world and the people tired of being subjected to a new ruling class — the party bureaucracy and the security services. Instead of creating a classless society, the Soviet leaders and their allies had merely replaced one class structure with another.

China

Following a prolonged civil war, the Communist Party of China, led by Mao Tse-tung (also written as 'Mao Zedong') (1893–1976), seized power in 1949. This was an even more unorthodox revolution than that in Russia. China was an almost completely agricultural society, with little industry and no history of socialist activity. It is true that the Chinese peasantry were ready for revolution, but this was in the hope of throwing off the exploitation of landlords and warlords rather than of creating a socialist state.

Like Lenin, therefore, Mao had to modify Marxist theory. This meant creating a socialist state among the peasantry. As in the Soviet Union, the farms were turned into collectives and production was controlled by the ruling Communist Party. Unlike the USSR however, Mao, attempted to avoid the formation of a ruling

The Cultural Revolution of Mao Tse-tung disrupted progress towards true socialism

class, in the form of a powerful bureaucracy, by encouraging the people — i.e. the peasants — to challenge authority and to ensure that the party and its officials remained accountable to them. In this way, he hoped to create a purer form of popular socialism. For about three years from 1966 he instituted the *Cultural Revolution* — a continuous process by which all figures of authority were challenged by the people. Millions of officials, teachers, intellectuals, magistrates and managers were either killed or forced to work as lowly peasants to teach them humility.

However, this 'continuous revolution', proved to be excessively disruptive. It ensured economic equality and granted considerable power to the people, in contrast to the Soviet Union, but ultimately it failed. Once again, an attempt to adapt classical Marxist theory to particular circumstances had been unsuccessful. Following Mao's death, the regime began to introduce limited free markets, and more recently the country has begun to move rapidly towards full-scale capitalism. All that remains of the old communist regime is the one-party state and its prevention of any form of political opposition.

The Frankfurt School and critical theory

A group of Marxist philosophers who were concentrated in Frankfurt in the 1920s and 1930s, sought to explain why Marx's predictions of the final demise of capitalism had not materialised. The group was led by Theodore Adorno (1903–69), Max Horkheimer (1895–1973) and Herbert Marcuse. They developed the term 'critical theory', which they used to refer to a new form of philosophy that had moved away from Marx's traditional methods and was heavily influenced by the ideas of Sigmund Freud (1856–1939), the father of psychoanalysis. They also broadened the analysis of capitalism to include the idea of 'cultural hegemony'. This suggested that capitalism does not merely exploit workers in an economic fashion, but subverts the whole culture. It controls consciousness and all the instruments that control consciousness, such as consumption patterns, education, the arts and the media.

When fascism emerged in Europe, the Frankfurt School explained it as a distorted version of capitalism. It was, in other words, a stage of capitalism which had not been identified by Marx or Lenin. Fascism was for them the political representation of the monopoly power of capitalism. Just as capitalist enterprises had grown in size and power, coming to dominate whole markets, so fascism monopolised the political system for itself. The all-powerful state became the agent of all-powerful capitalism. This is how Marcuse expressed this idea, much later:

> The turn from the liberalist to the total authoritarian state occurs within the framework of the single social order. With regard to the unity of this economic base, we can say it is liberalism that produces the total, total-authoritarian state out of itself, as its own consummation at a more advanced stage of development.
>
> From *Negations*, 1968

In simpler terms, Marcuse claimed that totalitarianism is the inevitable outcome of the development of liberal society. Just as the Fabians argued that capitalism would inevitably develop into socialism, Marcuse asserted that liberalism would become totalitarianism in the modern age. He did not mean the traditional form of totalitarianism, such as the fascist case, but the complete control of the economy, culture and consumerism by monopoly capitalism and its agents.

Having become convinced that fascism and its struggle against liberal democracy marked the final crisis of capitalism, the Frankfurt School was dismayed that capitalism did not collapse after the Second World War, but instead emerged greatly strengthened. The school therefore disbanded and most of its members renounced Marxism. Only Marcuse remained convinced that their analysis was valid. Their influence did, however, extend into the 1960s and became a major factor in the militant New Left movements, which included radical feminism, anti-racism, consumerism and environmentalism.

Contemporary Marxism

Orthodox Marxism is now all but dead. Pockets of the faithful remain in the former Soviet Union and its ex-satellite states in Eastern Europe. Communist parties still exist in most democratic countries but they are small and have become completely marginalised. The end of the Cold War in 1990 and the apparent victory of liberal democracy and capitalism signalled the death knell of orthodox Marxism.

Some former communist regimes remain, but these have become distortions of their original Marxist forms. North Korea, for example, is little more than a dictatorship in which the state controls the economy, but there appears to be no movement toward a genuinely socialist system. The same is true of a number of former Marxist movements in Africa.

In a few countries where there is exploitation of the peasantry, Marxist guerrilla groups still seek revolution in the hope of liberating this exploited class and creating communism in the countryside. Nepal and Columbia, for example, are considerably troubled by their activities. Less economically developed countries were fertile ground for Marxism in the 1960s and 1970s, and these guerilla movements are their legacy. However, the influence of globalisation and the power of international organisations (for example, the World Trade Organisation and the International Monetary Fund) have persuaded these countries that industrialisation and the creation of free-market economies are the answer to their ills, rather than Marxist-inspired socialism.

We do not study Marxism today in the expectation that politics will be seriously affected by it in the future, but because it provides us with insights into how capitalism developed and how it was indeed able to save itself from the fate which Marx predicted for it. In a sense, therefore, it stands as a warning to current generations of what could happen if we fail to maintain careful controls over the development of capitalism.

Key Marxist leaders

Vladimir Ilyich Lenin (Russian, 1870–1924)

Originally named Ulyanov, Lenin changed his name as part of his attempts to escape the attentions of the Russian state, which saw him as a dangerous enemy. He engaged in revolutionary activity in the late nineteenth century, largely among the peasants, but then became an orthodox Marxist and turned his attention to the industrial proletariat. He spent the first part of the twentieth century agitating among the workers, writing a prolific quantity of books and pamphlets and escaping the attentions of the authorities. He eventually had to flee Russia, spending much of his time in exile.

When the first Russian Revolution occurred in February 1917, Lenin was in exile in Switzerland. However, aided by the Germans (he was campaigning for peace, so it suited the Germans to have him creating trouble in Russia), he returned from exile. Once back in Russia, he took leadership of a new party, the militant wing of the social democratic movement, known as the Bolsheviks. He persuaded the movement to take the opportunity of chaos in Russia to promote a socialist revolution. He and the Bolsheviks seized power in October 1917, having won the support of much of the disaffected army and working class.

Once in power, Lenin set about creating a workers' state, led by his party. He fought a civil war against the counter-revolutionary 'Whites' and finally claimed full control of the country in 1921. He then turned his attention to his political opponents and established the complete authority of the Communist Party (the new title of the Bolsheviks) by 1922. Lenin fell ill in that year and died two years later without leaving any clear heir.

Lenin claimed to be an orthodox Marxist, but he certainly amended Marx's theories considerably, adapting them to the circumstances of Russia and the state of European capitalism in the early twentieth century. The synthesis of Marxist and Leninist thought was known as *Marxist-Leninism* and became the ruling ideology of the Soviet Union, its satellite states in Eastern Europe and even of China after 1949. Lenin's contribution to Marxist theory is described below.

History and the revolution

Orthodox Marxist theory stated that revolution would only occur in advanced capitalist societies. Lenin, however, was anxious to create revolution in Russia, where the system would still be described, in Marxist terms, as merely 'primitive capitalism'. How could he justify this?

The basis of Lenin's ideas was a phase of capitalism which he simply called *imperialism*. In this late stage of capitalism, the advanced countries would begin to exploit the economically undeveloped countries in an imperialist fashion. Russia would be plundered for its cheap natural resources and labour, just as colonies further away had been for some time. Lenin described the process thus:

> The more capitalism is developed, the more strongly the shortage of raw materials is felt, the more intense the competition and hunt for sources of raw materials throughout the whole world, the more desperate the struggle for the acquisition of colonies.
>
> From *Imperialism*, 1919

In order to prevent Russia from falling irrevocably into the capitalist camp, a revolution could be created, after which socialism could be built from the bottom up. Marx had argued that the working class could only become truly socialist as a result of the experience of intensive exploitation. Although such conditions did not exist in Russia, socialism could be built through intense education and propaganda. The peasantry would be recruited to the socialist cause, thereby constructing a new revolutionary class.

In effect, Lenin was proposing the acceleration of the historical process described by Marx. If Russia could industrialise rapidly, if socialist consciousness could be created through education rather than experience, and if the Communist Party could lead the people to an egalitarian and classless society, the end result would be the final, communist stage of history.

Lenin's modification of the Marxist theory of historical development proved to be extremely influential upon the growth of communist ideology during the twentieth century. Many other states and revolutionary movements, which did not conform to Marx's classic description of pre-revolutionary society, attempted to create socialism by copying Lenin's model. States such as China, Cuba, Vietnam, Cambodia, North Korea and a number of African countries all sought to build socialism in non-industrial, peasant-based societies.

The Communist Party

Lenin was sceptical of the possibility that the working classes would rise up spontaneously to bring down capitalism and create their own state. He believed that, after the revolution, they would simply seek to improve their own conditions and would fail to dismantle capitalism and the bourgeois state which supported it. They would therefore need to be led by a small elite party that embodied orthodox Marxist ideology. In this way, the success of the revolution could be assured. This is how Lenin described the danger of spontaneity:

> There is much talk of spontaneity. But the spontaneous development of the working-class movement leads to its subordination to bourgeois ideology... Hence our task, the task of Social Democracy, is to combat spontaneity, to divert the working-class movement from this spontaneous, trade unionist striving to come under the wing of the bourgeoisie, and to bring it under the wing of revolutionary Social Democracy.
>
> From *What Is To Be Done?*, 1902

This lack of trust in the revolutionary instincts of the working class was to last throughout the existence of the Soviet Union. The revolutionary Leninist party turned itself into a dictatorial elite whose pronouncements became iron laws and which would tolerate no opposition. The party's policies became the only 'correct' version of Marxism and all its actions were justified on the grounds of that orthodoxy. Anyone who defied the party was therefore a traitor to the working class and had to be suppressed.

The state

Marx had insisted that the bourgeois state would have to be completely destroyed if socialism were to succeed. Lenin agreed with Marx's view and set about building a new state on the framework of the revolution. At first he tried to make the new state a workers' state, but soon discovered that workers were unable to run their own proletarian dictatorship. He therefore set about creating a new bureaucracy, very much along the lines of the state that had existed under the tsars. The problem which Lenin then encountered was that the revolutionary state, by necessity, would become enormous, since it was charged with the task of organising all production and distribution. This created the danger that such a huge machine would not be kept under political control and would therefore become a new exploiter of labour.

Furthermore, the state was to be the driving force behind the creation of socialism and the classless society. If it became too large and unwieldy, there was a danger that it would lose its sense of mission. To combat this possibility, the state was brought firmly under the control of the Communist Party, which was to give it constant direction. Every section and level of the state was directed by a parallel party committee (the term 'soviet' means committee in Russian). This created the great monolith of the Soviet state, which was to be so beloved of Lenin's successor, Stalin. The system came to be known as **democratic centralism**.

The communist state could not be pluralist in nature or hold free elections, because there could be no variations on Marxist-Leninist orthodoxy. Perversely, Lenin still described his state as democratic, but this was on the grounds that it governed in the interests of the working class and was creating equality. For Lenin, equality and socialist democracy were essentially the same thing.

Key term

Democratic centralism

The political system developed by Lenin was known as democratic centralism. It was not democratic in the liberal (or 'bourgeois', as Lenin would have it) sense. There was only one party, since there was to be no diversion from the central principles of Marxism, but there was to be open discussion within closed party circles. Once decisions were reached, however, political processes would end, and those decisions would be imposed on the party and the state. In theory, any individual who joined the party, and who was willing to work for it and maintain Marxist orthodoxy, could rise through the ranks. Under Stalin, democratic centralism became distorted and turned into the instrument of the rule of Stalin himself and his close advisers.

Joseph Stalin (Georgian, 1879–53)

Stalin was a close associate of Lenin and one of his inner circle during and after the Russian Revolution. After Lenin's death, Stalin engaged in a struggle for power against the other leading Bolsheviks, especially his arch rival, Leon Trotsky. By 1929, Trotsky was in exile and Stalin controlled the Communist Party and therefore the Soviet state. He proceeded to construct perhaps the most repressive totalitarian regime that has ever existed. When he died, under suspicious circumstances, in 1953, he was still in undisputed control of the all-powerful state he had built.

Stalin accepted Marxist-Leninism as his creed and claimed to be completing the work which Lenin had started. His theories of the state and the role of the Communist Party were essentially the same as those of Lenin, but carried to their extremes. In addition, Stalin added a number of key features to the Soviet state, which are described below:

The peasantry

Stalin did not share Lenin's faith in the peasantry as a socialist class. He believed they were unlikely to develop the necessary consciousness. He therefore sought to turn them into workers by industrialising the land. The farms were taken over by the state and turned into huge collectives where the former peasants worked for wages. The richer peasants were eliminated, either literally, or by forcing them to work in collectives.

In this way, Stalin overcame the problem of creating socialism in a country which had not yet been industrialised. However, as industry developed, many of the agricultural workers were moved into the towns and cities to work in the factories and the mines. Ironically, this process mirrored the effects of capitalist development. The failure of the Soviet Union to generate significant wealth meant that workers' incomes were kept barely above subsistence levels.

Socialism in one country

Because it was surrounded by hostile capitalist countries, some of which adopted fascism in the 1930s and 1940s, Stalin decided that he must cut off the Soviet Union from the outside world. He only traded with other socialist states and would not allow his people to travel to other countries. This isolationism was designed to ensure that socialist consciousness could develop without contamination from the outside world.

Stalin's hope was that the Soviet Union would be economically successful and able to combine prosperity with equality. This would create a perfect model, which other proletarian movements would wish to emulate. Until the time came when capitalist countries were taken over by revolutionary movements, using the USSR as their paradigm, the oppressive state would have to endure. Thus, the withering away of the state would not occur until there was no longer a threat from the antagonistic capitalist world. The attack on the USSR by Germany in 1941 and the later onset of the Cold War were used by Stalin to prove that it was necessary to retain the state as a means of defence.

Economic planning

Stalin accepted that capitalism was an extremely dynamic system and successful in creating wealth, albeit unequally distributed wealth, and he sought to ensure that the USSR could rival the richer countries in terms of productive output. The problem he faced was how to create incentives in a system where economic equality for virtually all workers and managers had been established. Without any profit motive, how was industry and agriculture to develop itself?

Classical Marxist analysis would suggest that, if the proletariat had developed true socialist consciousness, it would not need such 'bourgeois' incentives. Stalin, however, was nothing if not a realist. He recognised that, until true socialism had been built, incentives of some kind would be necessary. He refused to use economic incentives, since this would threaten socialism, and instead developed a system of Five Year Plans with stiff targets for production in all sections of the economy. The rewards for achieving targets were social honour and career advancement. The punishment for missing targets was loss of position and descent into menial forms of work. Stalin even created the myth of a model worker, **Stakhanov**, who always exceeded his targets, to inspire the workers.

Stakhanov, the model worker probably invented by Stalin

Key term

Stakhanovism

Stakhanov was a (probably mythical) worker who was held up as a model for others to follow. He always exceeded his production targets in the mines, and required no reward other than the knowledge that he had helped to build a socialist future. The principle of Stakhanovism, therefore, was that if every worker could emulate Stakhanov, the day when the whole world would embrace socialism could be brought forward.

Stalin's system of Five Year Plans ultimately failed. The USSR failed to keep pace with the capitalist world. Although Stalinism survived Stalin's death in 1953, it was inevitable that his brand of Marxism could not endure. When the gap between the prosperity of the USSR and that of the capitalist world was fully revealed in the 1980s, the end became inevitable.

Mao Tse-tung (Chinese, 1893–1976)

In the early part of the twentieth century, Mao was a land reformer who campaigned among the peasantry, urging them to overthrow their landlords and redistribute the land. In the 1920s, he became a communist and embraced Marxism. However, although he described himself as a Marxist-Leninist, he was never an orthodox Marxist thinker. He relied heavily on Stalin's support both before and after he took power and so, as a pragmatic gesture, embraced Stalinism. In fact, the two leaders had little in common. Stalin saw progress in terms of the development of industrial socialism, whereas Mao concentrated on the potentialities of the peasantry. After Mao's death in 1976, China fell into the hands of a small party elite which ran the country in an extremely authoritarian fashion. It was not until the late 1980s that the leadership began to dismantle the socialist system and to replace it, gradually, with free-market capitalism.

Following a prolonged civil war, Mao took power in 1949, declaring the People's Republic of China and claiming that it was to be a Marxist-Leninist state. There was, however, a great deal of originality in his thought and action. For example, Mao saw the peasantry as the principal revolutionary class. He reinterpreted Marx's view that the industrial proletariat was the only revolutionary class by arguing that in China the peasantry were as exploited as the proletariat in capitalist states. This meant that they too could be a truly revolutionary class.

Mao's main original contribution to the Marxist legacy was his insistence that socialism could be built under any economic circumstances, not just in an advanced capitalist state. In order to achieve this, however, it was necessary to destroy the existing culture, so that the new socialist culture could be constructed on a blank society. In the case of China, he instituted a series of mass campaigns, in particular the dramatic **Cultural Revolution**, to attack aspects of traditional Chinese culture. He encouraged the people to oppose reverence for the aged, the subjugation of women, deference to landlords and local officials, ancestor worship and the rigid class structure of the countryside. Once the existing social order had been destroyed, a pure form of socialism could be created among the peasantry and the growing industrial proletariat.

Key term

Cultural Revolution

The Cultural Revolution was the long-term struggle initiated by Mao and carried out by the Chinese peasantry against all those who claimed to be in authority. It was assumed that all authority figures were likely to abuse their power and exploit the people. Few escaped the campaign — party officials, teachers and lecturers, police chiefs and magistrates, were particularly targeted — and many lost their lives through violence or suicide. The main campaign lasted from 1966 until 1969 and left the country on its knees, with few people left who could organise it. Education virtually ceased and agricultural production slumped. The entire administrative system of China had to be rebuilt.

The Chinese communists under Mao exported their ideas to many other countries which were engaged in anti-colonial struggles or which were recently independent. Mao gave them a blueprint for creating socialism, whatever the circumstances. The most notorious example of this occurred in Cambodia, where the Khmer Rouge movement ruthlessly destroyed existing Cambodian society and replaced it with a totalitarian communist regime in 1975.

In addition, Mao developed the idea of *permanent revolution*, a theory originally attributable to Lenin's associate and Stalin's main enemy, Leon Trotsky. Rather than building socialism through a static, all-powerful party machine, Trotsky and Mao believed that the people should engage in a constant revolutionary struggle against all unaccountable wielders of power and anyone who seemed to be tending towards a bourgeois mode of thought and action. Thus the people could learn socialism in a practical way, rather than through education and propaganda.

Other Marxists

The contribution made to Marxist thought by a variety of other philosophers and revolutionaries is considered briefly below.

Leon Trotsky (Russian, 1879–1940)

By 1917, Trotsky was already a veteran revolutionary. However, he only joined Lenin's party just before the Russian Revolution. He was thought to be Lenin's natural heir and was therefore Stalin's closest rival. Having lost his power struggle with Stalin, Trotsky spent the rest of his life in exile before being murdered by a Stalinist agent in Mexico. Trotsky argued that the Soviet Union should not cut itself off from the rest of the world but should seek to promote revolution in other countries. He did not believe that socialist states could survive if capitalism were allowed to thrive elsewhere. He criticised Stalin's creation of a state bureaucracy, arguing that it had simply become a new oppressive ruling class and was preventing the development of socialism rather than creating it. Trotsky was certainly one of the most democratic of Lenin's party. He argued that the people themselves should guide government towards socialism and should not be subjected to excessive party control.

Antonio Gramsci (Italian, 1891–1937)

One of the founders of the Italian communist party, Gramsci sought to explain capitalism's success in preventing its destruction by revolution. The system had learned, he argued, to control its own development and so prevent class warfare. In addition, capitalism had developed a hegemony over society which extended well beyond mere economics. Capitalist culture dominated all political, artistic and cultural life. As a result, its control was all-pervading. The only way to combat this hegemony was to undermine capitalism on all fronts. This meant that a 'counterculture' would have to be created among the workers in order to build socialist consciousness.

Gramsci died largely as a result of being imprisoned by Benito Mussolini during the 1930s. His influence extended into the 1960s, when various left-wing movements sought to set up countercultures in opposition to the ruling capitalist ideology.

Frantz Fanon (French, 1925–61)

Born in Martinique, Fanon was a revolutionary, and was active in the Algerian resistance movement during the country's fight for independence from France. He focused on the peasantry of the poorest countries in the world, arguing that these were the most exploited class, and therefore the most revolutionary. The peasants must struggle against colonial rule, and having achieved independence, should promote a nationalist–socialist resistance to the economic imperialism of the great capitalist powers.

Herbert Marcuse (German, 1898–1979)

Beloved of the left-wing youth movements of the 1960s and 1970s, Marcuse was by that time the last remaining member of the interwar Frankfurt School of communism who was still Marxist. He described modern capitalism as a new form of totalitarianism that manipulated the consciousness of the masses. Capitalism, he asserted, created a one-dimensional view of the world, in which people were part of a mass society whose consumption patterns and lifestyles were totally manipulated. We are therefore all alienated as consumers, not as workers, as Marx had observed. The idea of class struggle was outdated for Marcuse. The new struggle concerned the need for people to liberate their own consciousness of the world. He was pessimistic that this could be achieved, but did see some hope among those sections of the community which were excluded from mass society — members of ethnic minorities, the poor, homosexuals, oppressed women and protesting youth. He described the possibility of the downfall of totalitarian capitalism as: 'nothing but a chance, only a chance.'

Regis Debray (French, 1940–)

Debray is the principal theorist behind the guerrilla movements that sprang up all over Central and South America in the 1960s and 1970s. He was a particular friend of the Cuban regime led by Fidel Castro. In post-colonial states that were dominated by Western capitalism, he saw small guerrilla organisations as the most effective revolutionary weapon. Broad-based peasant and worker movements were easily infiltrated or diverted from the course of socialism. The oppressed classes were best led by a tight-knit, elite group. The experience of armed struggle by such groups would give them the strength and commitment that would enable them to topple regimes that were much more powerful than themselves. However, the Cuban state remains the only lasting success of Debray's so-called 'revolution within the revolution'. Like Marcuse, Debray became popular with Western New Left resistance groups in the late 1960s and early 1970s.

Issues in Marxism

Was Marx a scientific or a utopian thinker?

The basis of Marx's claim to be scientific was that he relied almost totally upon empirical evidence. In other words, his ideas were developed from the experience of history. A potential weakness arises from this. Marx claimed that all previous versions of history had been corrupted by the ruling ideology of the age. In other words, history was always written by the ruling class to justify its own position. Marx, on the other hand, claimed that his explanation of history was purely scientific, and yet he offered no conclusive proof of this. How can we know that his version is not tainted by the same faults as previous analyses of history?

Marx does have something of an answer to this criticism. He examines history from the point of view of the material conditions of society, asserting that less concrete factors, such as politics, philosophy and religion, are all secondary to economic forces. These material conditions can, he claims, be studied scientifically. For example, the feudal system can therefore be explained in terms of the economic relationships between its various classes. The progress of feudalism towards its own destruction can therefore be explained by changes in the conditions of the real world of productive forces; in other words, by stresses in its economic structure. In the same way, an event such as the French Revolution can be explained scientifically in terms of the growing class struggle that France was experiencing in the eighteenth century. Those who explained the revolution in terms of philosophy — that is, as the culmination of the Enlightenment period — or of politics — as the corruption of the *ancien régime* — ran the danger of corrupting their own analysis by adopting a subjective approach to these developments.

If Marx really did analyse history in an objective, empirical manner, his argument that each age develops in a similar way could be justified. If the oppressed class in every past age did indeed inevitably destroy the system that created it, it seems reasonable that capitalism should behave in the same way and so come to the same end. Critics argue that there is no reason at all why capitalism should behave according to apparently unchangeable laws of history. Why, for example, should capitalism not have characteristics that guarantee its own survival? Marx had, in truth, admitted that capitalism was like no previous system — it was more productive and more dynamic than anything seen in history. There was, therefore, no reason why it should conform to past experience.

The main arguments of Marx and his critics can be reduced to a stark conflict. Marx claimed that there are fixed historical laws which allow us to understand how capitalism will ultimately be transformed into socialism following its catastrophic destruction. Against this is the view that historical laws of this kind do not exist, so the future course of capitalism cannot be predicted. The most cynical of his critics suggest that Marx was a utopian socialist who simply constructed a complex, quasi-scientific theory to justify its apparently inevitable creation.

Were Leninism and Stalinism distortions of Marxism?

Both Lenin and Stalin accepted that their theories were modifications of Marxist ideology, which they adapted to take into account the conditions of post-revolutionary Russia and the fact that the rest of the world remained capitalist. Since Russia had not been an advanced capitalist state, measures had to be taken to build socialism and industry at the same time.

Having said that, there are still serious criticisms that can be levelled against Leninism and Stalinism in terms of their deviation from Marxism. These accusations are described below.

Leninism

- Marx insisted that socialist consciousness could only be built upon the proletariat's experience of exploitation. Furthermore, that exploitation would have to be widespread and intensive. This was clearly not the case in Russia. Socialism was therefore built on artificial grounds.
- The small, elite revolutionary party that Lenin created excluded large sections of the working class, thus losing the spontaneous development of socialism which Marx had said would spread through the industrial proletariat.
- The state which Lenin built turned out to be similar to the state which it replaced. Indeed, Lenin actually employed many of the bureaucrats, police chiefs and security agents who had served the former Tsarist regime. Marx had stated that the nature of the state would have to be completely transformed and run almost exclusively by the workers themselves, to ensure it would work only in the interests of socialism.

➤ Lenin employed a large number of bourgeois intellectuals in his new government and party machine. Marx had accepted that some intellectuals would be needed to lead the revolution, but the driving force was to be the proletariat.

Stalinism

➤ The huge state machine which Stalin built turned into a new oppressive ruling class. Orthodox Marxist theory envisaged a state apparatus which was controlled by the working class rather than by professional bureaucrats and party officials.

➤ By creating a personality cult around his own leadership, Stalin denied the leading role of the proletariat.

➤ Cutting the Soviet Union off from other countries meant that Stalin failed to spread revolution throughout the capitalist world. The creation of a world revolution was the first duty of socialist revolutionaries.

Stalin's USSR deviated widely from Marxist ideology

➤ Support for the regime should have been built upon socialist ideology. Stalin, however, appealed to Russian nationalism to achieve this. Nationalism was despised by Marx as a form of false consciousness used to underpin capitalism.

➤ Above all perhaps, Stalin failed to deal with the problem of scarcity of resources in the USSR. This created competition among its people for those resources. Competition, however, forms the basis of capitalist economic organisation. Thus, Stalinist rule had recreated the conditions which spawned capitalism. This is how Trotsky criticised this development:

> The basis of bureaucratic rule is the poverty of society in objects of consumption with the resulting struggle of each against all. When there are enough goods in the store the purchasers can come whenever they want to. When there are little goods the purchasers are forced to stand in line. When the lines are very long it is necessary to appoint a policeman to keep order. Such is the starting point of the power of Soviet bureaucracy.
>
> From *The Revolution Betrayed*, 1936

Marxism today

The end of the Cold War

Although the years 1989–91 can be identified as the end of the great Marxist era, the truth is that Marxist-inspired communism had been in decline for many years before that. Indeed, many have argued that the regimes set up in the USSR, China, Cuba and elsewhere became politically corrupted within a short time of their establishment.

What was remarkable about the end of the Cold War was the rapidity with which Marxist systems were dismantled. Within a decade, the centralised socialist economies were transformed into free-market systems. Communist parties were quickly marginalised as new parliamentary democracy was introduced, with accompanying multiparty systems. Communist parties either disappeared altogether or transformed themselves into socialist parties, which accepted the existence of mixed economies and pluralist states.

Despite this, the quasi-Marxist regime in Cuba continued and the Chinese state remained officially Marxist, although it was rapidly introducing a free-market system. Currently, small communist guerrilla bands continue to operate in Nepal and various parts of southeast Asia and South and Central America, but they remain minor remnants of a once mighty ideological movement. There appears to be no way in which Marxism could re-establish itself in the foreseeable future.

A word of caution needs to be added, however. The current world hegemony of Western-style capitalism may not be permanent, particularly where the less economically developed countries of the world are concerned. Just as poor Muslim countries are embracing fundamentalist Islam in their struggle against Western values, other less economically developed countries could adopt Marxist or quasi-Marxist ideologies as a means of rallying the people against economic imperialism. Frantz Fanon's belief that those he called the 'Wretched of the Earth' — the exploited poor peasantry — may yet rise up against their oppressors could still vindicate Marx's analysis.

The relevance of Marx

If Marxism is in such a state of decline or even completely extinct, why should we continue to study it? There are four possible reasons:

1 We could accept Marx's analysis of history as perfectly valid. The fact that the final stage — the destruction of capitalism and its replacement by a worker's socialist state — has been neither widespread nor successful should not deter us. Marx's dialectic method and his assertion that economic relationships form the basis of any society remain interesting and cogent theories. Although historians are nearly unanimous in their belief that Marx's explanation of historical development is too simplistic and many other factors determine human development, this does not necessarily negate the basic truth that economics and technological change are the main driving forces of history.

Even if Marx's methodology does indeed contain fatal flaws, it is useful in provoking a critical analysis of history. The dialectic method of philosophical inquiry requires that a proposition is confronted by its opposite. Through this, we may hope to arrive at the truth. It is therefore feasible to use Marx's propositions as one side of such a process. In other words, Marx's theories may not contain the truth, but they can help us to unlock the mysteries of historical development.

2 Between 1917 and 1990, a large part of the world was governed by regimes which claimed Marxism as their political inspiration. It is therefore important that we understand the theories which underpinned those regimes. It is interesting to speculate whether these regimes might have endured and been successful had they not become hopeless distortions of orthodox Marxist ideology.

3 In terms of purely historical study, Marx's descriptions of nineteenth-century capitalism, especially in Britain, remain a magnificent body of work, containing insights and analyses which are rooted in empirical, scientific research. Even the most vehement opponents of Marx would have to admit that this aspect of his work informs us in a way which perhaps no other social theorist of the day was able to do.

4 Marx's method of studying past eras can still be useful when applied to the study of contemporary societies. His analyses of class, alienation, surplus value and the dynamic nature of capitalism can still be examined usefully, especially with reference to global forces. We may not accept his conclusions about how capitalism would develop and eventually be destroyed, but many of his insights remain either valid or simply interesting.

Marxism and socialism

It is necessary to clear up a possible source of confusion before making some comparisons between Marxism and socialism. Marx was, in a sense, a socialist. He saw socialism as the system which would succeed capitalism; it was, in essence, the negation of capitalism. Furthermore, he saw socialism as the essential precondition for the final transition of society to communism. The replacement of the capitalist state by the socialist state was the immediate objective of all left-wing revolutionaries in the nineteenth century. Marx numbered himself among these, especially when socialism split from anarcho-communism in 1872. The difference between Marx and other socialists, such as Auguste Blanqui in France and H. M. Hyndman in England, was that Marx believed socialism would evolve into a final historical stage in which the state would become unnecessary. In other words, Marxism, like anarcho-communism, could be described as 'socialism without a state'.

Marxism can be characterised as distinct from socialism in its revolutionary fervour. Marx insisted that socialism would almost certainly come about through bloody revolution. In this sense, he seems closer to anarchism than socialism. He belonged to a European tradition of revolutionary socialism which included syndicalists, radical peasant leaders and even nihilists.

Indeed, a great deal of Marx's later political thought was directed at leading the opposition to evolutionary forms of socialism. Those who believed that socialism could come about through democratic means, notably Eduard Bernstein in Germany, and those who thought that capitalism would spontaneously develop into socialism, for example the English Fabians, represented a huge threat to Marx's hopes for the success of the movement. Marx believed that, without revolution, socialism would become subverted. It would be sidetracked into believing that compromises could be made with capitalism on the road to a workers' state. Marx insisted that such compromises were the greatest danger to socialism. Trade unions, welfare provisions, higher wages and participation in bourgeois democracy would hold back the development of socialist consciousness. The proletariat would be duped into believing they were achieving emancipation, when in fact their cooperation would only help to maintain and strengthen capitalism's hold over society.

Marx was adamant that the capitalist state had to be dealt a shattering blow. No compromises would be successful. The true nature of capitalism could only be fully revealed by revolutionary activity. Without revolution, there would be no socialism.

Marx's followers can certainly claim that, in this respect at least, his fears about the subversion of socialism were justified. In the century after Marx's death, socialism did indeed become largely evolutionary in nature. In the advanced capitalist states — e.g. France, Britain, Germany — the developments which he had feared came to pass. Socialist parties gradually became increasingly moderate as the conditions of the working class were improved. By the end of the Second World War, there were few revolutionary socialists left outside China and the Soviet bloc. Socialism evolved into democratic socialism and then moderate social democracy. Capitalism won its battle against socialism, not by resisting the revolution, but by disguising its true nature from working-class movements that preferred compromise to confrontation. At least in this respect, Marx was right.

Exam focus

Using this chapter and other resources available to you, answer the following questions.

Short questions

Your answers should be about 300 words long.

1 What did Marx say was the nature of the state?
2 What was the basis of Marx's theory of history?
3 What was the basis of Marx's claim to be a scientific thinker?
4 What did Marx mean by ideology?
5 Why did Marx insist that the state would wither away under socialism?
6 Why did Marx think that revolution was inevitable?
7 What was Marx's view of social class?
8 What was Lenin's theory of the state?
9 What was Lenin's theory of the party?
10 What were Trotsky's main criticisms of Stalin?

Long questions

Your answers should be about 900 words long.

1　Assess Marx's claim to be a scientific thinker.
2　Is Marxism still relevant today?
3　Distinguish between Leninism and Stalinism.
4　Distinguish between Marxism and anarchism.

Further reading

Bottomore, T. and Rubel, M. (eds.) (1970) *Karl Marx: Selected Writings in Sociology and Social Philosophy*, Penguin Books.

McLellan, D. (1980) *Marxism After Marx: An Introduction*, HarperCollins.

McLellan, D. (ed.) (2000) *Karl Marx: Selected Writings*, Oxford University Press.

Singer, P. (2000) *Marx: A Very Short Introduction*, Oxford University Press.

Williams, B. (2000) *Lenin*, Longman.

Wood, A. (2004) *Karl Marx* (2nd edn), Routledge.

Wright, A. (1987) *Socialisms: Theories and Practices*, Oxford Paperbacks.

Chapter 6

Anarchism

Anarchism refers to a collection of political movements which have emerged at various times and in various circumstances since the end of the eighteenth century. All anarchists are united by the belief that each individual is sovereign, and should therefore be the sole judge of his or her own actions; that no person has the right to exercise power over another; and that the political state is an unnatural institution which should either be abolished or have a minimal, non-political, non-coercive role. These three beliefs define anarchism.

Anarchists have disagreed about what should replace the modern state and structure of society, and this has given rise to different strands of anarchism with varying objectives. Nihilists oppose any kind of social order and organisation. Syndicalists and communists favour common ownership of property, common norms of behaviour and voluntary communities which are self-governing, directly democratic, and in which all members share a common set of values. Anarcho-capitalists support private property and inequality, but oppose state regulation of any kind. There are a number of other anarchist traditions which combine a variety of beliefs about the best form of society and human conduct.

Introduction

There is a fundamental paradox in the anarchist tradition. On the one hand, all anarchists are united around three basic beliefs — the sovereignty of the individual, that no individual has authority over any other, and opposition to the political state. On the other hand, anarchists are fiercely divided about how these beliefs should be translated into social reality. Put another way, anarchists have agreed about the problems of modern society, but disagreed about how to solve them (see Table 6.1).

There can be difficulties in distinguishing between anarchism and communism, between anarchism and socialism, and between anarchism and extreme forms of liberalism (sometimes described as libertarianism). These issues will be tackled later in this chapter; at this stage it is useful to consider anarchism as a distinctive set of political traditions.

A further problem arises from the undeniable fact that there has never been any significant example of anarchism being put into practice on a significant scale. It is true that there have been examples of small anarchist communities, such as the many communes which sprang up among the youth protest movement of the 1960s and 1970s, the 1,000-strong Christiania community in Denmark set up in 1970 (now disbanding), and a brief anarchist period in Barcelona during the Spanish Civil War of the 1930s. However, these experiments have been small and short-lived. The tradition is therefore open to the charge that it is merely a utopian set of ideals, with no realistic hope of practical success. It is hard to counter this criticism.

Why, then, is anarchism so widely studied? The answer is twofold. First, as a philosophy, anarchism has been expounded by many profound and authoritative thinkers, from Jean-Jacques Rousseau, one of the inspirations behind the French Revolution of 1789, to the US philosopher Robert Nozick, a contemporary hero for those who support totally free-market capitalism. In the 200 years between Rousseau and Nozick, many other philosophers and political activists have written or marched under the banner of anarchism. In one way or another, they have had an important impact on the development of political thought.

Second, anarchism provides a comprehensive critique of virtually all aspects of modern society. Anarchists have forced us to

Table 6.1 Anarchism: a united tradition but a divided movement

Ideas common to all anarchists
- Belief in the complete sovereignty of the individual
- Belief that the individual is the best judge of his or her own actions
- Belief that no individual or body should exert power or force over any other individual
- Total opposition to the existence of the political state

Ideas that divide anarchists
- Most anarchists oppose private property, but some accept limited property as inevitable
- Some anarchists are individualists who oppose social organisation; others believe social communities are natural and desirable
- Some anarchists believe in common ownership and no system of exchange of goods; others propose exchange on the basis of mutual benefit
- Some anarcho-capitalists accept that the completely free market can be just
- Some anarcho-communists propose small, natural communities; others believe communities should be based on industrial or occupational groups

question such fundamentals as the nature and functions of the state, the importance of personal freedom, the basis upon which societies are founded, the role of private property and the system by which goods and services are exchanged and distributed. Such a critique can deepen our understanding of how modern society operates and how it is developing. Over the last two centuries, anarchists may have alerted us to the dangers of state power and taught us to guard our personal freedoms with greater determination.

Early developments

As is the case for a number of other ideologies, anarchism, as an influential movement, can be traced back to the time of the French Revolution at the end of the eighteenth century. Like both liberalism and socialism, it can be seen partly as a product of the Enlightenment.

The Enlightenment opened people's minds to the possibility that traditional forms of authority could be challenged. The French and US revolutions were largely the product of such thinking. Yet while these revolutionaries were determined to replace autocratic government with representative institutions, other philosophers and activists were putting forward far more radical ideas. Perhaps, they argued, former examples of political authority could be replaced with no government at all. Or, rather, they could be replaced by the self-government of each individual. Rousseau had already argued that this was the ideal situation, but had reluctantly come to the conclusion that it would be simply impractical. To be capable of self-government, he admitted, every individual would have to enjoy perfect enlightenment. 'Such men are gods', he asserted, dismissing the idea of self-government or direct democracy.

The most important anarchist philosopher of this revolutionary period came, ironically, from England — a country whose traditional forms of authority survived the revolutionary challenge, but produced one of their most effective critics. This was William Godwin, who was arguably the father of philosophical anarchism. He held an optimistic view of the nature of humankind, in direct contrast to contemporary conservatives, such as Edmund Burke. Godwin believed that people were capable of rational thought and moral perfection. Given the correct education and nurturing, coupled with the removal of the evils of the state, everyone was capable of governing his or her own actions, and of considering the well-being and feelings of others when deciding upon action. This was an original view of the state of humankind. It opened the door to thinking about government and society in new ways, unhindered by fears of disorder if social discipline were to be relaxed.

Godwin did not recommend revolution as the way to achieve his goals. He believed that education and reasoned debate would eventually lead to a society dominated by rational, moral human beings. They would not need government to direct their actions to good ends: a just, equal and ordered society could emerge naturally from the changes created in the human condition. He described how the state should be as restricted as possible:

> It is earnestly to be desired that each man should be wise enough to govern himself, without the intervention of any compulsory restraint, since government, even in its best state, is an evil. The object principally to be aimed at is that we should have as little of it as the general peace of human society will permit.
>
> From *Enquiry Concerning Social Justice*, 1792

This now appears intensely idealistic and utopian. It is true that Godwin did not see his dreams develop to any extent, but he provided a solid philosophical underpinning for the more active anarchists who were to follow.

During the nineteenth century, anarchist ideals gradually caught hold throughout Europe and eventually reached the USA. Anarchism took on different forms, largely depending upon which groups were involved, but all anarchists had an interest in overthrowing the existing order. The most disadvantaged groups were its main standard bearers. It was therefore the exploited peasantry in Russia who formed self-governing anarchist communes, the poorest members of the working classes in France and Northern Europe who supported socialist forms of anarchism, and the independent pioneers of the USA who sometimes became anarcho-individualists in order to preserve their independence from the growing power of federal government.

Revolutionary anarchism

In the middle of the nineteenth century, revolutionary movements of various kinds sprang up all over Europe. Most were socialist in nature and one — Marxist communism — was to become pre-eminent. These developments were a response to the inequalities and deprivations which were seen to be the consequences of free-market capitalism. At the time, there were no clear distinctions drawn between revolutionary socialism, communism and anarchism. They were merely tendencies within the same broad anti-capitalist, anti-landlord movement. As the century progressed, however, the differences between them began to widen, and in 1872, when the leading anarchist Mikhail Bakunin finally split with Karl Marx, anarchism was born as a distinct tradition.

Meanwhile, in those parts of Europe still dominated by agriculture, the final remnants of the old feudal order were breaking down. In some countries, notably Russia, the state remained dominated by landed interests, and anarchism caught hold among those members of the peasantry who were impatient to create social justice. This was mainly to be achieved by seizing land from estate owners and redistributing it among the poorer peasants. Revolutionary anarchism, in these instances, was therefore localised. However, the champions of the peasants, such as Peter Kropotkin, understood that if social justice on the land were to be achieved, the centralised, autocratic state would also have to be destroyed.

Revolutionary socialists and Marxists all proposed that the capitalist state should be taken over by the working class and run by that class in the interests of greater equality and common ownership of the means of production. Revolutionary anarchists shared their hatred of capitalism and the state that supported it, but insisted that the whole apparatus of the state should be completely abolished. While socialists attacked the existing state in order to bring an end to capitalism, anarchists hoped to destroy the state *for its own sake*. In some ways, the destruction of capitalism was for many anarchists a by-product of the abolition of the state. This was the basis of the Bakunin–Marx conflict referred to above.

Three main strands of revolutionary anarchism emerged. The first was *nihilism*, the most violent and revolutionary of all the left-wing creeds. Its proponents included the notorious Russian Sergei Nechaev (1847–82) and the German radical Max Stirner (1806–56). They wished to destroy the state and set all individuals free without providing any prescription as to how post-revolutionary society should be formed. In practice, they were opposed to social order *per se*. Members of the second strand were known as *communists*. Many were closely associated with Marx and, later, with Vladimir Ilyich Lenin, disagreeing with them about means rather than ends. The anarchists rejected the Marxist–Leninist insistence that revolution should usher in an interim workers' state; for anarchists, *all* states are evil. Anarcho-communists, such as Peter Kropotkin and Mikhail Bakunin, wished to move directly from the capitalist state to a no-state organisation of self-governing communities (these were often known as communes, from the French term for a small village or community — hence the term communist). Members of the third strand were known as *individualists*. These anarchists, many of whom were from the USA, were less concerned with the fate of the state, or with the destruction of private property, than they were with the sovereignty of the individual. They were not revolutionary in the sense of proposing violence, but in that they wished to see individuals withdrawing from the state so that it would become irrelevant to their lives. They preached resistance rather than revolution in its traditional form. Celebrated US pioneers such as Henry Thoreau (1817–62) and Benjamin Tucker (1854–1939) were its leading exponents.

During the nineteenth and twentieth centuries, revolutionary anarchists were responsible for a number of assassinations, insurrections, industrial strikes and violent demonstrations. The philosophy of those who sought to bring down the state by the use of violence — by no means the belief of all anarchists — was that by constantly attacking and undermining the state, it would lose its will to survive and be ripe for toppling by an increasingly exploited working class. During the Spanish Civil War (1936–39), anarchists hoped to fill the void which would be left if the anti-fascist forces were to prevail. (In the event, the fascists under Francisco Franco (1892–1975) took power, and the anarchist movement melted away or moved underground.) As recently as the 1960s and 1970s, anarchist cells have committed atrocities as a means of undermining the state. The Baader-Meinhof Gang in Germany and the Italian Red Brigade are notable examples.

In the event, revolutionary anarchists were unable to attract sufficient support from the working classes to bring down any of the states which they attacked. Successes proved to be both modest and short-lived.

Core values of anarchism

The sovereignty of the individual

Those who treat anarchism as merely a branch of socialism or communism are mistaken, primarily because anarchists insist that each individual is completely independent of all other individuals. For anarchists the individual is sovereign. Socialists and communists, on the other hand, see humankind as essentially social, arguing that there is a natural interdependence among people and that we prefer to achieve goals collectively rather than individually.

A word of caution is needed here. First, the most celebrated of the nineteenth-century anarchists, Mikhail Bakunin, disagreed with this fundamental anarchist belief. He suggested that we are bound by a form of natural law which dictates that we behave in a social rather than an individualistic manner. He asserted that 'social solidarity is the first human law, freedom is the second law'. By this he meant that, although we are free, sovereign individuals, we do not have the free will to deny our social nature. In other words, we are free individuals within the natural laws of society.

Mikhail Bakunin believed that people are naturally social

Most anarchists, however, are convinced that we are total individuals. Furthermore, they insist that this does not conflict with the needs of society. Given free will, any moral human being will either form natural communities with other people (as the communist Peter Kropotkin argued), or will pursue his or her own self-interest without interfering with fellow individuals (as the individualist anarchist Benjamin Tucker asserted). Rational, moral human beings do not need to be told to behave with sympathy for others, since they will naturally do so. This means that we could live in society, adjusting our conduct to the needs of others, without feeling constrained or controlled.

Bakunin expressed the idea of the sovereignty of the individual in his great work, *Social and Economic Bases of Anarchism* (1872):

> To be personally free means every man living in a social milieu not to surrender his thought or will to any authority but his own reason and his own understanding of justice.

Individualist anarchists, for example Godwin, Stirner and Thoreau, stress individual liberty to a greater extent than communists such as Bakunin and Kropotkin. They are less concerned with the need to create a free and just society and more interested in restoring individual liberty. They stress that no individual has the right to exercise power over any other. This eliminates all possibility that we may be governed by any government or by any laws.

The nature of liberty

Perhaps the best way to explain the anarchist view of freedom is to contrast it with the liberal view. Both anarchists and liberals begin with the basic belief that all individuals are born free and ought to remain so. However, liberals concede that freedom cannot be unconditional. If an individual, in exercising his or her freedom, interferes with the freedom of another, this is unacceptable. In other words, we cannot exercise our own freedom at the expense of the freedom of others. This means that we can only be free within laws, for without them we live in fear of encroachments on our liberty by the exercise of freedom by others. It follows from this that we have to submit ourselves to some kind of government and that government's laws. The typical liberal view, therefore, sees freedom in terms of its restrictions (so-called *negative* liberty). As Rousseau remarked, we may need to be *forced to be free.*

Anarchists firmly reject this view. They see negative liberty as external restraint and this offends their basic principle of individual sovereignty. How then, do anarchists avoid the problem that, if everybody considers themselves to be completely free, the world will dissolve into a state of war and of constant fear, the nightmare envisaged by the English philosopher Thomas Hobbes? Their solution is twofold:

1 They have an optimistic view of human nature. (There are some exceptions to this among anarcho-individualists, but they are not in the mainstream.) As long as we are allowed to live a moral and enlightened existence, we will take into account the interests of others. We have a natural empathy for our fellow humans and will adjust our actions accordingly.

2 This positive view allows for the liberal conception of external restraint to be replaced by internal restraint, which William Godwin called *private judgement.* In a world where we are all returned to our natural state, uncorrupted by the evils of modern society and the repressive state, artificial laws become unnecessary. Bakunin took this view a stage further by asserting that humankind in a natural state is bound by natural laws. These have been replaced in the modern world by artificial, man-made laws. Natural laws govern our conduct towards our fellow creatures. When we obey them, we do not feel constrained since we are acting naturally. For many anarchists, therefore, a new order can be established, governed by natural, rather than state-enforced, laws.

Critics of the anarchist view of liberty concentrate on their assertion that humankind is naturally 'good'. If this claim is mistaken, the whole anarchist conception of freedom fails. Liberals and conservatives have been united in the belief that the natural goodness of people is either an illusion or is, at best, inconsistent. An answer to this was provided by Rousseau, Godwin and Bakunin, all of whom argued that individuals are neither good nor bad; in other words, an individual is not born with any internal moral code. (Bakunin suggested, however, that an individual does soon learn to understand natural law.) Thus, if society could create a community of morally perfect people, humankind could live together without state-enforced laws, because individuals would control their own behaviour naturally.

Rousseau ultimately rejected the anarchist utopia on the grounds that such a society could only be very small scale in nature. Godwin, Bakunin and others remained more optimistic. The Italian anarchist Enrico Malatesta (1853–1932) expressed the idea of a society of free, caring individuals in sentimental fashion: 'Men must love each other and look on each other as members of one family, if things are to go well with them' (*Anarchy*, 1906).

Critique of the state and consent theory

Although anarchists have disagreed about the precise character of human nature, they have all agreed that the state should be abolished. Their critique of the state offers a number of reasons for this. These are given below.

The state is oppressive

The state is oppressive and represents the few who seek to oppress the many. This is close to the Marxist view, which describes the state as the 'management committee' of the ruling class in any age. Historically, the ruling class was the aristocracy and landed gentry; in the modern age, it is seen as the forces of capitalism, which exploit workers, peasants in less economically developed countries, and consumers everywhere. Enrico Malatesta summarised this view:

> The basic function of government everywhere in all times, whatever title it adopts and whatever its origin and organisation may be, is always that of oppressing and exploiting the masses, of defending the oppressors and exploiters; and its principal, characteristic and indispensable, instruments are the police agent, the tax collector, the soldier and the gaoler.
>
> From *Anarchy*, 1906

The state removes freedom

The state takes away our freedom. It subjects us to laws and controls that are artificial, offending the basic principle of individual sovereignty. In a colourful diatribe against government, the French anarchist Pierre-Joseph Proudhon (1809–65) expressed this principle as follows:

> To be governed is to be at every operation, at every transaction, noted, registered, enrolled, taxed, stamped, measured, numbered, assessed, licensed, authorised, admonished, forbidden, reformed, corrected, punished.
>
> From *General Idea of the Revolution in the Nineteenth Century*, 1846

The state is corrupting

In common with many liberals, anarchists believe that the act of governing is in itself corrupting. Those who come into government may do so with good motives, but inevitably lose their idealism and become exploiters themselves. Lord Acton expressed this view with his famous maxim: 'power tends to corrupt, and absolute power corrupts absolutely'. The socialist novelist George Orwell (1903–50) satirised the dangers of power in his 1945 work *Animal Farm,* which he mainly wrote as a critique of the Soviet Union, a state which had been born of high ideals but had descended into totalitarianism. In 1870, Mikhail Bakunin wrote a passage which looks as reasonable today as he believed it to be so then:

> Nothing is as dangerous for man's morality as the habit of commanding. The best of men, the most intelligent, unselfish, generous and pure, will always and inevitably be corrupted in this pursuit. Two feelings inherent in the exercise of power never fail to produce this demoralization: contempt for the masses, and, for the man in power, an exaggerated sense of his own worth.
>
> From *Federalism, Socialism, Anti-Theologism*

The state is unnatural

Anarchists see the state as an artificial form of society. The anarchist view is either that humankind should be free to form voluntary, natural communities (usually small-scale ones) or that the individual should be free to withdraw altogether from any political organisation. The political state denies this freedom and creates an unnatural community. For this reason, anarchists oppose nationalism, since the nation, although arguably a natural organism, is usually expressed through statehood and so becomes unnatural. Peter Kropotkin was perhaps the most important exponent of the view that humankind should naturally form self-governing communes, arguing that this was how people had organised themselves throughout most of history. Once the state was abolished, he hoped, humankind could return to such an age.

   This final critique of the state is central to anarchist belief. If communities are voluntary, they argue, there should be no need for government and laws. If we freely choose to enter a community and support its accepted norms of behaviour, we do not need any compulsion to conform. The state, in contrast, is an artificial organisation. Not everyone will wish to conform and so there must be compulsion.

Anarchist responses to consent theory

At this point, it is useful to confront anarchist opposition to the state with the liberal argument. Liberals understand that states, by their nature, threaten individual liberty. Since the days of the English philosopher John Locke in the late seventeenth century, liberals have developed a theory of political consent to overcome this difficulty. If the people come together voluntarily to set up government over themselves, the state is no longer seen as an imposition. If we consent to be governed, we accept justified curtailments of our liberty. This can be seen most clearly in the philosophy behind the American Constitution, which was written in 1787.

The early liberal view is also known as contract theory. This suggests that the state represents a contract between the governed and the government. The people consent to obey the laws created by the state, while the state is bound to safeguard the liberties of the people as far as possible. If the state fails to honour the contract, the people have the right to dissolve it.

At first sight this seems reasonable. Not so, say anarchists. They offer three main objections:

1 Individuals cannot give up their own liberty in this way if they are to remain true to their real nature. Liberty is a birthright which cannot be conceded. Its abandonment would be a denial of our humanity.

2 Consent theory implies that there will be a majority and a minority. In setting up the state, even by free agreement, the majority oppresses the minority. The US individualist anarchist Henry Thoreau asserted that 'a government in which the majority rule in all cases cannot be based on justice'. Thus, only if all the people offer their consent could the setting up of a state be justified. This seems an unlikely event. In any case, it is invalidated by anarchists' third objection.

3 Even if consent is justly arrived at, it cannot be binding on future generations. For the state to be legitimate, therefore, it would have to be subject to continuous consent. This is clearly impractical, unless the community is extremely small (an Israeli kibbutz might fit the bill). Political states, which force laws on people, can never claim consent unless it is expressly given at all times. In practice, therefore, those anarchists who have made specific proposals for setting up communities suggest that any decisions which have to be made should be reached through direct democracy.

Opposition to property

Not all anarchists have opposed private property. Some contemporary anarcho-capitalists (sometimes known as libertarians), such as the US philosopher Robert Nozick, have asserted that private property is acceptable as long as it has been legally and justly obtained. These thinkers are anarchists in that they believe the state should not be allowed to interfere with the ownership of property and its uses. In addition, the nineteenth-century French anarchist Proudhon reluctantly came to the conclusion that property was a necessary evil in a modern society. As long as the ownership of property was not used to exploit others — either workers or consumers — and the distribution of property was not too unequal, it could be justified. This is explored further in the section on mutualism (see p. 212).

Unlike most anarchists, Pierre-Joseph Proudhon accepted that private property is necessary

Despite these two exceptions, most anarchists believe that social justice can only be achieved if private property is abolished. The inequality it causes is not the only reason for their objection. Many anarchists see the state as the protector of property interests; without a state, property owners feel vulnerable and insecure. Indeed, Rousseau, a precursor of anarchism, suggested that property had been the fundamental cause of humankind's oppression. Kropotkin, who of the great anarchists probably came closest to pure communism, put it this way:

> In common to all socialists, the anarchists hold that the private ownership of land, capital and machinery has had its time; that it is condemned to disappear, and that all the requisites for production must, and will, become the common property of society, and be managed in common by the producers of wealth.
>
> From *Revolutionary Pamphlets*, 1892

A variety of proposals have been made by anarchists for replacing private property with common ownership. However, they all have one aspect in common which decisively separates anarchism from socialism — that the state should not be the vehicle for common ownership. Communities, trade unions, groups of industrial workers and cooperative organisations might all take over the means of production and use them for the common good, but the idea of public ownership being under the control of the state would clearly offend the core principles of the movement.

Critique of capitalism

As has been noted, some contemporary libertarian anarchists support the maintenance of free-market capitalism, provided it is genuinely *free market*. However, most anarchists, both in the nineteenth century and today, see capitalism as the root of a number of social ills.

Above all, capitalism is opposed by most anarchists because it exploits, and in doing so negates true freedom. Nineteenth-century anarchists, such as Bakunin and Kropotkin, were like Marxists and other socialists in seeing the working classes and the downtrodden peasantry as victims of capitalist exploitation. They would only be truly free when capitalism was overthrown.

The most vociferous of the anti-capitalist anarchists were the anarcho-syndicalists, who flourished in the late nineteenth and early twentieth centuries. They proposed that the workers should seize control of the instruments of capitalist domination and run them in the interests of all. Georges Sorel, who is often classified as a socialist, led the syndicalist movement in France. For him and his followers, the 'natural' community was the fellowship of workers engaged in the same industry. Such a fellowship should be self-governing and independent of any centralised state. Exceptionally violent in their revolutionary outlook, the syndicalists believed that once capitalism had been undermined and then destroyed, most of the functions of the state would become redundant.

Contemporary anarchists have turned their attention to the ways in which international capitalism is exploiting workers and peasants in poorer countries and exploiting consumers in more economically developed countries. Many, known as eco-anarchists, see the degradation of the natural environment as a direct consequence of capitalism. These activists, often seen demonstrating at meetings of world leaders and the World Trade Organisation (WTO), attack both national governments and international institutions, including the WTO itself, the International Monetary Fund (IMF) and the World Bank. These supranational organisations are viewed by anarchists as the heirs of the nineteenth-century capitalist state.

On a more philosophical level, anarchists have argued that capitalism creates inequality. Inequality is, in itself, a threat to freedom, since those who enjoy greater prosperity have the opportunity to dominate the less well off. For most anarchists, social justice is tied up with the concept of liberty, because, they argue, we are all born both free and equal, with equal needs. Capitalism, and the state which supports it, sponsor inequality and, indeed, have celebrated it. Mainstream anarchists therefore oppose both. Anarchists reject religion and nationalism, too; they see both as artificial creations designed to rob people of their personal liberty.

The reasons why anarchists oppose capitalism, and various other institutions, are summarised in Table 6.2.

Table 6.2 What anarchists are opposed to and why

Institution	Reasons for opposition
The state	It oppresses the individual, supports private property and represents the government of the many by the few
Private property	It creates inequality, gives rise to oppressive laws and is a denial of the natural right to the fruits of the earth
Law	Laws are a denial of individual liberty
Capitalism	Goods and services are exchanged on an unfair basis and workers are exploited, creating inequality and giving rise to an oppressive state
Religion	It presents a false view of the world and encourages authority to be exercised by some individuals over others
Nationalism	Nations are artificial, not natural, communities. Nationalism leads to conflict and war

Types of anarchism

Anarcho-communism

This has been the dominant form of anarchism. It is sometimes described simply as 'collectivism', or even as 'communism'. However, both these terms have also been applied to Marxism and socialism, which are distinctive movements. The use of the full term 'anarcho-communism' is therefore preferable.

The principal exponents of this branch of anarchism are Mikhail Bakunin, Peter Kropotkin, Elisée Reclus (1830–1905) and Enrico Malatesta, all of whom presented an alternative to socialism and Marxism in response to the perceived evils of capitalism. Anarcho-communists were at the height of their influence towards the end of the nineteenth century and in the early twentieth century — the same period in which Marxism and revolutionary socialism were prominent.

The anarcho-communists proposed dissolving the state — either by violent or peaceful means — and replacing it with small-scale communes (favoured by Kropotkin and Malatesta) or federations of workers (Bakunin's view). Despite differences in emphasis, the various anarcho-communist groups agreed that these communities would display the following characteristics:

➢ They would be voluntary: each individual would have the right to join a community or to leave it. Communities might vary in their organisation and values, but individuals would not be forced to conform as their decision to join would be taken freely.

➢ They would be self-governing and there would be no overarching authority to bind them together.

➢ Internally, they would be governed by some form of direct democracy. This is perhaps the most problematic aspect of such communism. What would happen to minority opinions? Would minorities be forced to accept majority decisions and so become oppressed? This was the very situation anarchists hoped to escape. It is in this context that anarchists can be seen at their most optimistic. They argued that the process of democracy would produce a unanimous conclusion, or minorities would accept majority opinion without feeling oppressed or else leave the community and find another more to their liking. Critics naturally see this as impractical and utopian.

➢ On the whole, the communities would be self-sustaining. This would avoid excessive need for cooperation with other communities. Too much interdependence, anarchists feared, might result in the restoration of capitalist exchange systems, inequality, rivalry and the need for administration, which might turn into government. Where exchanges were essential, they would take place on the basis of mutual benefit. Instead of the capitalist exchange system, which involves negotiated prices on the basis of supply and demand, mutual-benefit systems would involve exchange being calculated on the basis that both parties to the transaction would benefit fairly. Kropotkin described his own proposals for this kind of system as 'mutual aid', and his vision is perhaps the one most likely to come to people's minds when they think of anarchism. Malatesta was involved in establishing communes based on mutual benefit exchange among the Italian peasantry in the nineteenth century, while Kroptkin was an inspiration behind the Jura Federation in the Swiss–French border country after 1873. Mutual benefit exchange is the basis of the kibbutz system in Israel, the Christiania experiment in Denmark, and many independent subsistence communities in the USA.

➢ Goods and services would be distributed within the community on an equal basis, according to need. All production and distribution would be organised collectively.

➤ Kropotkin believed that membership of a community should be on the basis of a natural empathy between individuals. Just as prehistoric humans and many species in the animal kingdom naturally formed social, cooperative groups, so should modern humankind. Bakunin, on the other hand, argued that workers in the same industry would have a natural affinity, so occupation would be the most successful basis for cooperation.

The philosophy behind such mainstream anarchist thought is best summarised by Reclus:

> But whether it is a question of small or large groups of the human species, it is always through solidarity, through the association of spontaneous, co-ordinated forces that all progress is made... We know that, if our descendants are to reach their high destiny of science and liberty, they will owe it to their coming together more and more intimately, to the incessant collaboration, to this mutual aid from which brotherhood grows little by little.
>
> From *Evolution and Revolution*, 1891

Anarcho-individualism

Although anarcho-communism can be seen as the classical form of anarchism, the individualist movement was also extensive and influential. Its principal authority was the nineteenth-century German radical, Max Stirner. His best known work, *The Ego and His Own*, was published in 1845 and became something of a bible for anarcho-individualists. His main influence, however, was not in Europe but in the USA.

Stirner differed from the anarcho-communists in that he had a specific view of human nature. For him, humankind was driven principally by egoism, i.e. the drive to pursue its own self-interest. He asserted that notions of individuals being naturally sociable and cooperative were false. The state was to be opposed mainly on the grounds that it denied people's egoism, controlling their behaviour and forcing them into unnatural social relations. Stirner summarised this view in a famous and unequivocal passage:

> Therefore we two, the State and I, are enemies. I, the egoist, have not at heart the welfare of this human society, I sacrifice nothing to it, I only utilise it.
>
> From *The Ego and His Own*, 1845

Thus Stirner rejected the state and human society as denials of human nature.

The USA proved to be more fertile ground than Europe for these beliefs, largely because of the deeply-rooted sense of human rights, support for individual liberty and suspicion of the state which flourished there. As well as this, socialism, a key opponent of individualist ideas, had made little progress in US society. In Europe, on the other hand, the collectivist movement was well advanced and the state was seen as the main way in which social justice could be delivered.

Three followers of individualism in the USA were Josiah Warren (1798–1874), Benjamin Tucker and Henry Thoreau. Warren and Tucker proposed replacing the existing system with cooperative capitalism, which was to be based on two main principles. First, the state would cease to exist and all individuals would be freed from obedience to any laws. Second, individuals should exchange goods and services with each other on the basis of *labour value*, rather than exchange value. All products would be valued according to the amount and quality of labour which had gone into their production. This would replace the capitalist system, which valued goods according to the forces of demand and supply, rather than their intrinsic value. The seller would therefore receive the full value of his or her labour, while the buyer would not have to pay more than a product's true value. This meant that profit would cease to exist.

The schemes of Tucker and Warren were designed to achieve three main objectives. The first was to create social justice without the interference of the state. The second was to create greater (though not complete) social equality. Third, individuals would be truly free, in that they would no longer be slaves to either the state or to the exploitative nature of capitalism.

Thoreau was less well known in his own lifetime, but was rediscovered by members of the youth-protest movements of the 1960s. His best known work, *Walden*, became a manual for those who opted to withdraw from society and to form self-sufficient, independent communes. Thoreau's opposition to government was less rational than that of other anarchists, but perhaps displayed more common sense. He simply believed that most government was bad government. He admitted that sometimes governments did act in the interests of the people, but this was rarely the case. Therefore, he decided, we should be free to obey or disobey, whichever suited our purpose. This is how Thoreau summed up this view:

> The authority of government, even such as I am willing to submit to, — for I will cheerfully obey those who know and can do better than I, and in many things even those who neither know nor can do so well, — is still an impure one. To be strictly just, it must have the sanction and consent of the governed. It can have no pure right over my person and property but what I concede to it.
>
> From *Walden*, 1854

Unlike Tucker and Warren, Thoreau was not particularly interested in how people might interact. He was solely concerned that the individual should resist the control of the state and, if necessary, withdraw from it altogether.

Although both individualist and communist anarchists oppose the state and capitalism, and both revere individual liberty, the similarity ends there. The anarcho-individualists reject the idea that the state should be replaced by a different kind of social order. For them, there should be no replacement for the state. They also reject the collectivist form of production proposed by the communists, in the belief that this would merely recreate the state by another name. For them, economic and social relations between individuals should be conducted on a free, voluntary basis.

The modern heirs of the egoism of Stirner, the utopian ideas of Warren and Tucker, and the dreamy romanticism of Thoreau, have accepted the need for the restoration of individual self-determination, but have been forced to reach an accommodation with capitalism. For this reason they are often known as anarcho-capitalists.

Anarcho-capitalism

The effects of economic development, increased industrialisation and specialisation of labour in the modern age have rendered the ideas of the nineteenth-century individualists obsolete. Some idealists have suggested turning back the clock and recreating more primitive forms of existence, but they are rare and isolated examples. More commonly, opponents of the state have accepted that the capitalist system of production and exchange is so entrenched that it must be adapted to no-state circumstances.

The most prominent of the contemporary anarcho-capitalists (i.e. modern anarcho-individualists) is Murray Rothbard (1926–95) of the USA. Rothbard shared Stirner's view that we are all self-interested individuals, but had a more optimistic view of what a world would be like in which everyone is able to pursue that self-interest freely.

Rothbard believed that virtually all the functions of the state can be replaced by the activities of the free market. For example, law and order could be maintained if individuals or groups simply purchased security on the open market. All welfare services could be provided by private enterprise, as could transport, housing and even planning. Furthermore, he argued, if a totally free-market system of exchange were introduced, individuals would become enlightened, understanding that if transactions took place on a fair basis this would benefit everyone in society. When a dispute arose between individuals, they could resort to private arbitrators with both parties agreeing to abide by the final decision. Why would individuals enter relations with others under such uncertain circumstances? Rothbard's response was that enlightened individuals, with free choice, would only participate if justice were guaranteed. Free-market capitalism is, claimed Rothbard, self-regulating. The state therefore becomes redundant.

Rothbard's colleague, Robert Nozick, is perhaps not strictly an anarcho-capitalist, preferring to be described as a libertarian or 'ultra liberal', but he is part of the same movement as Rothbard. Nozick accepted the need for a minimal state, rejecting the view that all state functions could be provided by the market, but he shared the anarchists' antipathy towards the state. He accepted that private property is an essential aspect of modern life, along with the inequality that inevitably results from capitalism.

Nozick argued that the economic model he proposed would not result in complete disorder. This was because the system of free relations between free individuals results in a balance of interests, which would, as Rothbard had claimed, be self-regulating. In Nozick's world, there would therefore be no taxation, no welfare state and only minimal laws to protect people from each other. The presence of a state means that this is not quite anarchism, but in purely economic terms it is capitalism without any state interference, which amounts to virtually the same thing.

Mutualism

The anarchist doctrine of mutualism expounded by Pierre-Joseph Proudhon bridges the gap between anarcho-communism and anarcho-individualism.

Ironically, Proudhon coined the best known anarchists' slogan, 'all property is theft', even though he was one of the few anarchists to accept that private property might be tolerated, provided the exploitative aspects of capitalism could be eliminated. He understood that it was essential for small-scale entrepreneurs to own their own means of production. Without this they would lose their independence. Proudhon proposed that peasants should own modest amounts of land, that most workers should be independent, and where large-scale industry was inevitable, that workers themselves should own the means of production. Like the US individualists Warren and Tucker, Proudhon devised a system of exchange which would assign values to goods based on the labour hours used to produce them. Money was to be replaced by 'labour notes' and free credit was to be made available to all, giving individuals the opportunity to set up their own enterprises or to buy land.

Proudhon was not, however, part of the anarcho-individualist tradition. He believed that people should live in small, self-governing communities. As long as the exploitation of workers, peasants and consumers was removed, he argued, people could live in harmony without the need for a coercive state. In this way he attempted to reconcile individual ownership of property with social harmony.

Like the US individualists, Proudhon was an important influence over the establishment of both producer and consumer cooperatives from the 1840s and the commune movements of the 1960s and 1970s. There is even an echo of Proudhon's idea of valuing goods by labour input in the current 'fair trade' scheme, which covers a variety of commodities from less economically developed countries where labour has been exploited by the 'unfair' operation of world markets. However, as was the case for much of the anarchist movement, mutualism was swamped in the late nineteenth and early twentieth centuries by the growing popularity of socialism and Marxism among the working classes.

Anarcho-syndicalism

Syndicalism was the name adopted by some revolutionary socialists — mainly French — in the late nineteenth and early twentieth centuries to denote a movement based on the power and organisation of trade unions. Most syndicalists proposed the overthrow of capitalism by workers and peasants and the replacement of the state by a workers' organisation which would impose worker and peasant ownership of industry and land. In practice, this meant industrial democracy, in which each industry was self-governing on the basis of direct democracy. There would be a centralised state organisation, however, which would organise the distribution of goods and carry out various security functions of government.

The anarchist wing of the syndicalist movement had similar objectives, but opposed the retention of the state. It argued that the self-governing industries and cooperatives would be able to arrange a fair system of exchange, distribution, security and welfare, without the need for a central state. Supporters of this branch are sometimes described as radical syndicalists.

The anarcho-syndicalists gained a reputation as the most violent wing of the anarchist movement. Their French leader, Georges Sorel, asserted that the capitalist state used violence and coercion to maintain its rule and that this should be challenged by even greater violence from the workers. The main weapon they used was the strike — a way of undermining capitalism that it could not combat. Sorel believed that a general strike, in which all workers participated, would actually bring down the state altogether. Such activities became known as **propaganda by deed**.

Key term

Propaganda by deed
This term refers to the tactic used by the most radical, revolutionary anarchists. When they commit violent acts, the state is forced to respond in an equally violent manner. In this way, the truly oppressive nature of the state is revealed. Anarchists hope that the violent response of the state will persuade people that it is founded on force and so should be resisted.

As the twentieth century progressed, syndicalism began to decline. The violent revolutionary wing was largely absorbed into socialism, while the non-revolutionary part of the movement evolved into a more moderate form, known as *guild socialism*. The guild socialists took their inspiration from the old craft guilds (metal workers, masons, tailors and so on) that had flourished in the Middle Ages. The guilds were largely self-governing and were granted charters of independence by monarchs over several centuries. This romantic historical image was naturally attractive to anarchists, since it represented a world in which the state's functions were reduced to a minimum and where the collective freedom of natural communities could be safeguarded. However, growing prosperity among the working classes, and the decline of crafts in general, meant that the movement withered away.

Nihilism

The term nihilism is derived from the Latin word *nihil,* meaning 'nothing'. There is no such movement as nihilism — the term is usually applied to individuals. Max Stirner has been described as a nihilist, as has Sergei Nechaev, an associate of Mikhail Bakunin.

Nihilists believe that all forms of social order are an unjustifiable denial of individual liberty. They have therefore attacked all forms of organisation, not merely the centralised state. Nihilists recommend the completely free exercise of egoism and the unfettered use of **terror**. If the world that results becomes extremely disordered and violent, then so be it, they assert.

Key term

Terror

In reference to the state, terror means the public use of violence to maintain order. This may simply include the regular appearance of police and troops on the streets, but it could also involve public trials and the execution of dissidents. When used by revolutionaries, terror might include assassinations, destruction of property and violent demonstrations. In such cases, its purpose is to reduce the will of the state to continue to govern, and of the people to support that state.

In the modern world, nihilism has a good deal in common with the philosophical movement known as *existentialism*. Existentialists argue that life can only have meaning, and we can only achieve self-realisation, if we throw off society's constraints. Life has meaning for us if we are able to impose ourselves upon it. If we allow society — i.e. its morality and its value system — to impose itself on us, we are guilty of 'bad faith'. Such bad faith is a denial of our humanity. It follows that true existentialists should act according to their own personal will and their own conscience.

However, few existentialists propose the destruction of society and the state. They merely argue that we should impose ourselves on society and the state, not vice versa. Therefore they should not be described as anarchists (even though many may describe themselves as such).

Nihilism has also influenced fascism. In common with existentialists, many fascists argue that it is our destiny and our duty to impose our own will upon society. Decisive action, for fascists, is a heroic enterprise: rational organisations should be challenged for the very reason that they *are* rational, and therefore lack direction and dynamism; moral and social restraints can be thrown off in the interests of progress. Thus, we come full circle. The most left wing of all political creeds becomes almost synonymous with possibly the most right wing.

Contemporary anarchism

Anarcho-capitalism and libertarianism may be considered modern versions of anarchism, but there are many other activists around today who describe themselves as anarchists and remain anti-capitalist.

The problem with identifying anarchism today is twofold. First, there are no great contemporary anarchist thinkers. The nineteenth century produced a stream of influential anarchists, such as Bakunin, Stirner, Kropotkin, Reclus and Leo Tolstoy (1828–1910). There have been many contemporary theorists expressing important critiques of the modern state, including Herbert Marcuse, Louis Althusser (1918–90), Jürgen Habermas

(1929–) and Noam Chomsky (1928–), but none of them has headed a coherent political movement. Second, the term anarchism itself has been taken over by disparate groups of activists who have specific grievances rather than a comprehensive opposition to the state and attachment to individual liberty. Many environmentalists, feminists, campaigners on behalf of less economically developed countries and radical socialists who have described themselves, or been described, as anarchists, oppose authority largely on the grounds that it stands in the way of their goals.

Protesters in Washington DC march against the IMF and the World Bank in 2000

That said, there is a recognisable world movement which stresses the dangers of globalisation. Just as the nineteenth-century state and the capitalism it sponsored oppressed workers and peasants, so contemporary international bodies (e.g. the WTO, the IMF and the World Bank) and the world trade system they uphold oppress the poor workers and peasants of the less economically developed world. This is the argument of the current radical anti-authority movement.

It is also the case that traditional anarchism proposed alternatives to existing authority systems, even though they were often seen as utopian and impractical. In contrast, modern anarchism is simply anti-authority. Environmentalists, such as Ernst Schumacher (1911–77) and Murray Bookchin (1921–), have recommended a return to more social, small-scale, primitive forms of organisation to preserve the environment, but they are rare exceptions. In practice, modern anarchism is largely confined to the anti-globalisation movement.

The key beliefs of the main anarchist movements are summarised in Table 6.3.

Table 6.3 Summary of key beliefs of the main anarchist movements

Anarcho-individualism	Anarcho-communism	Contemporary anarchism
• Human beings are essentially egotistical	• Human beings are essentially social	• Human beings are both individuals and have social responsibility
• Society is in general a denial of individualism	• Free societies enable individuals to achieve true freedom	• The human race needs to return to simpler forms of social organisation
• Individuals should be self-sufficient as far as is possible	• Economic cooperation is a natural activity	• Individuals should be self-sufficient and free to engage in free trade
• Trade between people should be conducted on the basis of mutual benefit, not based on market forces	• Goods should be produced and distributed communally	• Completely free trade is to the benefit of all

Key anarchist thinkers

William Godwin (British, 1756–1836)

Married to Mary Wollstonecraft (1759–97), an early feminist, and father of Mary Shelley (1797–1851), the author of the novel *Frankenstein*, Godwin was an unsuccessful clergyman who turned to philosophy when he became disillusioned with the Church of England.

Godwin rejected the concept of original sin, believing that people are born neither good nor bad. He was optimistic that each individual, through education in morality and rationality, could be made into a perfectly moral human being.

In his main work, *An Enquiry Concerning Political Justice* (1792), he claimed that government would have no purpose in a rational, moral society. Governments have operated in their own interests and have resisted the progress of rationalism to protect themselves. Should a rational society be established, the state would become redundant and disappear. In its place would be left a natural society, dominated by reason and based on benevolent cooperation. Everyone in such a society would understand what actions would be in the best interests of all and behave in such a way as to bring these about.

Godwin's philosophy has been criticised for being overoptimistic and unsystematic in proposing an alternative to the state. He developed vague proposals for small, independent communities, but his theories were relatively unspecific. Nevertheless, he was a key figure who influenced the more extensive anarchist movement that followed.

Mikhail Bakunin (Russian, 1814–76)

A minor aristocrat by birth, Bakunin spent the middle part of the nineteenth century attaching himself to various revolutionary movements before developing his own distinct theory of anarchism. He was closely associated with Marx until 1872, when the two disagreed irrevocably. Bakunin criticised Marx's insistence that, following revolution, a worker's state should be established — the so-called 'dictatorship of the proletariat'. Bakunin, who was by no means implacably opposed to the concept of the minimal state, argued that the continuance of a powerful state would wreck the goals of the revolution. Along with Peter Kropotkin, he became the leading exponent of anarcho-communism.

Bakunin's theories began with the belief that individuals are born neither good nor bad. Their characters are entirely moulded by their experience of life. A perfect society could therefore produce perfect people. A perfect society was, for Bakunin, one in which every individual put the needs of society as a whole above his or her own selfish ends. He believed that humankind could only be free when living in cooperative communities where self-interest did not exist.

His analysis of capitalism and its exploitative nature was similar to that of Marx, as was his vision of the revolution that would come. However, he believed that the state should be abolished immediately and replaced by a federal system of communities, each based on the occupation of its members. These communities would be self-governing and cooperate with others on a mutually beneficial basis.

Bakunin's legacy was to make anarchism an intensely community-based ideal, rather than an individualistic doctrine. Of all the leading anarchists, he perhaps placed the least stress on the sovereignty of individuals and the most on their natural sociability (see Box 6.1).

Box 6.1 Bakunin on the corruption of power

Before the liberal Lord Acton coined his famous dictum that 'power tends to corrupt, and absolute power corrupts absolutely', Bakunin demonstrated the same principle even more forcefully:

> Nothing is as dangerous for man's personal morality as the habit of commanding. The best of men, the most intelligent, unselfish, generous, and pure, will always and inevitably be corrupted in this pursuit. Two feelings inherent in the exercise of power never fail to produce this demoralisation: contempt for the masses, and, for the man in power, an exaggerated sense of his own worth... If there were established tomorrow a government or a legislative council, a parliament made up exclusively of workers, those very workers who are now staunch democrats and socialists, will become determined aristocrats, bold or timid worshippers of the principle of authority, and will also become oppressors and exploiters.

From *State and Revolution*, 1870

This passage becomes prophetic when considering the way in which the communist revolution in the Soviet Union became corrupted under Stalin. The causes of Bakunin's break with Marx in 1872, on the issue of the corrupting effects of the state, are clearly illustrated here.

Peter Kropotkin (Russian, 1842–1921)

Like Bakunin, Kropotkin was from an aristocratic background and closely associated with the Marxists. He supported Lenin during the Russian Revolution, but soon became disillusioned and took no part in the Bolshevik government. He was in exile for much of his adult life, the most productive part of which was spent in the Jura region of France. An anarchist federation had been set up there by establishing a series of self-governing peasant communes. It was the traditional peasant communes of the kind Kropotkin observed there, where goods and work were shared on an equal basis, upon which he founded his beliefs.

Kropotkin was perhaps the most scientific of the leading anarchists, and drew inspiration from the animal kingdom when considering human society. In his best known work, *Mutual Aid* (1902), he argued that humankind, like the higher elements of the animal kingdom, would naturally form small-scale cooperative communities. The modern state had destroyed these natural formations and created an oppressive, as well as unnatural, situation. Kropotkin rejected the Darwinian theory that competition is the normal state of affairs for all species and forms an essential part of their development. Rather, he argued, the more successful species were those that lived in cooperative communities, such as apes, elephants and many types of insect. He supported his call for mutual aid by drawing on the relationship between human and animal environments:

Therefore combine — practise mutual aid! That is the surest means for giving to each and to all the greatest safety, the best guarantee of existence and progress, bodily, intellectual and moral. That is what Nature teaches us; and that is what all those animals which have attained the highest position in their respective classes have done.

From *Mutual Aid*, 1910

Kropotkin's system of mutual aid was based on small, self-governing communities, which would, as far as possible, be self-sufficient. When cooperation between communities was essential, it would be negotiated on a mutually beneficial basis.

He formed close associations with Bakunin, Reclus and Malatesta in the latter part of the nineteenth century. Indeed, their ideals were so similar that they could have formed an anarchist party. However, the notion of a political party offended their anarchist principles. It implied authority and hierarchy, both of which were unacceptable, so they resisted the temptation.

Kroptkin died considerably disillusioned with the state of communism in Russia under Lenin. It is perhaps fortunate that he did not live to see the excesses of the Stalinist regime.

Peter Kropotkin's theory of mutual aid was supported by his observations of the animal kingdom

Georges Sorel (French, 1847–1922)

The greatest anarcho-syndicalist, Sorel also had the reputation of being one of the most violent representatives of the mainstream anarchist movement. It is perhaps true that anarchism's reputation for violence (which is not totally justified) was earned largely by him. He believed that the ability of the revolutionary to act in a decisive way was inhibited by traditional morality. It was therefore necessary for the aspiring anarchist to be rid of any moral restraint whatsoever. This provided Sorel with carte blanche to carry out any atrocity, no matter how abhorrent. His main work, *Reflections on Violence*, is a clear indication of his priorities.

Sorel is best known in philosophical circles for his theory of the 'great myth'. He ascribed to 'myth' an unusual meaning. For him it was a great dramatic event which would completely transform humanity's view of the world. He therefore referred to the 'myth' of the proletarian revolution or the 'myth' of the general strike. Following these events, the world would never be the same again, and nor would our social consciousness.

Sorel's socialist ideas revolved around his faith in the qualities of the working class, especially the skilled working class. Once freed of oppression by the bourgeois state and monopoly capitalism, this section of the working class was capable, he believed, of striking a decisive blow for liberty and establishing a new age of freedom and social justice.

By a strange irony, Sorel became as popular with fascists as he had been with anarchists and socialists. His rejection of rational philosophy in favour of the efficacy of dynamic action (a view similar to that of Friedrich Nietzsche (1844–1900) appealed to the fascist psyche. He shared their view that power should be obtained through struggle, completely rejecting any notion of democracy.

Sorel was a leading figure within revolutionary socialism and anarchism in the early part of the twentieth century, but his extreme views and espousal of violence eventually alienated most of his supporters.

Henry Thoreau (US, 1817–62)

Thoreau is best known for writing *Walden*, which describes the 2 years he spent living in a log cabin by Walden Pond in Massachusetts, attempting to be self-sufficient. His experiences there became a model for the hippy communes of the 1960s and 1970s.

Thoreau was a romantic and believed that human fulfilment was best achieved through creative work. He hated both industrialisation and capitalism since they took away an individual's natural creativity. However, by withdrawing from society and becoming self-sufficient, the creative way of life could be restored. He is part of the tradition to which the English socialist and craftsman William Morris (1834–96) and the anarchist poet Herbert Read (1893–1968) also belonged.

Another aspect of Thoreau's anarchism was his hatred of the oppressive state, which removes an individual's freedom. Were the state to disappear, he believed, a natural, individualistic and creative way of life could be restored. However, he had no specific plans for how this could be achieved and remains something of a popular, but impractical, oddity within the anarchist tradition.

Murray Rothbard (US, 1926–95)

Rothbard was a key representative of the modern movement known as anarcho-capitalism or extreme libertarianism.

He called his theories 'Austrian Economics' — a revival of ideas which had been developed in the 1930s. Although neo-liberals argue that most goods can be provided by free markets, they accept that the state must exist to provide some services, such as defence and law and order. They also suggest that some social laws, for example concerning morality and drug use, are needed to maintain social stability.

Rothbard and the anarcho-capitalists go a step further than this. Anarcho-capitalists suggest that all services can be provided by private enterprise. There is therefore no need for the state at all. The philosophical basis for this belief lies in natural rights doctrine. If we are born with natural rights, there can never be any justification for the state interfering with our actions. We should be free to exchange goods with whoever we wish, on whatever basis, or with nobody at all. Similarly, the state has no right to intervene in our personal conduct, even if we may harm ourselves. As regards actions which interfere with others, it is up to them to take steps to protect themselves.

In answer to claims that a democratic society and state will also provide all we need, Rothbard asserted that popular democracy is a myth. In reality, as all other anarchists have claimed, government is the exercise of power by the few over the many.

Like Sorel, Rothbard has followers among right-wing as well as left-wing groups. Although he is placed among the anarchists, his views are difficult to categorise accurately. However, some of Rothbard's words are an appropriate summary of the anarchist world view:

> My own basic perspective on the history of man is to place central importance on the great conflict which is eternally waged between liberty and power. I see the liberty of the individual not only as a great moral good in itself, but also as the necessary condition for the flowering of all other goods that mankind cherishes: moral virtue, civilization, the arts and sciences, economic prosperity. But liberty has always been threatened by the encroachments of power, power which seeks to suppress, control, cripple, tax and exploit the fruits of liberty and production.
>
> From *Conceived in Liberty*, 1975

Issues in anarchism

Are anarchists utopians?

One of the main charges made against anarchists is that they are unscientific and therefore hopelessly utopian. Their views of an ideal society may well be worthy of support, but they are impractical. The main criticisms are as follows:

- Anarchists have a mistaken and overoptimistic view of human nature. Conservatives, in particular, argue that human nature is at best unpredictable or changeable, and at worst flawed. Humankind is too self-interested for there to be any hope of establishing a society in which there is no political authority. Of course, anarcho-capitalists, extreme libertarians and anarcho-individualists, such as Stirner and Rothbard, accept this view — that individuals should be able to pursue their own interests. They argue that the interaction of free individuals will create its own natural balance, which does not need regulation. Liberals respond to this by suggesting that no such acceptable balance will exist, and since we will therefore always need to be protected from each other, some kind of state is essential. Thus, both conservatives and liberals claim that anarchism will result in chaos.
- Anarcho-communists have suggested that it is possible to set up a social system based on equality and social justice, in which there will be collective ownership of the means of production. The main criticism of this concerns the nature of property. Conservatives assert that private property is an essential element in a stable society,

while liberals have always seen property as a natural right. A system without property, therefore, would be either disordered or unnatural, or both.

➢ Many critics, from different ideological traditions, have suggested that the drive to power is a natural instinct of humankind. Conservatives, in particular, view people as naturally unequal; there will be some who will succeed and others who will be less successful, some who will lead and others who will follow. Abolishing the state or any other form of political authority is therefore unnatural and will not succeed.

The anarchist response to these criticisms varies. The radical individualists are unconcerned. They believe that individuals should simply be given their liberty, and the outcome of the free exercise of that liberty, whatever it may be, will be natural and can be justified on that basis.

The anarcho-communists, on the other hand, offer a more specific response. The nature of humankind may appear to be inconsistent, selfish and unreliable, but this is because we have been corrupted by a flawed society. If we are indeed the products of our social environment, as Malatesta and Bakunin, for example, claimed, then it is inevitable that a society which lacks morality will produce people who lack morality. If we create a society which is based upon cooperation, morality, justice and liberty, its inhabitants will demonstrate these qualities.

A third view, held by Godwin, for example, is that if individuals are provided with a rational and moral education, they will spontaneously create a just society without the need of government. If individuals can learn to govern their own actions in such a way as to produce good outcomes, then government becomes unnecessary.

Can anarchists reconcile individualism and collectivism?

Although anarcho-individualists indeed accept that collectivism and individual liberty cannot be reconciled, thereby rejecting collectivist ideas altogether, mainstream anarcho-communists believe that they can. How can this belief be justified?

The main thrust of the anarcho-communist argument is that free individuals will naturally form themselves into social groups without feeling any compulsion to do so. They will therefore retain their freedom. As long as everyone in society is equally free and equally rational, they will be able to live harmoniously in social groups. Bakunin expressed this idea as follows:

> Thus, too, the freedom of all is essential to my freedom. And it follows that it would be fallacious to maintain that the freedom of all constitutes a limitation upon my freedom for that would be tantamount to the denial of such freedom. On the contrary, universal freedom represents the necessary affirmation and the boundless expansion of individual freedom.
>
> From *Social and Economic Bases of Anarchism*, 1872

Kropotkin took this a stage further. He saw human freedom in terms of collective identity, arguing that we are only truly free if we live in natural social units. If we are left to live as individuals, we lose our liberty because we will come into conflict with others. He called this principle *free communism* to distinguish it from Marxist schemes which involved the enforcement of collectivism.

Finally, Godwin believed that the answer lay in who was doing the restraining. As long as we are rational and moral, we will not need to be compelled to behave in a collectivist, cooperative way. By exercising what he called 'private judgement', we will express our freedom by restraining ourselves, not by being restrained by social compulsion. 'Each man should be wise enough to govern himself', Godwin asserted. Individuals would govern themselves by willing what is for the good of society as a whole, he argued, 'to promote the general happiness'. Thus, we can live in freedom, without government, in a collectivist social environment.

Marx was sceptical of this anarchist argument. After the revolution, the working class could not expect both individualism and socialism immediately. There would need to be a prolonged period of dictatorship by the proletariat until the people's consciousness had changed radically. Eventually, he insisted, the state would wither away and a new communist age of freedom would be ushered in. Unlike the anarchists, he believed that freedom and communism would not be able to coexist for some time to come. The outright opponents of anarchism, of course, claim that communism and freedom will always be irreconcilable.

However, the main objection to anarchist claims that individualism and collectivism can be reconciled is that any form of collectivism inevitably involves a loss of liberty. Collectivism simply cannot work, critics assert, without the need for some system of authority and some sacrifice of individual liberty.

Is anarchism a single ideology?
As is the case with many such questions, the answer is probably 'yes and no'. In short, anarchism is a single movement in that all anarchists share the same basic principles. These are:

1 All individuals have the right to absolute personal sovereignty.
2 No person has the right to exercise power over another.
3 The existence of the political state can never be tolerated.

Individuals who subscribe to these three principles are justified in describing themselves as anarchists.

However, it is impossible to put all those who have described themselves as anarchists into the same political tradition. The following movements can be identified, all of which have described themselves as anarchist:
➤ nihilism
➤ anarcho-capitalism or libertarianism
➤ anarcho-individualism
➤ anarcho-communism
➤ anarcho-syndicalism

Furthermore, there are movements which have added opposition to the state to their primary goals and so have been included in the anarchist tradition. These include feminism and environmentalism. All of these movements propose the abolition of the state but there are fundamental differences in the kind of social order (if any) they would put in its place. For some, there would be no state of any kind; for others, there would be a state which represented a transformed society.

It is also true that different anarchists have even disagreed about **human nature**, from Stirner, who sees us as basically egotistical and self-interested, to Bakunin, who sees us as naturally driven towards social organisation and cooperation. While Sorel and Stirner are pessimistic about human nature, Godwin and Kropotkin are intensely optimistic.

Key term

Human nature
All political philosophies and ideologies have developed theories about human nature. This means that they make assumptions about what is the natural state of humankind, i.e. how people behaved before society came about. Some ideologies, such as socialism, have an optimistic view of human nature — they believe we are naturally sociable and cooperative. Others take the pessimistic view that humankind is not naturally social, and may even be excessively selfish. Conservatives have tended to see people as unreliable, and driven by appetites rather than reason. The purpose of developing such theories is to help create a natural form of society suited to humankind's basic character.

To confuse the issue further, anarchists have disagreed over the means of bringing about the anarchist utopia. Most anarchists have been revolutionaries and accept the need for a dramatic, often violent transformation of society into a stateless existence. Some, however, have been pacifists. The most notable example was perhaps the Russian novelist Leo Tolstoy (author of *War and Peace* and *Anna Karenina*), who opposed revolution, preferring instead a gradual, voluntary transition to anarchism. Tolstoy was a wealthy, aristocratic landowner who freed his own peasants and encouraged them to form self-governing communes. Some individualists, such as Thoreau, have recommended that we should simply withdraw from society and so free ourselves from the oppression of the state.

In summary, therefore, anarchists are united on the three basic principles. However, they disagree fundamentally both about the form of social order they would prefer and the means by which this can be brought about.

Anarchism and liberalism

Both anarchism and liberalism were born out of Enlightenment thinking and both place liberty at the centre of their political universe. They also share a strong suspicion of the power of the state. It is therefore interesting to ask whether anarchism is really an extreme form of liberalism. In order to address this question, we need to look at three aspects of the two philosophies:

> Are there fundamental differences in how they view liberty?
> How do they view the state?
> What kind of society do they propose to replace the existing order?

These questions are considered in turn under the three different headings below.

Freedom

In summary, liberals make the fundamental assertion that the most important kind of liberty involves the absence of external restraint. This has become known as 'negative liberty'. Anarchists have no problem in agreeing that this kind of liberty is essential. However, whereas liberals accept that there must be laws and limitations on the individual to ensure that his or her freedom does not interfere with the freedom of others, anarchists say that this will not be necessary. In their idealised, perfectly moral society, each individual will exercise internal restraint, often described as 'private judgement'.

In this sense, the answer to our initial question might be 'yes': anarchism is an extreme version of liberalism in that there would apparently be a greater degree of personal liberty in the anarchist world, although both worlds would be similar in that they would be remarkably free. There is, however, a crucial distinction. Anarchism will countenance no laws. Anarchists insist that all laws are incompatible with freedom, while liberals argue that we cannot be free without laws.

The two philosophies do, perhaps, agree on the form of liberty known as 'positive freedom'. Both claim that the societies they propose would maximise individualism and the fulfilment of personal progress and creativity. The freedom they promote would liberate individuals from the restraints of societies which restrict choice and opportunity and discourage the achievement of self-realisation. In that sense, therefore, liberation has a positive outcome and the anarchist aim of creating total liberation goes much further than liberalism.

The state

As with freedom, there is an apparent affinity between the two doctrines regarding their view of the state. Both oppose the excessive exercise of power and see the state as the actual or potential enemy of freedom. There is, however, a vital distinction. Liberals see the state as essential to the preservation of liberty (provided, of course, it is a 'liberal' state). It protects individuals from each other and from accumulations of power. Anarchists, on the other hand, insist that all forms of state are unacceptable. It is inevitable, they argue, that states will exercise the power of the few over the many. However benign it may appear, the state must, by its very nature, use force against its citizens. How else is it able to perform its functions? Anarchists reject all forms of power and force, even if the state claims that they are used for good ends.

This is clearly not a difference of degree, but a fundamental distinction. Liberals accept the existence of a limited state, but anarchists will never support any kind of state. They argue that even limited states will eventually become powerful states. Ironically, anarchists find it easier than liberals to support Lord Acton's famous warning about the corrupting nature of power. Acton intended his slogan as a liberal motto.

The free society

The anarcho-individualists and anarcho-capitalists share with liberals a desire to see a society which is as free as it possibly can be. Indeed, classical liberals and social Darwinists share with anarchists the belief that every individual can only reach his or her full potential in a free society. They all believe that the freedom of the individual should stand above social constraints. Of course, anarchists hope and expect that individuals will use their liberty exclusively for 'good' ends, whereas liberals accept that individuals are likely to pursue their own self-interest, and are therefore likely to create a highly competitive world. However, there is certainly a case for arguing that some extreme liberals envisage a society close to an anarchist world of autonomous individuals motivated by egoism. The world of evolutionary competition espoused by Herbert Spencer seems similar to Max Stirner's conception of a complete absence of social order, with individualism being granted free rein.

However, when collectivist forms of anarchism are considered, notably the anarcho-communism of Bakunin and Kropotkin, crucial distinctions between the ideologies emerge. The liberal community comes about through an agreement among the people to set up government over themselves. This community is based on a kind of social contract and usually stems from national identity. Once the community is established, consent is assumed, say liberals, and it is necessary to reserve the use of force against those citizens who defy the restraints within that community. For anarchists, communities must be totally voluntary and therefore natural. The use of force becomes unnecessary because the community comes into being naturally and not through an artificial contract.

A second key distinction concerns the role of private property. Liberals see the existence of property as a right enjoyed by all individuals. Almost all anarchists (Proudhon being a notable exception) oppose the preservation of private property. They believe that property inevitably creates injustice, inequality and corruption. It also leads inevitably to the emergence of power relationships.

Conclusion

The anarchist principles of the absence of a state and private property, and the voluntary nature of the political community, all make for fundamental and irreconcilable differences between liberalism and anarchism. In terms of values, it may well be argued that anarchism is an extreme form of liberalism, but this is certainly not the case when considering their fundamental beliefs on the nature of freedom and of the free society.

Anarchism and socialism

On what grounds do socialists and anarchists conflict?

First, we must eliminate any comparison between anarcho-individualism and socialism. Clearly these two traditions have very little in common and in many ways they can be seen as ideological opposites. Socialists insist that humans are social animals whose instincts for cooperation and mutual sympathy are stronger than their egoism. For socialists, the pursuit of self-interest is unnatural and the result of capitalism rather than a prerequisite for it. By contrast, anarcho-individualists believe that egoism is a fundamental feature of human character, and that any form of social organisation restrains egoism and is therefore unnatural.

However, collectivist forms of anarchism have a good deal in common with socialism, making comparisons between the ideologies more complex. The points of similarity include the following:

➤ Both traditions see major problems arising from the existence of private property. Indeed, both Marxists and anarcho-communists oppose private property altogether. Less extreme forms of socialism have allowed some scope for the possession of property, but temper this with a need for some common ownership.

➤ Anarcho-communists and socialists hold similar views of human nature. Both accept that individuals can achieve all or much of their self-realisation, and the fulfilment of their own aspirations, through collective action. In extreme circumstances, this means collectivising all resources. For moderate socialists, it would only involve collectivising some, but not all, of the means of production and distribution.

➤ Both traditions have a strong sense of equality. They both support equal rights and equality of opportunity, and share a sense that each individual has equal worth. Marxists and quasi-Marxist socialists agree with anarchists that there should be an equal distribution of rewards in society according to need. It is true that moderate socialists accept degrees of inequality as natural, but even they accept that every individual is worthy of equal respect, dignity and opportunity.

Thus, anarcho-communism and socialism have much in common and in many ways they have common roots — in their opposition to capitalism, inequality and the dominance of the state by a ruling class. However, this should not disguise their fundamental differences.

The most striking contrast concerns the position of the state. All anarchists would abolish the state. Whatever its function, the state is always a denial of liberty and individualism. It does not matter to anarchists that a socialist state might abolish private property and impose economic and social equality (as in the USSR or communist China). Once the state's outward appearance is stripped away it is revealed as the government of the many by the few, say anarchists, whatever its apparent objectives. Furthermore, all states will inevitably become politically corrupt because the exercise of power is as oppressive to leaders as it is to subjects. The leaders of the state become victims of their own drive to exercise power. This drive can be intoxicating and therefore addictive. The experience of the communist-socialist states of central and Eastern Europe certainly appears to have borne out this anarchist assertion.

In the 1870s, the role of the state split the anarchists and Marxists. Anarchists insisted that the revolution which was to overthrow capitalism would lead immediately to a stateless society and a communist order. Marxists argued that there would need to be an interim phase after revolution in which an oppressive workers' state would be established in order to build socialism and protect the achievements of the revolution. Anarchists predicted that such a state would not wither away, as Marx had declared, but would endure as a new form of ruling class.

So-called state socialists, including the early British Fabians, the French Socialist Party, Eduard Bernstein and Tony Benn, have all seen the state as a vital component in the realisation of socialist goals. They see welfare, equality, common ownership and collective action of all kinds as best organised by the centralised state, as this is the only way of ensuring universal equality. For anarcho-communists, however, equality would naturally follow from the establishment of free, voluntary communities. The state would lead to the negation rather than the facilitation of freedom and equality.

Finally, a more philosophical distinction should be considered. Socialists tend to believe that freedom and individualism are developed by the establishment of equality. This means that the principal enemy of freedom is inequality. This is not acceptable to anarchists. For them, liberty is an individualist concept, which perhaps has more in common with the classical liberal view of freedom. Equality cannot guarantee such freedom; only the complete abolition of the state, its laws and the compulsory herding of people into unnatural communities can do so. Natural anarchist communities can combine individual liberty with both equality and mutual cooperation. Socialism, complain the anarchists, simply involves too much compulsion. On the other hand, socialists argue that anarchism is utopian and unrealistic in believing that equality and collective freedom can be achieved without being organised by some form of state.

Is anarchism merely unscientific socialism?

An important criticism of anarchism in all its forms is that it is an unscientific, utopian philosophy, the product of romantic dreamers or violent revolutionaries who know what they are against, but lack any rigorous conception of how a new social order should be formed. A detailed critique of anarcho-communism, in particular, would include the following features:

➢ lack of a theory of history
➢ lack of a coherent view of humankind
➢ incoherent view of a social order
➢ lack of a coherent conception of class

It is certainly true that anarchism does not have its own Marx, a theorist who could demonstrate a natural historical progress towards a no-state society. It is also the case that anarchists differ greatly in their views of human nature. Bakunin believed there was no such thing as human nature or natural morality, and argued that an individual is, at birth, neither good nor bad. Kropotkin and Tolstoy firmly believed that man is naturally sociable, but individualists such as Stirner and Tucker see man as a solitary, egotistical figure. This lack of unanimity over human nature makes it extremely difficult to accept a single ideological position. It certainly weakens any claim that anarchism is a rigorous, rational philosophy.

It is often argued that anarchism fundamentally lacks a scientific explanation of the nature of society and the role of social class in particular. This suggests that anarchists are simplistic in their social vision, looking no further than phenomena such as excessive authority, oppression and exploitation.

This may be overcritical. Most anarchists have shared a set of distinct values with socialists that are fully identifiable. These include equality, community, cooperation, common ownership and mutual respect. In this regard, anarchism, whether or not it is scientific, can be seen as a form of socialism that simply opposes the institution of the state.

Exam focus

Using this chapter and other resources available to you, answer the following questions.

Short questions
Your answers should be about 300 words long.
1 What do anarchists mean by 'liberty'?
2 Distinguish between a liberal and an anarchist view of freedom.
3 Why do anarchists oppose the state?
4 How do anarchists view human nature?
5 On what grounds do anarchists oppose private property?

Long questions
Your answers should be about 900 words long.
1 To what extent is anarchism merely a utopian aspiration?
2 'All anarchists agree about ends, but disagree about means.' How true is this statement?
3 Distinguish between individualism and collectivism in the anarchist tradition.
4 Is anarchism merely an extreme form of liberalism?
5 Is anarchism a separate ideology or merely a branch of socialism?

Further reading

Marshall, P. (1993) *Demanding the Impossible: A History of Anarchism*, Fontana.

Miller, D. (1984) *Anarchism*, Everyman.

Nozick, R. (2001) *Anarchy, State and Utopia*, Blackwell.

Thoreau, H. D. (1962) *Walden*, Bantam.

Wolff, R. P. (1970) *In Defence of Anarchism*, Harper and Rowe.

Woodcock, G. (1962) *Anarchism: A History of Libertarian Ideas and Movements*, Penguin.

Chapter 7

Fascism

Fascism is the name commonly given to a number of political movements and regimes that flourished mainly between the First World War and the Second World War. It is a synthesis of right-wing nationalism, so-called radical conservatism and concentration on the state and its leader as the vehicle for the collective aspirations of a nation. Fascism directly opposes pluralist and popular forms of democracy, rejecting them in favour of totalitarian forms of rule, in which a single leader is placed at the apex of power and no rival authorities are allowed. In a fascist state, each individual's self-interest must be subordinate to the interests of the state and its leader. Fascists value self-sacrifice, personal dynamism, struggle and inequality. In the German (i.e. Nazi) form of fascism, these virtues were to reach their height.

Introduction

Most of this chapter is concerned with the general term 'fascism'. There is often some confusion between the terms fascism and Nazism, but this is relatively easily to resolve. Nazism can be safely treated as a particular form of fascism; it stressed certain aspects of fascist ideology more than others, but nevertheless it was content to describe itself as fascist (Adolf Hitler himself often used the terms interchangeably). Nazism is, of course, associated specifically with the Third Reich which controlled Germany from 1934 to 1945. The characteristics which distinguished Nazism from other forms of fascism (for example, in Italy or Spain) are examined later in this chapter (see pp. 245–46).

As political movements, both fascism and Nazism were totalitarian in nature. It is therefore important to be clear about the meaning of the term 'totalitarian' before proceeding. There have been many theories about and explanations of totalitarianism, but for the purposes of this book a relatively brief and uncontroversial definition will suffice. Thus, a totalitarian state is one that exhibits most or all of the following features:

➤ The state — that is, all the permanent institutions of the country, including the law-enforcement system, armed forces, permanent apparatus of government, etc. — claims the right to control all aspects of the lives of its people.

➤ There is little distinction between what is private, e.g. family life, arts, media and business, and what is public, e.g. the organisation of education, transport, welfare services, law and order etc. The state has the power to regulate both.

➤ The usual pluralist aspects of democratic government are absent. There is only one ruling party, there are no properly contested elections (if there are elections at all) and pressure groups, religions and trade unions are either banned, suppressed or controlled by the state.

➤ Government is dominated by a single leader or ruling elite that claims total power, accepts no opposition and is not directly accountable to the people. However, totalitarian rulers do claim to embody the collective will of the people.

➤ The regime uses terror — the public display of force — to secure the obedience of the people.

➤ Propaganda and mass psychology are used to try to secure the support of the people.
Note this summary could be applied to communist (sometimes called 'soviet-style') regimes as well as to fascist and Nazi governments. It may also describe — in part at least — some regimes which have flourished more recently, such as Saddam Hussein's Iraq or the military government in Burma.

Rationalism and romanticism
It is difficult to understand the nature of fascism without first examining the distinctions between rationality and romanticism. These are both ways of thinking and forms of political action. Fascists pride themselves on both their rejection of rationality and their adoption of romantic ideals, which they consider to be vastly superior. Indeed, fascism should be considered in terms of the conflict which existed in politics and philosophy between rationalism and romantic idealism.

The Enlightenment era — roughly corresponding to the eighteenth century in Western civilisation — ushered in new rational ways of viewing the world and society. Rational thought claimed to be able to discover explanations for virtually everything in the world, based on scientific, objective evidence. Alternatives to this rational thought had included explanations which proposed that the will of God was behind most events, or general theories adopted by prominent individuals. It was common to explain the world simply as a reflection of God's grand plan or of his will.

In the Enlightenment age, rationalism was applied to a wide range of areas. In the physical sciences, the ideas of Isaac Newton became dominant; in religion, rational,

Protestant thinkers replaced the conservatism of the Roman Church. Rationalism also pervaded artistic fields, such as architecture, painting and even music, where Wolfgang Amadeus Mozart was the primary example.

For the purposes of this book, however, it is rationalism in the fields of philosophy and politics that is of most concern. France spawned a number of celebrated thinkers, many of whom became collectively known as 'les philosophes'; Voltaire (the pen name of François-Marie Arouet), Jean-Jacques Rousseau and Charles-Louis Montesquieu (1689–1755) are examples. There were many too in Germany (e.g. Friedrich Hegel), England (e.g. John Locke, John Stuart Mill, Jeremy Bentham), in Scotland (e.g. David Hume (1711–76)) and in the USA (e.g. James Madison). These philosophers and political theorists were largely concerned with the problem of how to set up and run a government along rational lines. There was a pressing need for this since in many countries the traditional form of government — monarchy backed by a hereditary aristocracy — was breaking down as the people sought political power and influence.

Rational government involved such principles and practices as government by consent, democracy (either direct or representative), accountability, the protection of individual rights and constitutionalism. In addition, the objectives of government were to be discovered by rational means. This could mean scientific methods of discovering which actions would be in the best interests of the people (the clearest example of this being utilitarianism) or effective ways of converting the demands and needs of the people into political action — that is, various kinds of democratic arrangements.

The typical fascist of the twentieth century rejected these modes of thinking and forms of action, preferring romantic ideals and actions based on emotion rather than reason — in other words, acting from the heart rather than the head. Two concrete examples of fascist behaviour serve to illustrate this point.

First, there is the fascist response to the problem of how best to serve the interests of the people. Instead of using scientific formulae to do this, fascists favour the inspirational leadership of a single ruler (a man — fascists were all anti-feminist), who could exercise his superior judgement. He would know what was best for the people better than the people did themselves. The petty self-interests of the people were to be disparaged — far superior to mere economic contentment was the noble cause of the dynamic pursuit of glory for the nation. This was indeed a romantic rather than a rational goal.

Second, there is the fascist objection to democracy. Different kinds of democracy can be seen as the rational means by which political demands can be converted into action. Fascists reject traditional liberal democracy. They believe it is a weak and directionless way of conducting politics. The people — who effectively govern a liberal democracy — are too easily swayed by short-term popular movements. Furthermore, the people are prone to changing their minds and to seeking short-term advantages, often at the expense of long-term ideals.

Again, the power of the romantically inspired leader is preferable to the feckless, unreliable demands of the masses. The leader is likely to be dynamic and determined, and to embody higher ideals than those of the ordinary people. It was clear to many Germans in the early 1930s that the pluralist and chaotic politics of the Weimar Republic, which preceded the Third Reich, was failing them. Instead they chose Hitler, a great orator who had successfully presented himself as a convincing romantic hero. He promised them deliverance from the humiliation of the post-First World War settlement and offered in its place dreams of a return to the past glories of the German nation.

It should be pointed out at this stage that some fascists have argued that leadership-based regimes can be described as broadly democratic. The basis of this argument is that the leader is governing *for* the people. It is not democracy in the sense of government *by* the people (as Abraham Lincoln (1809–65) had proposed in his famous Gettysburg Address) but it could be described as government *on behalf* of the people.

The interwar crisis of democracy

Democracy in most European countries suffered a series of major crises between the two world wars. Having survived a strong challenge from communism and revolutionary socialism after the First World War, Europe, like the USA, was hit by the Great Depression. Democratic governments struggled to deal with the crisis of economic decline.

The political systems of countries such as Germany, Italy and France were highly pluralistic in nature, with multi-party scenarios in which no single political force was able to exercise dominance. There were frequent changes of government with weak coalitions rapidly coming and going. Party politicians proved themselves to be, on the whole, remarkably ineffective. Under the combined pressures of economic crisis and challenges from extreme political movements of both the left and the right, conventional politics often could not cope, and was characterised by constant vacillations and compromises. Moreover, in those countries that had suffered defeat in the First World War, especially Germany, many of the postwar politicians were associated with wartime failure. Liberal democratic politics was therefore discredited.

Fascism arrived on this scene, initially in Italy in the early 1920s, and supplied answers to some of these problems. Its leaders appeared to be strong and dynamic, whereas the liberal democratic politicians were weak and lacked vision. The fascists were looking forward to promised future solutions and greater glories so that their countries could escape their current depression; the democrats were backward looking and negative in their attitude. Above all, the fascists were able to inspire a popular following on the basis of their message and personal qualities, while other politicians seemed to be slaves to constantly shifting public opinion. Liberal democratic politics, claimed the new fascists, had failed.

The theoretical origins of fascism and totalitarianism

Fascism and totalitarianism have similar origins. This section considers the dominant philosophies and ideas that shaped them both.

General will

In the late eighteenth century, the French philosopher Jean-Jacques Rousseau considered the shortcomings of popular democracy, a system which was emerging at the time as a possible replacement for monarchical governments. Democracy, Rousseau argued, would tend to develop into majority rule and this would not necessarily serve the best interests of the people collectively. Indeed, he mistrusted any political system based on people's self-interest. His notion of a *general will* suggested that a people had some kind of collective identity that stood above mere self-interest. But how could the general will be determined if the democratic process was so flawed? Rousseau's answer was that an individual ruler, a kind of philosopher leader, would be identified. This ruler would understand the collective interests of the people and govern the state accordingly.

Rousseau's notion of general will and an all-powerful leader who could enforce it has been seen by many as a philosophical justification for totalitarian rule. Indeed, it could be argued that his ideas were the inspiration behind the rule in France of Napoleon Bonaparte, which commenced not long after Rousseau's life had ended.

Organic state

At the end of the eighteenth century and into the early nineteenth century, the German philosopher Friedrich Hegel transformed perceptions of history and society. He saw the state as an organic entity, which was gradually developing through history to a perfect form. He believed that the Prussia of the turn of the eighteenth century was evolving into such a state. What Hegel meant by a perfect state was one in which the interests of the people collectively would coincide with the interests of individuals. There would be a harmony between the purposes of government and the purposes of the people. This has been interpreted (falsely, many claim) as meaning that a state can be reduced to a single organic whole and could therefore be governed in a non-democratic, perhaps totalitarian, manner. This interpretation is based on the assumption that the will of each individual will be subordinate to the collective will of the state.

Nationalism

A close contemporary of Hegel was the German nationalist Johann Fichte. Fichte's philosophy controversially suggested that human destiny lay in a kind of romantic nationalism — an emotional attachment to one's circumstances of birth. Nationalism, especially German nationalism, was the ultimate expression of the human spirit. Fichte's ideas closely match the ideals of the fascists who were to emerge over 100 years later.

Racialism and social Darwinism

Fascism, especially in its Nazi form, is strongly associated with racialism. The two main influences behind fascist racial theories were Arthur de Gobineau (1816–82) and Houston Chamberlain. Both these thinkers considered racial identity to be a key factor in the development of civilisation. Gobineau placed different races into a hierarchy, with the purest and therefore strongest at the top (e.g. Germanic peoples) and inferior races (e.g. Asian peoples) at the bottom. Chamberlain saw the history of modern civilisation in terms of a struggle between Aryan or Teutonic (i.e. North European, Germanic) peoples and the Jews. These theories accord closely with fascist radical nationalism, which was based on racial and cultural superiority. Indeed, Chamberlain was one of Hitler's closest advisers in his early days as a populist politician.

Closely linked to the racial theories of Gobineau and Chamberlain were ideas that emerged from the work of Charles Darwin on evolution, in particular his so-called 'survival of the fittest' analysis. It should be pointed out that Darwin himself firmly denied that his biological theories could be adapted to human society in any strict sense. Nevertheless, many political thinkers of the latter part of the nineteenth century did just that, and created a movement known as 'social Darwinism'. This movement suggested that, as in the animal kingdom, humans were engaged in a struggle for superiority over each other, especially in their economic life and, even more importantly, within capitalism. Far from being a problem, this evolutionary struggle served to strengthen society, just as a similar process did for the genetic lines of animal species. The struggle ensured a dynamic society in which only the strongest would emerge in positions of economic and political power.

Cycle of elites

In Italy, Benito Mussolini was influenced by the work of Vilfredo Pareto (1848–1923). Pareto argued that political power would inevitably rest in the hands of a small elite at the top of society. He suggested that most ordinary people are incapable of taking control of their lives and are certainly not fit to be actively involved in the organisation of the state. He also asserted that, although the state will be dominated by such an elite, there will always be a rival group gathering its power and unity in the background. Governing elites will, he suggested, inevitably begin to decline, lose their effectiveness and become decadent. While this is happening, the new aspiring elite will consolidate its forces and will eventually topple the ruling group. This would become a recurring, cyclical process. It embodied ideas such as strength through struggle and the power of unity, which were particularly attractive to fascists.

Superman

Finally, we must turn to the most controversial of all the influences on fascism — the German philosopher Friedrich Nietzsche. It is a mistake to describe Nietzsche as a fascist — he was not. Three reasons can be given for this. First, of course, he predates fascism by several decades. Second, he wrote little about politics (he was more concerned with the broader issues of civilisation and the human condition). Third, he did not suggest, as is often claimed, that nations should be ruled by all-powerful, totalitarian dictators. He certainly did believe that some individuals were endowed with superior will and imagination and that they would tend to dominate societies, but this was not a recipe for the kind of government which fascists were to set up.

Much of Nietzsche's reputation and influence were in fact propagated after his death by his sister, Elizabeth Foerster-Nietzsche (1846–1935). She put together a distorted collection of extracts from Nietzsche's writings, titled *The Will to Power*. It was this work which was taken up by fascists as a philosophical justification for their ideas and actions. In it, the famous idea of the *Übermensch* was developed. This 'superman' was an individual whose vision, will and dynamism would make him superior to all others and would inspire a whole nation to heroic action. Small wonder that leading fascists should seize upon this concept and use it for their own purposes.

Friedrich Nietzsche's philosophy was appropriated by fascists

Nietzsche certainly discussed the conflict which exists within civilisations between rationalism and romanticism, as described above, but he seemed to favour a balanced harmony between them. The crisis of modern civilisation was, for him, that this harmony had been destroyed and that rationalism (in religion as well as the arts and government) was sapping society of its dynamism and future potential. Fascists were particularly impressed by the notion that they were in a position to deal with this crisis.

Core values of fascism

Irrationality

Fascism is characterised as an anti-rational (or 'irrational' — either term can be used) doctrine. As has been shown, its origins lie to some extent in a romantic, irrational reaction against Enlightenment thinking. Scientific, reasoned analyses of history and society offered by thinkers such as Karl Marx (proponent of scientific socialism) or Bentham (who favoured liberal utilitarianism) in the nineteenth century were seen as flawed and uninspiring. They were flawed, argued fascists, in that they ignored the influence that great individuals had upon history and social development. At the same time, efforts to attract the support of a nation in future enterprises would surely fail if they were based on dry, rational arguments. People do not have the capability of understanding and responding to reasoned analysis; rather, they need to be inspired by emotional appeals and by the example of heroic deeds from the past. Unsurprisingly, fascists were therefore anti-intellectual and highly sceptical of philosophy. They preferred action to thought and the exertion of will over people to reasoned arguments.

These ideas were linked closely to their attitude towards the role of individuals in social development. Scientific philosophers, such as Hegel and Karl Marx, seem to have suggested that society is subject to historical forces beyond humankind's control. Marx asserted that it was the nature of economic relationships and systems which explained the true character of any society. Historical change, according to Marx, occurred as a result of changes in these basic economic conditions. For fascists, this is a one-sided view of historical change which carries two problems. The first is that such an analysis omits the role of individuals in history. The great heroes, monarchs, adventurers and warrior leaders were significant figures who were to be admired and emulated. Figures such as Charlemagne (?742–814), the legendary William Tell and Napoleon had engaged in great struggles, often when the forces of history were against them. Their triumphs illustrated the potential of the human spirit and strength of will. Second, if individuals came to believe that they were merely powerless pawns in a great historical process, it would sap their drive and energy. Societies would then prove to be weak and directionless — a total denial of the human spirit.

Mythology

The Renaissance political theorist Niccolò Machiavelli (1469–1527), in his famous work *The Prince*, advised rulers that they should only tell the truth to their people if it were absolutely necessary. What was important was that they maintained their own rule in the interests of the state and its security. If deceiving the people would preserve the peace and create order, rulers should ignore morality and do so. Machiavelli added that if they could manipulate public sentiment, too, so much the better. Fascist leaders certainly behaved in this way. Another example followed by fascists was that of ancient Greek societies which developed a mythology inhabited by heroes, gods and goddesses, based less on historical truth and more upon a representation of the kind of virtues rulers hoped to promote among the people.

Both of these ideas — manipulating the emotions of the people and encouraging individual virtues — lend themselves to the extensive use of myths to justify the state's actions. The most sinister use of myth concerned attitudes towards the Jews in Nazi Germany and its conquered territories. The blame for Germany's defeat in the First World War was placed firmly on the shoulders of Jews and communists, with no objective evidence for this. Gobineau and Chamberlain used history to justify the oppression and elimination of the Jews. Their quasi-scientific studies claimed, without real substantiation, that the struggle against the Jews was part of Germany's more glorious history. Stories about the heroic deeds of the Teutonic knights in the Middle Ages were told in German schools under the Third Reich, and young men re-enacted the knights' glories in their own lives.

In Italy, Mussolini and his close adviser, Giovanni Gentile (1875–1944), developed an entire mythology around Italian history. Drawing on the glories of the Roman Empire they created the illusion that Italy was destined to recreate its imperial past. Even the fascist symbol of authority, the *fasces* (a bundle of rods), was of classical Roman origin. Indeed, the idea that Italy was an established, single nation was itself largely mythological.

Ironically, it was a nineteenth-century anarchist, Georges Sorel, who influenced Mussolini in his use of the 'great myth'. Sorel asserted that reasoned arguments and rational theories could not inspire people to create revolutions and to transform society, a view all facists came to believe. What they needed was a myth, a vision of what the future could hold, to inspire them. The Italian fascists adapted this idea to lead the Italian people toward a new golden age, and a new imperial future for Italy.

The virtues which fascists worshipped, such as heroism, struggle and honour, were glorified in fascist history books, and a great following for the works of Richard Wagner (1813–83), the German romantic composer, emerged in the 1930s. Wagner's grand operas portrayed the lives of German historical figures, arguably employing some of the most romantic and inspiring music that has ever been written.

Will to action and struggle

Adapting Nietzsche's worship of 'will to power', fascists were driven by a desire to achieve great deeds, to transform whole societies and to leave behind them evidence of their masculine virtues. Such decisive action could not be the result of philosophy and rationality, or the outcome of a democratic process. It could only be realised through the dynamic actions of the state's leaders. Mussolini's apparently trivial boast that he could 'make the trains run on time' was symbolic of a deeper belief. This was that the fascist leader could cut through complexity, bureaucracy and human frailty in order to bring about heroic outcomes.

In both Germany and Italy there is still evidence of will to action in the form of great monuments, motorways, public buildings and memorials (a feature, in fact, of all total-itarian regimes, whether fascist or not). The passage below illustrates the importance of such dynamism:

> Fascism wants men to be active and to engage in activity with all their energy; it requires that they should be manfully aware of the difficulties besetting them and ready to face them. Life is conceived as a struggle in which a man is bound to win for himself a really worthy place... As it is for the individual, so it is for the nation, and for all mankind.
>
> From *Enciclopedia Italiana* (largely by Giovanni Gentile), 1932

Being able to act decisively involves a struggle against those forces which threaten the will of the individual. The features of modern society ranged against will to action and struggle include popular democracy, intellectualism, self-interest, religion and bourgeois (i.e. middle-class) values. Individuals have a duty to struggle against such obstacles, whether or not they succeed. It should be noted that fascists did not believe women possessed the necessary virtues to carry out such a struggle, so will to action is exclusive to men.

Just as individuals are engaged in this struggle, so too are nations and entire civili-sations. The ancient Romans succeeded in conquering virtually the whole of the known world, the Italian fascists pointed out, while the German people were engaged in a historic rivalry with the Jews and all they stood for, a myth adopted by the Nazis. The struggle of wills that exists in any dynamic society gives rise to a Darwinian process of 'survival of the fittest', which ensures that only the individual with the most superior will to action will rise to the highest position in the state. This is explored further in the section on leadership below.

Warfare

A consideration of a number of values common to fascism makes it clear why most fascists became obsessed with the need to engage in warfare. Will to action, the virtues of struggle, self-sacrifice and heroism, and the subjection of the individual to the purposes of the state, point to warfare being the ultimate expression of all of them together.

Nietzsche declared: 'The Nation that gives up war and conquest is ripe for democracy and rule by shopkeepers....' (*Beyond Good and Evil*, 1886). This sums up the fascists' attitude. Democracy represents weakness, while 'shopkeepers' refers to the notorious pursuit of self-interest engaged in by members of what Marx called the 'petite bourgeoisie'. This class considered their own interests to be more important than those of the collective. Fascists despised this trait, and yet ironically it was the bourgeoisie which proved to be among Hitler's greatest supporters in Germany.

Another reason for the fascist obsession with warfare is that fascists are radical, right-wing nationalists. The interests of the nation are often seen in terms of its rivalry with other powerful nations, the need to protect it from expansionist nations and, above all, as a desire to express the nation's superiority. In order to prove such superiority, at least in the first half of the twentieth century, strong nations sought to conquer weak ones. Note Italy's invasion of Abyssinia in 1936 and Nazi Germany's ambition to conquer all Slavic peoples.

Leadership

The existence of a single, all-powerful leader is perhaps the best-known feature of fascist regimes. Hitler, Mussolini, Francisco Franco and (arguably) Juan Peron (1895–1974) in Argentina are all closely associated with fascism. Although the existence of such a leader is not a defining characteristic of fascism, it is true that all fascist regimes have had one.

Two features of the typical fascist society give rise to dominant leadership. The first is the process of struggle and will to act which replaces democracy. It becomes inevitable that he who rises to the top will be strong simply because he is the product of such a struggle. This outcome is celebrated by fascists as a superior way of selecting political leadership to that of democratic choices. Under democracy, people

Benito Mussolini, Il Duce

choose leaders on the basis of who will give them what they want, or who can merely command the support of the majority. This does not necessarily mean that they will be the best individual to lead a state to future glories. As regards collective leadership, fascists argue that this suffers from the problem of being divided, lacking a singular vision and therefore becoming too weak. Nietzsche famously predicted that each modern society would fall under the control of a superior individual, his famous *Übermensch* (superman). This leader, he predicted, would demonstrate a more superior 'will to power' than any of his rivals.

Key term

Übermensch

This concept was developed by Nietzsche. He proposed that a society may produce one individual who demonstrates higher qualities than any other members of that society. This 'superman' would demonstrate his superior will to power by rising above the sheep-like quality of most other people. He would stand above the concepts of good and evil: all that would matter to him is that he be able to act, and inspire others to act, in a decisive way. The concept of the *Übermensch* is in direct contrast to democracy, which reduces mankind to behaving with a herd instinct. Great men, Nietzsche insisted, can inspire the collective instincts of the people. Fascists were attracted to this aspect of Nietzsche's work and shared his Darwinian approach to the emergence of great leaders. They agreed that leadership should be the result of a struggle for power, not rational processes like democratic elections. Like Nietzsche, fascists believed that such leaders need not concern themselves with any notion of morality.

The second feature is that the fascist state needs, above all, unity of purpose. Democracy, argue fascists, cannot create this. It has to be provided by a single leader who can embody the collective will of the state and its people. In a 1939 speech, Hitler stated:

> He [the leader] shapes the collective will of the people within himself and he embodies the political unity and entirety of the people in opposition to individual interests.

Mussolini took this belief even further, suggesting that he, Il Duce (the leader), was effectively infallible and therefore his orders had to be obeyed without exception. If an individual or group were to defy the leader, they would also be defying the collective will of the people, and this would be a crime against the state itself (see Box 7.1).

As a result of these beliefs, fascist leaders have tended to demonstrate similar characteristics. They have all recognised the importance of oratory, since the people need to be inspired. They have demanded, and usually achieved, complete obedience to their will. Above all, however, they have promoted a grand vision for their respective nations. They were rarely concerned with the petty politics arising from conflicts between different groups in society (i.e. pluralist democracy), preferring to deal in grand projects, heroic dreams and historical destiny.

Box 7.1 The fascist ten commandments

These commandments were issued to Italian fascist troops in 1931. They contain within them a number of key fascist principles.

God and Fatherland: all other affections and duties come after these.

Whoever is not ready to give himself body and soul for his country, and to serve the Duce [Mussolini] without discussion, is not worthy of wearing the Black Shirt. Fascism repudiates lukewarm faith and half-characters.

Use your intelligence to understand the orders that you receive and all your enthusiasm for obedience.

Discipline is not only a virtue of the soldiers in the ranks, it must also be the practice of every day and all circumstances.

A bad child and a negligent student are not fascists.

Organise your time in such a way that work will be a joy, and your games work.

Learn to suffer without complaining, to give without asking, to serve without waiting for reward.

Good actions, like actions in war, must not be done in halves; carry them to their extreme consequences.

In actual circumstances, remember that good lies in audacity.

And thank God every day for having made you a fascist and Italian.

Opposition to democracy

It is clear from the fascist view of leadership that democracy is simply inappropriate in a fascist regime. Indeed, many fascists, including Hitler, saw it as a positive evil. Examining three types of democracy reveals the various objections proposed by fascists.

First, there is democracy in the form of rule by the majority. Fascists saw no grounds for the majority being necessarily right. Rather, just as the liberal/anarchist philosopher Rousseau had asserted in the eighteenth century, they saw democracy as merely an arithmetical expression of the most dominant self-interests. Fascists are concerned with the collective, organic will of all. This may not be recognised by the people themselves, but can be understood by the one brilliant individual who is the fascist leader. Combining opposition to this kind of democracy with his notion of the necessary qualities for political leadership, Hitler included the following critique in his political testament, *Mein Kampf* (1925):

> The majority represents not only ignorance, but cowardice. And just as a hundred blockheads do not equal one man of wisdom, so a hundred poltroons [weak individuals] are incapable of any political line of action that requires moral strength and fortitude.

Second, there is pluralist democracy. Under this system the political process allows open access to political institutions for various groups in society and attempts to mediate between their various claims. This kind of politics, fascists argue, lacks strength of will and any sense of direction. It is the politics of self-interest, whereas fascists wish to see self-sacrifice for the higher purposes of the state as a whole. Moreover, pluralist democracies often appear to be chaotic, and certainly all the prominent fascist leaders despised the weaknesses that emerged from these political systems. The Weimar Republic, which existed in Germany until Hitler's elevation to power in 1933–34, was known for its lack of coherence and weak coalitions which were unable to deal with the country's pressing problems.

Finally, there is liberal democracy, which emphasises the freedom and rights of individuals. The problem fascists have with this is that they expect individuals to put aside their own selfish interests and instead to sacrifice themselves to the collective interest of the state. Giovanni Gentile put this simply enough in the *Enciclopedia Italiana* (1932): 'If liberalism spells individualism, Fascism spells collectivism.'

Organic society

In many ways, the concept of the organic society represents a direct alternative to liberal, pluralist democracy. Throughout the nineteenth century, European philosophers described the virtues of a society in which the interests of individuals and the state as a whole could amount to the same thing. This meant that people would no longer see themselves as completely free individuals, but rather as parts of a single whole.

For conservative thinkers such as Hegel, or for liberals such as T. H. Green, the concept of the organic society (or **organicism**) could be the answer to the problem of how we can all become free without jeopardising the collective interests of society. If we, as individuals, desire the same kind of life which society as a whole desires, we do not lose our freedom. In fact, the concept's proponents saw this as a higher form of freedom than the traditional kind of individual liberty which was so celebrated in the nineteenth century. The organic society, then, displays a strong sense of social harmony and common purpose along with individual fulfilment.

Key term

Organicism

This term is common to traditional conservative and fascist traditions. It refers to the belief that society is a single, living and evolving whole. An organic society has a life of its own over and above the individual lives of its members. The concept implies that all members of a society are interdependent.

Fascists adopted these ideas and carried them a stage further. For them, the organic society — which was to be represented by an all-powerful state — was everything. Individual will was to be completely suppressed in the interests of the state. Individuals were expected to obey the will of the leader, as it was he alone who represented the destiny of the organic society. Thus, a concept which had originated as an attempt to explain true freedom became a vehicle for totalitarian rule. The *Enciclopedia Italiana* (1932) summarises the fascist view:

> Being anti-individualistic, the fascist system of life stresses the importance of the State and recognises the individual only in so far as his interests coincide with those of the State.

Nationalism

All fascists have been radical nationalists. In this context, 'radical' describes a kind of nationalism which is neither liberal nor passive in nature. Instead, nationalism is seen by fascists as a collective and positive movement.

As has been shown, fascism is obsessed with the idea of uniting people into a single, organic whole. Fascists therefore worship any aspect of human life capable of binding people, for which purpose the common circumstances of birth and history which a nation enjoys are clearly ideal. Historically, the concept of nationhood certainly seems to have been the most powerful binding force, perhaps rivalled only by religion. Indeed, many fascists actively sought to promote nationalism as a kind of religion, or a replacement for it.

A word of caution is needed here. Different fascists have used nationalism in different ways. For the Italian and Spanish fascists, nationalism was merely a vehicle for uniting the state. For them, the state (which expressed the collective will of the people) was paramount. If the promotion of nationalism could safeguard and preserve the interests of the state, then it was a useful political force.

In the Third Reich, however, nationalism took on an altogether more important position. The unification, glorification and final world triumph of the German nation were the ultimate goals of the Nazi form of fascism. The role of the state was to serve the interests of the nation, thus reversing the roles of state and nation as existed in fascist Italy and Spain. Hitler described this view:

> The State is only a means to an end. Its end and its purpose is to preserve and promote a community of human beings who are physically as well as spiritually kindred.
>
> From *Mein Kampf*, 1925

Hitler deployed a range of emotional appeals designed to inspire his people. As we have seen, a series of historical myths was a powerful feature of his message. He also played upon the fears and resentments of the German people by claiming that threats to their power and integrity were presented by the other great powers, as well as by Jews and communists. Above all, however, he unveiled a golden future for Germany, in which it would reunite all its scattered peoples, restore its lost territories, conquer weaker peoples and take their land for further expansion. Referring back to a partly factual, partly mythical history, he promised to restore Germany to its former glories. He claimed that Germany had the potential to become the highest form of civilisation the world had ever seen. For many Germans, this proved to have an overwhelmingly attractive appeal. Individuals might not be willing to sacrifice themselves to the abstract concept of the state, but they were willing to follow Hitler anywhere in the name of German nationalism.

Racialism

Before considering this aspect of fascism, two terms need to be clarified. *Racism* is normally used to denote a particular state of mind rather than a political theory. Racists are prejudiced against certain racial groups and are likely to see their own race as superior to others. *Racialism*, on the other hand, is a quasi-scientific set of theories about race. It often results in a feeling of racial superiority, and a system of discrimination or worse, but racialist theories claim some kind of rational basis for their beliefs (see Chapter 4, p. 145). As mythology played a large part in the appeal of fascism, it was hardly surprising that racialist theories were usually based on such myths. For the purposes of this section, however, we will run together the two concepts of racism and racialism and refer to them as *racialism* collectively. In other words, fascists were often racists, racialists or both.

It is a common error to believe that fascism and racialism are essentially the same thing. This is not the case. The main reason why the two movements are confused is, of course, that the Nazi regime was intensely racialist in nature. There is, however, nothing necessarily racialist about fascism. Many fascists movements were scarcely racialist at all. Nevertheless, it would be unrealistic to argue that there is no link between the two, and the reasons for this are outlined below.

First, the National Socialist (i.e. Nazi) movement in Germany was extremely racialist. Hitler and his followers synthesised their fascist creed with an intense form of racialist nationalism. By the mid-1930s, Hitler's Germany had become a model for other fascist regimes to follow, and part of that model was racialism. Mussolini, having met Hitler and fallen under his spell, showed signs of imitating the Nazi regime. As a result, the Italian fascists became anti-semitic and began rounding up Jews and handing them over to the Third Reich. In the UK, meanwhile, the fascist leader Oswald Mosley had shown no partic-ular signs of racialism until he too began to copy Hitler's political style and developed an anti-semitic approach.

The second link is more sinister. As has been shown, nationalism is a key aspect of all fascist movements. Understandably, race is a powerful element in nation-alist feeling. Many nations see racial or ethnic identity as the key element in their unity and shared experience. Small wonder, then, that fascists should stress the racial

Adolf Hitler supported Nazism, which blended fascism with extreme racialism connections among people when seeking to promote social unity. This combination of nationalism and racialism is best expressed by the German term *Volksgemeinschaft*. This is the collective expression of nationalism, based on a particular race and its shared history — a potent cocktail and fascists knew it.

The Nazis carried their racialism several stages further. They adopted a number of 'scientific' theories about race to justify their policies on racial purity, conquest of other peoples and, ultimately, genocide.

However, if fascism is considered as it existed in South America, Spain, the UK and parts of central Europe, there is no reason to place racialism as one of its more significant aspects.

The most important elements of fascism are summarised in Table 7.1.

Table 7.1 Summary of the principal features of fascism

Feature	Explanation
Irrationality	Fascists oppose the imposition of rational ideas upon society. Rationalism, fascists argue, leads to a lack of direction, dynamism and positive action. Fascists are also anti-intellectual.
Mythology	Myths are versions of the truth. They are manipulated by fascist regimes in order to inspire the people. In particular, fascist histories are selective, emphasising heroism, civilisation and national legends.
Will to action and struggle	The ability to convert one's individual will into decisive action and the successful exercise of power is the highest ideal of leadership.
Warfare	War is the ultimate expression of the sacrifice of the individual to the collective will of the nation. It is also the highest example of individual heroism.
Leadership	The role of the fascist leader is to embody the collective will of the organic society. He will be the individual who demonstrates the highest virtues of fascism.
Elitism	All societies tend towards control by a superior elite. The strength and unity of the ruling elite give society its dynamism.
Organic society	Society should be an organic whole and not merely a collection of individuals. Individualism must be sacrificed to the needs of the state.
Nationalism	All fascists are nationalists. The unity and success of the nation is the highest human ideal. The nation is the embodiment of the collective identity of the people.

Fascism, Nazism and totalitarianism

The Nazi form of fascism

National Socialism — or Nazism, as it is commonly known — was undoubtedly the most notorious form of fascism. It was peculiar to interwar Germany and, as such, assumed a character of its own, though there have been imitators since, usually known as new-Nazis. Below is a summary of the ways in which Nazism added to the fascist creed and, to some extent, modified it.

1 As the full name National Socialism suggests, the Nazis extolled some of the virtues of socialism. This is confusing since they engaged in a violent struggle against socialists and communists in the 1920s and 1930s. The reason for this is that it was only some of socialism's values that they supported — the Nazis certainly did not share its aims. This aspect is explored further later in this chapter (see pp. 257–258).

2 Like all types of fascism, Nazism was a radical nationalist movement. Indeed, between the two world wars German nationalism was of an especially expansionist type. While the Italians under Mussolini were seeking to build an overseas empire that would rival those of Britain and the other European powers, Hitler sought to dominate mainland Europe.

3 As well as being expansionist, German nationalism had a particularly racialist character. This is often described as volkism, a synthesis of nationalism, racialism and cultural superiority.

4 Nazism placed the nation at the apex of human experience. The collective identity of the people (or 'volk', as they were always termed), its history and its future were all bound up in the concept of nationhood. The state, made up of the political and administrative organs of the country, was secondary to the purposes of the nation. In short, the state served the nation. This was not the case with other fascist movements, which placed the state above the nation. The exercise of power became a political aim for Nazis, rather than a romantic nationalist ideal. For most fascists outside Germany, the nation served the purposes of the state.

5 Perhaps surprisingly, the Nazi form of fascism is often said to have been less totalitarian than other regimes of an apparently similar nature. Hitler was prepared to allow civil society — i.e. intermediate groups such as trade unions, religions, business groups and youth organisations — to flourish. Only political parties (other than the Nazi Party, of course) were banned outright. The price these groups paid for their independence was that they should agree to serve the interests of the state and the fatherland, as expressed by the Führer himself. Of course, the Third Reich condemned millions to death, but these people were considered to be 'social outsiders'. The racially acceptable Germans remained relatively free as long as they served the Third Reich when called upon to do so.

The totalitarian nature of fascism

Note that not all fascist regimes are totalitarian. In truth, they varied a great deal. In Spain and Portugal, for example, fascist dictatorships endured into the 1970s. Had they approached Italy or Germany in terms of their use of terror, it is unlikely that they would have been tolerated for so long. These regimes are perhaps more appropriately described as *autocracies*. This term suggests the dominant rule of a single leader and almost certainly a one-party state. It implies that opposition to the ruling party will be outlawed. However, there is no sense in such regimes of 'totalness' of power. In contrast, fascist Italy and Nazi Germany were certainly totalitarian by most definitions of the word.

In his famous novel about totalitarianism, *Nineteen Eighty-Four*, George Orwell develops a dystopia in which a totalitarian regime exercises absolute control over all language, knowledge, information, history and even the individual and collective psychology of the people. This extreme characterisation of totalitarianism was not designed to be a literal description of any real regime. It was, Orwell suggested, closer to the Soviet Union under Stalin than it was to fascism, but he argued that it did demonstrate the tendencies of such regimes. The manipulative propaganda, public displays of force, insistence that the leader alone could interpret the will of the people, and the cult which grew up around fascist dictators, were all present in Orwell's novel. *Nineteen Eighty-Four* simply took these elements to their logical extremes.

Hannah Arendt (1906–75) searched for features common to fascism and Soviet **totalitarianism**. She found several. In particular, she observed how such regimes develop a bureaucracy or administrative structure designed to organise terror. Virtually all the atrocities of the Third Reich were governed by a legal code. The discrimination, suppression and final annihilation of the Jews, for example, were carried out in an organised, disciplined way. The Italians, too, created a highly bureaucratic state designed to ensure fascist control over all aspects of life. Like Orwell, Arendt saw mass psychology as a vital tool of totalitarian rule. The ability to manipulate and bend the emotions of the people to political ideas and actions was vital in exercising total rule. Emotional attachment to the regime replaced people's allegiances to other social movements, such as religion, alternative ideologies, trade unionism or the pursuit of individualism.

Key term

Totalitarianism

This term is used to describe a certain kind of regime in which the state claims to have total authority and control over every aspect of life. These aspects include politics, the economy, ideology, public information, all associations and the general lives of its subjects. Nothing is considered to be outside the business of the state. The politics and ideology of the state reside in the hands of a single leader or a ruling elite.

J. L. Talmon (1916–80), in his 1952 work, *The Origins of Totalitarian Democracy*, looked back to Rousseau's ideas of a superior individual (Rousseau had described this figure as 'the legislator') who could understand what was in people's hearts and could therefore express and implement the 'general will' — that is, the collective will of the people. The general will was to be emptied of individual self-interest and would be superior to any democratically determined course of action for a society. This description certainly suggests the perfect fascist leader who understands the destiny of a nation better than the people do themselves. Of course, any connection between Rousseau and fascism involves a distortion. Rousseau's ruler was to be accountable to representative assemblies and would be distinctly moral and benign in character. Above all, in theory at least, he could be removed if he failed to fulfil his role.

Key fascist thinkers

Benito Mussolini (Italian, 1883–1945)

Mussolini virtually created fascism in Italy in the 1920s. Moving gradually away from his original belief in socialism, he seized power in 1922 after the celebrated 'march on Rome' by his Blackshirt movement. Originally, fascism was a reaction against the chaos of pluralist democracy that followed the First World War and the petty infighting among the socialists and communists. While democracy was proving to be impotent, socialism was too concerned with abstract theory and ideology to offer practical solutions. In contrast, Mussolini became obsessed with the idea that action was superior to theory. Indeed, his creed could have been taken straight from Marx's famous maxim: 'The philosophers have only interpreted the world in various ways; the point, however, is to change it'. The 'march on Rome' was a classic example of how dynamic action can overcome political weakness.

Mussolini's main contribution to fascism (other than the name itself — he consciously adapted the term *fasces*, a bundle of rods, to represent the aspirations to tight social unity held by his movement) was his theory of the state. For him, the state could represent the collective identity and will of a people. In order to achieve its aims, it would have to become all embracing and command absolute obedience. Together with Giovanni Gentile, his close associate, Mussolini created a major exposition of fascist beliefs in the *Enciclopedia Italiana* in 1932. The following passage from the *Enciclopedia* sums up his attitude towards the state:

> When one says fascism, one says the state. The fascist conception of the state is all-embracing; outside it no human or spiritual values can exist, much less have value. Thus understood, fascism is totalitarian, and the fascist state — a synthesis and a unit inclusive of all values — interprets, develops and potentiates the whole life of a people.

For Mussolini, the main purpose of the Italian state was to become an imperial power, rekindling the glories of the Roman Empire and rivalling the likes of Germany, France and Britain. Ultimately, he failed to carry all his people with him. There was much less support for fascism in Italy than there was in Germany. In the end, his people turned on him and he was effectively lynched in 1945.

Giovanni Gentile (Italian, 1875–1944)

From the beginning of fascism, Gentile stood at Mussolini's shoulder. He is the nearest figure fascism has to a philosophical father, being close (although not identically so) to what Marx was to communism. His principal contribution to early fascism was to develop the idea of a society which could be utterly unified; no divisions and no class distinctions could be allowed to divert attention away from the state's collective purpose.

Gentile also expanded the idea of the perfect fascist leader. Of course, he meant Mussolini, but the theory could apply to any such dynamic figure. The individual who could represent the fascist state would have to exhibit superior qualities to all others in society. This individual would be excessively masculine (what the Spanish would term 'machismo'), dynamic, self-sacrificing and, above all, would understand the destiny of the state.

By putting the two concepts together — the all-powerful state and the dynamic leader — Gentile took both ideas a stage further, in that the leader and the state were effectively the same thing. Opposition to the leader was therefore treachery against the state.

Giovanni Gentile could be described as the philosopher of fascism

Adolf Hitler (Austrian, 1889–1945)

It is easy to ignore the fact that Hitler was much more than an anti-semitic, totalitarian and militaristic ruler. However distasteful his beliefs might have been, it must be recognised that he could lay some claim to creative political thought.

We must first dismiss Hitler's more outlandish racial theories, which he learned from his close associates Houston Chamberlain and the philosopher Alfred Rosenberg (1893–1946). Between the three of them, they concocted a number of theories about the history of the German people, their former glories and how their civilisation had declined because their bloodline had been mixed with so-called inferior races. His anti-semitic beliefs should also be placed in context. Many Europeans at the time were anti-semitic, although Hitler managed to convert his prejudices into an extremely sinister conspiracy theory, which was to culminate in the Final Solution.

However, as regards his theories of the nature of the state and its leadership, we must take his philosophy more seriously. He despised democracy, liberalism and intellectualism. For him they represented political weakness and a betrayal of the true *Volksgemeinschaft*, i.e. the collective identity of the people. Hitler opposed communism too, not so much because of its goals, as its promotion of class conflict at the expense of national unity. In place of these discredited ideologies, he proposed a philosophy of the state and the nation, which would be synthesised to create the most powerful political force in history.

Hitler also concerned himself with a fundamental political problem: how can the true, inner desires of the people be made coherent, and therefore converted into real, decisive action? He argued that democracy of a traditional kind could never achieve this. It needed the creative will, understanding and will to action of the leader. This concept was summarised by Hitler's adviser, Ernst Huber, in a speech he gave in 1935:

> In his [the leader's] will the will of the people is realised. He transforms the mere feelings of the people into a conscious will.

Houston Chamberlain (English, 1855–1927)

Although Houston Chamberlain was an Englishman, he was married to the daughter of the composer Richard Wagner and was obsessed with all things German. He was a key figure in the early development of Hitler's political and racial thought. Following the theories of the French thinker Arthur de Gobineau, he extolled the role of racial purity in the success of civilisations. For him, history was characterised by an epic struggle for supremacy between different peoples. What gave a people strength was the exclusivity of its bloodline. This quality had created the Greek and Roman civilisations and, with a macabre irony, also accounted for the success of the Jewish people.

Chamberlain argued that the Germanic 'volk' had traditionally demonstrated superior racial qualities. What was needed in the twentieth century was a new drive to restore the genetic purity of the race. The Germans could then re-engage in a Darwinian struggle against inferior peoples — a struggle in which they would inevitably triumph.

Alfred Rosenberg (Estonian, 1893–1946)

Like Chamberlain (and indeed Hitler himself), Rosenberg was not born in Germany. He was an Estonian who, as a student, became obsessed with Germany and German civilisation. He was of ethnic German origin, however, along with millions of others of similar heritage who were scattered throughout eastern and central Europe in the nineteenth century. Many of these ethnic Germans flocked to the Nazi cause and proved to be even more zealous than those who had been born in Germany itself.

On his return to Germany, Rosenberg threw in his lot with Hitler and the National Socialists, becoming editor of the party's newspaper, the *Voelkischer Beobachter* (*People's Guardian*). He collaborated closely with Hitler in the writing of *Mein Kampf* and subsequently established himself as the central philosopher of the Nazi movement. However, as the 1930s continued, his position in the party declined and he spent the war in relative obscurity. He was tried at Nuremberg and executed in 1946. His main influence, therefore, lay in the early development of Hitler's thought.

Rosenberg's main contribution was to the racialist theories of the Nazis. He held similar views to Chamberlain in that he saw European history in terms of a struggle between Aryans and Jews. The Aryans — or Germans, or Nordic people, as he variously described them — displayed superior qualities to all other races. They exemplified honour, intellect, artistic qualities, organisation, action and purity of spirit. For Rosenberg, the pursuit of racial purity and superiority had replaced religion in its ability to inspire men to great deeds. He expressed this view in his best known work, *The Myth of the Twentieth Century* (1930):

> The German people is not marked by original sin, but by original nobility. The place of Christian love has been taken by the National Socialist, Germanic idea of comradeship...which has already been symbolically expressed through the replacement of the rosary by the spade of labour.

Rosenburg can also be credited with developing the notion of Lebensraum (literally meaning 'living space'). This theory claimed that if a people could demonstrate superior qualities, they were justified in taking over land occupied by inferior peoples. If blood were spilled in conquering such land, this would give legitimacy to its occupation. Poland and Russia clearly fell into this category for the Nazis.

Rosenberg was the main philosopher of the peculiarly racialist form of fascism developed by Hitler and his party. Ironically, this proved to be his undoing — as has been shown above, fascists tended to despise intellectuals and rationality. Rosenberg was ultimately dismissed by his colleagues for placing philosophy above action. Fascists are pragmatists and resist being bound by rigid social theories of the kind which he promoted.

Issues in fascism

Why are fascists irrational?

In many ways, fascism can be defined in terms of its opposition to the exercise of rationalism in politics. Fascists observed the exercise of a variety of rational ideas in the lives of nations and found them to be wanting. Liberalism, for example, in one form or another, had dominated the nineteenth century. What it had done, argued fascists, was to underpin capitalism, which had brought about economic depression in the 1920s and 1930s and produced a political system — democracy — which had proved to be directionless and impotent.

On a more romantic level, fascism favours dynamic action undertaken by individuals who are not inspired by reason, but by heroic myths and a sense of destiny. People, they assert, are inherently unequal. Any philosophy which attempts to make them equal must therefore be flawed. Socialism and Marxism, which propose economic equality, interfere with the natural processes of economic struggle. Liberalism advocates equal rights, which is translated into equality within the political system. For fascists, the political process can only be dynamic and healthy if it is based on unequal powers. Those with superior attributes should prevail and will deserve to do so.

An examination of the relationship between fascism and nationalism reveals a further reason for opposing rationalism. People's allegiances to nation and race are not rational ideas, but intensely romantic and even quasi-religious. The German fascists referred to this as *gemeinschaft,* a collective sense of identity.

This opposition to rationalism is shared with many conservative movements. When faced with political problems, conservatives prefer to solve them with pragmatic solutions, rather than by resorting to fixed principles. Fascists face obstacles in a similar way, seeing them as opportunities to display the virtues of strength of character and will to action.

Key distinctions between Nazism and fascism

Nazism and fascism are not identical, although the Nazi regime was undoubtedly also a fascist regime. National Socialism did not begin life as a fascist party, but became so as the influence of the Italian experience began to take hold. When it became apparent that the Nazis could not hope to gain sufficient power to achieve their aims through the democratic process, it was almost inevitable that they would adopt fascism as an alternative. Indeed, Hitler's struggle to secure leadership of the National Socialist Party can be seen as the triumph of fascism over rationalism within the movement.

As we have seen, the position accorded to the state differs between the typical fascist and Nazi. Put another way, Nazism placed nationalism on a considerably higher level than other fascist movements did. For the Italian fascists, for example, a great deal of their appeal to nationalist sentiment was mythological in nature. The purpose of nationality was to create allegiance to the state, rather than being an end in itself. Even the state was considered subordinate to the nation. Gentile summed up this view:

> It is not nationality which creates the state, but the state which creates nationality, by setting the seal of actual existence on it.
>
> From *The Genesis and Structure of Society*, 1937

If the position of nationalism helps us to distinguish between Nazism and fascism, so too does the character of that same nationalism. For the Nazis, nationality was defined almost entirely in terms of racial identity. For fascists in general, nationalism was crucial, but not to the same extent as it was for the Nazis, and it was not necessarily racial in character. Furthermore, German nationalism and the German nation were considered by the Nazis to be superior to all other examples.

Why do fascists honour war and conquest?

War and conquest automatically come to mind when thinking of the fascist legacy. This is hardly surprising since many fascist regimes were exceedingly belligerent and often expansionist. Of course, not all fascist regimes engaged in warfare; Spain and Portugal, for example, remained neutral during the Second World War (although both supported the Germans and Italians in economic and diplomatic ways). Despite this, it is not unjustified to associate fascism with warfare. There are three reasons for this: international Darwinism, self-sacrifice and the German concept of Lebensraum.

First, fascist historians and philosophers characterised history as a struggle for supremacy between races and nations. Indeed, it was seen as a natural outcome of radical nationalism that a people should wish to demonstrate its superiority over others.

They argued that this is as much a natural part of life as procreation and survival. The true life force of a people could only be realised effectively in warfare, the ultimate expression of heroism and will. It was the natural outcome of a Darwinian struggle.

Second, fascists encourage all individuals to sacrifice their own interests to those of the state and the nation. The ultimate form of self-sacrifice is to fight and therefore risk or give one's life for one's country. Gentile suggested this idea in the following words:

> The State educates its members to citizenship, makes them aware of their mission, urges them to unity... The State hands down to future generations the memory of those who laid down their lives to ensure its safety.
>
> From *The Genesis and Structure of Society*, 1937

Finally, fascists, especially in Nazi Germany, believed that superior peoples had the right to expand their territory in order to nurture their civilisation. Hitler expressed the concept of Lebensraum as far back as 1925:

> When the territory of the Reich embraces all the Germans and finds itself unable to assure them a livelihood, only then can the moral right arise, from the need of the people, to acquire foreign territory. The plough is then the sword; and tears of war will produce the daily bread for generations to come.
>
> From *Mein Kampf*, 1925

These were not idle thoughts. Hitler's military activities bore out his ambitions. First, the Germans recovered territory lost in the 1919 Treaty of Versailles. Then the scattered German peoples in Austria, Czechoslovakia and Poland were annexed back into the Reich. Finally Russia and eastern Europe were invaded in an attempt to expand the German empire.

Fascism and democracy

Can fascists claim to be democratic?

Although fascism opposes all traditional forms of democracy, there are grounds for fascists to make some claim to be democratic rulers. J. L. Talmon's interpretation of Rousseau's ideas could be said to support the argument that the ideal fascist leader can be democratic. This is because the leader will embody the collective will.

In a telling 1935 speech, Ernst Huber summarised the relationship between the leader, the individuals in society and the collective identity of the people:

> It is possible for [the leader], in the name of the true will of the people which he serves, to go against the subjective opinions and convictions of single individuals within the people if these are not in accord with the objective destiny of the people.

This suggests that the fascist leader does serve the people; he is neither a monarch whose people are merely subjects, nor a self-serving dictator. Democratic rulers also see themselves as servants of the people (famously, US president Bill Clinton used to refer to the people as 'the boss'), but in a different way. The role of the traditionally democratic ruler is to ensure that the demands of different groups in society are considered and weighed against each other. The leader is also expected to respect the rights of individuals in that society.

This is not the case with a fascist ruler. As Huber asserts, the fascist leader serves the collective will of the people, not the demands of individuals and groups. The problem arises, of course, with determining what the collective will is. The fascist response is that it is the leader who can discern the collective will (harking back to Rousseau's idea of the general will being recognised by the 'great legislator'). This poses a further difficulty. How can we be sure that the leader's interpretation is a valid one? Fascists propose two answers to this.

The first concerns the way in which the leader emerges. He is the product of a struggle between individuals, the outcome of which will determine who has both the superior will and the superior judgement. By definition, the victor in this struggle must be whoever is best placed to understand the will of the people. The second answer asserts that the collective will of the people and the historical destiny of the nation are essentially the same thing. By understanding the history and future destiny of the nation, the true collective will of the people can be discerned.

Critics of this nationalist interpretation of democracy point out that fascists were guilty of trading in myths, half-truths and the quasi-scientific theories of figures such as Giovanni Gentile, Houston Chamberlain and Alfred Rosenberg. In other words, national aspirations were actually the vision of the leader himself and not the genuine collective will of the people.

Why do fascists oppose democracy?

Note that it is the liberal, pluralist, parliamentary forms of democracy which fascists despise, not the 'totalitarian democracy' described above.

It is an indication of fascism's relationship to democracy that it flourishes wherever democracy appears to be failing. This remains true today. If democracy fails to deliver stability, prosperity and progress, fascists or their close imitators argue that this is the result of a loss of human spirit, dynamism and direction. This has been seen in recent years in Russia, Serbia and Italy, where quasi-fascist parties have achieved some, albeit modest, success.

Traditional democracy recognises the diversity in society, spawning political parties whose aim is often to further the interests of a particular class or group. Fascists abhor this style of politics since their concern is to unite a people, not to encourage divisions.

As for the simpler concept of majority rule, this is equally rejected by fascists as a result of their total distrust of the motives of the popular majority — the feckless, directionless people who lack the discipline of strong leadership. In *Mein Kampf* (1925), Hitler argued that a single leader was always superior to the majority rule:

Does anybody honestly believe that human progress originates in the composite brain of the numerical majority and not in the brain of the individual personality.

It was perhaps Oswald Mosley, the British fascist leader in the 1930s, who best exemplified fascist opposition to parliamentary styles of democracy. He blamed the failure of governments to deal with the Great Depression on the frailties of the parliamentary system, vowing to replace it with the leadership of himself and a ruling elite. The problem was, he claimed, that democratic politicians believed the state should not interfere in the economy and society. He argued that the state *should* take control of society to solve its problems and move forward. The liberal idea of limited government was an error. Far from being limited, the state should be all embracing.

Oswald Mosley, founder of the British Union of Fascists

Liberal democracy had become closely associated with the operation of free-market capitalism. Thus capitalism too exercised the minds of the fascists between the two world wars. This is discussed below.

Fascism and capitalism

What was the fascist attitude to capitalism?

Capitalism had brought great prosperity in the nineteenth century, but during the 1920s and 1930s it appeared to be losing its momentum, culminating in the disastrous slump after 1929. Marxists and socialists offered clear alternatives to free-market capitalism, as did the emerging fascists.

The socialist response to capitalism's problems was to suggest extensive state interference in economic activity to ensure both investment and a just distribution of rewards. Marxism represented the most radical of the socialist solutions. These ideas might have been attractive to the fascists, given their love of the collective state; indeed, it is no coincidence that many fascists began their political lives as socialists, Mussolini and Mosley being prime examples. However, capitalism represented the kind of Darwinian struggle fascists revered, and socialism threatened that quality.

Despite favouring social Darwinism, fascists opposed the phenomenon of class conflict that capitalism had created. All the enemies of capitalism between the world wars recognised that this was intensifying. However, while socialists objected to capitalism on the grounds of its exploitative nature and promotion of inequality, fascists were concerned that it was preventing societies from making progress. The conflict of interest between the working classes and their capitalist masters was sapping society of its unity and true purpose.

The issue for fascists, therefore, was how to reconcile the dynamism and competitive spirit of capitalism with the needs of the state. The result was a middle way known as the corporate state. It was in Italy that the corporate state, or corporatism, had its clearest manifestation.

What was fascist corporatism?

Fascists held the concept of the national community above all other social organisations. Two major groups potentially threatened this community: organised labour in the form of trade unions, which clearly had their own self-interested agenda, and capitalist business interests.

The answer, which was developed mainly in Italy and was copied in Spain under Franco, was to create a **corporate state**. Under the auspices of the fascist party, capital and labour were obliged to work together to strengthen the national community, rather than competing with each other for ascendancy. This arrangement was not state nationalisation, as socialists proposed, nor was it completely free-market capitalism. It was an entirely original form of economic organisation.

Key term

The corporate state (corporatism)

This term refers to a way of organising the state that was first developed in Mussolini's Italy. It operated by bringing into the state apparatus the representatives of organised labour and capitalist employers. The fascist state could then act as a mediator, ensuring that the goals of these organisations were reconciled, but also served the interests of the state and the nation. After the defeat of fascism, it was also used in non-fascist states, including Britain, as a means of reconciling class interests and maintaining the national interest, rather than merely that of the ruling party and its ideology.

In Italy, a highly organised structure was created to impose corporation. The Italian economy was divided into 22 corporations, each of which involved a contract between employers and unions. Disputes were to be settled on the basis of what was best for the Italian state, rather than private interests. Unsurprisingly, fascist party officials were always on hand to 'facilitate' (in fact, to enforce) such agreements. In this way, strikes, demonstrations, lockouts and protracted negotiations could be prevented. In Spain, a slightly less organised corporate system was introduced, and Mosley also proposed the system for Britain.

In Nazi Germany, Hitler was not prepared to go this far, instead implementing an informal kind of corporatism. While the state kept the trade unions firmly under control, banning and suppressing communist groups altogether, Hitler reached a number of bilateral agreements with industrialists. In return for a relative degree of autonomy, German companies such as Krupp and Bosch agreed to serve the interests of the state when called upon to do so. When war broke out, these companies were called upon to honour their agreements.

Some have characterised fascist corporatism as a kind of socialism, and it is certainly true that most fascists were more sympathetic to the working class than to big business. However, the key distinction was that the state did not engage in economic activity on its own account. More tellingly, fascists did not use the corporate state to create greater equality, the main aspiration of socialism.

Fascism and socialism

In what senses is fascism a form of socialism?

There is much controversy over the full name of Germany's form of fascism, 'National Socialism'. Some suggest that the term 'socialism' was retained simply for the purposes of attracting working-class support. They argue that it had no substance other than as a cynical example of opportunism.

Others, however, have observed a more substantial link. Certainly, fascists saw much to admire in the solidarity of working-class movements. Socialism and fascism are both collectivist doctrines, suggesting that they extol the virtues of social rather than individually motivated action. Similarly, both movements are deeply suspicious of capitalism, seeing it as being based on the pursuit of self-interest at the expense of the social good.

Finally, it should be said that many fascists, notably Oswald Mosley and Hitler's rival in the Nazi party, Ernst Röhm (1887–1934), admired the struggle in which the working class was engaged, both against capitalism and often against the physical conditions in which its members had to work. Fascists revered groups such as miners, engineers and farm workers, since they fought to bend nature to the needs of the whole community.

As the 1930s continued, however, fascism became increasingly antagonistic towards socialist parties and movements. In the end, it was characterised by opposition to, rather than sympathy for, socialism.

Why have fascists opposed socialism?

Ultimately, what fascists cannot accept about the socialist movement is that it pursues the interests of only one section of society — the working class. It therefore denies the concept of the national community. Fascists see socialism as a divisive movement, engaged in splitting society on the basis of class, rather than uniting it.

The more scientific socialists, notably Marxists, are opposed by fascists for the further reason that they propose rational analyses of society. Fascists would say that they have downgraded the role of individual human endeavour. Neither fascists nor socialists support selfish individualism, but fascists do accept the creativity of the individual human spirit and its potential for creating social change. In contrast, socialists see progress as the result of the harnessing of social forces, rather than through the actions of heroic individuals.

A consideration of the socialist goal of equality reveals a further reason why fascists are so hostile towards the movement. Fascism thrives on the notion of human inequality. By engaging in struggle, both individually and collectively, those with superior powers will prevail and those who are inferior will be dominated by them. The progress of civilisation depends upon such inequality since it guarantees that those who possess higher qualities will maintain control. Fascists argue that socialism attempts to make people equal when they are not. This is unnatural and will inhibit progress.

Finally, it is necessary to return to the theme of nationalism that dominates fascist thinking. Socialists are essentially internationalists. They see the plight and struggle of the working class as transcending national boundaries. The more radical socialists and Marxists even see nationalism as a form of false consciousness that has been employed to disguise the true nature of capitalism. By encouraging nationalism and patriotism among the working class, they argue, its real exploitation by capitalism is masked. For fascists, especially in Nazi Germany, the denial of national aspirations and solidarity is a positive evil.

Footnote on contemporary fascism

Political theorists and historians suggest that fascism was a phenomenon which could only have existed within the context of the interwar period. Social, political and economic conditions, as well as information technology, have changed so radically that a truly fascist regime could never re-emerge. Increased globalisation means that the kind of narrow, bigoted nationalism which fascists promoted could never again take hold. Furthermore, the nature of modern warfare and the existence of a single superpower — the USA — would thwart the military aspirations which national fascist parties have demonstrated.

On the other hand, there have been examples since 1945 of quasi-fascist movements coming to power, or at least having a significant impact on various political systems. It seems that whenever significantly alienated groups emerge in a society, whenever democracy seems to have run out of solutions to social and economic problems, quasi-fascist groups are able to flourish and threaten the established order. Issues such as widespread immigration, racial tension, economic recession and excessive state inter-ference all lead to extreme right-wing groups gaining support. The Freedom Party in Austria, neo-Nazi groups in remote areas of the USA, the British National Party and the French National Front are all recent examples of this occurring. However, a search for a truly fascist *regime* that has existed since 1945 is bound to encounter difficulties. It is possible that Saddam Hussein's rule in Iraq, or the brief dominance of Serbian nation-alism after 1990, could be seen as fascist, but as a coherent, widespread doctrine, fascism remains a historical phenomenon.

Exam focus

Using this chapter and other resources available to you, answer the following questions.

Short questions

Your answers should be about 300 words long.

1 Why are fascists usually described as irrational or anti-rational?
2 On what grounds do fascists emphasise leadership?
3 Why is the concept of the state so important to fascists?
4 Distinguish between fascism and Nazism.
5 What is the relationship between fascism and nationalism?
6 In what ways is fascism totalitarian in nature?
7 Why is fascism often associated with racialism?
8 In what sense, if any, can fascism be associated with socialism?

Long questions

Your answers should be about 900 words long.

1 Is fascism merely a radical form of nationalism?
2 Why have fascists been so interested in conquest and war?
3 Was Nazism merely a racist form of fascism?
4 Why and how have fascists opposed democratic politics?
5 In what ways were fascism and Nazism totalitarian in nature?

Further reading

Eatwell, R. (1997) *Fascism: A History*, Penguin.

Gregor, N. (2000) *Nazism*, Oxford University Press.

Kallis, A. A. (2003) *Fascism Reader*, Routledge.

Passmore, K. (2002) *Fascism: A Very Short Introduction,* Oxford University Press.

Paxman, R. O. (2004) *The Anatomy of Fascism*, Allen Lane.

Thurlow, R. C. (1987) *Fascism in Britain: A History, 1918–85*, Blackwell.

Chapter 8

Feminism

Feminism first became a politically significant movement in the 1960s, although its earliest origins lie in the eighteenth century. It is usually divided into two main 'waves'. The first wave began around the time of the French Revolution and lasted until the early 1960s. It had three, relatively limited, main aims. First, it sought to obtain equal legal and property rights for women; second, to extend the franchise to women; and third, to expand the range of opportunities open to women in fields such as politics, the professions and higher education. The second wave began in the 1960s and was much more ambitious in its aims. Second-wave feminists desire equality (or at least the choice of equality) for all women with men. Liberal feminists have sought to reform society in order to achieve equality, while the various types of radical feminists have proposed revolutionary methods to achieve their aims. The aims of the radical feminists have been far more extensive than those of the liberals on the grounds that patriarchy (i.e. male supremacy) — the principal enemy of feminism — is deeply rooted.

Introduction

Feminism is not like other ideologies. Above all, it is relatively limited in its objectives. Most (although not all) feminists limit their aims to improving the equality and/or status of only half the population. Feminism is an extremely fragmented movement, to an even greater extent than conservatism and socialism. The militant feminists of the 1970s, the period when the movement was at its height, bore little resemblance in their political outlook to the early advocates of women's rights in the eighteenth, nineteenth and early twentieth centuries.

Feminism is the most modern of the ideologies described in this book. It is certainly a critique of contemporary society and so could never be accused of being a purely historical phenomenon (as arguably Marxism or fascism have become). Indeed, in its current form, feminism is a challenging and vibrant movement which is relevant to virtually all aspects of contemporary society.

Feminism is unusual too in that there have been no conventional political parties based on the movement; nor have there been organised and influential pressure groups, at least in Europe. Feminism as an ideology has flourished within parties, within intellectual and academic circles, in the media and in popular opinion. Although the superior status of the men who largely run states has been threatened by feminism, the modern state has not been challenged by the movement in the same way as it has been by ideologies such as fascism, communism, socialism and anarchism. It is therefore remarkable that feminism has been so successful.

The first wave

Prior to the French Revolution, there were sporadic examples of writers and movements which had proposed equal rights for women, but these were never systematic and were certainly never converted into action. On the whole, the Enlightenment failed to inspire thinkers to consider the inferior social and economic position of women. However, the wave of rationalism and free thinking which swept Europe in the latter part of the eighteenth century, culminating in the French Revolution, did create the possibility for the development of original ideas about women in society.

Mary Wollstonecraft was one of a very few thinkers who took the ideas of the Enlightenment and applied them to the status of women. She saw women as naturally equal to men, perfectly capable of rational thought and possessing the same rights. These ideas were explained in her best-known book, *A Vindication of the Rights of Woman* (1792). Wollstonecraft challenged the conservative assumption that women are less rational than men, and that it is, therefore, natural for them to be subordinate to men. This was a radical idea, since the concept of a natural inequality between the sexes was a powerful one in the eighteenth century. As well as Wollstonecraft's ideas, the novels of Jane Austen (1775–1817) satirised the conventional view of women's inferiority, lack of reason and, therefore, lack of potential. However, neither Austen nor Wollstonecraft made any lasting impact in terms of enhancing women's status in society. Their ideas were too advanced and met with little support among women themselves.

More successful was Harriet Taylor (1807–58), wife of the great liberal philosopher, John Stuart Mill. (Ironically, both Wollstonecraft and Taylor were married to more celebrated husbands — Wollstonecraft was the wife of the great early English anarchist, William Godwin.) Taylor and Mill wrote *On The Subjection of Women* in 1869. In this important feminist text, they advocated equal legal rights for women, including the vote. However, Taylor and Mill's main contribution to the advancement of sexual equality was sponsorship of the Married Women's Property Act in the same year. This allowed women to retain their own property even after marriage. The Act had the effect of allowing women much more freedom in determining who they would marry, and gave them the opportunity to separate from unsatisfactory husbands without losing their wealth. In practice, of course, it was significant only to the well off. For the majority of women, such advances were irrelevant.

Votes for women was to become the principal aim for the first-wave women's movement. In 1869, the National Women's Suffrage Association was formed in the USA. The first realisation of votes for women occurred in New Zealand in 1893 and the British suffrage movement came into existence in 1903. Women over 30 years of age obtained the vote in Britain in 1918, the US constitution was amended in 1920 to enforce women's suffrage, and in 1928 British women were granted the same voting rights as men.

Women's suffrage was seen as the first stage to achieving equality in other areas

The campaign for women's votes was the key element in first-wave feminism because it was assumed that, once the vote had been granted, other benefits would follow. Women would, it was hoped, take up positions in legislatures in increasing numbers, and female voters would use their electoral power to demand equality. Although advances of this kind were certainly made, with women gradually being admitted to higher-education institutions and to professions such as medicine and the law, these successes were limited. Why, then, was first-wave feminism so unsuccessful? There are several possible reasons:

➢ Male pre-eminence in politics was still heavily entrenched.
➢ Campaigners underestimated the degree to which culture was patriarchal. In other words, the depth of male dominance was not appreciated. Granting women the vote did not scratch the surface of patriarchy.
➢ The movement was almost completely dominated by the middle classes. Most middle-class women were conservative in outlook and considered feminist ideas too radical, so they limited their demands to the franchise.
➢ There was still insufficient economic pressure to release women from their traditional roles of wife and mother. A much greater increase in the demand for female labour, especially skilled and educated labour, was required in order to free many women from traditionally inferior roles.

These factors meant that little progress was made until second-wave feminism arrived in the 1960s. This is how Betty Friedan (1921–) described the issue:

> The problem lay buried, unspoken, for many years in the minds of American women. It was a strange stirring, a sense of dissatisfaction, a yearning that women suffered in the middle of the twentieth century in the United States. Each suburban wife struggled with it alone. As she made the beds, shopped for groceries, matched slipcover material, ate peanut butter sandwiches with her children, chauffeured Cub Scouts and Brownies, lay beside her husband at night — she was afraid to ask even of herself the silent question — 'is this all'?
>
> From *The Feminine Mystique*, 1963

The second wave

The second-wave women's movement can be seen as part of the wider political phenomenon of the 1960s called the *New Left*. Radical thinkers were developing a theory based on their observation of the growth of what was to become known as *mass culture* or *mass society*. Mass culture had a number of characteristics:

- Consumption was becoming the most significant element in people's perception of themselves. In other words, an individual's consumption patterns had begun to define what sort of person he or she was. This replaced a traditional class analysis of society, whereby people defined themselves in terms of social class, which was largely identified by occupation and income.
- This development meant that producers and sellers in capitalist societies were able to manipulate cultural attitudes and needs in order to promote consumption of their products and services.
- To facilitate their task, it was convenient for producers to create a mass culture. This made it much easier to control that culture and to persuade people to buy mass-produced goods. The media were recruited in this enterprise, especially television, so the whole culture was penetrated.
- Mass culture was aimed at those groups in society which were predominantly white, male, aged over 25, heterosexual and well off. These groups were the cultural leaders and possessed the most spending power. Other groups were therefore excluded. The poor, black and Asian people, the young, gays and, of course, women were largely ignored by mass society. Either they had insufficient income to benefit from the new prosperity, or their spending patterns were determined by others. The New Left saw them as being *alienated* from the mass culture. Radical activists campaigned on their behalf, first helping them to become conscious of their alienation and, having become so, encouraging them to create a *counterculture* which could liberate them.

Movements which were spawned by the New Left revolution included black rights activists, gay rights campaigners, anti-poverty drives, 'youth in protest' ('yippies') and second-wave feminism.

The key moment in the birth of the second wave was the publication of *The Feminine Mystique* in 1963 by Betty Friedan. This book galvanised the women's movement. It gave rise to a liberal form of feminism and also provided material that was used by a more radical group of writers and activists. Friedan called the position of women 'the problem with no name'. This was to be the case no longer. The problem became known as *patriarchy* and the women's movement was retitled *feminism*.

By 1970, feminism had matured as a movement, but it had split into two main branches — liberal feminism and radical feminism. The liberal wing remained firmly within the mainstream of political thought. It proposed reforming society, largely through piecemeal and gradual advances in the women's cause. The radicals, on the other hand, were revolutionary in their thought and aspirations. Shulamith Firestone (1945–) argued that women must throw off the main source of their oppression — their place in the reproductive process — and therefore their reliance upon men. Germaine Greer (1939–) saw women's inferior status in terms of the way in which popular culture portrayed them, while Kate Millett (1934–) argued that male domination did not begin and end with public life, but infected all aspects, both private and public, of the relations between men and women.

Meanwhile, those on the political left were synthesising feminism and socialism. They saw the subjugation of women in economic terms. For them, women would be truly liberated only when class oppression was removed. Indeed, the most extreme of the socialists — the Marxists — supplemented the study Karl Marx had made of developed capitalism by pointing out that female labour had become a vital element in the exploiting process, and that working-class women formed the most exploited of all classes.

Indeed, radical feminism had such a rich variety of perspectives on women's oppression that to talk of one single movement may be mistaken.

Postfeminism

By the end of the 1970s, many of the goals of conventional forms of feminism had been achieved. Women enjoyed legal equality in all economically developed states, male attitudes were finally responding to the constant bombardment of feminist thought and women were making rapid advances towards equal status in fields such as politics, the professions, education, sports, the arts and media and even (albeit more slowly) in business. Discrimination on the grounds of gender was outlawed everywhere in the Western world and a wide range of social and economic legislation was passed to allow women to free themselves from traditional roles. Changing attitudes and new laws in areas such as marriage and divorce, sexual relations, abortion, birth control and state welfare were providing women with life choices and greater freedom to realise self-actualisation — i.e. the achievement of their own chosen goals.

However, rather than resulting in the disappearance of the women's movement, the effect of these developments was to fragment the feminist ideology into many different branches, often described as postmodern feminism or poststructuralist

feminism, sometimes even as the 'third wave'. The concept of a single women's liberation movement became outdated. New perspectives on women's conditions were
developed and with these came new ideas about how to liberate women. For example,
the lesbian movement proposed that all women should abandon relations with men
and instead form women-only cultures with no physical relations with men remaining.
Matriarchal feminists argued that the male–female hierarchy should be reversed and
women should become the dominant gender. The most radical of all the feminists even
suggested that technological advances in the procreation of children meant that it
might be possible to do without men altogether, so that an exclusively female society
could be created.

Postfeminists have concentrated on individual issues as well as the position of women
in general. Pornography, for example, has attracted a great deal of their attention, with
feminists divided over whether pornography exploits women or men. Others have
concentrated on the plight of women in societies where arranged marriages (especially
child brides), the denial of women's rights to careers and female circumcision exist.

Core values of feminism

As has been shown, feminism became a divided movement in the 1970s. Core values
are therefore difficult to identify and limited in number. However, some principles have
been shared by all feminists and these are outlined below.

Patriarchy

At its most basic level, patriarchy can be defined as a system of discrimination against
women by men. The key word here is 'system'. It implies that a number of different
phenomena are connected in some way. The discrimination against women and/or their
oppression and exploitation therefore has different aspects, but aspects that are interconnected. The women's movement has always identified individual examples of
discrimination, for example legal inequalities, exclusion from certain activities such as
politics and business and unequal rights in marriage. These do not necessarily add up
to a system. Radical forms of feminism distinguish themselves by their insistence that
there is a whole clutch of aspects that depend on each other.

For example, the traditional (now largely eliminated) discrimination against women
in education — i.e. obstacles placed in the way of educational success — underpins male
dominance in many occupations. If women are denied education and training in some
fields, they cannot challenge men's prominence in those fields. On a more subtle level,
sexist attitudes towards women, which suggest that the qualities they typically possess
are inferior to the qualities apparently held by men, clearly hinder women's career development. More obviously, the tendency to maintain a female workforce of part-time
workers, undertaking menial jobs, ensures that women retain an inferior status in the
workplace.

For feminists, patriarchy therefore has a variety of facets, including the psychological, sexual, political, economic and cultural aspects of the relations between men and women. The fact that these features are connected has given patriarchy its strength and endurance. Its all-embracing nature explains the immense difficulty feminists have had in dislodging it.

Although patriarchy is a core value of feminism, different branches of the movement have emphasised different aspects of the concept. Socialist feminists have stressed the economic exploitation of women; liberals have tended to emphasise the political and cultural aspects of patriarchy. Radical feminists have concentrated on sexual and psychological forms of exploitation, particularly emphasising how the role of the father in a typical family is a model for the dominance of men in wider society. This is how Kate Millett described this phenomenon:

> Patriarchy's chief institution is the family. It is both a mirror of, and a connection with, the larger society; a patriarchal unit within a patriarchal whole.... Serving as an agent of the larger society, the family not only encourages its own members to adjust and conform, but acts as a unit in the government of the patriarchal state, which rules its citizens through the family heads.
>
> From *Sexual Politics*, 1970

Otherness

The idea of the 'otherness' of women is a difficult concept, since it encompasses elements of psychology such as the notion of consciousness. In general terms, it refers to the fact that women are considered to be fundamentally different from men, not merely in the biological sense, but in every other sense too, and economically, culturally and psychologically in particular.

On one level, then, otherness is merely an explanation of the subjection of women to men, but it has a greater significance as well. Women, feminists say, have 'internalised' their otherness. By this they mean that it has not only been imposed on them by men, but they have also come to accept it for themselves. This is largely the result of women's perceptions that they have a separate role as a result of their biological differentness. Men can never understand this otherness since it is a product of biological identity. Note that the biological role of women has been assigned an inferior role in society.

Thus, women are not just inferior in the eyes of men, but are inferior in their own eyes too. Furthermore, otherness is part of a woman's 'unconscious' being — that is, women are not conscious of their own acceptance of their inferiority. It was the French philosopher Simone de Beauvoir (1908–86) who first recognised this phenomenon as long ago as 1950. Betty Friedan, too, argued over a decade later that women's acceptance of their inferior roles is a learned response which appears in early childhood. This is therefore exceedingly difficult to dislodge. Women must first become conscious of their subjugation before they can begin to struggle against it.

For liberals, otherness can be combated if the common experience of women changes. When they are granted equal status with men, women will shed their own sense of inferiority. The more radical feminists, however, have been less optimistic. To attack the psychological effects of deep conditioning, it will be necessary for women to set up a complete counterculture against patriarchy. In this way, the consciousness of women themselves can be altered. Indeed, the most radical feminists have insisted that women separate themselves completely from male culture in order to free themselves and take control of their own inner being.

Gender

Gender refers to the role and consciousness of women, which has been assigned to them by society and which they learn for themselves from an early age. The acknow-ledged founder of second-wave feminism, Betty Friedan, is largely responsible for recognising the importance of **gender**, as opposed to **sex**, which refers to biological distinctions.

Betty Friedan distinguished gender from sex

Key terms

Sex and gender

The difference between these two words is crucial to feminists. 'Sex' refers to the biological differences between men and women. These are, of course, natural and unalterable. Women give birth and are physically weaker than men. This produces unavoidable distinctions. 'Gender', on the other hand, refers to typical male and female roles which are the product of upbringing. They are not inevitable and will vary according to the social environment and the consciousness of the individual. Feminists propose changes which could modify or even eliminate such gender differences.

Women learn 'womanly' roles from an early age. On a superficial and less signifi-cant level, they come to expect that they will fulfil traditional female roles such as child rearing, cookery, housework and caring occupations in general. This is illustrated most effectively by pointing out that, before feminism became influential, women would typically aspire to be nurses, while men might expect to become doctors. On a deeper and more important level, however, the female gender role is considered to be inferior to that of men. Indeed, women used to grow up commonly accepting that they would play an inferior role to men in society. In fields of social power, such as politics and business, it was expected that men would fill the leading positions. It was accepted that the majority of women would not expect to pursue a career, settling instead for a lifetime of housewifely pursuits.

The process by which women learn to expect that they will play such gender roles, and by which men expect them to conform, is clear. It can be seen in patterns of children's play, in relationships between sons and fathers and daughters and mothers, and in the traditional literature and value systems of every society. Gender roles have been transmitted in the past through educational practice (e.g. domestic science and needlework for girls, woodwork and metalwork for boys) and in the workplace (e.g. male bosses and female secretaries). Feminists have pointed out that gender stereo-types can also be absorbed in more subtle ways, for example through language and the arts.

All feminists, whether they are reformists or revolutionaries, agree that gender is critical to the inequality suffered by women. They therefore argue that an attack should be mounted on such stereotypes. Liberals argue that women must be given choice and the opportunity to determine their own gender roles, as well as total equality with men. Radical feminists, however, wish to destroy the concept of gender altogether and rebuild women's culture from scratch.

Equality

Equality between men and women should be included as a core feminist value with some caution. While equality is a clear objective for liberal feminists, it is a problematic concept for more radical elements of the movement. However, all feminists agree that, while there are important biological differences between the two sexes, in terms of gender — the learned roles of men and women — there should essentially be no differences. Rather, there is natural equality, and society should reflect this fact.

For liberals, equality means full political, legal, social and economic rights for women, and implies total equality of opportunity. Women should have equal access with men to educational opportunity, public offices and all positions within the economic structure. Success in achieving this has been uneven. In education and employment in general, equality has largely been attained, while in economic life a remarkable degree of male dominance remains.

Although radicals might accept that equality for women is an essential goal, they would see such an aspiration as extremely limited. Some see female culture as superior and would therefore seek to place women in a superior position to men, rather than merely an equal one. Others see superiority and inferiority as irrelevant. These feminists, who include Germaine Greer, have argued that male and female cultures are essentially incompatible and therefore the issue of superiority becomes an irrelevance. Any sense of superiority should be replaced by one of separateness.

Liberation

The women's movement is often described as 'women's liberation' ('women's lib' for short). This implies that men have somehow kept women in a subservient, even enslaved, position. For liberals, this control is seen as less sinister than the kind of enslavement which many radical feminists have identified, but for all feminists libera-tion is essential if women are to make significant progress.

Betty Friedan, a liberal, refers extensively to the cultural domination of women by men. It is men who control the culture, therefore women have found it difficult to escape from its clutches since such patriarchy is all-pervading. However, by raising their own consciousness and by liberating their minds, women have found it possible to evade this cultural hegemony. Having liberated their consciousness, women have been able to demand and achieve equality of opportunity and to open up worlds that had previously been closed to them.

It is the radical socialist feminists who hold the most vehement views on liberation. For them, women's enslavement is economic. They are used as a cheap source of labour, both within the home and in the workforce in general. By closing off opportunities to them, men have forced women into inferior, subservient economic roles. This is in the interests of both capitalism and of patriarchy. For women to achieve true freedom, therefore, the economic structure would need to be transformed so that economic exploitation would become unpopular.

Both liberal and socialist feminists, however, would agree that patriarchal capitalism needs to be transformed if women are to be liberated. This is how Kate Millett described women's economic situation:

> Since woman's independence in economic life is viewed with distrust, prescriptive agencies of all kinds (religion, psychology, advertising etc.) continuously admonish or even inveigh against the employment of middle class women, especially mothers. The toil of working class women is more readily accepted as 'need', if not always by the working class itself, at least by the middle class. And to be sure, it serves the purpose of making cheap labour in factory and low grade service and clerical positions. Its wages and tasks are so unremunerative that, unlike more prestigious employment for women, it fails to threaten patriarchy financially or psychologically.
>
> From *Sexual Politics*, 1970

Types of feminism

Liberal feminism

This description refers to feminism, or at least the women's movement, as it existed during the 'first wave' — from the eighteenth century to the late 1960s — and to the reformist elements of the movement from the 1960s onwards. The label 'liberal' implies a number of characteristics and principles, which are as follows:

- Liberals do not propose a revolutionary transformation of society. Rather, they would reform some aspects of society in order to achieve their aims. In the context of feminism, therefore, liberals reject the insistence of the radicals and the socialists that there must be a revolution (albeit a peaceful one) if women are to achieve equality and emancipation. The fundamental structures of modern Western societies — capitalism, pluralist democracy, multiculturalism, etc. — do not need to be changed significantly. Women can win equality within these structures.

➤ There should be a clear divide between public and private life. For liberals, some aspects of our lives are not the concern of the state, the law and public attention in general. If people choose freely to live their lives in a certain way, and this does no harm to others, their lifestyles are of no concern to the rest of us. On the other hand, conduct which does affect others is the concern of society as a whole, and therefore of the state. For example, if employers routinely discriminate against women in recruitment and career promotion, it is a public, not a private, concern. On the other hand, if a woman chooses to play a subordinate role to her male partner, this is clearly private and of no concern to others.

➤ This distinction between public and private spheres leads to the further conclusion that each individual woman must have the right to decide how she wishes to lead her own life. Betty Friedan, in her book *The Second Stage* (1983), reacted against what she saw as the excesses of the radical feminist movement by insisting that women should feel free to take up the traditional roles of what she described as 'love, nurture, home'. The radicals seemed to suggest that such roles should be forbidden to women.

Liberal feminism has therefore concentrated on reform, largely through the law and changing public attitudes to the position of women. Table 8.1 sets out most of the principal legal and attitudinal changes that liberal feminists have sought, and, to a large degree, achieved.

Table 8.1 Some liberal-feminist initiatives

Legal reforms	Attitudinal changes
Equal pay for women doing work of equal value to men. • This has been achieved in law in the UK, but is not always the case in practice. In the USA and elsewhere, it is a similar story.	Promoting the belief that women have exactly equal capabilities to men, except in purely physical work. • There can therefore be no rational basis for discrimination in employment.
Outlawing discrimination against women in employment, education, commerce and other fields.	Raising educational expectations for girls and young women. • In fact, girls have overtaken boys at most educational levels. However, there is still subject-based bias, for example boys are more likely to achieve science and technology qualifications, whereas girls tend to specialise in the arts.
Proposing positive discrimination (known in the USA as affirmative action) for women. • This forces organisations to favour women in some cases. Although voluntary schemes are in operation, especially in the UK, legal requirements remain rare.	Creating a climate of opinion which places women in the workplace in an equal position with men. • The critical issue is that women are not discriminated against at work because they are not considered to be as committed to their careers as men.

Legal reforms	Attitudinal changes
Legal guarantees for women of maternity leave, childcare facilities at work and help for female lone parents with childcare, enabling them to work.	It should be reasonable for women to choose a professional career over home roles, or to be able to combine the two without being seen as neglectful homemakers.
Legal right to abortion.	Women should have complete control over their own bodies. • This includes control over contraception and sexual health.
Legal protection against violence and rape in marriage and other relationships with men. • This includes better safeguards for women reporting rape and fairer treatment for them in court proceedings.	Police and courts' attitudes to rape and domestic violence should be altered so that full protection is afforded to women and more cases are brought to court.

The liberal issues described in Table 8.1 are not exhaustive. The rights of women with regard to pensions, social security benefits and divorce, for example, continue to exercise the liberal women's movement. There is a continuing struggle to change attitudes towards women too. The idea of 'political correctness' has fallen into disrepute (should we, for example refer to the *herstory* of the women's movement, rather than its *history*?), but the role of language remains important for all feminists. Language transmits cultural attitudes from one generation to the next. For feminists it is therefore vital that stereotypes which suggest female inferiority are eliminated from language.

Liberals have difficulties with women's issues that arise in 'traditional' societies. The apparently inferior position of women in Muslim communities (a view disputed by many Muslims), forced arranged marriages (especially of very young girls), and female circumcision are all examples of such issues. Although modern Western societies object to these practices, liberals find themselves in a dilemma: do we have the right to interfere in the cultural mores of other societies, however abhorrent we may find them? Although there is no absolute solution to this problem, liberals have attempted to solve it by supporting women's movements within the societies affected. This means that reforms would be internal, rather than imposed by external feminist groups.

There are still tasks for the liberal-feminist movement to achieve — full-scale equality and equality of opportunity for women do not yet exist. However, there is no doubt that since Betty Friedan's ideas were first propounded in 1963, huge progress has been made.

Radical and militant feminism
Radical — sometimes described as 'militant' — forms of feminism have their origins in the New Left movement that emerged in the 1960s. The New Left sought to emancipate all alienated groups in society, including ethnic minorities, the very poor, gays and

disabled people. Women, of course, formed the largest group of all. Although Friedan stimulated the formation of modern feminism, the radicals argued that her views were indeed valid but failed to identify the fundamental causes of women's oppression. Whereas Friedan argued that women were merely *suppressed*, the radicals declared they were *oppressed*. While Friedan argued for female *emancipation*, the radicals were seeking social *revolution*.

Like all radical political movements, feminism of this kind is highly fragmented. It is therefore important to begin by examining the principles which unite radical feminists. These principles are as follows:

➤ Patriarchy is extremely pervasive and it exists in all aspects of life, both private and public.
➤ Although there are important biological differences between men and women, there is no justification for suggesting that gender differences exist, or, if they do, that they are important.
➤ All relations between men and women are inevitably oppressive.
➤ The solution to the problems of women in society cannot be achieved by mere reform, but must involve a radical transformation of the structure of society.

Of all the radical beliefs concerning the origins of patriarchy, sexual oppression probably forms the most important critique. Germaine Greer and Shulamith Firestone in particular see sexual relations as the crucial element in the oppression of women. For them, the other aspects of patriarchy are merely reflections of the basic fact that personal relations between men and women involve exploitation and subservience. Furthermore, both men and women have been complicit in this relationship.

It is necessary to refer to Marxist theory for a moment to understand Firestone's thesis. Marx argued that all societies can be understood in terms of the particular class structure and class conflict that characterises them. The dialectic conflict that occurs between the classes is critical and creates its own reflection in terms of politics and philosophy. Firestone audaciously substitutes sex for class in her analysis of history and claims that it is sexual conflict which characterises every society. The title of her most famous work, *The Dialectic of Sex*, indicates the nature of her philosophy. Clearly the implication is that until sexual equality is brought about, social conflict in general will continue and women will remain an alienated 'class'.

Greer does not share Firestone's scientific analysis of patriarchy, but agrees that sex is the critical factor. For Greer, sexual differences should not be

Germaine Greer argues that sexual differences should be celebrated

suppressed, but restored and celebrated with mutual dignity. Male dominance has removed female sexuality and subverted it for men's own purposes. If women's identity can be liberated and restored to its genuinely free state, there can be healthier relations between men and women. This is how Greer expressed the importance of sexual difference:

> Liberation struggles are not about assimilation, but about asserting difference, endowing that difference with dignity and prestige and insisting on it as a condition of self-definition and self-determination.
>
> From *The Whole Woman*, 1999

Greer believes that a revolution must occur in relations between men and women, so that genuine liberation can be realised and women can achieve fulfilment on their own, and not on men's, terms. She sought to refute the last remnants of **Freudian theory** in this context.

Key term

Freudian theory

Freud's theories are extensive and highly complex, but a key issue in relation to feminism concerns his assertion that women suffer from an undeniable sexual inferiority. This stems largely from 'penis envy'. Women grow up with the belief that men must be more powerful since they possess a penis, while women do not. Most, though not all, feminists reject this analysis, arguing that male superiority arises from social conditioning, not fundamental biological inferiority. Nevertheless, some postmodern feminists have resurrected interest in Freudian theory; they suggest that his beliefs about sexual difference are valid and assist our understanding of patriarchy.

Kate Millett identified the consciousness of women themselves as an agent of oppression and the family as the origin of inferiority consciousness. It is the traditional family unit, Millett asserted in *Sexual Politics* (1970), which is the source of female oppression. Women's consciousness, as well as men's, is conditioned from an early age within the family. Based on what they see at home, children learn that women are subordinate and economically exploited in the home. Once that consciousness is in place, it becomes difficult to dislodge. Furthermore, once men have achieved a dominant role in families, it is inevitable that they will achieve dominance in all other walks of life. Unsurprisingly, Millett therefore attacked the institution of the family in her opposition to all-pervasive patriarchy.

It can be seen from this brief review of some of the principal elements of radical feminism that there are a number of different explanations as to how patriarchy has come about. It is therefore inevitable that radical feminists propose a variety of ways of combating the male oppression of women. The proposals of three of the most celebrated radical feminists — Millett, Greer and Firestone — are discussed below.

Kate Millett (1934–): androgynous society

Millet's object was to create an androgynous society in which there would be no significant gender differences between men and women — a state of genuine equality. Of course, sexual differences would remain, but gender would no longer be a significant element in society.

Since the family was the main cause of gender difference and women's oppression, the family would have to be destroyed. In its place, women should form their own communities in which female consciousness would be raised. By removing themselves from relations with men, women would gradually throw off their alienation and become conscious of their own independent worth. After a long period of consciousness raising, relations between men and women could resume, but on an equal basis. Thereafter, male and female subcultures could exist in some harmony.

Germaine Greer (1939–): sexual liberation

The term 'women's liberation' probably applies more to Greer than any other prominent feminist. Women, she asserts, have been oppressed and rendered powerless by their relentless exploitation by men. The key revolution is therefore not in the structure of society, but in the consciousness of both men and women.

Women must reassert their identity, freeing themselves from all situations in which they fall under the control of men, including in the family, at work, in politics and in social life in general. Above all, however, Greer proposes sexual liberation. The traditional, male-dominated sexual relationship must end and be replaced by relations on a totally equal basis. The family, which she (like Firestone and Millett) sees as a crucial agent of oppression, should be replaced by communal forms of living, or, possibly, women should live alone.

Shulamith Firestone (1945–): removing men's reproductive role

The most modern of the radical feminists, Firestone holds perhaps the most revolutionary beliefs. She sees the family unit, together with the biological differences between men and women, as having made women's inferiority inevitable. She points out that, in the modern world, women can perform their reproductive roles without men. Artificial insemination means that sexual relations are outdated. This, she triumphantly announces, removes the main cause of male control — the reliance women have on men when they are rearing children.

For Firestone, this gives rise to the possibility of a women-only community. Women, she argues, are all capable of forming lesbian relationships, or, short of that, can certainly make a life without men. Firestone's more radical followers have suggested that the need for men will disappear altogether and the world will cease to recognise sex or gender differences. However, for Firestone the vision of a community of free women without the need for men was enough.

The passage by Andrea Dworkin below (Box 8.1) demonstrates not only a desire for liberation, but also the sheer anger of some feminists.

Box 8.1 **Dworkin on pornography**

The US feminist Andrea Dworkin's (1946–2005) attack on patriarchy concentrated on the propagation of pornography. This is a short extract from her book, *Pornography: Men Possessing Women* (1981):

In the system of male sexual domination explicated in pornography, there is no way out, no redemption; not through desire, not through reproduction. The woman's sex is appropriated, her body is possessed, she is used and she is despised: the pornography does it and the pornography proves it. The power of men in pornography is imperial power, the power of the sovereigns who are cruel and arrogant, who keep taking and conquering for the pleasure of power and the power of pleasure.

Socialist and Marxist feminism

It is perhaps surprising that one form of Marxist feminism actually predates radical feminism. Friedrich Engels, Marx's collaborator, turned his attention to the plight of women after Marx's death. In *Origin of the Family, Private Property and the State* (1884), he suggests that before the existence of private property there had been a matriarchal society. It was only when private property and a system of exchange of goods emerged that patriarchy came about. More recently, under capitalism, the subjugation of women became more intense, with women being exploited both at home and in the workplace. Women could only be emancipated, Engels argued, when capitalism and private property were abolished. He therefore urged women to join the class struggle, even though revolution appeared to be man's work. He believed that the raised consciousness of women could help to support the broader revolutionary movement.

The analysis Marxists offered of women's position under capitalism was principally that they had been reduced to the status of an exploited part of the workforce; they were a reserve body of labour that could be brought into action, for low wages, when production levels rose, only to be discarded when the inevitable economic slump followed. Furthermore, those women who remained at home to raise children and do housework were also exploited. At home, women were free labour, releasing men to leave the home and earn wages. Capitalism, Marxists claim, relies upon the exploitation of women to make labour more available.

Many socialist feminists have adapted Marxist analysis in their attempt to understand the subjugation of women. The main thrust of their critique concerns inequality, both in the workplace and in the home. The British feminist Juliet Mitchell (1940–) sought to link the psychological causes of women's inferior status — to be found mainly in the home — to their economic position. By fostering a sense of inferiority in the home, men are able to exploit women in the workplace. The consciousness of women is therefore manipulated in such a way that they are unable to liberate themselves unless the whole capitalist edifice is destroyed.

However, not all socialist feminists have been Marxists. There is a general sense that the creation of socialism — in particular imposing equality by changing the structure of ownership of the means of production and the system of exchange — will liberate women. Under an economic system that creates equality, women will not only become entitled to equal rewards, but will also cease to be dominated by a patriarchal society. This belief has a long history. It originated in the utopian socialism of figures such as Charles Fourier and Robert Owen (see Chapter 2). Fourier, in particular, argued that a truly socialist society would liberate women altogether from the imprisonment of marriage and the family. Indeed, modern socialist feminists see the family as a model of the exploitation in the wider economic world. For some, the answer lies in paying women (or indeed men) for housework and child rearing as if it were any other professional occupation. As a result, women would not have to face an artificial choice between unpaid house-work, which places them under the economic control of men, and a paid career. For more radical socialist feminists, the answer lies in the destruction of the family as an institution.

Third-wave feminism

Modern feminism is sometimes referred to as the 'third wave'. Modern feminists accept that most of the specific aspirations of women have been achieved, at least as far as liberal feminists are concerned, and therefore seek a new identity for women and the women's movement. To some extent, they are reacting against the revolutionary ideas of the radicals and the socialists. They argue that ideas such as oppression and exploita-tion can no longer be sustained as criticisms of modern society. Women now have the full range of opportunities for which they campaigned. Although equal pay has not been achieved, women have been considerably empowered and are moving inevitably towards full equality in the economic structure. What kind of new identity, then, should women be seeking in a postfeminist world?

For many liberal feminists, such as Friedan herself, the postfeminist woman should feel free to adopt the traditional role of mother and wife. This freedom in itself is the main achievement of feminism: women have a voluntary choice in undertaking this role, rather than being forced to do so. Raising children and creating a loving home are digni-fied and noble occupations. Women, Friedan says, should cease to treat them as inferior to paid occupations.

Other modern feminists declare that women have achieved equality and equality of opportunity, and that they should use their new-found liberation to take a leading role in society. A world in which women can play a leading role is bound to be a better world. Above all, liberated women now have choices that they did not have before. They are in a position to enjoy the fruits of the individualistic world which has been created by social democracy and neo-liberalism.

Table 8.2 summarises the different types of feminism.

Table 8.2 Summary of the three main types of feminism

Liberal feminism	Radical feminism	Socialist/Marxist feminism
• Reforming rather than revolutionary • Seeking equality of opportunity for women • Seeking legal, political and economic equality for women • Accepting that women may choose their own lifestyles and relationships • Pursuing a number of issues which affect women in general, such as abortion rights, violence in the family, rape • Campaigning to change attitudes to women which suggest they are inferior	• Fundamental, revolutionary change needed to the nature of society • Belief that patriarchy does not recognise the boundary between private and public spheres • Firm rejection of the validity of gender differences, while accepting that biological differences are important • In order to liberate women, a new society must emerge in which consciousness of gender difference is eliminated	• Belief that the oppression of women is economically based • Women are used and abused as a source of cheap or free labour • The exploitation of women in the family is a model of the wider economic exploitation of women • Capitalism relies upon the exploitation of women in order to guarantee the superior position of men • Equality for women relies upon the destruction of capitalist exploitation in general

Key feminist thinkers

Mary Wollstonecraft (English, 1759–97)

Married to William Godwin, the early English anarchist, and mother of Mary Shelley, the author of *Frankenstein*, Wollstonecraft died shortly after the birth of her daughter. Her best-known work is *A Vindication of the Rights of Woman*, published in 1792 and one of the earliest feminist tracts.

Nowadays, Wollstonecraft's views would not raise any eyebrows, but in the world of the 1790s she was considered a radical. She was fundamentally a liberal who believed that all people — i.e. women as well as men — are rational beings entitled to rights, freedom and dignity. The women of her day, however, were denied all of these. They were effectively enslaved, as they were tied to their husbands and not allowed any legal independence. She observed that the main problem was the lack of true

Mary Wollstonecraft argued for the education and legal independence of women

education most women suffered. Education, according to Wollstonecraft, was the answer to women's plight.

Wollstonecraft offered a number of practical measures to counter this inequality. She argued that women should enjoy full civil rights, be entitled to their own property and be allowed to pursue a career whether they were single or married.

Nevertheless, Wollstonecraft was not so radical as to suggest that men and women should be equal in all spheres of life. She recognised that, by virtue of biological necessity, women would be most likely to follow careers as wives and mothers. What she campaigned for was that women should at least have the choice, and, if they chose marriage, that they should enjoy more fulfilled lives as a result of their independence. She saw no reason why women should be considered inferior to men, but at the same time she knew that most women would choose to play a secondary role in society. Should they do so, however, it would make them no less virtuous than men.

John Stuart Mill (English, 1806–73) and Harriet Taylor (English, 1807–58)

Mill and Taylor were husband and wife. They collaborated to produce *On the Subjection of Women* in 1869. Like Wollstonecraft, neither was especially radical by modern standards, but at the time their ideas were extremely controversial.

Their views on the relations between men and women, and on the inferior social status of women, were based on two simple principles. The first was that men and women are born equal in terms of rationality, judgement, intellect and entitlement to rights. Of course, there are biological differences, but there is no evidence for male superiority. The second was that the inferior position of women was based largely upon economic considerations, and that these considerations were designed to retain the superior position of men.

The implications of these principles were that there should be no occupations or any public offices from which women were excluded. In short, women should enjoy full equality of rights and opportunities.

However, it was in the fields of votes and property ownership that Mill and Taylor's beliefs were to have the most significant influence. The Married Women's Property Act, which was passed in 1869, the same year as *On the Subjection of Women* was published, gave women the right to own property even after marriage. Prior to the Act, women effectively passed all their property to their husband on marriage. This situation had had two main effects. First, it made wealthier women vulnerable to fortune-hunting suitors and limited their choice of husband. Second, it made divorce virtually unthinkable for a woman, since she would be left without any property at all: men owned all joint property after divorce.

Mill campaigned for women's suffrage and hoped to have it included in the Second Reform Act of 1867 (see Box 8.2). The failure of his campaign led to the formation of the suffrage movement in Britain, which pressed for votes for women for the next 50 years.

Box 8.2 John Stuart Mill on the equality of women

This passage is taken from *On the Subjection of Women* (1869):

> On the other point which is involved in the just equality of women, their admissibility to all functions and occupations hitherto retained as the monopoly of the stronger sex, I should anticipate no difficulty in convincing anyone who has gone with me on the subject of the equality of women in the family. I believe that, there, disabilities elsewhere are only clung to in order to maintain their subordination in domestic life, because the generality of the male sex cannot yet tolerate the idea of living with an equal.

Betty Friedan (US, 1921–)

Friedan is known as the mother of second-wave feminism. Her ground-breaking book, *The Feminine Mystique* (1963), heralded the emergence of modern feminism. She went on to found the National Organisation of Women (NOW) in the USA, which continues to campaign for women's rights and equality.

The basis of Friedan's thought was an attack on Freudian explanations of women's inferiority. Freud had argued that women were inevitably inferior because of their biological distinctions. It was in particular their lack of a penis, and the phenomenon of 'penis envy' women consequently suffered, that consigned them to their inferior role. 'Anatomy is destiny', said Freud. Not so, replied Friedan. She asserted that women's destiny had been moulded by their long experience of social conditioning. This conditioning had its origins deep in history and was therefore well rooted in society. The typical consciousness of women in 1960, said Friedan, had in fact been developed in the Victorian era. It had nothing to do with biological differences.

Why is it, asked Friedan, that women develop such strong expectations that they will fulfil the limited role of wife and mother? Why do they not expect to pursue careers that will lead them into more fulfilling and public roles? She believed the answer lies in the way girls are raised. Limited expectations are built into their psyche at an early age. Family life, the education system and other cultural institutions, such as religion, reinforce the idea that women should not aspire to be anything more than wives and mothers.

Before Friedan, it was commonly believed that traditional female roles were biological in origin. Women gave birth and cared for infant children, the argument ran, so it was natural that they should remain in the home. Challenging this assumption was a radical act in Friedan's day.

The process whereby a male-dominated culture propagates assumptions of women's inferiority has become known as **sexism**. In order to combat it, Friedan recommended a sustained campaign by women's groups to open up opportunities for women, change public (i.e. both male and female) attitudes toward women, challenge male domination everywhere and obtain legal and political equality. Friedan was therefore a liberal: she did not propose a revolutionary transformation of society, but rather reforms within the existing social structure. In other words, she believed that the relationship between men and women could be fundamentally changed without making significant changes to society in general.

Key term

Sexism

This is a collective term for the range of ways in which men propagate the inferiority of women. It particularly refers to cultural attitudes which tend to perpetuate the belief that men are superior. Sexism exists in cultural fields such as education, language, the media, the arts and psychology. Feminists argue that sexist attitudes are based purely on myths and have no objective basis.

Friedan later demonstrated her liberal outlook still further by arguing that women should feel sufficiently free to choose the more traditional role of wife and mother. Indeed, she accepted that many women do possess a deep need to nurture children and to provide a loving home for a male partner. Although feminism had made great advances, she argued, it was dangerously close to losing sight of some women's genuine desires. This is how she expressed her concern:

> In the first stage, our aim was full participation [of the women's movement], power and voice in the mainstream. But we were diverted from our dream. And in our reaction against the feminine mystique, which defined women solely in terms of their relation to men as wives, mothers and homemakers, we sometimes seemed to fall into a feminist mystique which denied that core of women's personhood that is fulfilled through love, nurture, home.
>
> From *The Second Stage*, 1983

Kate Millett (US, 1934–)

The 1970 publication of Millett's book, *Sexual Politics*, sent shock waves through the feminist movement, and indeed through all radical political communities. Millett agreed with Betty Friedan that the roots of patriarchy lie in the traditional structure of the family, but she went much further than Friedan in her analysis. She argued that patriarchy had invaded the whole of human culture and society, so that it existed in politics, business, the arts, the media and all aspects of social life.

Millett claimed that the relationship between men and women is a power relationship. It is therefore political in nature, because politics is about power. Men exert power and oppression over women everywhere. They use this power to place women in inferior roles. The biological differences between the sexes are exaggerated and distorted by men in order to suggest that their dominant role can be justified by such differences. Furthermore, Millett asserted that men exert psychological control over women. In doing so, they have been able to persuade women to accept their inferiority as though it were true. Women learn that if they are to survive in the male-dominated world, they need to adopt a 'feminine' attitude, which is determined by men.

Millett declared that patriarchy is not restricted to public life. It exists in private relations between men and women, including their sexual relations. Men do not just seek to dominate in the workplace, but in the home and the bedroom too. There is no escape for women: patriarchy is everywhere and has invaded women's minds, taking a firm hold over their consciousness.

What is the answer to this patriarchy? Unsurprisingly, Millett offers a radical solution. Women, she argued, must develop their own consciousness, which should be completely separate from men. They must have no relations with men, including sexual relations, and must instead form their own communities.

Kate Millett recognised that patriarchy dominates the private as well as the public sphere

(Millett herself was bisexual or lesbian and recommended that women should follow her lead or be celibate.) Rather like the anarchist communes that were formed in the late 1960s and early 1970s, the female commune was to be self-sufficient.

In Millett's ideal, **androgynous** world, power relationships between the sexes would come to an end and true gender equality would emerge. The characteristics of men and women, having become identical, would lead to the end of patriarchy, or indeed any relationship of power. Male–female relations could then resume on the basis of true equality.

Key term

Androgyny

This term literally refers to a state in which an individual is neither exclusively male nor female. In radical feminist thought, notably that of Kate Millett, the term is used to describe a world in which gender differences are abolished, and the consciousnesses of men and women are identical. This would result in the end of patriarchy.

Germaine Greer (Australian, 1939–)

It would perhaps be wrong to suggest that Germaine Greer has been a major contributor to feminist thought, but she deserves consideration on the grounds that she has done a great deal to popularise feminist ideas. She has been accomplished in using the media to put across feminist ideas and even once posed nude (an obviously ironic gesture) to publicise her views.

Greer's emphasis has been on sexuality. Male domination, she claimed, has repressed female sexuality and prevented women from being able to express themselves and achieve self-realisation. Greer argues that the unsatisfactory nature of male-dominated sexual relations is bad enough in itself. However, more importantly, it is symbolic of the way in which oppression prevents women from developing. The term 'women's liberation' can be applied most appropriately to Greer's thought — her belief was that liberation of the mind could be achieved if women could free themselves from exploitative relationships with men. She also turned her attention to the radical belief that '**the personal is the political**'.

Key term

'The personal is the political'
This term was developed by the radical feminist Carol Hanisch (1941–) in 1970. It suggests that the dominant position of men and the political power they exert over women are not confined to public life alone. All relations between men and women are political, Hanisch argued. Family life, sexual relations, work relations and politics itself are all aspects of the politically based power relationship between men and women. The concept is also associated with Kate Millett and Germaine Greer.

A major problem for Greer lay in the fact that she was heterosexual and therefore not willing, as Kate Millett suggested, to give up relations with men altogether. Furthermore, like Friedan, she recognised that childbearing and homemaking were reasonable occupations for women. Greer proposed two solutions to these problems. The first was to recommend sexual freedom, which would avoid the potential enslavement involved in an exclusive relationship. Second, she addressed the stifling effect of the traditional nuclear family. To avoid this, she recommended a form of group living that would be close to the idea of the extended family. This arrangement would mean that children could be raised and relationships freely engaged in without the dangers of subjugation by dominant males.

Shulamith Firestone (US, 1945–)

Firestone's principal work, *The Dialectic of Sex*, which was published in 1970, centred on the significance of biological differences between men and women. What she attempted was a Marxist analysis of history, in which sex was substituted for class. Firestone saw the alienation of women as solely the result of sexual oppression. The economic, political and physical oppression of women by men emanated from biological differences and the assumption that male sexual characteristics were superior.

Just as Marx had predicted that the oppressed class would rise up against its capitalist oppressors, so Firestone assumed that the oppressed sex would rise up against men. The catalyst for this was to be technology. With the possibility that women could reproduce without the active involvement of men came the possibility of a world without sexual conflict.

Taking her quasi-Marxist analysis to its logical conclusion, Firestone foresaw the emergence of a sexless (her substitute for classless) society, which she referred to as androgyny. This was a society without significant gender differences, in which no individual could therefore suffer inferiority or claim superiority on the grounds of biological difference. Women would have the choice of whether to form completely separate communities or to coexist with men on an equal basis.

Firestone was not a Marxist as such, but rather adapted Marxist historical analysis to suit feminism. She can therefore be seen as a feminist-Marxist, instead of a Marxist-feminist — in other words, a true radical, but not a pure socialist. Her ideas found relatively little support within the women's movement, partly because they were simply too radical and partly because her use of Marxist philosophy was considered both artificial and unsustainable.

Issues in feminism

Distinctions between liberal and radical forms of feminism

This is perhaps the most common issue encountered by students of feminism. It might initially seem relatively simple and possible to understand in the same way as the distinctions between socialism and social democracy, or between liberal and conservative forms of nationalism. In reality, however, it would be a mistake to assume that there is a clear distinction between the two sets of beliefs.

It is true that radical feminists have sought to stress that there is little in common between their analysis and that of the wider women's movement, which began in earnest with Mary Wollstonecraft, and was transformed into a full-scale political organisation by Betty Friedan nearly 200 years later. From the liberal perspective, however, there has been a good deal of common ground which all feminists have shared. It is therefore useful to list the aspirations and values that unite all feminists. These have included the following:

Common principles and beliefs

- The inequalities women have endured are not based on any natural inferiority. There are certainly differences between men and women in society as a result of biological reality, but these do not imply that men are superior in any way.
- Male dominance originates in the early social conditioning of both men and women. It is therefore the task of all feminists to alter social consciousness so that the equality of women is accepted.
- Women must be able to take control of their own circumstances of life, rather than allowing men to determine them on their behalf. In other words, what and who women are is the business of women themselves.
- All aspects of male–female relations that exploit, degrade or control women should be eliminated. Women must be emancipated so that they can make their own choices and never fall under the control of male-dominated social structures.
- The status of women as 'victims' must be combated. This raises issues such as rape, violence in marriage, prostitution and pornography.

This impressive range of issues add up to a major area of common ground. However, a casual observer in the 1960s and 1970s might have failed to realise that the huge increase in activity by women and women's groups disguised a fundamental fracture in the broader movement. By 1970, it was becoming more clear that the women's movement had indeed broken apart, and while liberal feminists were claiming victory after victory, the radicals were warning against such triumphalism. They believed that the fundamental causes of women's oppression had not been addressed. The principal ways in which radical feminism has been distinct from liberal feminism are as follows:

Key distinctions of radical feminism

- Patriarchy does not distinguish between public and private spheres. The liberals had certainly made many gains in public life, but they left the private circumstances of women to individuals. This was a mistake, the radicals argued. The roots of exploitation lie in private life, families and the sexual relations between men and women. They must be addressed first if true emancipation is to be achieved. This means that the most basic building blocks of society and its structure must be dismantled and reformed.
- Radical feminists warned that by failing to transform society, the liberals were winning illusory victories. Without dramatic changes in consciousness of sex and gender differences, there can never be true freedom for women.
- The economic exploitation of women does not stand in isolation from other forms of exploitation. Whereas liberals see economic equality and freedom as the key to all other forms of women's liberation, radical feminists argue that all forms of exploitation are interconnected and should not be treated separately. For example, the exploitation which is entailed by pornography and prostitution, or suffered by women who find themselves trapped in violent and alienating relationships with men, are part of the same system of patriarchy. Granting women economic independence alone will not bring them true freedom.
- On the whole, radical feminists believe that women will only achieve true consciousness of their role and genuine self-realisation if they separate themselves from male-dominated culture. By contrast, liberals aspire to achieving all their objectives within the existing culture.

Why are sex and gender so important to feminists?
Before Betty Friedan published the *Feminine Mystique* in 1963, the issue of sex and gender was either ignored or confused. It is true that the early French feminist Simone de Beauvoir had declared that 'one is not born, but becomes a woman' in the 1950s, and that her assertion made a firm distinction between sex, which is biological, and gender, which is socially determined. However, de Beauvoir did not mean to make this distinction for its own sake. She was more concerned with the superiority of men and the

inferiority of women being an artificial social creation rather than a natural state of affairs. It was Friedan and the later feminists who took de Beauvoir's assertion and used to it to define sex and gender.

Early feminists, such as Wollstonecraft and Taylor, believed that gender distinctions arose directly from biological differences between men and women. They therefore saw them as natural. Women would inevitably have to play a different role from men in society because they were the natural raisers of children. They did not see gender roles as a separate problem, created by men for their own purposes.

However, modern feminists have identified gender differences as a product of men's attitude towards women, rather than as merely a product of women's attitude to themselves. They argue that they have therefore been able to envisage the true liberation of women. Such an analysis has created horizons for women well beyond anything that had been expected before the 1960s.

Once gender had been identified as a social product, the way was cleared to understanding how women could realise their true potential. For liberal feminists, developments such as economic equality and equality of opportunity would mostly eliminate gender differences. Radical feminists did not oppose these aspirations, but argued that there would need to be a revolutionary change in consciousness itself if gender were to be abolished completely as a social phenomenon.

Sex, on the other hand, would continue to differentiate between men and women for all but the most radical of feminists. For liberals, it should be a matter of choice as to whether the biological distinctiveness of women is important to individuals. For radical thinkers, there is less clarity over this issue. Some radicals have argued that women can play a superior role by virtue of their sex; for others, it simply implies 'otherness', i.e. recognition that women will inevitably have a different consciousness of the world. The idea of androgyny goes even further, proposing that there could be a world in which men and women become elements of the same gender.

Despite these different responses to gender within feminism, there is no doubt that when sex and gender were identified as separate concepts, the women's movement attained a new, higher level of ambition after the 1970s.

Can a conservative be a feminist?

At first sight, conservatism and feminism appear to be utterly incompatible. While nobody would deny that there is a consensus among all but the most trenchant neo-conservatives and reactionaries that women deserve economic equality, and should not be subjected to discrimination, there seem to be clear conservative objections to the more fundamental feminist beliefs. These are as follows:

➢ Feminist beliefs threaten the traditional family structure. Conservatives see the conventional family as an essential foundation of a stable society.

➢ Conservatives argue that social change should be natural and evolutionary. Feminists, by contrast, have sought to promote social change on the basis of fixed principles and utopian dreams. Conservatives insist that if women are to achieve liberation and equality, this should occur naturally.

> Most conservatives insist that the biological circumstances of women are natural so the role of wife and mother is also natural. By challenging this fact, conservatives suggest that feminists are defying nature.

> It has always been a conservative value that individuals should be free to lead their own private lives as they wish. Many feminists, especially the radicals, seek to dictate to women how they should conduct themselves and even what consciousness of the world they should adopt. Conservatives have always resisted Jacobinism — the tyranny of ideas — and they see the more militant forms of feminism in this light.

Despite these apparent objections it would be wrong to deny dogmatically any possible connections between the two movements. It is certainly reasonable for a conservative to believe that society can embrace female equality and the reduction of gender differences without risking disintegration. It is even conceivable that a conservative could accept that there are valid forms of family other than the standard nuclear model. It is also true that there has been something of a conservative reaction within the feminist movement against radical perspectives. These conservative feminists wish to restore women's ability to choose a traditional role for themselves. They admit that it might be reasonable to propose that women may be more appropriate homemakers than men, given their biological status. Conservative feminists insist, in common with other feminists, that women should have free and informed choices, the resources and opportunities to choose for themselves, and must not allow themselves to be governed by patriarchy.

Exam focus

Using this chapter and other resources available to you, answer the following questions.

Short questions

Your answers should be about 300 words long.

1 What do feminists mean by the term 'patriarchy'?
2 Why do feminists say 'the personal is the political'?
3 What are the main distinctions between liberal and radical feminism?
4 Why do some feminists relate Marxism to feminism?
5 How and why do feminists distinguish sex and gender?

Long questions

Your answers should be about 900 words long.

1 'Feminism is not a single movement, but a loose collection of doctrines and beliefs about the problems faced by women.' Discuss.

2 'All feminists are radical and none is conservative.' To what extent is this true?
3 On what grounds have radical feminists criticised liberal feminists?
4 Has feminism succeeded?

Further reading

Beasley, C. (1999) *What is Feminism? An Introduction to Feminist Theory*, Sage.
Dworkin, A. (1981) *Pornography: Men Possessing Women*, Women's Press.
Firestone, S. (2003) *The Dialectic of Sex*, Farrar Straus Giroux.
Friedan, B. (1963) *The Feminine Mystique*, W. W. Norton.
Humm, M. (1989) *The Dictionary of Feminist Theory*, Harvester Wheatsheaf.
Kemp, S. and Squires, J. (1998) *Feminisms*, Oxford University Press.
Randall, V. (1987) *Women and Politics*, Palgrave Macmillan.
Segal, L. (1999) *Why Feminism? Gender, Psychology, Politics*, Polity Press.
Tong, R. (1989) *Feminist Thought: A Comprehensive Introduction*, Routledge.

Chapter 9

Environmentalism and ecologism

Before examining the issue of the environment as it exists within politics, it is necessary to define the terms environmentalism, ecologism and green politics. These terms have been used in a variety of ways and contexts, so there are no precise, universally accepted definitions. However, the following will suffice for the purposes of this book.

Environmentalism refers to a general political concern for the environment that stops short of being ideological. Environmentalists may be moderate or radical. They do not believe that society needs fundamental transformation for them to achieve their aims.

Ecologism refers to a movement that seeks to change the nature of humankind's relationship to its physical environment. It is largely based on the science of ecology, which suggests that it is an ideology in the full sense of the word: it is built on solid scientific evidence, not merely an arbitrary set of goals. That is, ecologists propose fundamental changes to the nature of society in order to bring about equally fundamental changes in humankind's relationship to its environment.

Green politics refers to the wide variety of political issues that relate to environmental considerations. Green parties seek to influence public policy, secure the election of representatives, and may even aspire to share power with broader-based parties (as is the case in Germany). The terms 'greens' and 'green politics' do not necessarily suggest an ideological approach to the environment. Green politics is ideological for some people, of course, but for most it includes a range of issues, such as conservation, emissions control, genetically modified food production, and preserving areas of outstanding natural beauty, rather than presenting a single unified vision of a reformed society. In practice, the green movement is now a collection of both political parties and pressure groups. The most important of the pressure groups, Friends of the Earth and Greenpeace, have become international, but every country has spawned its own environmental campaign groups.

Introduction

None of the three movements outlined above existed in any coherent form until the 1960s. Before then, concern for our physical environment and our relationship to it had been expressed in a variety of contexts, but no systematic form of environmental politics had been developed. During the nineteenth century, for example, rapid industrialisation caused anxiety about the destruction of the natural environment and the deteriorating quality of air and water. But these remained marginal issues in politics and failed to exercise the interest of policy makers. Indeed, it was not until 1956 that the Clean Air Act was passed in the UK to control the production of air pollution. By the 1960s, however, a growing number of environmental issues were beginning to emerge. These are examined below.

Biodiversity

One of the earliest environmental concerns of the 1960s was the threat posed to many animal and plant species by a number of developments, including industrialisation, urbanisation, rapid population growth, intensive agriculture, industrial methods of whaling, fishing and poaching, and the degradation of natural environments. On one level, this threat was seen as a general quality of life issue, but later, as environmentalism developed into a deeper political philosophy during the 1970s, it became a **biodiversity** issue. Biodiversity was also associated with ecologists who took a **holistic** view of the living world, seeing all species as interconnected. Should the variety of species decline, it was argued, the whole of nature, including humankind, would be adversely affected. It was therefore a mistake to think of conservation in terms of individual species, argued ecologists: the threat to biodiversity was a crisis for nature itself.

Key terms

Biodiversity

This term refers to the belief that the fullest possible range of the Earth's plant and animal species should be preserved. There are two main bases for this view. The first is that biodiversity is desirable for its own sake (a shallow ecology view). Life will be enriched by the existence of many different living species. The second is the more radical view that life is one single web (a deep ecology perspective). If parts of the natural world are lost, the whole of nature suffers. This is part of the holistic attitude to the environment.

Holism

This refers to the view, largely associated with Fritjof Capra (1939–), that the natural world is a single, organic whole. All aspects of nature are interconnected, so change or damage to some parts will affect the whole. Capra insisted that we will not necessarily find conventional scientific solutions to environmental problems. So-called 'new physics' suggests that we cannot be sure how natural phenomena are connected. When one part changes, we are unable to predict how the rest will be affected. From this belief in uncertainty, it follows that we should avoid interfering with any part of nature because we cannot be certain of the consequences of our actions.

Air and water quality

As the quality of air and water declined, a trend that occurred especially in urban regions and those parts of the world experiencing rapid industrialisation, the problem was seen largely in terms of human health. Water pollution was a direct threat to people's wellbeing, because it led to widespread disease, while poor air was identified as a cause of longer-term health problems, such as cancer, asthma and respiratory ailments in general. However, both types of pollution were having an increasing impact on plant and animal populations too.

The problem of air quality took on a new, more frightening dimension in the 1980s, with the realisation that the ozone layer had been damaged by chlorofluorocarbon (CFC) emissions, and that the release of 'greenhouse gases' — as a result of industrial processes — was causing global warming. Widespread concern over these developments, fuelled by increasing numbers of scientific studies which confirmed the damage and its long-term effects, led to environmentalism entering the world stage. Water and air pollution do not recognise national borders, and the ways in which countries behave affect the rest of the world. Transnational agreements and organisations are therefore required to combat pollution. This has proved to be the greatest of the challenges facing the movement in general.

Destruction of habitats

The best-known example of this phenomenon is the ongoing destruction of the world's rainforests. The southward expansion of the Sahara desert is viewed with similar alarm, as is the gradual shrinking of the Caspian and Aral Seas in central Asia. The destruction of habitats has three main consequences. First, rainforest loss has adverse effects on the atmosphere — it exacerbates the greenhouse effect, leading to global warming and rises in sea levels. Second, the destruction threatens the traditional habitats and ways of life of local human populations. Third, many animal and plant species have become endangered by the loss of their natural habitats. Note that environmentalists are as fearful of the loss of traditional human communities as they are of the loss of plant and animal species.

Resource depletion

Global economic growth has led to the rapid depletion of a wide variety of the world's resources. Dwindling energy supplies has been the primary concern, but the supply of other commodities is also threatened. Attention has focused on fossil fuels, mainly oil, but minerals, timber and other natural products are running out alarmingly quickly as well. Fear of such a dramatic depletion of physical resources is exemplified by '**space-ship Earth**' theory. Environmentalists have argued that we cannot rely forever on discovering new resources or improved technology in energy production. The answer lies, they argue, in dramatic reductions in our resource use. The more radical elements in the environmental movement, including the anarcho-environmentalists, have argued that a completely new attitude to economic growth must be developed. The socialist and anarchist wings of environmentalism see capitalism itself as the culprit, given its insatiable desire for growth, and have therefore campaigned to replace it with new economic structures that limit growth.

Key term

Spaceship Earth

This phrase refers to the belief held by most environmentalists that the resources of the Earth are finite. Just as a spaceship uses its supplies which will inevitably run out, so too will the Earth run out of resources. In order to prolong the Earth's life, therefore, we must use up its resources more slowly. Some campaigners, such as James Lovelock (1921–), have questioned this analysis, suggesting that we can rely upon renewable sources of energy in the future and ought to be developing them as quickly as possible.

Core values of environmentalism and ecologism

It is difficult to identify the core values of environmentalism and ecologism because in each case there is more than one tradition to consider. However, there are a small number of ideas that are shared by all or most environmentalists and ecologists.

Opposition to anthropocentrism

Anthropocentrism refers to the notion that humankind is the centre of the natural world and that the human species may therefore use nature for its own purposes. This is seen as being largely the result of the belief held by Abrahamic religions — Judaism, Islam and Christianity — that God created the world for man's benefit and gave him 'dominion... over all the Earth' (Genesis 2:26).

This is seen as false consciousness by most ecologists. For them, humankind is simply a part of nature as a whole, with no special status above that of all other living things. This view is not confined to ecologists. Hindus and Buddhists, for example, see humankind as part of the eternal circle of nature. Humans come from nature and will return there in a constant cycle of death and rebirth. The Jains, a Hindu sect, particularly emphasise this perspective on human life; they insist that all living things should be protected and respected, as humans are part of the same living organism as all other forms of life.

If we can free ourselves from our anthropocentrist obsession, therefore, we will learn to respect our natural environment. The depletion of resources is a classic example of this objection to anthropocentrism. Humans assume that the Earth's resources belong to them and that they may therefore use them as they wish. Environmentalists argue that we are not entitled to view them in this way. The Earth's resources are part of the whole of nature, so we are depriving nature itself when we selfishly deplete them.

Natural quality of life

The issue of what constitutes a good quality of life is highly contentious. Critics of modern international capitalism argue that the system sees quality of life largely in terms of the consumption of goods and services. In crude terms, the more we are able to consume, the better off we consider ourselves.

Environmentalists have two objections to the consumption model. The first is that the constant desire for increased material wealth is depleting the world's resources too rapidly and threatening the natural environment. In this sense, the price that must be paid for consumerism is simply too high. The second objection is that quality of life does not consist solely of conventional forms of wealth. Instead, they argue, the state of the natural environment is a key element in the quality of life. If, therefore, we curb our desire for consumption, we will reap great rewards in environmental terms.

Anti-industrialisation

It would be wrong to suggest that all environmentalists and ecologists are opposed to industrialisation. However, to varying degrees, environmentalists have seen industrialisation and economic growth as fundamental threats to the natural environment. The most liberal of these campaigners have proposed compromises with industrialism. They see industrial development as inevitable and believe that it is utopian to expect humankind to control it.

At the other end of the spectrum are those groups who wish to see the tide of industrialisation turned back. Indeed, for many radical, deep ecologists, industrialisation is the main cause of our environmental problems. They propose a return to simpler ways of life; self-sufficiency and the curbing of constantly rising levels of demand would lie at the centre of this new world. As is explained further below, anarcho-environmentalists see political institutions as accomplices in the relentless capitalist process of exploiting the world's resources, without concern for the future or for the health of our 'biosphere'. For anarchists, we will not be able to protect our environment unless the political structures which underpin capitalism are destroyed.

Perhaps the leading exponent of this concern with industrialisation was the radical economist Ernst Schumacher, who coined the term 'small is beautiful'. Schumacher argued that the scale of production was considerably too large and human communities had become oversized. Humankind must therefore return to a more appropriate scale of living and production. Schumacher also challenged the notion that human wants are infinite and will therefore always grow. We can, he asserted, curb our insatiable desire to consume more and more. We can return to a more natural way of living in small communities, which are integrated with the natural world rather than merely exploiting it.

Types of environmentalism and ecologism

Liberal environmentalism

Liberal environmentalism can be defined using the same approach as that taken with other ideologies. This means that the 'liberal' elements of the environmental movement are among those that do not propose revolutionary change and which believe that their objectives can be largely achieved within existing social structures. Of course, any distinctions between the liberal and radical wings of an ideology are bound to be blurred and environmentalism is no exception. For our purposes, it is sufficient to include those environmental issues which constitute the mainstream green movement in a review of liberal environmentalism.

Moderate environmentalism of this type generally places humankind at the centre of the natural world. The concerns these environmentalists express mainly relate to the future of humanity. If the environment is degraded, this will threaten humankind and its future development. Unlike the deep ecologists, the liberal green movement tends to see environmental issues in isolation from each other. The holism that characterises the more ideological elements of green politics is largely absent. The main issues that concern liberal environmentalism include the following:

➢ biodiversity and species preservation
➢ preservation of areas of natural beauty
➢ pollution control
➢ habitat protection
➢ organic farming
➢ opposition to genetically modified foods
➢ opposition to nuclear energy
➢ concentration on the use of renewable resources
➢ protection of the habitats of traditional societies

Although liberals in general have a wide range of global concerns, the moderate green movement has tended to concentrate on what the individual can do in his or her own home and personal life to alleviate environmental problems. Typical examples of this are recycling, energy-saving consciousness, 'green' houses with a variety of devices for conserving energy, and natural forms of gardening.

Of course, the deep ecologists criticise this kind of environmentalism as tinkering around the edges. They argue that it fails to deal with our relationship with the Earth. Such measures merely treat the symptoms of the problem; deep ecologists say that we must identify and deal with fundamental causes, which concern humankind's basic relationship with the natural environment.

The Green Party principles given in Box 9.1 are anthropocentric. The protection of the environment is seen in terms of the welfare of the human race and future generations. Indeed, many of these principles can be seen as ultra-liberalism. They are as much about how humans should live together in harmony as about how we can live in harmony with nature. The principles are also relatively moderate in their tone. The Green Party urges us to adopt a new mode of living and looks forward to a more localised and direct form of democracy, but it suggests nothing that would shake the existing social and political structures. This is the essence of the liberal agenda — recognition that conventional politics does not take enough account of environmental concerns, but expressing no desire to rebuild society from the bottom up and to develop new kinds of human consciousness.

Box 9.1 Core principles of the British Green Party, issued in 2001

Life on Earth is under immense pressure. The environment around us is faced with massive destruction. Conventional politics has failed us because its basis is fundamentally flawed.

The Green Party isn't just another political party. Green politics is a new kind of politics guided by these key principles:

1 Humankind depends on the diversity of the natural world for its existence. We do not believe that other species are dispensable.

2 The Earth's physical resources are finite. We threaten our future if we try to live beyond those means, so we must build a sustainable society that guarantees our long-term future.

3 Every person should be entitled to basic material security as of right.

4 Our actions should take account of the well-being of other nations and future generations. We should not pursue our well-being to the detriment of theirs.

5 A healthy society is based on voluntary co-operation between empowered individuals in a democratic society, free from discrimination, whether based on race, colour, sex, religion, national origin, social origin or any other prejudice.

6 We emphasise democratic participation and accountability by ensuring that decisions are taken at the closest practical level to those affected by them.

7 We look for non-violent solutions to conflict situations, which take into account the interests of minorities and future generations in order to achieve lasting settlements.

8 The success of a society cannot be measured by narrow economic indicators, but should take account of factors affecting the quality of life for all people: personal freedom, social equality, health, happiness and human fulfilment.

9 Electoral politics is not the only way to achieve change in society and we will use a variety of methods to help to effect change, providing those methods do not conflict with our other core principles.

10 The Green Party puts changes in both values and lifestyles at the heart of the radical green agenda.

Shallow and deep ecologism

The term ecologism can be used in two contexts. It may refer to the science of humankind's relationship with other humans, the animal world and the physical environment. Its other meaning is as a collection of interconnected beliefs about what humankind's relationship to the natural world *ought* to be. It is therefore a political and a quasi-ideological movement. Ecologism in this sense can be further divided into two branches — shallow ecology and deep ecology.

Shallow ecology

Shallow ecology can be treated as mainstream. It is characterised by a number of beliefs:

➤ Humankind should consider itself a 'steward' of the natural world. Rather than simply exploiting the world for its own purposes, humankind has a duty to protect the Earth and ensure its survival.

➤ Humankind must protect the Earth and its resources for future generations. In other words, we must not ignore the consequences of our exploitation of the Earth. In practical terms, this implies energy conservation, use of renewable resources and protection of habitats.

➤ The richness and diversity of the plant and animal world are ends in themselves. They do not merely exist on Earth to serve us; their life has value in itself.

➤ Although shallow ecologists do not share the holistic view of their more radical colleagues, they understand that humankind's manipulation of the Earth for its own purposes may have consequences far beyond what can be perceived. The depletion of the ozone layer is an example of this.

➤ Whereas liberal environmentalists treat various issues separately, shallow ecologists have a sense that the environmental movement should be all-encompassing. Ecologism is a state of mind which can be applied to all issues that affect the natural world (deep ecologists take this further by seeking a new consciousness). Thus, we should not separate issues such as emissions control, biodiversity and habitat protection from each other, but treat them as a single problem.

➤ Shallow ecologists use science to develop and reinforce environmental theories. However, note that they do not tend to apply philosophy or religion to their belief system, as deep ecologists do.

Jonathan Porritt, one of the pioneers of the green movement in the UK, made a useful distinction between liberal environmentalism and ecology. He accepted that for most liberals (who are usually middle class), environmentalism exists to support humankind's own self-interest. In other words, we will care for the environment if this will be to the benefit of humankind. For genuine ecologists ('deep greens', Porritt called them), concern for the environment should not be self-interested. We should consider the welfare of the natural environment for its own sake.

Deep ecology

The first distinction between shallow and deep ecology was made by the philosopher Arne Naess (1912–), who articulated the idea in 1972. While not disparaging the efforts of shallow ecologists to raise awareness of issues such as biodiversity, air quality control and protection of the oceans, Naess argued that these were 'shallow' concerns which failed to appreciate that ecologism was a philosophy that should exist for its own sake. Although the shallow ecologists wished to see a better balance between the natural world and humankind's needs, Naess claimed that they still placed humans on a higher level than the rest of the Earth. Ecologism, Naess insisted, must consider the natural world as a system within which humankind has equal status with other

Arne Naess argued that raising awareness of environmental issues was not enough

species. Environmental protection is worth doing simply because it is worth doing, not merely because it satisfies humankind's desire to live in a more pleasant world. Instead of thinking about humankind's relationship with the natural world, we should see ourselves as part of a single whole.

The animal rights movement, although not necessarily part of the environmental mainstream, demonstrates a deep ecological attitude. By seeing animals as part of our own natural world and deserving of as much respect as we expect to have for ourselves, the movement has reached a deep level of consciousness. It has, in other words, freed itself from anthropocentrism.

Murray Bookchin (1921–), an anarcho-environmentalist whose views are explored further below, deploys a similar argument. For him, all life on Earth is part of a single web in which every part is equal in importance to every other part. Thus, it is not acceptable for humans to consider themselves to be superior to the rest of nature any more than it is correct to consider elephants to be superior to microorganisms just because they are larger.

Bookchin's view involves a radical change in human consciousness — one of the defining features of deep ecology. Naess expressed the idea of developing a deeper consciousness by identifying different levels of involvement with ecology. At the lowest level (which he termed level four), we are merely concerned with environmental issues on an individual basis, perhaps concentrating on those aspects that we meet in our own lives. We do what we can at this level but make no fundamental changes to our lives. At the highest level (level 1), we can achieve self-realisation. This means that our whole lives can be conducted in accordance with the philosophical principles of ecology (see Box 9.2). We immerse ourselves in consciousness of the natural world and see no separation between it and ourselves.

Box 9.2 **The eight-point platform**

Written in 1984, and largely the work of Arne Naess and George Sessions, the eight-point platform is a kind of deep ecology manifesto and statement of principles.

1 The wellbeing and flourishing of human and non-human life on Earth have value in themselves. These values are independent of the usefulness of the non-human world for human purposes.

2 Richness and diversity of life forms contribute to the realisation of these values and are also values in themselves.

3 Humans have no right to reduce this richness and diversity except to satisfy vital needs.

4 The flourishing of human life and cultures is compatible with a substantially smaller human population. The flourishing of non-human life *requires* a smaller human population.

5 Present human interference with the non-human world is excessive, and the situation is rapidly worsening.

6 Policies must therefore be changed. These policies affect basic economic, technological and ideological structures. The resulting state of affairs will be deeply different from the present.

7 The ideological change will be mainly of appreciating life quality (dwelling in situations of inherent value) rather than adhering to an increasingly higher standard of living. There will be a profound awareness of the difference between bigness and greatness.

8 Those who subscribe to the foregoing points have an obligation directly or indirectly to try to implement the necessary changes.

James Lovelock, a scientist, represents a part of the deep ecology movement that can be characterised as 'Earth first'. This places the whole of the Earth, both animate and inanimate parts, above the interests of humankind. In some ways, Lovelock is not as radical as Bookchin and Naess — for example, he argues that nuclear energy is to be tolerated and even encouraged — but he does represent an important branch of the deep ecology movement. This branch accepts that technology can be harnessed to serve the interests of the planet as a whole. Indeed, to a certain extent, Lovelock suggests that Earth is capable of making its own adjustments to humankind's influence. What matters to Lovelock and his supporters is that we understand that everything on Earth is interconnected. Furthermore, we cannot possibly know how these interconnections work, and so must avoid activities whose consequences for Earth are uncertain, and possibly irreversible.

Although deep ecology is not a cohesive, united movement, it does have one element which brings together all its members. This is that humankind must be prepared to change its whole consciousness if the environment is to be saved. It is not sufficient merely to be aware of environmental issues and place them at the centre of the political universe: our whole being must become one with nature.

The key beliefs of liberal environmentalism, shallow ecology and deep ecology are summarised in Table 9.1.

Table 9.1 Summary of mainstream environmentalism and ecologism

Liberal environmentalism	Shallow ecology	Deep ecology
Concern for the environment is centred upon the interests of humankind.	Humans should care for the environment for its own sake.	Humans must develop a new consciousness that sees humankind as an intrinsic part of the natural world.
Environmental issues can be treated separately.	Different aspects of the natural world are interconnected, so our treatment of nature should take this into account.	The Earth is a single, complete organism. Humans are part of that whole.
Environmental problems can, in theory, be solved within existing political and economic structures.	Existing political and economic structures must be transformed so that they place environmental issues at the centre of their concerns.	There must be a total change in all economic, social and political life so that humankind can be placed more naturally within its physical environment.
Most environmental issues are fundamentally economic in nature.	Ecology is largely scientific in nature.	Ecology is a synthesis of science, philosophy and, in some cases, religion or even mysticism.

Anarcho-environmentalism

Although there are active groups of feminists and socialists who have synthesised their primary ideological position with an environmentalist stance, it is perhaps today's anarchists and quasi-anarchists who form the main group of 'specialised' environmentalists — that is, those who see no barrier between their specific political aims and a radical attitude to ecology.

The main thrust of modern anarchism — whether environmentally based or not — has concentrated on anti-globalisation. Anarchists argue that the problems created by globalisation are various. Their beliefs include the following:

➤ Opposition to the behaviour of multinational and transnational corporations. They accuse these organisations of destroying traditional cultures, exploiting cheap labour forces through low wages and bad working conditions, and destroying local environments and community-based forms of self-sufficiency. The incident at Bhopal in India in 1984 is perhaps the most notorious example of such exploitation and has acted as a touchstone issue for many anarcho-environmentalists. The Union Carbide Company's chemical plant exploded, causing at least 20,000 immediate deaths and many more subsequently, with hundreds of thousands suffering illness and homelessness. Bhopal became a symbol of multinational exploitation of the developing world. Several instances of badly maintained and managed supertankers running aground, causing huge damage to wildlife and natural habitats from oil pollution, also illustrate a lack of consideration for the environment. The same is true of the activities of oil companies in Alaska.

➢ Opposition to the policies of international organisations such as the World Trade Organisation, the International Monetary Fund and the World Bank. These organisations stand accused of forcing poor countries to restructure their economies in order to ensure that such states can boost export earnings. Anarcho-environmentalists argue that this has had a disastrous effect on both traditional communities and the ecology of such countries. Forests have been cut down, intensive agriculture has caused deserts to expand and native plant and animal populations have come under pressure.

Protest over the treatment of the Bhopal victims, Michigan, USA

➢ Attempts to reach international agreements on environmental control have been blocked by the influence of multinational companies. The USA's reluctance to comply with such agreements has been singled out as the critical factor in its resistance to cooperation. Anarcho-environmentalists recognise that environmental issues have to be dealt with on an international basis, but argue that agreements can never be successful as long as the governments of the main industrial countries are dominated by business interests.

It should be stressed that these concerns are not the monopoly of anarchist groups. Many liberal environmentalists are also critical of international organisations and corporations, but propose reforms rather than revolutionary methods to change the way in which environmental issues are solved.

The anarchist's case rests on their assertion that humankind must adopt a simpler, more natural way of living and producing. This involves the withdrawal of giant corporations from the world stage and the replacement of international political organisations with community-based social structures. Much of the inspiration for these ideas can be traced back to the nineteenth- and early twentieth-century anarchist Peter Kropotkin and his modern US counterpart Murray Bookchin.

Bookchin's ideas centre on the destruction of all forms of social hierarchy. For him, humans are naturally equal and society should reflect this equality. He argues that by forming small, self-sufficient communities similar to those proposed by Kropotkin, such equality can be achieved. However, he extends his ideas into humankind's relationship to the natural world, rejecting the notion of hierarchy here, too. All living things, he insists, have equal status in nature. Thus, if there are no hierarchies in nature, humans cannot claim to be superior. Life, he says, is a web, not a pyramid. Bookchin's holistic and egalitarian view of nature is expressed in Box 9.3.

Box 9.3 Murray Bookchin on the 'web of nature'

In this passage from *The Ecology of Freedom* (1982), Bookchin explains his philosophy:

If we recognise that every ecosystem can also be viewed as a food web, we can think of it as a circular, interlacing nexus of plant–animal relationships (rather than a stratified pyramid with man at the apex) that includes such widely varying creatures as microorganisms and large mammals. What ordinarily puzzles anyone who sees food-web diagrams for the first time is the impossibility of discerning a point of entry into the nexus. The web can be entered at any point and leads back to its point of departure without any apparent exit. Aside from the energy provided by sunlight (and dissipated by radiation), the system to all appearances is closed. Each species, be it a form of bacteria or deer, is knitted together in a network of interdependence, however indirect the links may be. A predator in the web is also prey, even if the 'lowliest' of the organisms merely makes it ill or helps to consume it after death.

In many ways, Bookchin is perhaps the deepest of deep ecologists. His ideas are inspired by science, philosophy and religion, as well as by his anarchist politics. Although he can be seen as an anarchist, his theories can be applicable to all radical ecologists.

Key environmentalist and ecologist thinkers

Arne Naess (Norwegian, 1912–)

Naess is possibly the most philosophical of today's leading ecologists. His belief system, which has become known as deep ecology, has three fundamental bases. These are romanticism, science and philosophy.

Naess's romantic view of nature has led him to understand that humans have a deep spiritual relationship with nature, which has largely been lost in modern, complex civilisation. His theme, which is echoed by writers, musicians and religious traditions such as Buddhism, involves the natural affinity that all living creatures have for each other and for the physical landscape which surrounds them. In the high mountains, where Naess has spent much of his life and from which he draws most of his inspiration, this oneness with nature is most apparent.

As regards science, Naess's theories are closely related to Lovelock's 'Gaia' thesis (see p. 301). The Earth, says Naess, is a biosphere — a single living organism in which all parts of it are interrelated biologically and spiritually. As humans, we must develop a deep understanding of both the relationships between the different parts of nature and our own personal relationship with the biosphere.

It is in the field of philosophy that Naess's contribution to the ecology movement is perhaps most original. Indeed, it has been ascribed its own name — **ecosophy**. He argues that on a personal level we seek to achieve self-realisation — that is, the fulfilment of our deepest desires for harmony within the world that surrounds us, both human and physical. Philosophers of many kinds, including Marxists, anarchists, existentialists and feminists, have sought to explain how best we can achieve such self-realisation. Naess emphasises the search for total harmony with the natural world we inhabit; for him, the highest level of human consciousness is to reach an understanding that we have relationships with the whole of nature and that all parts of nature itself are interconnected. What affects nature, for good or ill, also affects us. Once we achieve self-realisation, Naess declares, we will also have developed a full understanding of how we must interact with the natural world.

Key term

Ecosophy

Mainly associated with Arne Naess, this term refers essentially to the synthesising of environmentalism with philosophy. Most environmentalists have been concerned with ecological science and the practicalities of protecting our biosphere from harm. Naess, however, links a philosophy of life — mainly how we can achieve self-realisation — with a full understanding of our relationship with the natural world.

However, Naess's beliefs are not purely philosophical. Having achieved self-realisation, he says, we can better understand the practical ways in which we, as individuals, can protect and nurture the environment. In the case of a farmer, for example, this will involve emphasising natural methods, avoiding pesticides, protecting wildlife and recycling materials. For an individual involved in business, it will mean conserving energy, avoiding pollution and caring for the physical environment. For a feminist, it may mean exploring feminine consciousness in order to discover ways in which women can contribute to the environmental movement both practically and politically.

James Lovelock (English, 1921–)

A scientist by calling, Lovelock developed his theories while working on the NASA space programme in the USA during the 1960s and 1970s. His particular field was the assessment of whether life existed, or had existed, on other planets. He is best known for his development of the concept of the *Gaia*. Gaia was the Ancient Greek goddess of the Earth, and it is upon the Earth as a whole that Lovelock bases his ideas.

He sees the Earth (and indeed any planet) as a single, organic, living whole. Most interestingly, Lovelock includes the inanimate parts of nature — even the rocks — among that whole. Humankind is but a part of the organic Gaia. We are not separate from it nor even passengers on it. However, human society has developed its own consciousness of the world, believing that as a species it is superior to all the other parts of the whole and that the Earth can be manipulated for humankind's own benefit.

Lovelock argues that the Earth is a self-regulating organism. If any part begins to change significantly, the rest of nature will adjust itself in order to recreate a balance. For example, if temperatures began to rise for some reason, the plant life on the planet will adjust in order to change the composi-

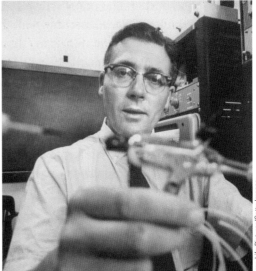

James Lovelock controversially supports the use of nuclear power

tion of the atmosphere and restore temperatures to their normal level. A second example of this mechanism concerns the salinity (salt concentration) of the seas. From time to time this may rise or fall, threatening sea life, but there will be an adjustment to restore salinity to a compatible level.

The processes that maintain the Earth's balance are exceedingly complex, something on which all environmental scientists and theorists agree. Lovelock therefore asserts that humankind should resist the temptation to interfere with natural processes since it can have no idea of the consequences of its actions. As he says: 'We'll never know enough...hands off!' Although to some extent the Earth will be able to adjust itself to human interference, we have become so intrusive that eventually this will not be possible. In particular, the tiny microorganisms that make up life on Earth are affected by human action so fundamentally that the very basis of life may be threatened.

The implication of Lovelock's theories is that we must avoid taking any actions (including towards inanimate objects) which will affect the balance of the Earth. We must be sensitive to natural processes and allow the Earth to find its own balance. In particular, Lovelock considers energy production to be the most damaging human activity of all. He recognises that humankind needs energy to sustain itself and argues that nuclear energy is the way forward, rather than renewable forms which will never satisfy our growing needs. Whereas most environmentalists oppose the use of nuclear power, on the grounds that it produces waste products which will remain a threat for thousands of years and because of the ever present danger of a catastrophic accident, Lovelock believes that this is the price we have to pay. Nuclear fission produces virtually no interference with the balance of the Earth, so its long-term consequences are less severe than those of any other known method of energy production.

Fritjof Capra (Austrian, 1939–)

Of the three thinkers discussed in this section, Capra is perhaps the one most inspired by the physical sciences, especially physics. Like Naess and Lovelock, he is closely associated with Schumacher College, a centre for environmental research in England. Capra's science is complex, but some accessible conclusions are described below.

Capra challenged the explanations of the biosphere offered by traditional forms of science. Since science had suggested that the different parts of the natural world could be studied separately and that they could therefore also be manipulated separately, fundamental errors were made in our understanding of the natural environment. The alternative to these scientific models offered by Capra was holism. The holistic approach asserts that all living organisms are interconnected and form one great whole. Furthermore, Capra says, this does not just occur on a macro level — e.g. the seas, atmosphere, animal and plant species — but on a micro level. The building blocks of life, including microorganisms, cells and, indeed, parts of cells, are all interconnected and communicate with each other in ways which we have not even begun to understand.

The idea of the Earth as being a single entity with interrelated parts was held by the ancient world in the form of mysticism and religion. Although ancient people had little science as we understand it today, they had a fundamental understanding that all life is part of a single whole and that energy flows through all of it in a continuous stream. These ideas can still be seen in traditional medicine (e.g. acupuncture and reflexology), in religions (e.g. Buddhism, Jainism and Taoism), and in a mystical understanding of the energy forces which pass through the Earth (e.g. lay lines).

Capra accepts that science will probably never be able to fully make sense of all these interconnections. Similarly, many astrophysicists assert that we will never fully understand the workings of the universe. However, an understanding that the Earth is a single organism must inform the way in which we treat our natural environment. Above all, Capra attacks anthropocentrism — the belief that humankind is at the centre of nature and is separate from and superior to it. We must replace this belief with ecocentrism — the reality that nature, as a single whole, dominates all life, and that we humans are merely a part of that whole and equal to all other parts.

Issues in environmentalism and ecologism

Are environmentalism and ecologism ideologies?

An ideology is a set of ideas which have coherence and are therefore interlocking. These ideas propose the transformation of society in a fundamental way. Ideology therefore involves revolutionary rather than evolutionary change, which is created by positive, purposeful actions, rather than being gradual and natural, without any specific political aims.

According to these criteria, liberal environmentalism cannot be seen as an ideology. The environmental movement as a whole certainly shares a common value — that our physical environment should be protected and that humankind must readjust its relationship to the natural world. However, liberal environmentalists do not believe that any transformation of society and its structures is necessary. For example, there is no need to reform capitalism in any fundamental way. Capitalism, liberals argue, can be regulated and moderated in order to take environmental concerns into account. Similarly, liberal environmentalists have no specific political goals other than a desire to place environmental concerns high up or even at the top of the political agenda.

Evidence of liberal environmentalism's lack of ideological credentials is that it does not seek to change the relationship between humans and nature in any fundamental way. In short, it remains anthropocentric. By retaining humankind's place at the apex of the natural world, liberals are failing to propose revolutionary change. The fundamental structure, or 'hierarchy', as Bookchin would call it, remains unaltered. Liberal environmentalism is therefore better described as a political movement rather than as an ideological one. Despite this, it is worth noting that it is an extremely coherent political movement, far more unified in its principles and objectives than mainstream, democratic political parties.

When we turn to the radical ecologists the picture changes considerably. The deep ecologists, led by Capra and Naess, criticise the shallow ecologists on the grounds that they are not sufficiently ideological. The key reason for this concerns human consciousness. At the deepest level of ecologism (Naess's level 1), humankind achieves self-realisation through the development of a complete subjugation of human consciousness into the continuous flow of natural forces. This can be compared to the Marxist concept of total socialist consciousness, which can become so deep-rooted that no alternative form of consciousness is possible. The shallow ecologists, on the other hand, do not seek such depth of consciousness, but merely modify anthropocentrism in the interests of the natural world. This can arguably be described as radical, but shallow greens remain reformers rather than revolutionaries.

Deep ecologists certainly demonstrate values and principles, as well as a liberated consciousness, that give their movement an ideological coherence. This coherence is evident in two senses. First, their philosophy involves a fundamental change in social structures. Industrialisation must be firmly controlled and even turned back; capitalism must be replaced by simpler forms of production and distribution; the acquisitive, consumer society must be turned into one which caters for needs, not wants. Second, it proposes a completely new attitude towards nature. Humankind must not be separated from nature, but must see itself as part of it, equal to its other parts and part of nature's wholeness. For Capra, this relationship is a flow of energy, whereas for Bookchin it is a web; but in both cases, humankind becomes part of nature, not separate from it. These characteristics seem to be both coherent and purposeful.

Similarly, those who combine environmentalism with other ideologies — anarchists, socialists and feminists in particular — can be seen as ideologues. They are ideological in the sense that they have adopted an ideological approach to social transformation in general, and have linked social revolution to fundamental changes in humankind's relationship with the natural environment.

The answer to this question must therefore be that liberal environmentalism is not in any sense ideological; that a weak case can be made for describing shallow ecologists in such terms; but that deep ecology certainly is an ideological movement.

Is ecologism merely a utopian philosophy?

Many deep ecologists, especially Arne Naess, would be proud that their beliefs might be described as a 'philosophy', but would object to them being termed utopian. This is because the term 'utopian' implies 'unrealistic'. In other words, are the radical ecologists merely romantic dreamers?

Certainly, there is a strong case to be made for describing ecologism as a philosophy rather than a political movement. We should, perhaps, separate 'green politics' from 'green philosophy'. Such a philosophy need not have highly specific ends and might have unforeseeable consequences for society. The Enlightenment of the eighteenth century can serve as a model for this idea. The original Enlightenment philosophers, most notable of whom was René Descartes, were not ideologues in the sense that Marxists or anarchists have been. Rather, they changed our consciousness of the world in fundamental ways without specifying any political objectives. The philosophical developments they made gave rise to specific political movements at a much later stage in human social progress. Yet we would not describe the Enlightenment period as utopian in character. In fact, the contrary is true — it is seen as an age when new truths were revealed to us, which led humankind to a 'higher' form of civilisation. It may be that deep ecology will one day be recognised as a similar philosophical revolution whose consequences may be prove to be as fundamental and significant as those that followed the ideas of Isaac Newton, Descartes and Darwin.

However, the problem of where to place deep ecology in human consciousness has been exacerbated by the fact that its adherents have associated themselves with mysticism and religions like Buddhism and Taoism. The latter have been seen as little more than philosophies of individual self-realisation, rather than social religions that provide ethical codes. To make matters worse, mysticism is often criticised as 'quackery', with no basis either in science or the human imagination.

A specific charge which can be levied against Naess, for example, is that he proposes to turn back progress and return to simpler ways of living that do not acknowledge industrialisation and technological advances. He goes so far as to assert that the 'natural' human population of the Earth is only 100 million, a tiny fraction of its current number. Clearly this 'natural' level cannot be achieved and must therefore be viewed as intensely utopian. Admittedly, the notion of returning to simpler forms of community and economic organisation has long been explored by anarchists, and may therefore be seen as a perfectly reasonable alternative to modern, complex societies. Such communities can be created within existing human society (like the Israeli kibbutzim, for example).

However, the ecology movement demands that all humankind would have to eschew progress, dismantle most industry and adopt simple technologies. Since the aim of the movement is environmental, it would be futile if only some people adopted new forms of communal living. In order to make an environmental impact, we must all make fundamental changes to our way of life.

However, the picture is perhaps not so stark for deep ecologists. We could, for example, take one basic principle from the movement — that humankind is part of nature and not superior to it or merely separate — and adopt it as a fundamental consideration in all our activities. If we change our consciousness, seeing ourselves as interdependent organisms within the total Gaia, and understand that we must avoid taking actions the environmental consequences of which we cannot predict, it may be possible to sustain lifestyles modern humankind can find acceptable. We could therefore continue to engage in industrial processes, provided we only use non-polluting, renewable forms of energy. We could retain sophisticated economies while always replacing any resources we take from the Earth. Agriculture could develop in such a way that the rest of the living world remains unexploited. Respect for all life forms cannot be seen as utopian, nor need the retention of biodiversity be viewed as revolutionary.

The most powerful claim which ecologists can make is that humankind really has no alternative. The inevitable result of our present attitude towards the natural environment is disaster. They can therefore say that it is utopian to believe that humankind can survive without a fundamental change in consciousness. The ecologists are, in fact, the realists; it is the rest of humanity which is utopian.

What is the impact of globalisation on the green movement?

In some ways, globalisation has had the effect of bringing the green movement to the forefront of international ideology. When environmentalists were nationally based, their concerns seemed parochial. The emergence of truly global environmental issues, such as ozone depletion, global warming and biodiversity, forced the movement to itself become global in nature. This has chiefly occurred in two ways.

First, the two main organisations that campaign on environmental issues — Greenpeace and Friends of the Earth — have become global organisations. Their campaigns are international and they have increasingly focused their attention on international organisations and conferences. The great environmental conferences of recent times — Rio (1992)

Greenpeace protesters run out in front of US President George W. Bush's cavalcade, the Mall, London

and Kyoto (1997) — were characterised by intense lobbying on the part of both organisations.

Second, a new quasi-anarchist, anti-globalisation movement has grown up separately from the more conventional environmentalist lobby. The groups that make up this movement, whose philosophy and aims are varied, argue that conventional methods of campaigning are futile. They believe that an anthropocentric and exploitative attitude to the environment is so entrenched within international organisations and multinational companies that radical methods must be employed. Such methods have included mass demonstrations and even attacks upon property, especially where international conferences are being held.

The main problem for environmental groups is that, no matter how much influence they may have over national governments, environmental problems are now so extensive that only global action can be effective. Furthermore, the administration of the most influential country, the USA, has shown relatively little interest in green issues, and the US Green Party, led by Ralph Nader (1934–), has made virtually no impact on electoral politics.

Globalisation has therefore been a two-edged sword for the green movement. On the one hand, it has united environmentalists throughout the world (a development facilitated by the internet) and has prompted enormous amounts of scientific research into issues such as climate change, movements in animal populations and habitat degradation. On the other hand, it has presented environmentalists with a host of new problems. The power of large corporations and international financial organisations is immense. Their interests in trade, technology, energy resources, development and industrial issues have pushed environmental considerations to one side. For such groups, short-term gains take precedence over the long-term dangers of adverse environmental impacts.

There is also a considerable amount of tension concerning the issue of the economic development of poor countries. The green movement has argued for genuinely sustainable development in such countries. They should, greens say, be presented with opportunities to develop their own natural and organic economic systems. If this can be done, these countries will retain a vested interest in environmental protection. Self-sufficiency and traditional social structures will mean that natural habitats will be protected and the damaging effects of rapid industrialisation will be avoided. For example, if India had developed its own chemicals industry, using its own technology controlled by local communities, Bhopal would never have occurred. If the native peoples of South America were given the opportunity to exploit the rainforests in a sustainable way, their traditional way of life would be protected, their natural habitat would survive and the problem of global warming would be reduced.

Against this view is ranged pressure from international economic organisations for rapid economic development to bring less developed countries out of poverty. Saddled with huge debt and massive social problems, together with fast-growing populations, the temptation for these countries is to take the short-term view and accept aid that will create immediate growth. This has a seriously damaging impact on natural environments.

Thus, environmentalists have had to become concerned with issues of economic development. It could be argued, however, that global ecology issues cannot be separated from economic considerations since they are essentially the same thing.

Is ecologism science or politics?

As has been shown, the origins of both deep and shallow ecology are both scientific and philosophical. Indeed, leading authorities such as Arne Naess and Fritjof Capra would argue that no meaningful distinction can be made between science and philosophy. Such a distinction is historical, they argue, and has no place in modern ecological thinking. Furthermore, these ecologists have rejected the conventional science, especially physics, of Newton and his followers. Newtonian science presents the world as a kind of machine, the workings of which can be discovered by observation and empirical research. If a part of the machine is damaged, it can be repaired in isolation from the rest of the machine.

Instead, deep ecologists propose an alternative philosophy of science which challenges the basis of known physics. No part of the natural world, they argue, can be seen in isolation from the whole. At the same time, the natural world is constantly experiencing instability; every time it does so, new elements enter the system to change its dynamics. It is therefore mistaken to adopt a fixed view of how nature works, which is what conventional science does. We must instead adopt a new synthesis of philosophy and science that accepts the instability of nature and the unknowability of all the implications of humankind's impact upon it. Whether we accept Capra's idea of nature as constant energy and matter flows, or Bookchin's idea of it as an enclosed web of life, we must adopt new methods of studying and understanding the complexity and inherent chaos of the natural world.

Deep ecology is therefore neither science nor philosophy in isolation. If it is not a science in the usual sense of the word, can it be seen as political? If philosophies are political in nature, the answer is 'yes'. However, politics suggests more than this. Philosophy forms the basis of political development, but does not replace it. Deep ecologists propose new forms of consciousness and attempt to educate us into thinking about the relationship between our lives and the natural world, but this does not translate as politics. It may be left to others to create the specific forms of action which can facilitate this new consciousness. The French Revolution is a model for this. It was certainly inspired by Enlightenment thinkers such as Jean-Jacques Rousseau, Thomas Paine and Voltaire, but it was the revolutionaries themselves who translated their philosophy into political action.

The liberal environmentalists and shallow ecologists, as represented by green pressure groups, Greenpeace and Friends of the Earth, are clearly political. They have developed manifestos for action and seek to influence decision makers in specific ways. This is uncontroversial. However, the deep ecologists have challenged these groups on the basis that they remain anthropocentric. Without changing fundamental human consciousness, attempts to salvage the planet from environmental disaster will be unsuccessful. In other words, by making compromises for the sake of political gain, such pressure groups fail to confront the real, profound issues.

To summarise this discussion, therefore, it can be said that ecologism is certainly a science, but one which is based on a completely new philosophy. It is not political in the conventional sense, since it proposes changes to the basis of our ethics and our relationship with nature, and is unspecific about its precise political objectives. The liberal environmentalists, by contrast, are intensely political, but are criticised by their radical colleagues for failing to understand the importance of the new philosophy of science. Thus, they cannot claim to be true ecologists. They are simply well-meaning liberal campaigners.

It is worth finishing with the words of Aldo Leopold (1887–1948), who wrote *A Sand County Almanac*, published posthumously in 1949. This passage from his work does not propose political action, new science, or even philosophy, but a new system of human ethics:

> All ethics so far evolved rest on a single premise: that the individual is a member of a community of interdependent parts. His *instincts* prompt him to compete for his place in that community, but his *ethics* prompt him also to cooperate (perhaps in order that there be a place to compete for). The land ethic simply enlarges the boundaries of the community to include soils, waters, plants, and animals, or collectively: the land.

Exam focus

Using this chapter and other resources available to you, answer the following questions.

Short questions

Your answers should be about 300 words long.

1. What do environmentalists mean by 'anthropocentrism'?
2. Outline the meaning and importance of the term 'Gaia'.
3. What are the main distinctions between ecologism and environmentalism?
4. What is meant by the term 'deep ecology'?
5. Why are some environmentalists also anarchists?

Long questions

Your answers should be about 900 words long.

1. What are the main distinctions between liberal environmentalism and the different forms of ecologism?
2. 'Anthropocentrism is the main enemy of environmentalism.' Explain and discuss.
3. Explain the importance of holism in the ecology movement.
4. Is ecologism a philosophy or a science?

Further reading

Baxter, B. (2000) *Ecologism: An Introduction*, Georgetown University Press.

Capra, F. (1997) *The Web of Life*, Flamingo.

Dobson, A. (2000) *Green Political Thought*, Routledge.

Goodin, R. (1992) *Green Political Theory*, Polity Press.

Naess, A. (1990) *Ecology, Community and Lifestyle*, Cambridge University Press.

Young, S. (1993) *The Politics of the Environment*, Baseline.

Websites

Greenpeace: www.greenpeace.org

Friends of the Earth: www.foe.co.uk

The UK Green Party: www.greenparty.org.uk

Schumacher College: www.schumachercollege.org.uk

Chapter 10

Conclusions

Political ideology has been crucial in the development of world politics. However, as the nature of politics changed dramatically after the Cold War and as the twentieth century came to an end, the relevance of ideology to the contemporary world of political ideas has been re-evaluated.

End of ideology theory

Hegel and Marx

Theories about the end of ideological thought and practice have been around for a long time. The philosopher Friedrich Hegel and his best-known follower, Karl Marx, both viewed history in terms of a constant process of ideological conflict. The internal conflict that characterised each ideological age would eventually lead to the dissolution of that age and the dawning of a new age. This new age would in its turn go through the same process of development and change.

Both Hegel and Marx envisaged an end to this process. For Hegel, ideological development was coming to an end in the Prussia of the early nineteenth century. In that society, he argued, a complete form of freedom had been attained, alienation had ended and a final social harmony had been created. There was no foreseeable challenge to this unity, no ideological conflict and therefore no ideology.

Marx believed that ideologies arise out of class conflict — the dominant ideology of a ruling class clashes with an emerging consciousness, which in time turns into a rival ideology. For Marx, ideology would cease to be relevant when there was no ruling class, since ideology reflected the system the ruling class created. In a classless society there could be no more ideological conflict, and therefore no more ideology.

Burnham

Both Hegel and Marx based their views of ideology on their theories of historical development. The more recent end of ideology theory has not been based on theory, but on empirical observations (see Table 10.1). One of the first such contributors was the US social theorist James Burnham (1905–87). Burnham's highly influential work, *The Managerial Revolution*, was published in 1941, at the dawn of the post-fascist age. He argued that in the West, and ultimately throughout the world, societies would be dominated by an elite group of managers, bureaucrats and technological experts. Ideologically based political movements would become irrelevant. Instead, the problems of politics would become managerial problems.

In Burnham's world (partly echoed by George Orwell's 1948 novel *Nineteen Eighty-Four* and presaged in the work of the Czech writer Franz Kafka (1883–1924)), a new kind of totalitarianism would emerge. All political problems would have technical solutions, not ideological ones. The general population would therefore be forced to accept the government of the new management class. The ordinary man and woman would be incapable of understanding the technicalities of these solutions and so would surrender all political power to the technocrats. Ideology would be of no use since it would not address modern managerial issues. The question 'why?', which is posed by ideologues, would be replaced by that of 'how?'.

Bell

From the 1960s, Daniel Bell (1919–) replaced Burnham as the standard-bearer for end of ideology theory. Indeed, his 1960 work *The End of Ideology* popularised the expression. For Bell, ideology is a fundamentally Marxist concept and therefore based on class conflict. Like Marx, he argues that if society is no longer characterised by class conflict, ideology becomes irrelevant. However, Bell was not referring to a communist society, as Marx was, but to postmodern industrial society. Although there were still class distinctions in the 1960s, there was no significant political conflict between those classes. Bell's ideas have been criticised for being too narrow; he is accused of focusing on the importance of class and ignoring other forms of social conflict that may emerge and give rise to ideological conflict. The examples of race and gender refute Bell, and most recently religion has once again come to play a major part in ideological conflict.

Foucault

The French philosopher Michel Foucault (1926–84) examined the conflict between science and ideology. Science and ideology propose two opposing versions of truth. Science claims to study the world in an empirical fashion and to arrive at basic truths by objective study. Scientists have rejected ideology on the grounds that it is a corrupted view of the world that has been distorted by political consciousness. Ideology, on the other hand, claims to understand truth through a more creative process that combines empirical knowledge with political theory.

For Foucault, this dispute is illusory. He argued that power and power relationships characterise society. In the absence of any such thing as an objective truth, what exist in society are versions of the truth. The most powerful of these versions will, naturally, be developed by those who hold social and political power. This truth–power relationship replaces ideology as the only significant way of understanding humankind's consciousness of the world.

Furthermore, Foucault rejected the idea that human nature is fixed. What we are as humans is created for us by society. There can only be perceived truths of human nature. This view further undermines ideology, since those who support an ideology base their beliefs on fixed views of human nature. Ultimately, Foucault's rejection of the concept of truth led him to declare that ideology is no longer relevant.

Fukuyama

Perhaps the most celebrated end of ideology theorist is the US philosopher Francis Fukuyama (1952–). Fukuyama believes that ideology has become irrelevant to modern society because all the major ideological conflicts which have beset the world in the modern age have become outdated. The defeat of communism in particular prompted him to suggest that the final triumph of Western political values had arrived. He argues that liberalism and its companions — democracy and capitalism — have triumphed (see Box 10.1).

For Francis Fukuyama, liberalism has triumphed over other ideologies

---

Box 10.1 **The triumph of liberalism**

In this passage from *The End of History and the Last Man* (1992), Fukuyama describes the triumph of liberal principles.

The most remarkable development of the last quarter of the twentieth century has been the revelation of enormous weaknesses at the core of the world's seemingly strong dictatorships, whether they be of the military-authoritarian Right, or the communist-totalitarian Left. From Latin America to eastern Europe, from the Soviet Union to the Middle East and Asia, strong governments have been falling over the last two decades. And while they have not given way in all cases to stable liberal democracies, liberal democracy remains the only coherent political aspiration that spans different regions and cultures around the globe. In addition, liberal principles in economics — the free market — have spread and have succeeded in producing unprecedented levels of material prosperity, both in industrially developed countries and in countries that had been, at the close of World War II, part of the impoverished Third World. A liberal revolution in economic thinking has sometimes preceded, sometimes followed, the move towards political freedom around the globe.

Fukuyama believed that human society has been moving towards a world in which all individuals show respect for each other and for each other's individuality. Civilisation will have reached its height when this mutual respect becomes firmly entrenched. For Fukuyama, ideology can only be seen in terms of conflict. If there is no conflict, there is no ideology. Fukuyama's theories gave rise to end of history theory.

These theories about the end of ideological thought are summarised in Table 10.1.

Table 10.1 Summary of end of ideology theory

Theorist	Views
James Burnham (1905–87)	Ideological rule will be replaced by a new managerialism. Political competition will be based on elites who claim to be able to manage modern industrial society most successfully.
Daniel Bell (1919–)	Ideologies are reflections of class conflict. In modern, post-industrial society, class conflict is of no great significance. Therefore ideologies have become irrelevant. Like Burnham, Bell believed managerialism would replace ideological politics, especially with regard to the USA.
Michel Foucault (1926–84)	Ideology proposes a single, exclusive version of social truth, based on a fixed view of human nature. Foucault rejects the idea that there can be any such thing as objective truth, because truth is a reflection of the view of the world held by those who exercise power. Furthermore, there is no such thing as human nature.
Francis Fukuyama (1952–)	Liberalism has values that have finally triumphed and human civilisation will be based, from now on, on liberal values. Since ideologies exist because of conflict, the absence of conflict makes ideology meaningless.

End of history theory

End of ideology theories have also been described as 'end of history' theories. The two theories have been brought together because many analysts have interpreted historical change in terms of ideological conflict. If ideologies cease to be important, history will come to an end. This is not in the sense that events will cease to happen, but that there will no longer be any discernible transitions from one age to another. History will simply be a continuous stream of events and changes without revolutionary transitions.

All the major developments of history, such as wars, revolutions, social movements and religious schisms, are reflections of a struggle in which humans are engaged. This struggle is what Fukuyama calls *recognition*. He asserts that history is the history of this struggle. As humans, we all have beliefs, faiths, aspirations and cultural and economic lives to which we adhere and we desire that other humans recognise this. A fully mature society is one in which mutual recognition among all peoples has been achieved on the basis of equal treatment. In this society, people can all live in a state of mutual respect and equality, irrespective of whether they hold a religious faith, are patriotic nationalists, play different roles in the economic system or have different life aspirations. This, says Fukuyama, is the essence of a liberal democratic society. Furthermore, different nations can achieve mutual recognition on the same basis.

If liberal democracy can indeed survive, if it contains no internal contradictions (as Marxists had claimed it would do), Fukuyama sees no reason why it should not continue. The historical struggle for recognition being over, history comes to an end. For Fukuyama, then, the triumph of liberal democracy is the end of history. However, the emergence of new challenges to liberal democracy has forced Fukuyama to amend his views on the issue of its apparent victory. In particular, he has had to recognise that new ideological schisms may arise, notably between neo-conservatism and progressive liberalism.

Ideology today

There is no doubt that Fukayama was right in arguing that liberal democracy had won the Cold War. All over the world, Marxist-inspired regimes collapsed and were replaced by partially or fully liberal, capitalist systems. It is also true that all the major developed countries of the world have consistently elected liberal-based governments. It therefore seems that the ideological element of Western politics has declined.

However, there are three ideological movements that are providing challenges to liberal democracy. Ironically, one of them — neo-conservatism — is a movement to which Fukuyama once belonged. The other two are religious fundamentalism and the anti-globalisation movement.

Neo-conservatism is a reaction against the moral decadence and excessive individualism of modern free-market liberalism. Modern post-industrial society, the neo-conservatives argue, is under threat of collapse as a result of the many social problems caused by excessive freedom and lack of moral restraints. Drugs, crime, family break-down, teenage pregnancy, sexually transmitted diseases, prostitution and pornography are all symptoms of this moral and social decay.

Led by US philosophers such as Leo Strauss and Irving Kristol (1920–), the neo-conservatives propose a society which is dominated by a state-imposed moral code. They promote the spread of fundamentalist religious beliefs and have demanded that governments adopt a more authoritarian approach to law and order issues. This is far removed from the liberal, tolerant and individualist society that was spawned in the 1950s and 1960s and which had triumphed over communism. The schism between neo-conservatism and progressive liberalism is seen at its most stark in the USA, a society which has become severely divided by ideological conflict. As yet, this conflict has been contained within conventional politics, but these deep divisions threaten to break out into a more fundamental political struggle, challenging national unity itself.

On a global level, the clearest threat to Western liberal democracy comes from religious — mainly Islamic — fundamentalism. Like the neo-conservatives in the USA, religious fundamentalists hate the decadence of Western society and have reacted against the influence of Western capitalism on traditional societies. The manifestations of this struggle — seen by many as ideological in nature — are well documented and their future development is worryingly uncertain.

However, the growth of non-Islamic forms of fundamentalism should not be ignored. In the Middle East, ultra-orthodox Jews have been prominent in maintaining a high degree of confrontation between Israel and the neighbouring Arab states, including against the Palestinians. In India, Hindu nationalists have rekindled sectarian conflict with the country's large Muslim minority. At the end of the twentieth century, India and Pakistan appeared to be close to armed (possibly nuclear) conflict over Kashmir, a dispute that was fuelled by religious extremism on both sides.

The anti-globalisation movement, although in its infancy, might become increasingly significant. This is inspired by anarchism, quasi-anarchism and ecologism. Other groups, such as socialists and feminists, have also attached themselves to the movement, seeing it as a potentially liberating force. As yet, anti-globalisation is more coherent in terms of what it opposes than what it proposes, but it is a growing force and an increasing challenge to the hegemony of global free-market capitalism.

As a result of these ideological reactions to liberalism and capitalism, many US citizens have argued that liberalism itself must take on an ideological fervour if it is to survive in an increasingly hostile world. It may well be, then, that liberal democracy itself will become an aggressive ideology.

Claims that ideology is an outdated concept are clearly premature. It may be that ideological traditions such as Marxism and individualist anarchism are in decline, and that nationalism will ultimately succumb to globalisation, but new ideologies seem to be emerging to take their place. It is too soon to assume that the 250 year history of ideology is at an end.

Chapter 11

Answering examination questions

This section is a guide to answering typical examination questions on political ideologies. It explains how to tackle each type of question, gives worked examples, lists generic essay questions and explains the command words used by examiners.

Short questions

The demands of short questions on ideologies generally fall into the following categories:
- Defining political principles as used by the followers of an ideology, e.g. the meaning of freedom, equality, order, the state.
- Explaining distinctions between the ways in which different ideologies have used principles, e.g. comparing how liberals and anarchists view freedom, or how liberals and anarchists view the state.
- Explaining typical ideological attitudes towards certain phenomena, e.g. the conservative attitude to human nature or Marx's attitude to social class.
- Giving short descriptions of how ideologies demonstrate internal distinctions, e.g. liberal and radical feminism or collectivist and individualist anarchism.

It is vital to focus clearly upon the question, to avoid unnecessary analysis where none is required and to ensure that as many relevant facts and illustrations as possible are included within the limited time available.

Examples
Three examples of short questions are given below, together with suggestions on how to structure a response.

Question 1 What do feminists mean by the term 'patriarchy'?

This is an example of a requirement to explain an important concept used within an ideology.

Short introduction
This should give a generalised description of patriarchy as a system of rule by men. You should give information such as the notion that it arises from the model of the family in which fathers are traditionally dominant.

Main answer
It is important when describing a concept or principle that you explain how different branches of an ideology have used the term. In this case, you should explain that liberals see patriarchy as the general domination of society by men. Give examples, such as the position of men in employment and politics, and refer to discrimination. Mention that radicals, however, see partriarchy as a more complete, all-embracing system. Explain that 'the personal is the political'. Illustrate ways in which radicals have insisted that patriarchy exists in public and private life, including personal relationships. Note that socialist feminists see patriarchy as economic in nature and explain why; add that other radical feminists have emphasised the sexual nature of patriarchy (e.g. Greer). Your answer should contain some references to leading authorities.

Conclusion
Write a sentence or two summarising what you have said, emphasising the fact that there are different usages, but that there is also a common meaning.

Question 2 What is a typical conservative attitude towards human nature?

Note that 'typical' invites some degree of critical analysis. As the answer shows, there may not be a typical attitude.

Short introduction
This should explain that there really is no 'typical' attitude. Instead, there is a traditionalist attitude and perhaps two modern versions. State how influential this concept is on the whole philosophy of conservatism, since it affects issues such as the role of the state, authority and morality. In particular, explain that conservatism was originally a reaction against Enlightenment thinking; it opposed the view that humans are rational beings, seeing them as being driven more by appetites than by reason.

Main answer
Explain the traditional view, for example as exemplified by Burke. This includes pessimism about human nature, humankind's imperfectability, original sin and related ideas. Then give the modern view, which accepts that individuals can be improved through education and the creation of a more moral society — the 'traditional values'

argument. Contrast this with the neo-conservatives, who have reverted to the pessimistic view, citing decadence, family breakdown, crime and so on as proof that humanity needs firm moral guidance and perhaps even religious observance. You could quote authorities such as Strauss or Kristol. Perhaps you could note that conservatism thus appears to have come full circle.

Conclusion

Return to your two main themes. First, state that there is a basic traditional, fundamental view, and second, explain that there have been adaptations of this view by modern conservatives, although some basic principles remain.

Question 3 Distinguish between an anarchist and a liberal view of freedom.

'Distinguish' questions are common and can be tricky. It is important to make sure you draw distinctions and don't just assume them. Avoid the temptation to describe one view and then the other, thereby leaving the reader to identify the differences. Distinctions must be clearly identified and stressed.

Short introduction

Make general comments about the importance of the concept to both ideological traditions. State that it might initially appear that there are no significant distinctions, but that you will show this is not the case.

Main answer

The liberal, at least classical liberal, view was that freedom is 'negative'. Explain negative liberty and emphasise that it means an absence of external restraint. Contrast this with the anarchist view that people should exercise private judgement. We do not need external restraint to indicate good actions as opposed to bad ones. Quote Godwin, for example, on how moral individuals use private judgement well.

Then go on to discuss positive liberty. Liberals see it as a widening of opportunity and choice. The anarchist view is similar, but concerns self-realisation. Explain this term. Show that, for liberals, the state can promote liberty, whereas anarchists insist that liberty can only be genuine within voluntary societies.

Third, explain that anarchists propose that the social existence we choose must be voluntary and a matter of free choice. For liberals, by contrast, political society arises from collective consent. We are free because we have consented. Anarchists do not accept that consent represents free choice.

Conclusion

Write one or two sentences explaining that both philosophies see freedom as fundamental and place it at the centre of their belief system, but note that it arises from different premises in each case. Stress again that the whole basis of a free political society — liberal consent versus anarchist voluntarism — is disputed.

Essay questions

Generic questions

Whichever politics course you are taking, certain generic questions will arise. The actual wording of these common types of question may vary, but the essential elements of a good response are the same. By learning the material for these answers and practising them, you can give yourself the basis for a good examination answer. Of course, it is imperative that you address the specific demands of the actual question too.

Below is a list of generic questions that commonly arise in ideologies examinations. It is not exhaustive, but it is based on the questions that have appeared in recent years.

Anarchism
- Distinguish between individualist and collectivist anarchism.
- Do you agree that anarchists are united on principles but divided on ends?
- Is anarchism nothing more than utopianism?

Conservatism
- Distinguish between traditional and New Right conservatism.
- Distinguish between neo-liberalism and neo-conservatism.
- How has the conservative attitude to the state and society evolved?
- To what extent has the modern Conservative Party abandoned traditional principles?

Environmentalism and ecologism
- Distinguish between deep and shallow ecology.
- Examine the importance of anthropocentrism in the environmental movement.
- Examine the importance of holism among ecologists.

Fascism
- Why is fascism described as a philosophy of irrationalism?
- Are all fascists necessarily racists?
- What are the main distinctions between fascism and Nazism?
- Why do fascists emphasise leadership?
- Why do fascists worship warfare?

Feminism
- Distinguish between liberal and radical feminism.
- Why have feminists argued that the personal is the political?
- In what ways have feminists disagreed about the nature of patriarchy?
- Has feminism succeeded?

Liberalism
- Distinguish between classical and modern liberalism.
- Why have liberals traditionally been suspicious of the state?
- Why do liberals stress limited government and constitutionalism?

Marxism

> Examine Marx's claim to be a scientific thinker.
> Why did Marx believe that revolution was inevitable?
> Is Marxism still relevant today?
> How much were Leninism and Stalinism distortions of Marxist theory?
> What were the main distinctions between Leninism, Trotskyism and Stalinism?

Nationalism

> Distinguish between liberal and right-wing nationalism.
> Is nationalism necessarily racist in character?
> Is nationalism necessarily expansionist in nature?

Socialism

> Distinguish between revolutionary and evolutionary socialism.
> Do you agree that socialism has disagreed more about means than ends?
> To what extent has modern social democracy abandoned traditional socialist principles?
> What have been the most typical socialist attitudes towards capitalism?

Command words

Most essay-based questions include important command words or phrases. Here are the most common ones and suggested approaches:

To what extent?

Make sure you give an evaluation. Put it in the introduction and the conclusion and assemble evidence to back it up. The answer to this kind of question would usually be 'a great deal', or 'the arguments are balanced', or 'not very much'. Note that none of these answers is a simple 'yes' or 'no'.

Discuss

This usually follows a quotation. You are being asked to explain its meaning. Explain why the quotation has been said and then evaluate it. It is acceptable to challenge a statement or to support it fully, but it is generally best to give a balanced assessment. Ensure that you assemble enough evidence to support your conclusion.

Distinguish

As was shown in the third short question example, it is vital to bring out the points of distinction and not just let the reader work them out. Go through each of the key points in turn. This a better technique than simply describing each point of view and then attempting a few distinctions at the end.

Why?

The answer to 'why?' is 'because', and your answer should be a full version of 'because'. Make sure you answer the question and use relevant evidence.

And finally...some dos, don'ts and misconceptions

➢ do write a plan
➢ don't cross out your plan
➢ do write an introduction
➢ do explain how you intend to answer the question
➢ don't start your essay with a long historical background that is not directly related to the question
➢ do address the question directly
➢ don't ignore what the question asks
➢ do plan your time
➢ don't run out of time
➢ do use bullets if you *are* running out of time
➢ don't use bullets in any other circumstances
➢ do refer to leading authorities
➢ don't attempt to quote them at length
➢ do use as many real-world examples as you can
➢ do write a conclusion which states concisely what your conclusions are

Bibliography

General reading

Adams, I. (1998) *Ideology and Politics in Britain Today*, Manchester University Press.

Adams, I. and Dyson, R. W. (2003) *Fifty Major Political Thinkers*, Routledge.

Crick, B. (1994) *In Defence of Politics*, Penguin.

Eccleshall, R. et al. (2003) *Political Ideologies: An Introduction*, Routledge.

Goodwin, B. (1997) *Using Political Ideas*, Wiley.

Heywood, A. (2002) *Politics*, Palgrave Macmillan.

Heywood, A. (2003) *Political Ideologies: An Introduction*, Palgrave Macmillan.

Leach, R. (1996) *British Political Ideologies*, Prentice Hall.

McLellan, D. (1995) *Ideology*, Open University Press.

Plamenatz, J. (1972) *Ideology*, Macmillan.

Rosen, M. and Wolff, J. (eds) (1999) *Political Thought*, Oxford University Press.

Vincent, A. (1995) *Modern Political Ideologies*, Blackwell.

Websites

The internet is not the most useful medium for finding additional information about political ideologies, but by using leading search engines, and keying in the names of major thinkers, you can find interesting biographies, critiques, summaries and quotations.

The best general site is probably Wikipedia, which can be accessed at http://en.wikipedia.org. It has an excellent search engine, which is particularly useful for finding information about major authorities and works on each ideology. It is interesting to view the current policies of the main UK and US political parties in relation to the ideologies that originally underpinned them. The three key UK party websites are:

www.conservatives.com

www.labour.org.uk

www.libdems.org.uk

For information on political parties in the USA, see the following:

www.democrats.org

www.rnc.org

www.politics1.com

Classic works

The following list includes many of the great works that have been written within each ideological tradition. They are available in virtually all large academic libraries.

Liberalism

Hobhouse, L. *Liberalism*
Locke, J. *Two Treatises of Government*
Mill, J. S. *On Liberty*
Rawls, J. *A Theory of Justice*
Rousseau, J. *The Social Contract*
Smiles, S. *Self Help*

Socialism

Benn, T. *Arguments for Socialism*
Giddens, A. *The Third Way*
Laski, H. *Democracy in Crisis*
Shaw, G. B. (ed) *Fabian Essays in Socialism*
Tawney, R. H. *Equality*
Winstanley, G. *The Law of Freedom*

Conservatism

Burke, E. *Reflections on the Revolution in France*
Disraeli, B. *Sybil*
Friedman, M. *Capitalism and Freedom*
Hayek, F. *The Road to Serfdom*
Hobbes, T. *Leviathan*

Nationalism

Carr, E. H. *Nationalism and After*
Kedourie, E. *Nationalism*

Marxism

Lenin, V. I. *What is to be Done?*
Marcuse, H. *One Dimensional Man*
Marx, K. *The German Ideology*
Marx, K. *Critique of the Gotha Programme*

Anarchism

Kropotkin, P. *Anarchism*
Nozick, R. *Anarchy, State and Society*
Thoreau, H. *Walden*
Wolff, R. *In Defence of Anarchism*

Fascism

Hitler, A. *Mein Kampf*
Mussolini, B. *The Political and Social Doctrine of Fascism*
Nietzsche, F. *The Will to Power*

Feminism

de Beauvoir, S. *The Second Sex*
Friedan, B. *The Feminine Mystique*
Greer, G. *The Female Eunuch*
Millett, K. *Sexual Politics*

Environmentalism and ecologism

Bookchin, M. *The Ecology of Freedom*
Capra, F. *The Web of Life*
Lovelock, J. *Gaia: A New Look at Life on Earth*
Thomas, K. *Man and the Natural World*

Index

Page numbers in red refer to key term definitions.